JAMES MADISON

JAMES MADISON

AMERICA'S FIRST POLITICIAN

JAY COST

BASIC BOOKS

NEW YORK

Basic Books
Hachette Book Group
1290 Avenue of the Americas, New York, NY 10104
www.basicbooks.com

Printed in the United States of America

First Edition: November 2021

Published by Basic Books, an imprint of Perseus Books, LLC, a subsidiary of Hachette Book Group, Inc. The Basic Books name and logo is a trademark of the Hachette Book Group.

The Hachette Speakers Bureau provides a wide range of authors for speaking events. To find out more, go to www.hachettespeakersbureau.com or call (866) 376-6591.

The publisher is not responsible for websites (or their content) that are not owned by the publisher.

Print book interior design by Trish Wilkinson

Library of Congress Cataloging-in-Publication Data
Names: Cost, Jay, author.
Title: James Madison : America's first politician / Jay Cost.
Other titles: America's first politician
Description: First edition. | New York : Basic Books, 2021. | Includes
    bibliographical references and index.
Identifiers: LCCN 2021019211 | ISBN 9781541699557 (hardcover) | ISBN
    9781541699540 (ebook)
Subjects: LCSH: Madison, James, 1751–1836. | Presidents—United States—
    Biography. | Statesmen—United States—Biography. | United States—
    Politics and government—1783–1809. | United States—Politics and
    government—1809–1817.
Classification: LCC E342 .C67 2021 | DDC 973.5/1092 [B]—dc23
LC record available at https://lccn.loc.gov/2021019211

ISBNs: 978-1-5416-9955-7 (print), 978-1-5416-9954-0 (ebook)

LSC-C

Printing 1, 2021

For James and Evelyn

CONTENTS

AUTHOR'S NOTE

FOR THE CONVENIENCE of the reader, I have altered some of the spelling, capitalization, punctuation, and typographical emphases of historical passages to make them conform to modern conventions. No substantive changes of any sort have been made to direct quotations.

PREFACE

IN 1827, CHARLES Ingersoll, a Philadelphia lawyer and politician, gave a public toast for James Madison in which he declared, "If Washington was the father of our country, Mr. Madison is entitled to be considered the father of that Constitution." When Madison died in 1836, former president John Quincy Adams paid tribute with the same moniker, and so Madison has been remembered ever since as the Father of the Constitution.[1]

There are certainly good reasons to bestow upon Madison such an august title. He gave 167 speeches, made seventy-two motions, and served on four committees at the Constitutional Convention in 1787, and he bequeathed to history a voluminous set of notes on the proceedings. Most importantly, Madison authored the Virginia Plan—a bold call for a total redesign of the national government that set the agenda for the convention and established the foundation upon which the Constitution would be built.

Yet Father of the Constitution is not a nickname Madison would ever have used. The fourth president was always the

first to remind his fellow countrymen that the nation's founding charter was a joint effort and that no single person could
claim paternity. And while his demurral can be chalked up to
his characteristic modesty, he still had a point. Though Madison arguably contributed more to the creation of the Constitution than any other single delegate, there were a half dozen or
so others whose efforts also mark them for special distinction,
including John Dickinson, Oliver Ellsworth, Gouverneur Morris, John Rutledge, and Roger Sherman. To single Madison out
as *the* father of the Constitution undervalues the efforts of these
delegates.

And yet Ingersoll's sobriquet has been stubbornly sticky, perhaps because Madison's contributions to the continuing project of establishing the new government after the Constitutional
Convention was finished can feel enigmatic, or even contradictory. He sometimes comes across the pages of history like a
man without fixed political principles. He argued against political parties in 1787 but helped create the Republican Party
(today referred to as the Democratic-Republican Party) in 1791.
In the 1790s, he argued that powers not clearly established under the Constitution, like chartering a bank, were forbidden, but
he looked the other way when the government incorporated the
territory of Louisiana in 1804, for which there was no explicit
constitutional sanction. Then, as president in 1816, he signed
into law a charter for a new national bank.

Unfortunately, Madison did little over the years to clarify exactly what he was on about. This might be why some biographers
have been so aggressive in periodizing Madison, breaking his life
up into discrete, manageable chunks where his positions can be
properly identified. Irving Brant started this trend back in the
1940s with his magisterial six-volume biography, published over
twenty years, with each entry's title identifying the Madison of

that moment: *The Virginia Revolutionist, The Nationalist, Father of the Constitution,* and so on. More recently, Noah Feldman took this approach to its logical conclusion by naming his biography *The Three Lives of James Madison: Genius, Partisan, President,* implying that Madison somehow transitioned from embodying one role to another over the decades. Nearly two hundred years since his death, it seems that Madison remains a difficult man to pin down. Better to think of him as two, maybe three different men.

But Madison was, of course, a single person—a brilliant and deep thinker who made careful arguments about what republican government should look like. The facts of his life have been well told, by these and many other books dating back to William Cabell Rives's *History of the Life and Times of James Madison,* the first volume of which was published before the Civil War. Yet the story still feels somehow incomplete, like pieces of a puzzle that have not been put together. To create a full portrait of Madison, we must connect his constitutional theory to his career in government, looking carefully at his life in the public realm to find the continuities between the theory and practice of politics. When we do, we find a man uniquely committed to the potential for well-ordered republican politics to solve the essential problem of government.

Philosophers since the very beginning of Western civilization have been confounded by a riddle embedded deep within human nature. People cannot create justice among themselves spontaneously. We are too selfish to place the needs of our neighbors or the community ahead of our own desires. This is the primary task of the state: to act as a neutral third party to settle our disputes and promote our common interests, because we cannot do so on our own. The problem is that government is also made up of people, and so it likewise has a tendency toward corruption, pursuing the interests of the leaders rather than the people at large. The ancient Greeks like Aristotle were aware of this problem, as were historians and philosophers from the Roman era like Polybius and Cicero. During the Renaissance, it was on the mind of Machiavelli, and in the Enlightenment it was a central concern for intellectuals such as Montesquieu and David Hume.

By the time Madison reached adulthood in the 1770s, the general consensus was that there were two forms of government capable of addressing this essential problem. The first was a small republic where the citizens alone would rule. In a smaller polity, like the city-states of Venice and Florence, the people would have generally homogenous interests, minimizing the scope of political conflict, and they could keep a careful eye on their leaders, reducing the chance for corruption. So long as the people possessed a basic level of virtue, such a government could be sustained. For governments ruling over larger territories and more diverse peoples, the solution was to blend economic classes together in shared governance, balancing the rule of a monarch, the landowning few, and the people at large. Great Britain, for instance, was praised by Montesquieu as a successful commonwealth for having established Parliament as a partner in government with the monarch.

But neither of these solutions would work in the United States in 1787. Obviously, there could be no mixed system—the colonists had overthrown the British king a decade earlier and had no interest in establishing a new one, nor, for that matter, did the country have a class of nobility. The thirteen states seemed compact and homogenous enough to function as small republics, and the constitutions they drafted after declaring independence were pristinely democratic by the standards of the age. Yet the states, gathered loosely under the Articles of Confederation, behaved atrociously in the early years of the country, consistently undercutting the national interest and mistreating their own citizens. It seemed to some as though the American experiment in self-government might have been a mistake. Perhaps the people would prove unable to rule themselves after all.

Madison had been acutely aware of these problems since his midtwenties. In 1777, he joined the executive council of Virginia, where he saw the problems of state government firsthand. In 1780, he entered the Continental Congress, and what he witnessed there horrified him: petty squabbles that disrupted the business of Congress, selfish states that undermined the war effort, and a stubborn refusal by so-called statesmen to address the problems plaguing government at all levels of American society. Having been immersed in the classics of the Western canon from a young age, Madison understood these myriad problems in light of that ancient dilemma of securing dispassionate justice for a passionately selfish species.

His solution, however, was new. Previous thinkers had it exactly backward, Madison thought. Republican government was in fact precarious in a state or city but could be stable in a large nation. The problem in small republics was that single factions could take control of the government and pervert it to their own ends. The commercial elite in Massachusetts, the poor farmers in Rhode Island, and the Anglican laity in Virginia were each numerous enough that they could dominate their respective states. Consequently, the majority could abuse the rights of the minority. On the other hand, all of the states together would form an expansive nation so diverse that no group could rule by itself. Factions would check one another, and eventually the only way past such a stalemate would be to meet in the middle. In this process of finding common ground, something approaching justice and the public interest might be achieved, without the need for a king or a class of nobility. The implication was that, if practiced on a large and diverse enough scale, *politics itself* could solve the essential problem of government.

Madison took this idea to the Constitutional Convention in Philadelphia in 1787, and while his fellow delegates altered his proposals in important ways, his notion of an "extended republic" was the core innovation in the nation's founding charter. Madison offered his most thorough defense of these ideas in his famous essays *Federalist* 10 and 51, widely read by students, scholars, and good citizens to this day. These essays expounded the grand theory of American politics, and Madison as much as anybody can claim to be its innovator.

But this was hardly the end of his contribution to the American system. He was also the first great practitioner of this new style of national politics, establishing a model of republican statesmanship that has endured ever since. It was not enough, Madison believed, to establish a system of government whose purpose was to find equitable common ground. The United States also needed leaders who took this to be their personal mission. Compromises must be made. Seemingly competing interests must be reconciled. And above all, government should not privilege one group over another, for favoritism is contrary to the bedrock of justice upon which all government should be founded.

It is at this point that Madison has so often been misunderstood, in both his own time and through subsequent generations. Alexander Hamilton, the brilliant financier-statesman who had coauthored the *Federalist Papers* with Madison, was surprised to discover in the early days of the new republic that Madison opposed his program of using the powers of the national government to consolidate and strengthen the country's financial system. Hamilton wanted the government to pay the national debt at full face value, assume the debts of the states, charter a national bank, and support the nascent industrial sector—and Madison opposed him at every turn. This, to Hamilton, seemed like a great betrayal of their joint venture to establish a more powerful national government. Historians through the generations, especially those sympathetic to Hamilton, have chided Madison for his seeming inconsistency. But what Hamilton and his later defenders failed to appreciate is Madison's commitment to fair play. To Madison, Hamilton's system was too heavily biased in favor of the commercial interests of the large cities, whereas in a republic the benefits and burdens of policy should be evenly distributed across the populace.

So it goes for much of Madison's seemingly puzzling career. When we keep in front of us his commitment to this particular vision of republican politics, many of the contradictions begin to make sense. The way he practiced politics was an extension of how he designed it on paper, as a search for common ground among factions. So, just as Madison the republican theorist promoted a government structure that balanced the forces in society, so, too, did Madison the politician persistently seek that sort of balance. For him, there was no distinction between republican theories of politics and the republican practice of it. The depth of his commitment to a neutral government that advanced the public interest, treated citizens equitably, and respected individual rights is the through line of his public life. Though many politicians from this era had similar commitments, what we see in him is the most forceful expression of them, in both word and deed. It was in this way that his life itself served as the greatest instruction on how politics in a republic should function.

There were limits to Madison's genius, and important ones at that. He was at his best when he was presented with a puzzle, tasked with placing different elements together in their proper order. But he was hardly a visionary, especially in fields outside of politics. His brand of hyperrealism meant that he served well as a ballast for a friend like Jefferson, whose imagination often got the better of his reason. But Madison struggled to grasp emerging trends in society and economics, even as they were unfolding right before his eyes. He was slow, for instance, to appreciate the transformation of the United States into a market economy, a development that Hamilton had seen decades before Madison ever did. Having spent the first quarter century of public life in legislatures and conventions, Madison never appreciated the potentially vast scope of power that rested within the presidency, so he struggled to govern the country effectively during his two terms in the White House. And while he was a first-rank political theorist, his understanding of the Constitution as a legal document was always hazy at best. His various positions on issues over the years fit seamlessly into his view of how republican politics was supposed to work, but he struggled to articulate a consistent constitutional justification for his political views. Even more profoundly, he never really understood the moral calamity of chattel slavery. He knew, on an intellectual level, that slavery was wrong. But the institution never really pricked his conscience; a slave owner himself, he was never moved to use his vast powers to try to lead the country out of slavery's pernicious grasp. And it was only very late in his life that he finally saw the threat that slavery posed to the ideals of liberty and justice that he had sought to instill in the republic.

What emerges from this story is hopefully a fuller portrait of Madison than we have had to date: not a man with uncertain opinions and inconstant views, but a single—and singular— man of politics. His lifetime mission was to forge a stronger union of the states around the principles of limited government, individual rights, and, above all, justice. Like any man in public life for so long, he had limits, and his mistakes were consequential. But his nearly half-century career is both intelligible and extraordinary. His life demonstrates that politics in a national republic, despite all its frustrations, can actually solve the essential problem of government. In this way, he was the first great American politician, not only establishing for us the rules of our constitutional system but also showing us how to govern within them.

1

BORN FOR POLITICS

IN SEPTEMBER 1716, Virginia governor Alexander Spotswood led a procession of settlers, rangers, and horses across the Swift Run Gap, through the Blue Ridge Mountains, and finally to the Shenandoah River, where they celebrated their expedition by getting good and drunk on what one traveler recorded as "an extraordinary variety of liquors." Along the way, they passed by the forks of the Rapidan River, a short distance from what would become Montpelier, the Madison family estate.[1]

The purpose of Spotswood's expedition was partially about public relations, a way of encouraging further migration westward. Through much of the seventeenth century, the colonial government had been attempting to navigate between, as the governor put it, "Scylla and Charybdis, either an Indian or a civil war." If the colony tried to expand into Indian territory too fast or too far, it risked conflict with the Algonquian-speaking tribes of the Tidewater, organized under the Powhatan Confederacy. Yet if the colony came to terms with the Native Americans, it risked a revolt among the lower classes who were hungry for more land. But by the turn of the century, the once-mighty Powhatan had been subdued, and the handful of native Piedmont tribes to the west were no match for the English settlers. Some, like the Manahoac, who had once occupied the lands that would become Montpelier, had already been wiped out by war and disease. Now the colonists could move west easily. In making his trip, Spotswood hoped to encourage Virginians to consider that possibility.[2]

This was the dawn of what has often been remembered as the "golden age" of colonial Virginia. Initially settled in 1607 at Jamestown, the colony in its first century of existence offered little evidence of the genteel manners and aristocratic breeding it would eventually become known for. Disease in the early days was rampant, wiping out thousands upon thousands of settlers; the Powhatan Confederacy was also a potent danger. Despite these threats, Virginia continued to attract a steady stream of immigrants—often poor, single men from England who were willing to risk the dangers for a chance at a better life. The great lure was the opportunity to grow and sell tobacco, which had become popular in Europe after it was introduced there in the late sixteenth century. Many men came over as indentured servants, working for a fixed time for a landowner until they could claim acreage of their own. As a consequence, farms in the early era tended to be small and family run, with easy access to the Atlantic Ocean along one of the four main rivers—the James, York, Rappahannock, and Potomac—or their tributaries. Town life during this period was almost nonexistent. Jamestown never counted more than a few hundred souls as residents, Williamsburg was not established until the 1670s, and Richmond would not be laid out until 1737.

The colony had introduced slavery early in its existence, but slavery did not overtake indentured servitude as the main source of cheap labor until the end of the 1600s. In 1680, enslaved people accounted for less than 7 percent of the total colonial population, but by 1740 they had become more than 33 percent. If tobacco kept the Virginia project afloat in the seventeenth century, slavery made it rich in the eighteenth, as small farms were eclipsed by vast plantations and wealth accumulated at the top of white society. Those who had the capital to buy land and enslaved people could take advantage of Europe's seemingly limitless demand for tobacco, while those who could not struggled to scratch out an existence.

Consequently, Virginia developed an informal aristocracy. Wealthy landowners did not receive titles from the Crown, but their vast holdings of land and enslaved persons gave them a position of social and political distinction. Ownership became essential to the identity of colonial Virginia, informing the early development of its republican thought. The reigning philosopher of the colony was not so much John Locke, whose radical theory of revolution would inspire the Declaration of Independence in 1776, but rather James Harrington, who had in the 1600s sketched a vision of an ideal agrarian commonwealth, which he called "Oceana." In Harrington's thinking, landowners were the anchor of all good government, for people are only free "in proportion to their property." If a man worked the land of another, or otherwise depended upon somebody else for his livelihood, his judgment could not be his own. The Virginians adopted this belief in the necessity of landownership and in it found an implicit justification for slavery. As William Byrd II—one of Virginia's most prominent aristocrats—wrote in 1726, "Like one of the patriarchs, I have my flocks and my herds, my bond-men, and bond-women, and every sort of trade amongst my own servants, so that I live in a kind of independence on everyone, but Providence." A man like Byrd was free not only because he owned land but because he owned fellow humans.[3]

As the wealthier planters in the Tidewater region began to establish themselves economically, they self-consciously modeled their lives on the tastes and manners of the English aristocracy, acquiring books, furniture, clothing, and all sorts of other refined goods from London. The simple, wood-frame homesteads of the seventeenth century were gradually replaced by the grand, brick-built Georgian manors of the eighteenth century. The Tidewater elite also committed themselves to the project of Enlightenment learning, a dedication embodied by Wren Hall, a grandiose, Georgian-style building constructed between 1695 and 1700 that housed the College of William and Mary. This was more than a building; it was a statement of purpose. Though still a colonial backwater, Virginia intended one day to be a great intellectual and economic force, with an educated citizenry and a refined set of manners.

Cutting against this aristocratic atmosphere was the west of the colony, where it was relatively easy to acquire land. A new life was available on the Piedmont—the vast steppe running north to south between the lowland Tidewater to the east and the Blue Ridge Mountains to the west—but not for everybody. One had to have an intrepid spirit to move into this virtually untamed wilderness, and also possess the means or the social connections to acquire enough land and enslaved people to make such a venture feasible.

Ambrose Madison—the grandfather of the future president—was one who had the necessary connections to make a fresh start in the west. He had certainly married well. His wife, Frances, was the daughter of James Taylor, a surveyor who had traveled with Governor Spotswood on his famed expedition. On his journey west, Taylor had taken careful note of promising land just east of the Blue Ridge Mountains near the Rapidan River that he might later claim. In the 1720s, Ambrose Madison and

Thomas Chew claimed nearly five thousand acres in what would later be organized as Orange County, Virginia.

The Madison clan had been in the Virginia colony since the middle of the seventeenth century, when John Maddison, a shipbuilder, initially acquired several hundred acres of land between the York and Rappahannock Rivers. John had a son named John Jr., who in turn had three sons: John, Henry, and Ambrose. They shortened the family name to Madison and together held about five thousand acres between them in the Mattaponi River drainage area. This placed them in the middle tier of Tidewater landowners—well above the class of small freeholders, but hardly at the level of the elites who dominated the top of Virginia society. In the future president's telling, his forebearers were "among the respectable though not the most opulent class." So when it became safe to settle in the Piedmont, young Ambrose could not resist the opportunity for upward mobility. After patenting the land, he sent agents out to clear forests and begin the process of building a new estate. Around 1729, Ambrose, Frances, and their children moved to the plantation, originally named Mount Pleasant, about halfway between Fredericksburg and the eastern side of the Blue Ridge and thirty miles northeast of the future site of Thomas Jefferson's Monticello.[4]

Early life at Mount Pleasant reflected the gap between the life these western planters hoped to build and the one they actually lived. The family homestead was extremely plain: a wood-frame, two-room farmhouse that sat on a stone-lined cellar. Compared to the grand mansions that wealthier planters were building in the Tidewater around the same time, it was quite humble. But the Madisons' possessions and lifestyle reflected a better sense of their aspirations. The interior of the house was well-appointed, with leather chairs, tables, curtains, rugs, a mirror, feather beds with bedsteads, and in all likelihood white plaster walls. The exterior kitchen included a wide variety of iron cookware, a brass skillet, scales and weights, two dozen drinking vessels, pewter plates, and stoneware—all signs that the Madisons enjoyed a refined cuisine. The plantation was also substantial; they brought with them dozens of animals, all manner of farm instruments, and more than two dozen enslaved humans.

The family's ambitions would not be fulfilled in Ambrose's lifetime, for he died in the summer of 1732, when his oldest son, James, was just nine years old. In the years that followed, Ambrose's widow took over day-to-day control of the estate until young James came of age in 1741. Fortunately for the family, James was well-disposed to the life of a plantation owner on the western frontier, and the estate thrived under his management. The demand for foodstuffs in Europe and the Caribbean induced many Virginia planters, including James, to diversify their crops, and Mount Pleasant eventually grew corn, wheat, apples, and even peaches. He also began a distillery and ironworks. It was, all in all, a thriving venture, which enabled him to purchase more land and more enslaved people. When Ambrose died in 1732, his estate counted twenty-nine enslaved people. When his son James died in 1801, Montpelier had more than one hundred enslaved people.

In keeping with the expectations of a country squire in colonial Virginia, James participated in government administration—in part as a form of public service, but also to establish himself as a man of power and importance. The most practical way to serve was in county government, especially for those on the Piedmont, far away from Williamsburg, where the royal governor, the executive council, and the House of Burgesses (the popularly elected legislature of the colony) sat. At various points, James would serve as overseer of local roads, justice of the peace, county lieutenant of the militia, and coroner. His sisters, meanwhile, married into well-to-do families, expanding the social reach of the Madisons in the local community. In 1749, James married Nelly Conway, whose family lived a short distance away near Fredericksburg. Eighteen months later, she gave birth to James Jr., the first of twelve children.

JAMES MADISON JR. spent his early years in the simple home originally built by his grandfather Ambrose, but by the time he was a teenager, the family had moved into a new house about four hundred yards away. Unlike the original homestead, this was an impressive brick building constructed in the Georgian style that wealthy planters in the Tidewater favored. The new home was two stories tall and two rooms deep, with a wide hallway running down the center. This was a home fit for a gentleman, large enough to receive and entertain guests while housing the growing Madison clan. At the time of its completion, around 1764, it was the largest brick home in Orange County, and thus a symbol of the local prestige the family had acquired. At some point after the construction of the new home, James Sr. would rechristen his plantation Montpelier.

Little "Jemmy," as young James was known by his family, was not required to do the backbreaking labor necessary to sustain a thriving plantation. That work, of course, was left to the enslaved workers, who in turn were monitored by a handful of white overseers. James Jr. was, moreover, physically limited in what he could do. When he reached full adulthood, he measured only five feet four inches, making him the shortest of America's presidents. With narrow shoulders and a thin waist, the adult Madison never weighed more than one hundred pounds. While his physical constitution may not have been suited for the frontier, he nevertheless was drawn to the life of the Virginia planter. From an early age, he would explore widely throughout the Montpelier estate, taking a keen interest in the natural world—an enthusiasm he would share with his neighbor and future friend, Thomas Jefferson. When James Sr. died in 1801, his son would take seriously the duties of plantation management, even as his political career continued to rise.

Those born into Madison's social station were first educated at home, learning mathematics from the family's account books and how to read from the Bible and the Book of Common Prayer. Often, these lessons were supplemented by scholastic readers or other books that happened to be in the family library. Unfortunately for young James, who took to reading early and eagerly, his father's literary selections were wanting, mostly religious and medicinal texts. Still, Madison's grandmother had sent away for an eight-volume collection of an old periodical named the *Spectator*, which, Madison would recall, inspired within him "an appetite for knowledge, and a taste for the improvement of the mind and manners." The purpose of the *Spectator* was to bring the high culture of the Enlightenment—ethics, philosophy, literature, aesthetics—to middle-class Londoners. Though its run was brief, lasting for only a few years in the early 1700s, the magazine had a wide, lasting influence, finding its way into the New World as aspiring colonists looked to experience a taste of English society. Madison was especially taken by the essays and poems of founding editor Joseph Addison. Toward the end of his life, Madison recalled that Addison "was of the first rank among the fine writers of his age" and his *Spectator* was "the best that had been written for cherishing in young minds a desire of improvement, a taste for learning, and a lively sense of the duties, the virtues, and the properties of life."[5]

At a certain point, however, there was not much more Madison could learn from his father's Book of Common Prayer or his grandmother's library. James Sr. had never been afforded much of an education, as he had been consumed from a young age with management of the plantation. He resolved that his children would have opportunities he did not, and he invested in the education of his eldest son, beginning when James Jr. was about eleven years old. Young James was sent to boarding school at the Innes plantation in King and Queen County, northeast of Richmond, under the tutelage of Donald Robertson. A former minister who had been educated at the University of Edinburgh, Robertson provided intensive instruction in Greek and Latin, including the works of Homer, Xenophon, and Justinian. Studies also included algebra, geometry, literature, French, and Italian. He may also have been introduced to the great works of Enlightenment political and moral philosophy as well as epistemology, including John Locke, David Hume, and Montesquieu, for Robertson owned copies of their works. In 1767, Madison returned home to continue his education under the direction of Reverend Doctor Thomas Martin, the rector of the Brick Church in Orange County and a graduate of the College of New Jersey (now Princeton). This was a fateful appointment, for it was probably Martin more than anyone else who influenced Madison's decision to attend the college himself.

Going to New Jersey in 1769 was Madison's first departure from the traditional path of the plantation gentry of Virginia. Most intelligent men of his age and social background attended William and Mary, as did Jefferson, John Marshall, and James Monroe. But with Martin's encouragement, Madison made a different decision. The reputation of the College of New Jersey was on the rise by the late 1760s, thanks to the efforts of its new president, John Witherspoon. On the other hand, the prestige of William and Mary had sunk after the departure of professor of natural philosophy William Small, who had instructed Jefferson. Madison's fragile physical constitution also played a factor. Williamsburg, in the far southeast corner of the state, had a swampy climate during the summer months that might endanger his health.

At this time, the College of New Jersey was housed entirely in Nassau Hall, which featured so centrally in school life that students often referred to the school as "Nassau." Built in 1756, Nassau Hall was the largest stone building in continental North America. All aspects of college life were contained within its walls: classrooms, kitchens, and space for lodging and lounging. At full capacity, its dormitory could hold more than 150 students, three per room in spartan quarters, though this did not seem to bother Madison at all. "I am perfectly pleased with my present situation," he wrote Martin shortly after his arrival, "and the prospect before me of three years confinement, however terrible it may sound, has nothing in it, but what will be greatly alleviated by the advantages I hope to derive from it."[6]

Madison's instruction under Robertson and Martin had been so advanced that, upon arrival at Nassau Hall, he took early exams in order to skip his freshman year. He was expected to translate Latin works by Virgil and Cicero into English, translate English into Latin, translate the Greek New Testament into English, and demonstrate facility in arithmetic, spelling, and grammar. He passed all of the exams and proceeded to undertake a vigorous course of study.

The academic studies at the College of New Jersey were intense. Witherspoon explained the details of his program in a 1773 letter: Freshman year was dedicated to reading Latin and Greek, "with Roman and Grecian antiquities, and rhetoric." In their sophomore year, pupils studied "a complete system of geography, with the use of globes," plus "the first principles of philosophy" and mathematics. Junior year was focused on math and science. In the senior year, students read the "higher classics," advanced further in mathematics and science, and went "through a course of moral philosophy." Witherspoon supplemented this with lectures to the juniors and seniors on "history, and afterwards upon composition and criticism," as well as instruction in French. Students were also required to give public speeches after prayers so "that they may learn, by early habit, presence of mind, and proper pronunciation and gesture in public speaking."[7]

Situated in the middle colonies, the College of New Jersey had a more ecumenical social climate, which impressed upon Madison a continental view of American life. Unlike Virginia, which had established the Anglican Church and suppressed religious minorities, often violently, New Jersey and neighboring Pennsylvania had a long tradition of tolerance and encouragement of immigration. Madison was thus able to meet people he never would have encountered if he had gone to William and Mary. For the first time in his life, he was stepping outside the narrow confines of the Virginia plantation gentry to see how the rest of his fellow colonists lived.

He found people deeply dissatisfied with colonial relations with Great Britain. Anti-Crown sentiment was widespread throughout North America by the time Madison arrived at college, but it was in the middle colonies—Delaware, New Jersey, and Pennsylvania—where these grievances took on an especially nationalistic flavor, as their central location made them the place where people from all over the eastern seaboard could meet and exchange views. In the fall of 1769, right at the start of his first semester, Madison sat in on the College of New Jersey's annual commencement, an event that impressed him greatly. He wrote to his father that in addition to awarding several bachelor's and master's degrees, the college granted a doctorate in law to John Dickinson, who had recently published a series of essays, entitled *Letters from a Farmer in Pennsylvania*, arguing against the taxes

Great Britain imposed upon the colonies. Also receiving an honorary degree was John Hancock, the Massachusetts merchant who would soon become a leading revolutionary figure. At the 1770 commencement, held the following July, Madison would note that all the graduates walked in "American cloth," signifying the nationalist ideals percolating throughout the nation and especially among the young.[8]

It was also in college that Madison discovered he had a talent for debate. He was a leading member of the American Whig Society, the famous debate club formed in 1769. While he had a very soft voice that made it hard for him to speak to large gatherings, he was a lively, engaging, and funny participant in the society's smaller, salon-style discussions. And his deep learning and carefully reasoned approach to argumentation made him a formidable opponent in any forensic combat.

Nevertheless, the bulk of Madison's time was dedicated to schoolwork. His personal character, in both private and public, was upright and serious. He detested idleness, drunkenness, and any indulgence that distracted from his academic duties. For instance, he advised his college friend William Bradford to "not suffer those impertinent fops that abound in every city to divert you from your business and philosophical amusements." Instead, he should show "indignation at their follies" and keep "them at a becoming distance." After Madison's death, his longtime manservant, an enslaved man named Paul Jennings who was born at Montpelier in 1799, would recall, "He was temperate in his habits. I don't think he drank a quart of brandy in his whole life. . . . When he had hard drinkers at his table, who had put away his choice Madeira pretty freely, in response to their numerous toasts, he would just touch the glass to his lips, or dilute it with water, as they pushed about the decanters."[9]

Jennings's recollections speak to the fact that Madison had enslaved people tend to him from birth until death. An enslaved

man named Sawney escorted Madison and Martin up to Princeton in 1769, and when Madison returned to Montpelier in 1772
he reentered the world of chattel slavery without any apparent
hesitation. His intensive study of Enlightenment thinking at the
College of New Jersey forced him to question many of the as-
sumptions that structured colonial life, but he never seems to
have given much thought to the racial hierarchies that undergirded the economics and social thinking of the New World. If
anything, his education reinforced the racism that infused life
at Montpelier. The Western world, in this view, had managed to
build a stable civilization upon the shaky foundation of human
nature. It had literally taken millennia to do it, and the whole
project had nearly been destroyed during the Dark Ages, but it
had been done. So, what of the Africans and Native Americans?
They were not civilized in this schema; rather, they were "sav-
ages," a word that recurs frequently in Madison's papers. Their
habits and traditions, their morals, their lack of learning, their
simplistic religions—all of this, and more, left them incapable
of sustaining the institutions of free government that had finally
begun to emerge in the Anglophone world. Accordingly, whites
were under no obligation to integrate them into Western civilization, for doing so would destroy it. Over the course of Madison's lifetime, people on both sides of the Atlantic would begin
to conclude that a commitment to freedom demanded an end to
slavery, but Madison was never to be counted among them.

The young Madison seems not to have suffered from home-
sickness during his time away from Montpelier. His correspondence with his father, though respectful and solicitous of his
family's well-being, had a decidedly businesslike feel to it. In
July 1770, for instance, he wrote to his father about returning to
Montpelier, but far from revealing a yearning to come home, he
was much more concerned about the logistics. "If I come home
in the spring, the purchase of a horse and travelling expenses, I

am apprehensive, will amount to more than I can reserve out of my present stock for those purposes so that it would not be amiss perhaps if you were to send a few [gold coins]." Like many other college students through the ages, the young Madison was not beyond pestering his dad for extra cash. Madison even prevailed upon his father to allow him an extra semester of postgraduate study with a focus on Hebrew. He finally returned to Montpelier in the spring of 1772, around the time of his twenty-first birthday.[10]

Several important themes from Madison's education give a sense of the politician and philosopher he would become. First, there was a grounding in the Bible and Christian theology, beginning from the time he first learned to read. All three of Madison's teachers were Christian ministers, and religion, accordingly, would play an important role in his intellectual development, even though he would never exhibit a particularly lively attachment to the faith. His theory of moral psychology was decidedly within the Christian tradition, in that it juxtaposed the inherent fallibility of man with the intrinsic value of human life. These two ideas need not go together, and in fact one could argue that they are in tension: Why should such value be placed on beings who eventually commit evil deeds? But these notions are yoked in the scriptures, and so they were in the secular thought of the age. Moreover, as a matter of political philosophy, Madison would follow the lead of the Gospels in placing the individual at the heart of existence, independent of the state or social community—a view that is notably different from the ancient thought of philosophers like Aristotle, and which would be rejected by many continental philosophers in the nineteenth century.

It is also noteworthy that Madison's college instruction came from outside the Anglican Church into which he was baptized. The main difference between the Presbyterianism of the College of New Jersey's Witherspoon and the Anglicanism of the Church of Virginia was not theological, for both were in the Calvinist tradition. Instead, the main point of contention was organizational. The presbytery system, especially as it evolved in the United States, was much more egalitarian than the hierarchical Church of Virginia. This was a welcome alternative for Madison, who did not care for the aristocratic undertones of Anglicanism.

Additionally, Madison's immersion in the classics of the Western tradition provided him a wealth of practical advice and philosophical instruction on all manner of subjects. Thucydides would instruct him in warfare, Aristotle in philosophy, Cicero in ethics, Polybius in politics, Justinian in law. It was only during the Renaissance that Europe had begun to match the erudition and sophistication of these classic works, at least outside the scholastic tradition of the Catholic Church. This made them essential texts for the Enlightenment project of statecraft to which Madison would dedicate his life. Time and again during the period of 1786 to 1788, when Madison and the other Founders were developing a new instrument of government, they would return to the ancients, who offered practical instruction on how to build a stable regime.

Finally, Madison was tutored in the British empirical tradition of the seventeenth and eighteenth centuries. This pushed Madison's thought in important directions. Empiricists like Locke held that all information is derived from sensory data, which in their view offered a firm foundation for understanding the universe. This inherently positive view of humanity's ability to learn inspired in Madison an optimism regarding man's control of his own destiny. He believed that human beings could utilize the lessons of history and philosophy to build durable institutions of government based on reason. In the *Federalist Papers*, he and Hamilton would refer to this as the "science of politics," an idea that is ultimately built upon the confidence he gleaned from the empiricists.

Yet this confidence in the potential for human understanding was tempered by Madison's rather dim view of the human capacity for goodness. For this, Madison was heavily dependent upon the moral theory of Scottish philosopher David Hume. Though Witherspoon's lectures were critical of Hume's epistemological skepticism and theological secularism, he nevertheless provided Madison with a fateful introduction to Hume's thoughts on psychology and politics. In him, Madison would find a fellow skeptic of the capacity for human beings to see beyond their own selfish passions and act for the greater good of the community. This would inevitably temper Madison's enthusiasm for democratic institutions, as he, too, doubted the virtue and prudence of the masses.

MADISON'S DEPARTURE FROM the College of New Jersey ensnared him in an existential crisis. Until that point in his life, he had been a model student. School had been the central purpose of his life. But now his studies were over. Madison's friend William Bradford was dealing with similar feelings. "If a collegial life is a state of bondage," he wrote Madison, "I am in love with my chains." Now, he would have to choose "what business I shall follow for life," an uncertain prospect that left him anxious. But "Jemmy," as Bradford affectionately called Madison, was going through something much more serious. For his whole life, he be would prone to what he would later call "sudden attacks, somewhat resembling epilepsy," that suspended his "intellectual functions." These had become quite severe around the time of his graduation from the College of New Jersey and continued after he returned to Montpelier. In November 1772, he wrote Bradford that he was "too dull and infirm now to look out for any extraordinary things in this world" because he did not "expect a long or healthy life." Bradford wrote back to register alarm and suggested to Madison that "you hurt your constitution" at college "by too close an application to study." Bradford added optimistically, "Persons of the weakest constitutions, by taking a proper care of themselves often out live those of the strongest"—a bit of folk wisdom that, in Madison's case, turned out to be true, as he would go on to live well into his eighties.[11]

Madison's lachrymose mood would eventually be broken by the cascade of events that led to the American Revolution. Relations between the colonies and Great Britain took a turn for the worse in 1773, when British prime minister Lord North secured passage of the Tea Act, which placed a modest tax on tea and gave the British East India Company the right to sell directly to the colonies, circumventing North American tea merchants. North reckoned that the colonists would accede to the tax because, on balance, the cost of tea would be lowered by cutting out the middlemen. But he badly miscalculated. In Boston, the Sons of Liberty allied with aggrieved merchants to dump a load of India's finest into the harbor. Parliament responded to the Boston Tea Party with the "Intolerable Acts" of 1774, which closed the Boston port, suspended representative government in Massachusetts Bay Colony, immunized British officials from being tried in local courts, and forced colonists to quarter the soldiers, imposing martial law.

After the Boston Tea Party, Madison's letters took on a noticeably revolutionary cast. In January 1774, he wrote to Bradford that "the frequent assaults that have been made on America, Boston especially, will in the end prove of real advantage" to the American cause. In the same letter, he advised his friend to study

British history, for he would "fall more in love with liberty" if he beheld the "detestable pictures of tyranny and cruelty" who had "swayed the British sceptre." In July 1774, he reported to Bradford that the people of Virginia were "generally very warm" in their sentiments toward Boston. Virginians "are very unanimous and resolute, are making resolves in almost every county, and I believe are willing to fall in with the other colonies in any expedient measure," even if it meant nonimportation of British goods. By August, he was advocating a wartime footing, suggesting to Bradford that the colonists should not "presume too much on the generosity and justice of the crown," and instead "begin our defense and . . . let its continuance or cessation depend on the success" of appeals for peace.[12]

This quick succession of events created sudden professional opportunities for Madison. Held in October 1774 in Philadelphia, the First Continental Congress called for a trade boycott with Great Britain and encouraged the colonies to begin organizing local defenses. As the most prominent citizen in the county, James Madison Sr. was named the head of the Orange County Committee of Safety. James Jr., as his son, was likewise appointed to the committee (while his uncle was named the clerk). Skirmishes in the Tidewater region between patriot militias and John Murray, Earl of Dunmore—the royal governor of the colony—throughout 1775 culminated in Dunmore ordering the burning of the town of Norfolk on New Year's Day 1776 and retreating to New York. With the British government having abandoned any present hope of reclaiming civil authority, Virginia became a self-governing commonwealth, but it did not have a charter by which to rule itself. It was for this purpose that voters around the state assembled at their local courthouses in the spring of 1776 to elect delegates to a new convention. James Jr. was a natural choice to represent Orange. He had not yet done anything to establish a reputation for himself in the field of public affairs, but he possessed the proper pedigree, which in eighteenth-century Virginia was essential. And, unlike his father, he did not have a vast plantation he had to oversee, so he could afford to travel to Williamsburg, the capital of the newly independent Commonwealth of Virginia, to participate in the assembly.

The young Madison had finally found the calling that had eluded him ever since he had come home from college. He would discover in politics not merely a duty that a gentleman of means and status was obliged to participate in, but rather a passion, a vocation that would define the rest of his life.

WILLIAMSBURG HAD SERVED as the seat of Virginia's colonial government since 1699. The center of daily life in Williamsburg was the Duke of Gloucester Street, with the College of William and Mary's Wren Hall to the west and the capitol building roughly a mile to the east. The street was lined with coffeehouses and taverns where the revolution had been planned and organized. As the royal governor had abandoned his post, the revolutionaries now assumed full control and settled into the capitol to write a new instrument of government.

The Virginia convention met at the same time as the Second Continental Congress. There, Richard Henry Lee—an early leader of the patriot cause in Virginia and a descendant of one of the colony's most prominent families—made the official motion for independence, while Jefferson, Virginia's most impressive young intellectual, drafted the Declaration of Independence. That meant the proceedings in Williamsburg would be dominated by the other prominent statesmen of the Old

Dominion—especially George Mason, Edmund Pendleton, and Patrick Henry. Madison, just twenty-five years old and a new-comer to politics, naturally took a back seat to these titans of Virginia statecraft.

The convention drafted a new constitution that placed the bulk of governing power in the new House of Delegates, which would replace the colonial House of Burgesses. This House of Delegates had the authority to select both the governor and the "privy council" that advised him. The convention also adopted the Virginia Declaration of Rights, a set of sixteen propositions that sharply limited the scope of governing authority. This doc-ument's primary author was George Mason. A wealthy planter and neighbor of George Washington, Mason was a quiet and imposing figure at the convention. While not a distinguished orator, he was nevertheless deeply knowledgeable about the his-tory and practice of republican government. Thirteen years later, when proposing the Bill of Rights for the United States, Madi-son would draw heavily upon Mason's declaration.

The opening passage of the Declaration of Rights boldly an-nounced that "all men are by nature equally free and indepen-dent," possessing "certain inherent rights" that cannot be taken by the government, including "life and liberty" as well as "prop-erty." These ideas, popularized by Locke, would find their most famous expression in Jefferson's opening to the Declaration of In-dependence. Mason then asserted that all government authority is "derived from the people" and that government is "instituted for the common benefit"—an idea that would become the basic tenet of American republicanism itself, affirmed in the preamble to the Constitution and later in Abraham Lincoln's Gettysburg Address. The Declaration of Rights also gave the right to vote to "all men, having sufficient evidence of permanent common interest with, and attachment to, the community." It further provided for due-process protections in criminal proceedings, freedom of the press, the subjection of the military authority to the civil, and religious toleration.[13]

It was on this last issue that Madison made his first mark in politics. The committee on religion, to which Madison was appointed, was tasked with amending Mason's original religion clause in the Declaration of Rights, which stated that "all men should enjoy the fullest toleration in the exercise of religion, according to the dictates of conscience." This was the forerunner to the First Amendment's "free exercise clause," which prohibits Congress from interfering with religious practices. But Mason still favored an established or government-supported church—namely the Church of Virginia, an Anglican institution. So, under the Declaration of Rights, dissenters from the state-supported church—be they Baptists, Presbyterians, or Quakers—could worship as they liked but would still be obliged to fund the Church of Virginia through their tax dollars. In Madison's view, this was unjust, and his alternative proposal supplemented Mason's right to free exercise with formal disestablishment: "No man or class of men," Madison suggested, "ought, on account of religion . . . be invested with peculiar emoluments or privileges."[14]

Madison's strong feelings about the issue sprung not from any deep sense of religious devotion but from his commitment to fairness in a republic. When he returned from college, he had been appalled by Virginia's treatment of the fast-growing Baptist population, which was especially concentrated in the Piedmont. Baptist services had a lively and egalitarian flair to them, which the Anglican gentry who ruled both church and state perceived as a threat. So, the colonial government restricted when and where Baptist ministers could preach and went so far as to prosecute those preachers who refused to follow the rules. From Madison's perspective, this was the sort of unjust outcome that happened when the government favored one faction over another. He had complained to Bradford that "ecclesiastical establishments" like the Church of Virginia "tend to great ignorance and corruption," promoting "pride, ignorance, and knavery among the priesthood" and "vice and wickedness among the laity." The established church also corrupted the government. Its clergy were a "numerous and powerful body," with "great influence at home by reason of their connection with and dependence on the bishops and the crown." They would "naturally employ all their art and interest" to get what they wanted, even if it meant the oppression of a minority.[15]

Madison's opposition to the established church anticipates a dominant political concern of his career: the government should not play favorites but rather act as a neutral arbiter that seeks to balance the interests of the various forces in society. He strongly believed that when it failed to do this, injustice and corruption were sure to follow. To be sure, this basic sentiment was not peculiar to Madison, but rather part and parcel of republican political philosophy in the eighteenth century. Mason's Declaration of Rights, after all, called for a government "instituted for the common benefit," under which "no man, or set of men, are entitled to exclusive or separate emoluments or privileges from the community." Yet Madison was unique in his deep commitment to this principle, whatever the implication; whereas Mason did not think it required disestablishment, Madison did.[16]

But in 1776, Madison was just a junior member of Virginia's political class, which still generally supported an established church. Edmund Pendleton, thirty years Madison's senior and a distant cousin, chaired the committee and opposed Madison's suggestion. Jefferson would recall that Pendleton "was the ablest man in debate I have ever met with." He was "never vanquished; for if he lost the main battle, he returned upon you, and . . . by dexterous maneuvers, skirmishes in detail, and the recovery of small advantages which, little singly, were important all together." By the end of the debate, Madison's injunction against "peculiar emoluments or privileges" was struck. The only remainder of his effort was a shift from Mason's original call "that all men should enjoy the fullest toleration in the exercise of religion" to a stronger phrasing fashioned by Madison: "All men are equally entitled to the free exercise of religion." Despite this clash, Madison and Pendleton never held a grudge against each other over the issue, and the convention would be the beginning of a fruitful professional relationship.[17]

ALL THINGS CONSIDERED, Madison's performance at the convention was a workmanlike beginning to what would ultimately be a remarkable political career. He was never bound to shine like Mason, Pendleton, or Patrick Henry, but he was a diligent participant who made a legitimate contribution to the important issue of religious liberty. Despite this notable contribution and his family pedigree, in April 1777 Madison lost reelection as a delegate to Charles Porter, whose victory was in large part a result of him supplying whisky to the county's voters—a gesture that Madison failed to duplicate. His defeat illustrates the populist subtext to Virginia republicanism. The gentry of the commonwealth dominated public offices, yet because the franchise belonged to all white male freeholders, the elites had to genuflect to the common men, at least on occasion. The young Madison refused to play along and suffered as a consequence.

But as a testament to Madison's rising reputation among the governing elite in the state, he was soon appointed by the new House of Delegates to serve on the privy council. Madison spent more than two years there, from November 1777 until December 1779, first under Henry as governor, then later under Jefferson. This thrust Madison into the day-to-day efforts of managing the Old Dominion. It was here he discovered that he had a real facility for the detail work required in government. He was more than happy to dig deep into the policy weeds, well past the point where others would find themselves bored or indifferent. Just as at the College of New Jersey, he was intensely committed to work, to the exclusion of virtually everything else in his life. He never missed meetings, never went home to see his family when government was in session, and seemingly had no interest in a love life. He enjoyed the work of the privy council so much that, when Orange County elected him to the House of Delegates in 1778, he declined the opportunity, as it would have required him to resign.[18]

Working in government at this time was truly a matter of service. Public officials in Virginia received an income, but it was quite modest, reflecting the dire financial situation of the nation during the Revolutionary War. Despite his paltry salary, Madison did not live a life of deprivation during his stint on the privy council—far from it. His cousin Reverend James Madison was an Episcopal minister who had in 1776 been named president of the College of William and Mary. Because of his position, Reverend Madison lived in the President's House, a fine, three-story brick home constructed in 1732 and 1733, and he invited his cousin James to lodge there, which he would do for the duration of his tenure on the council. As Madison explained to his father, it was "a much better accommodation than I could have promised myself." This was, in a small way, another illustration of the contradictions of life in Virginia. The new government had declared all men "naturally free and equal," but in practice much depended on who you were related to.[19]

Madison was evolving into a professional politician—one of the first in the nation. In Virginia, almost all politicians were also plantation owners who had to balance management of their estate with their service to the commonwealth. Madison, however, would not become the owner of an estate until his father died in 1801, and in the meantime he committed himself fully to a life of politics. While this cut against the ethos of the time, the old way was becoming outdated. The problems of public life in the United States were so pressing that they would soon require the full-time commitment of professional politicians, rather than part-timers who would always have to divide their attention. That Madison was able to make such a commitment meant that he could distinguish himself in the privy council.

The most immediate public-policy problem facing the government was the war. The Revolutionary forces were a hodgepodge. Some were under the command of officers such as Horatio Gates, Henry Knox, and George Washington, who were commissioned by the Continental Congress. Others, like the Virginia militia, functioned under the auspices of state governments—in this case, specifically the governor and thus the privy council. As such, Madison was charged with helping the governor oversee the militia. Public finance was another concern. The cost of the war was greater than the United States could pay in specie (or coins made of precious metals), so the government had taken to printing paper money not backed by gold. This led to rampant inflation throughout the country. Madison would be vexed by this problem for years to come, first as a member of the privy council then later as a delegate to the Continental Congress. Snowbound at Montpelier in the winter of 1779–1780, he committed himself to studying the problem and produced a treatise on currency—eventually published in 1791 in the *National Gazette* under the title "Money"—in which he argued that the value of currency ultimately depended on the trustworthiness of the government to repay its debts.

Most of Madison's time on the privy council was spent serving under Patrick Henry, who would be governor until 1779, when he was succeeded by Jefferson. Henry was the most forceful personality in all of Virginia politics. A legendary orator, he had taken a leading role in revolutionary politics over the previous decade. Though Madison and Henry would become bitter rivals in later years, they got along reasonably well during this time. Henry, who was never known for his attention to the details of government, certainly appreciated Madison's work ethic.

Jefferson's ascension to the governor's office inaugurated the great partnership between him and Madison. They had met in October 1776, when Jefferson joined the Virginia convention after his work at the Second Continental Congress concluded. At the time, Madison was young and demure, while Jefferson, nine years his elder, had already established himself as one of Virginia's most influential statesmen. Even so, Madison was a supporter of the reform agenda that Jefferson promoted in the House of Delegates. Ever the visionary, Jefferson saw the American Revolution as an opportunity not only to throw off the shackles of a distant and cruel tyrant, but also to reform and rationalize public policy in Virginia. To that end, he had introduced a systematic revisal of the laws, which called for free public education, an end to the slave trade, and the abolition of the system of "entail," an ancient set of rules regarding land ownership that concentrated property in the hands of a few. As a committed opponent of government-sanctioned privilege, Madison enthusiastically supported this agenda.

Madison and Jefferson would eventually become best friends, joined not only by shared backgrounds and interests but by the fact that they took great joy in each other's company. They both hailed from the Piedmont region of central Virginia. They both loved nature, science, and the life of the country planter, and their correspondence over the years would toggle among the many pastimes they shared. They both were firm believers in the Enlightenment notion that traditions should be subjected to tests of reason and discarded if found wanting. Beyond these intellectual and socioeconomic similarities, they simply got along well. Conversation between them always flowed easily, as both were much more comfortable in small groups than in large, formal settings. And their professional ambitions never clashed, for Madison did not presume to jump ahead of Jefferson in politics. He always deferred to his friend as the senior partner in their relationship, so there was never a doubt between them regarding the other's motives. Jefferson would go on to suffer a tremendous tragedy in 1782 when his wife Martha died, which made his friends all the more important to him, especially Madison, who would become a primary source of emotional and intellectual support. Jefferson, in turn, would inspire the ever-cautious Madison to dream bigger than he was otherwise inclined to.[20]

MADISON'S DILIGENT WORK in Williamsburg was far from glorious, but in due course it paid off. In 1779, the House of Delegates selected him to serve as a representative of Virginia at the Continental Congress. This was still technically the Second Continental Congress, the same that had declared independence three years earlier, but it had lost a lot of its luster. Many of the leading lights from the 1776 meeting—Jefferson, John Adams, John Hancock, Richard Henry Lee, and Benjamin Franklin—had moved on. Worse, the Congress had been saddled with a terrible governing charter. The Articles of Confederation, adopted in 1777, denied Congress the most basic of powers: to tax, to regulate commerce, even to enforce its own laws. And with the war for independence now dragging into its fifth year, there was real doubt as to whether this government was fit to prosecute the conflict.

Madison found this situation completely unacceptable, and the young Virginian would soon join a coalition of nationalists that would try unsuccessfully to expand the power of Congress. While the failure was frustrating for Madison, it was also useful. He was not only getting firsthand insight into how legislative politics worked in practice; he was also gaining a crucial understanding of the problems plaguing the national government, which would enable him to craft an alternative vision. And it was this vision that would eventually form the basis for the United States Constitution.

2

A POLITICIAN ON THE RISE

DELAYED BY UNUSUALLY heavy rains when traveling from Montpelier, James Madison took his seat at the Continental Congress in March 1780, shortly after his twenty-ninth birthday. This was his first entrance into national politics, the realm to which he would dedicate most of the next forty years of his life.

During Madison's tenure, Congress met in the Pennsylvania statehouse, today known as Independence Hall. Located on Chestnut Street in Philadelphia and completed in 1753, the building had originally held all three branches of the colonial government of Pennsylvania and was where the Declaration of Independence had been signed. Philadelphia was by that point a thriving and diverse merchant city of roughly twenty-five thousand people, thanks to the toleration and industriousness of its original Quaker settlers. Members of an English Protestant sect who refused to abide by the rules of the Church of England, the Quakers had emigrated to the New World in the 1680s in search of religious liberty. Having faced persecution themselves, they were quite tolerant of those with other beliefs, and as a result the colony had drawn a large influx of immigrants, especially from Germany. The Quakers were also intrepid businessmen, and Philadelphia had become a continental center of trade and commerce, which in turn attracted a vibrant artisan community, educational institutions, and even theaters. Though Quaker religious practices emphasized simple, unadorned manners, dress, and furnishings, the wealthy and diverse residents of the city enjoyed the finer things in life, and accordingly the town's social scene was quite lively by the standards of the day.

Madison's time in Congress—much like his time in the privy council of Virginia—was spent almost totally absorbed in work. His surviving correspondence suggests that letters home were few and far between and typically devoid of sentiment. Gone were the discursive missives to old friends like William Bradford, pondering questions of philosophy and looking back fondly on their college days. Instead, Madison's correspondence as it comes down to us is almost entirely dedicated to the business of government. Among politicians, Madison made a strong impression as a man of integrity. Chevalier de la Luzerne, who served as French minister to the United States from 1779 to 1784, described Madison as possessing "a sound and just mind. A man of learning, who desires to do good works and to improve himself, but who is not overly ambitious." Though Luzerne noted that Madison was a vigorous advocate for the interests of Virginia, he also thought him a man "of honest principles; zealous, without going to excess, for the honor of the thirteen states."[1]

While he was maturing into a respected leader, the young Madison was lacking in social graces. Martha Bland, the wife of Virginia delegate Theodorick Bland and a regular on the city's party circuit, recalled that Madison was "a gloomy, stiff creature." He may have been "clever in Congress, but out of it he has nothing engaging or even bearable in his manners." He was "the most unsociable creature in existence." She was probably not far from the mark. Madison was uncomfortable at parties, and even if he had possessed a disposition suited to the Philadelphia social life, he lacked the funds. Neither a man of northern commerce nor the owner of one of the larger plantations in the Tidewater, he was constantly pinching his pennies.[2]

Cold and halting at large social gatherings, Madison was warm and lively among a small group of intimates. While in Philadelphia, he stayed at a boardinghouse owned by Mary House and managed by Eliza Trist, her daughter, who lived there with her husband Nicholas and their son Browse. Madison would grow close to the Trists during his stay in Philadelphia, enjoying cheerful discussions in the evening after the business of Congress was concluded. Also staying at the boardinghouse were Joseph Jones and John Walker, two other delegates from Virginia, and William Floyd, a delegate from New York. The House residence became a home away from home for Madison, where he could put aside the stressful business of government, relax, and enjoy leisurely conversations that did not always have to involve politics. Jefferson—who had boarded at Mrs. House's during his stint in Congress—once noted the "raillery," or good-humored teasing, "you sometimes experienced from" the housemates, which he called "our family."[3]

Madison was particularly drawn to William Floyd's fifteen-year-old daughter, Kitty—the first known romance of his life. There are few verified facts about their courtship, Madison did propose marriage, and Kitty accepted. Unfortunately, it would end in heartbreak for the young delegate, as Kitty instead married a medical student named William Clarkson a few years later. Madison had written to Jefferson in April 1783 that "preliminary arrangements" for marriage were "definitive" and would be "postponed" until Congress adjourned at the end of the year, after which the pair would travel to Virginia. But by August, he wrote to Jefferson that the impending nuptials had been called off. The details remain sketchy at best, but it is a demonstration of how close Madison and Jefferson had become that the former was comfortable confiding in the latter about the unfortunate turn of events with Kitty. When Madison recovered the letter he sent to Jefferson many years later, he scratched out several portions related to Kitty—an indication that, whatever the specifics, he wished them to be erased from the historical record.[4]

Jefferson wrote to comfort Madison for the dissolution of his engagement to Kitty and encouraged him to cope by burying himself in work. Madison's "firmness of mind and unintermitting occupations," Jefferson suggested, would "not long leave" him "in pain." That is precisely what Madison did. He would not seriously pursue another woman for more than a decade, when he would fall head over heels for Dolley Payne Todd, whom he would marry in 1794.[5]

MADISON'S SERVICE IN Congress began at one of the darkest moments in the Revolution. While the French had joined the American cause in 1778, its fleet was engaged with the British in the Caribbean, leaving the British free to trawl the coastline of the United States. The winter of 1779–1780 was an unusually snowy one, and the Continental Army, encamped at Morristown, New Jersey, was running low on supplies. The British still controlled New York City, and, in a worrying development, British general Henry Clinton had taken the war south, reckoning that he could invade the less defended colonies of Georgia and the Carolinas, rally support among the loyalist population, and ultimately take control of Virginia. American efforts to thwart this plan by dislodging the British from Savannah, Georgia, had failed, and by the time Madison arrived in Philadelphia, Clinton was almost ready to lay siege to Charleston, South Carolina. Though Governor John Rutledge managed to escape, Charleston fell in May 1780, with a loss of some five thousand soldiers and three hundred cannons. As 1780 wore on, the situation would become more dire when Horatio Gates, tasked with rebutting the British invasion in the South, suffered a massive defeat at the Battle of Camden in August.

Meanwhile, Congress was a dysfunctional institution, as the Articles of Confederation strictly limited the power it could wield. With little hope of real action, debates in the body tended to be long, meandering, and ultimately fruitless. Often, members would be gone for months on end, which prevented the body from conducting essential business, since the necessary quorum could not be met. Many delegates were perfectly content with this situation. It was the states that had selected them, and few delegates were willing to trade their states' advantages away, even if it meant a stronger national government that could deal with the country's many problems.

Factional squabbling reared its ugly head in all kinds of matters—for instance, the question of what to do with the western territory. Did it belong to the country as a whole, or to the states that had claimed it when they were still colonies? This mattered because land sales were going to be a major way to pay down the public debts without taxing the citizenry, but unless the western territory was put into a common fund, some states would benefit while others would not. In fact, Maryland—which had no claims to western land—was so outraged over Virginia's insistence on extensive territorial claims that it had still not even signed the Articles of Confederation by the time Madison took his seat.

The question of western territory was especially fraught because it intersected with the biggest problem of the age: public finances. No issue dominated Madison's attention during his stint in Congress more than the interrelated problems of taxes, spending, and debt. The cost of financing the American Revolution was about $165 million in specie, which amounted to 15 to 20 percent of the country's total output of goods and services. This expense is proportional to the cost of the Civil War and World War I, both of which were substantial martial efforts. Funds for such massive endeavors must come from three sources: increased taxes, borrowing, or inflation. The problem for the Revolutionary generation was that the first two sources were grossly insufficient. The country simply lacked the wealth to raise the money through taxation. As Alexander Hamilton noted, "The war, particularly in the first periods, required exertions beyond our strength; to which neither our population nor riches were equal." While European governments and foreign creditors had provided the government with some resources, they were hardly enough.[6]

Unable to raise taxes or borrow enough money, Congress pursued the only means of large-scale finance available to it: inflation. Whenever it faced a cash shortfall, it would print "fiat currency," or paper money that could not be redeemed for precious metals. All told, fiat money accounted for nearly two-thirds of the total financing of the war. This was, as Hamilton noted, "originally an effect not a cause" of the country's financial distress; there really was no other choice. But inflation quickly began to spiral out of control. Congress printed $13 million in paper money in 1777 but increased it to $125 million by 1779. In April 1777, $2 in Continental money was roughly equivalent to $1 in hard currency. By April 1779, it took $16 worth of Continentals to match $1 in hard currency. When Madison took his seat in 1780, the exchange rate had ballooned to $60 in Continentals for $1 in specie.

The only hope of escape was to raise taxes to remove the excess money from circulation and keep inflation under control. But this exposed a design flaw in the Articles of Confederation, which granted Congress the power to print money but not to tax it out of circulation. That power rested exclusively with the states, which kept taxes too low and thus inflation too high. Faced with this dilemma, Congress's only options were to acquire the power to tax or give up its remaining control over the currency. It chose the latter. In a motion approved in March 1780, the legislature decided effectively to cede the power over the currency to the states. The states were instructed to tax the old money out of existence, and for every $40 of the old money they sent to Congress, Congress would return $1 in new money.

This was a terrible mistake. The war was a national crisis and required a national economic strategy. Congress's decision ensured that rather than a single response, there would be thirteen separate ones. George Washington summarized this anxiety in a letter to delegate Joseph Jones: "I see one head gradually changing into thirteen . . . and am fearful of the consequences of it." Washington's worries were not misplaced. The state governments had no desire to raise taxes on their constituents, so they only ever removed about half the old money from circulation. Meanwhile, Congress was left powerless to do anything, by its own volition. As Madison complained to Jefferson, Congress had once "exercised the indefinite power of emitting money on the credit of their constituents," which had given it access to the "whole wealth and resources of their continent." But now that the power had been given to the states, Congress was "as dependent on the states as the King of England is on Parliament."[7]

Congress made a similarly unwise decision on supplying the military. The Articles of Confederation gave it authority over the military, and by implication the responsibility for its provisioning. But because it lacked the power to tax, Congress was dependent on the states to supply it with the requested funds, which were often not forthcoming. So, Congress handed the responsibility of provisioning over to the states directly. Again, this made sense from the perspective of housing full power and responsibility within either Congress or the states, rather than spreading it across the two. But the states were once more reckless stewards of the national welfare. They rarely provided sufficient resources, and when they did they would often earmark them for their state's own troops, meaning some men at camp were better provisioned than others. Washington found this had a terrible effect on morale, for it "served to establish a contrast that embitters the sufferings of the rest."[8]

WATCHING CONGRESS TRY helplessly to constrain the states had a tremendous effect on Madison's views. He had come into Congress as a nationalist by instinct, his education at the College of New Jersey having given him a continental outlook. But watching in real time as the thirteen states mismanaged the war while Congress sat by unable to do anything gave Madison's disposition a decidedly political edge. He became increasingly convinced that there had to be a central authority to rule over the states, one with enough power to punish bad behavior and to act on behalf of the national good when the states failed to do their fair share.

He was not alone. The crisis in public affairs brought into existence a new faction in Congress. Before the war, divisions within the body had centered on the question of whether to terminate relations with Great Britain. After the Declaration of Independence settled that question, attention turned to how strong the new national government should be. As it became clear that Congress's decisions to divest itself of power over currency and military provisions had been wrongheaded, an informal group of nationalists began to emerge that called for strengthening the authority of Congress. Madison would become an energetic member of this team.

Generally speaking, the nationalists were men of property, and their numbers included the plantation gentry of the Virginia Tidewater and the South Carolina Low Country, whose extensive agricultural operations gave them an economic stake in the maintenance of an ordered society. The more prosperous farmers of the Virginia Piedmont, like the Madisons, had a similar interest. The nationalist faction also drew heavily from the merchants of the major cities in the North—Boston, New York, and Philadelphia—which had turned into busy hubs of international commerce even before the war and therefore had an incentive for stability. The manifest failure of the government to manage its affairs responsibly deeply threatened all of these men, who understood that without a competent government, the American experiment would surely fail.

The nationalists believed that the government was in need of serious reform, in two directions. First, Congress needed reorganization. It controlled both the legislative and executive functions of the government, meaning, for instance, that it was not only in charge of writing the laws authorizing spending and borrowing, but it was also responsible for carrying them out. As a large, diverse body, Congress struggled to act with the kind of efficiency necessary to manage a crisis such as the Revolutionary War. So, the nationalists secured a reorganization of the government into specific executive departments to be helmed by secretaries with vast discretion over public policy. The Philadelphia merchant and prominent nationalist Robert Morris became the superintendent of finance, where his influence stretched far and wide—much for the better. He brought a modern sense of public finance and accounting to the office and even pledged his own wealth as collateral for notes used by the government.

Second, Congress had to become a more powerful governing body. The currency issue had demonstrated that the states were too divided to come together for the sake of the national interest. The only solution was to empower Congress to force the states to behave themselves. On this matter, the nationalists enjoyed a single, lasting triumph: they persuaded the states to give Congress most of their claims to the western territory. Not only did this resolve many of the lingering tensions between the states, but it also established the precedent that the land belonged to the nation in common—a principle that would guide land policy for centuries to come.

Madison took a leading role on the issue of the western territory. Virginia had the most expansive claims to the western land, but its insistence on retaining them after the start of the war had grated on the smaller states, especially Maryland. With the possibility of a British invasion from the south now a reality, Virginia began to have a change of heart. In his first year in Congress, Madison backed a resolution, along with Joseph Jones, calling on Virginia to cede its lands. "As these exclusive claims formed the only obstacle with Maryland," Madison wrote Edmund Pendleton, "there is no doubt that a compliance with this recommendation will bring her into the confederation." Virginia made a conditional cession: it offered to give up the bulk of its territory, provided that land companies with dubious claims to Virginia's ceded land could not get hold of it.[9]

As Madison predicted, this was good enough to get Maryland to adopt the Articles, but Virginia's condition regarding the land companies turned out to be a snag. States without geographical claims to western lands had chartered companies that had purchased dubious titles from Native Americans who did not actually occupy the territory claimed. These companies began selling what were often faked land claims to buyers in the small states, then worked to influence Congress to retroactively legitimize their illegal claims. During his time in Congress, Madison was dogged in his opposition to these claims, offended that the land companies were trying to persuade the legislature to give them an unmerited bailout. The stickiness of the land dispute, which pitted the states against one another, combined with the energetic efforts of the land speculators ultimately kept a final compromise from coming together until 1783. Eventually, the states agreed to put the land into a common fund, controlled by the Congress. This in turn set the precedent enshrined in the Constitution, which grants Congress power over territory and the admission of new states.

Madison's approach to the land cession and his previous effort to disestablish the Church of Virginia together present the earliest portrait of his mature worldview. His perspective was broad-minded: he was an Anglican who sympathized with the Baptists; he was a Virginian who acknowledged that Maryland had a legitimate grievance about Virginia's domination of the western lands. He sought to craft a compromise that not only could work with each faction but would be good for the whole community. Nevertheless, his abiding sense of fair play kept him from negotiating with those he believed were operating in bad faith to "gratif[y] private interest at the public expense," as he put it in a letter to Jones. So, not only had he criticized the Anglican clergy—who in his view were idle and corrupt from their government subsidies—but he vigorously opposed the fraudulent companies looking to score windfall profits from congressional land policy. His resolute unwillingness to budge on this issue illustrates just how intensely he believed government should not play favorites.[10]

While the nationalists succeeded in reorganizing the executive departments and resolving the western land dispute, they otherwise failed to expand congressional authority. Even seemingly modest procedural tweaks faced serious opposition. The Articles of Confederation were unambiguous that the support of nine states was necessary for a proposal to become a law. But what about all the intermediate steps between its proposal and final passage, say, the creation of a committee to study an issue or the consideration of amendments to a proposed bill? The Articles themselves were silent, but Congress had adopted a rule that nine votes were required for every step. This ground legislative business to a halt, because many state delegations were regularly absent from Philadelphia. As an alternative, Madison and the nationalists argued that only a majority of a quorum (or five votes out of nine) should be necessary to conduct regular business. But they could not muster the votes for this change, as many anti-nationalists in Congress did not want the body to move expeditiously. A more effective legislature would do a better job of governing, which was exactly what the nationalists wanted but exactly what their opponents feared.

In 1781, the nationalists made a bold move to strengthen the national government, seeking to secure for Congress a 5 percent duty on imported goods, to be enacted and implemented by the states. Congress could not raise taxes itself, but maybe the states could be convinced. Superintendent of finance Morris threw the full weight of his office behind the proposal, warning in May 1782 that if the "scenes of distress and horror be reiterated and accumulated . . . the fault is in the states," for "they have been deaf to the calls of Congress, to the clamors of public creditors, to the just demands of a suffering army, and even to the reproaches of the enemy, who scoffingly declare that the American army is fed, paid, and clothed by France." These strong words seemed to have the intended effect. Most of the states began to sign on, and it looked as though success was finally at hand. But the triumph proved illusory. In November 1782, the Rhode Island state legislature unanimously rejected the impost measure. Madison was appointed to a committee helmed by Hamilton to respond to Rhode Island's decision and even to plead Congress's case in person. But before the committee members could depart, word came that Virginia had revoked its approval of the impost, arguing that if Rhode Island refused, it would too.[11]

Madison was not yet ready to throw in the towel, and in his efforts to save the impost, he made use of a legislative tactic that would become a perennial feature of American politics: the logroll. He knew that states should adopt the impost for the good of the nation, but he also grasped that they were predominantly motivated by selfish interests. So, he introduced a series of proposals that could serve as bait to each of them. As he said in Congress in February 1783, "The most likely mode of obtaining the concurrence of the states" would be to put together a plan "in the equitable interests of all of them." The idea was that each state would get some special benefit in exchange for enacting the impost, and Congress would in turn receive the power to tax. The main points of the logroll were the assumption of state war debts (good for indebted states like Virginia), an abatement on overdue requisitions from states that had suffered during the war (good for war-torn states like South Carolina), and the final cession of the western land (good for states with no claims like Maryland). To win over skeptics of a central taxing authority, the nationalists further agreed to allow the states to appoint the collectors of the tax, although Congress would retain the right to remove them.[12]

Unfortunately for Madison, Congress watered his plan down substantially, removing the assumption of the war debts, but even in its modified form the delegates from Rhode Island refused to support it—an ominous sign for its future prospects with the states. Still, Madison wrote an impassioned plea to the states, begging them to adopt the plan, arguing that it was necessary "to render the fruits of the Revolution, a full reward for the blood, the toils, the cares and the calamities which have purchased it." Washington added his endorsement to the plan, arguing that the choice to accept or reject the impost was a choice about whether the United States "will be respectable and prosperous or contemptible and miserable as a nation."[13]

The appeals went unheeded. Though the nationalists were right about the fundamentals—the Congress as organized was unfit to govern the United States—the moment of crisis, which opened the possibility for lasting reforms, had by that point passed. The nationalists had been victims of America's triumph on the battlefield. At the beginning of 1780, the country had been in the midst of a crisis, and many people were willing to entertain the idea of a stronger central government. But the tide of the war began to turn in the fall of that year, with a string of triumphs against the British southern offensive at Kings Mountain, Cowpens, and Guilford Court House. British commander Lord Cornwallis invaded Virginia in the spring of 1781, which gave the combined French and American forces an opportunity to strike a killing blow. Washington boldly marched his army southward and, with the help of the French fleet, pinned Cornwallis in Yorktown in October 1781. Though a formal peace treaty would not be signed until 1783, the war was effectively over. It was a stunning victory for America, but one that, at least for the time being, made the nationalist agenda seem less urgent.

As Madison's appointment to Congress was nearing its end, he prepared to depart Philadelphia in the fall of 1783. In September, he wrote a letter to Jefferson venting his frustrations with the legislature. Most of the same public problems and petty rivalries that had vexed the affairs of state when he had joined Congress in March 1780 lingered. The Department of Finance remained "an object of almost daily attack," which had finally prompted Morris's resignation—an event that would reduce public finance "to its crisis." Meanwhile, the states were squabbling over the extent of congressional authority. The impost still languished, soon to be abandoned altogether. While the nation had finally won its independence during Madison's time in Congress, the government itself could not be said to have been a success. The war had been won despite, not thanks to, the civil authority.[14]

AFTER MADISON FINISHED work at the Continental Congress, he paid a social visit to his old colleague from the Virginia convention, George Mason, whose vast plantation lay on the Potomac River, just south of Alexandria. The centerpiece of Mason's homestead was Gunston Hall, a mansion built in the Georgian style with an elaborate front porch and a rear view overlooking beautiful gardens in front of the river.

More than two decades Madison's senior, Mason was the godfather of Virginia republicanism, having authored the Virginia Declaration of Rights in 1776. Back then, Madison was but a junior partner in this great endeavor for self-government. But after dedicating seven years of his life to public duties, Madison had established himself as an essential member of the Virginia governing caste. Yet there remained a wide personal gulf between the two, one that could not be reduced to their difference in age. Mason was the archetype of the country republican. A man of independent means, whose enslaved people did the toiling to make the plantation prosperous, he could dedicate himself to the problems of government as he pleased. Montpelier, the Madisons' plantation in Orange County, was not nearly as profitable as Mason's, and more importantly it was the property of James Madison Sr. Montpelier was profitable enough that the twenty-five-year-old Madison could commit himself fully to public affairs in 1776. But by 1783, the thirty-two-year-old Madison was aware that, unlike Mason, he had very little that belonged to him personally. He had dedicated his life to the practice of politics, which offered little pay. He was still unwed and had no estate of his own.

His friends inadvertently made him keenly sensitive to his stunted personal life. Thomas Jefferson—whose wife, Martha, had died in 1782—wrote often to Madison, begging him to acquire some property near Monticello. James Monroe—Jefferson's former law student and friend, and Madison's replacement at the Continental Congress—was moving nearby, and Jefferson envisioned the three of them living near each other. "What I would not give [so] you could fall into the circle," Jefferson wrote dreamily, but Madison had to beg off. He simply did not have the money. "My situation," he complained, "is as yet too dependent on circumstances to permit my embracing it absolutely." Now that his time in Congress was finished, perhaps Madison might settle into a profession that could actually provide him some income independent of his father. The law was an obvious choice, and he wrote Edmund Randolph, his friend and longtime political colleague, that he had taken up a "course of reading" in preparation for "professional use of it . . . to provide a decent and independent subsistence."[15]

But his heart was not in it. There always seemed to be more interesting distractions, including visits from near and distant relatives who came to hear the latest news about life outside the Piedmont. Madison also busied himself with all kinds of scientific examinations, undertaking with Jefferson (who by this point was serving as American minister to France) to compare American mammals to their European counterparts.

He also traveled with some frequency. In the summer of 1784, he ran into the Marquis de Lafayette—the great French hero of the Revolutionary War—in Baltimore. Lafayette convinced Madison to travel to New York with him, where Madison watched a treaty signing with Native Americans. He had a splendid time on this trip with the Frenchman, who was feted by Americans wherever he went, though Madison found him equal parts vain and amiable. Much later in life, Madison edited a letter he had sent to Jefferson in 1784 that seemed to criticize Lafayette for his vanity. Lafayette would return to the United States in 1824–1825, when he would spend a good deal of time with Jefferson and Madison in central Virginia; no doubt Madison wanted his youthful criticisms of Lafayette not to be remembered, just as he struck passages from an earlier letter to Jefferson about Kitty Floyd. Madison also traveled to New York in 1786 to meet Monroe, who by then had become a close friend. The two would subsequently make a joint investment in land in the Mohawk Valley in upstate New York, although Madison's share was modest.[16]

THE MOST SIGNIFICANT factor keeping Madison from settling into a legal career was his passion for politics. Intermingled with his travels over the next several years, he would serve as a delegate from Orange County in the Virginia House of Delegates several times between his departure from the Continental Congress and the start of the Constitutional Convention. The state government had moved to Richmond in 1780, to protect itself from the British during the war (Richmond being farther inland than Williamsburg) and to be closer to the rapidly expanding western territories of the state. Laid out in 1734, Richmond had become a spot of commercial intercourse, as planters sold their tobacco and bought enslaved people. Even by the standards of the day, it was hardly a city of refinement like Philadelphia. By 1780, it was still extremely small, with just several hundred wood-frame buildings and a population of less than four thousand people. The state capitol building was only finished in 1784, so for several years a temporary building was used in the Shockoe Slip district of the city, about half a mile away. One German traveler likened it to an "Arabian village," and Madison never stayed longer in the city than his political business required.[17]

Madison being Madison, he threw himself fully into his service. His main effort was relaunching Jefferson's "Revisal of the Laws," a comprehensive set of proposals designed to sweep away the aristocratic vestiges of colonial Virginia and ground the commonwealth in the principles of reason, justice, and liberty. The endeavor had to be set aside because of the war, but with independence secured, Madison figured it was time to start once more the task of doing away with the old rules of colonial Virginia. Additionally, he wanted to revise the constitution Virginia had adopted in 1776. Though he had originally voted for its adoption, he had come to realize that the document was terribly defective. Of particular concern was the privy council, the body whose nominal purpose was to advise the governor but that in effect hamstrung him with a phalanx of counselors whose approval he constantly had to seek. Madison, having served on the council under both Patrick Henry and Thomas Jefferson, considered it "a grave of useful talents." As far as

Madison was concerned, the sooner reform happened the better, for "every day's delay settles the government deeper into the habits of the people, and strengthens the prop which their acquiescence gives it."[18]

As in any Virginia political matter, much depended upon the disposition of Henry, who remained an imposing presence in the Old Dominion, commanding the loyalty and support of a large portion of the House of Delegates. However, he was not a man of particularly fixed principles, so it was never clear to what ends he would steer his many followers. Henry initially seemed disposed to reforms. In the spring of 1784, Jefferson, Madison, and Joseph Jones, a Virginia politician who had worked with Madison at the Continental Congress, pitched Henry on a resolution calling for strengthening the Continental Congress, and the unpredictable orator appeared amenable to it. But the alliance turned out to be short-lived, as Henry quickly equivocated. He likewise refused to lend his assistance to strengthen the state constitution. Henry was possessed of an "adverse temper," Madison wrote to Jefferson, and showed "a more violent opposition than we expected." Jefferson wrote back to complain, "While Mr. Henry lives another bad constitution would . . . be saddled forever on us. What we have to do I think is devoutly to pray for his death." Henry at this point was still under fifty years old and the father of several young children—an illustration that, while Jefferson's public persona was of a national statesman, in private correspondence he could be acerbic, partisan, and intemperate.[19]

Madison and Jefferson caught a break when Henry was once again named governor in 1784. Given the constitutional constraints imposed upon the governor, it was a promotion that left Henry mostly powerless to influence the course of legislative events. That gave Madison an opportunity to advance his reform agenda, and he prioritized the relationship between church and state. While Henry and Madison had once worked together on the issue, Henry had grown concerned about the weakening morals in the commonwealth. He threw his considerable political weight behind an effort to subsidize all Christian denominations, thinking that public support for churches was necessary to restore civic virtue. Madison was aghast at this, as Henry's plan would essentially amount to a public bounty for preachers. The problem was that Henry, at least for the time being, seemed to have public opinion on his side. The measure enjoyed immediate and strong support from Anglican and Presbyterian clergy, who rightly saw it as a way to secure a permanent income for themselves. So, Madison elected to play for time. While the bill narrowly passed the House of Delegates early in the fall 1784 session, the motion for a third reading of the bill (necessary for its final approval) was delayed until the next fall.[20]

This gave Madison time to mobilize public opinion. By the spring of 1785, he had already begun to note a backlash to Henry's assessment from the small farmers who lived west of the Blue Ridge Mountains. It seemed that while the Presbyterian clergy were in favor of a government stipend, their parishioners were unwilling to abide the requisite tax increase. As for the Baptists, long persecuted by the government, any entanglement between the civil and spiritual authority was a nonstarter. What Madison needed was to focus public attention in a precise way, and for this purpose in June 1785 he wrote the "Memorial and Remonstrance Against Religious Assessments," the first great essay of his career.

The structure of Madison's "Remonstrance" is notably different from the form he would use in his later *Federalist* essays, which generally begin with a particular premise and work their way logically and carefully to a conclusion. The "Remonstrance" employs the opposite approach: asserting at the forefront that the assessment was unwise and unjust, then marshaling every argument he could muster against the bill, in hopes that at least a few of them would stick. This made sense given that the purpose of the essay was to build a sufficiently broad political coalition against the bill. Different arguments would appeal to different constituencies, so it was best to try a great deal of them. This meant, in turn, that the piece was not a systematic exposition of Madison's political thought. Nevertheless, the "Remonstrance" emphasized several important political ideas that would animate the remainder of Madison's career.

On the matter of religion and politics, Madison had been influenced by John Locke's *A Letter Concerning Toleration*. Locke, most famous for authoring the *Two Treatises on Government*, was widely hailed as the chief apologist for overthrowing the Stuart monarchy in Great Britain during the Glorious Revolution of 1688 and for proffering a theory of natural rights that had informed the Declaration of Independence. Locke also made important arguments against government regulation of religion, which Madison repurposed for the "Remonstrance." Like Locke, Madison affirmed that because religion was a matter belonging to the "conviction and conscience of every man . . . it is the right of every man to exercise it as these may dictate." Madison also followed Locke in arguing that because one's religious duties were prior, "both in order of time and in degree of obligation, to the claims of civil society," the right of religious conscience was a natural one. The legislature, therefore, had no rightful power to make laws about beliefs, and the civil magistrate was not "a competent judge of religious truth."[21]

Madison pushed the case further still than Locke had. Locke wanted the Church of England to remain the established church, with toleration for Protestant nonconformists (though not for Catholics). Madison, on the other hand, called for complete disestablishment of the Church of Virginia and unconditional toleration of all sects. In so doing, he previewed several ideas that would prove central to his future political theory.

First, Madison warned about the danger of government playing favorites among its citizenry, especially on the basis of religious beliefs. "Equality," he asserted, "ought to be the basis of every law," which meant the government could not bless certain religious denominations over others. A religious assessment such as Henry's would naturally benefit the denominations receiving subsidies and burden those sects that refused the bounties and the nonreligious who did not go to church. This notion of fairness undergirded Madison's entire philosophy, and several years later, in 1787, he would give it a fuller treatment in *Federalist* 10, where he argued that politics was essentially a matter of properly distributing the benefits and burdens of government. In a republic, he would write, "justice ought to hold the balance between them." Just as the "landed interest, a manufacturing interest, a mercantile interest, a monied interest," or "many lesser interests" should not be able to use government for their own ends at the expense of the others, he explained in the "Remonstrance," the Anglicans had no right to burden the Baptists or the agnostics.[22]

Second, Madison saw the abolition of religious establishments as necessary for constraining factional conflicts in society. In *Federalist* 10, he would call this "the violence of faction," or the inevitable tendency of humans to favor themselves or their kin over the good of all, which he saw as one of the gravest dangers for a free nation. In that essay, he would enumerate a long list of potential causes of factional strife, and he saw religion as one such force. "The regulation of these various and interfering interests forms the principal task of modern legislation," he would write, which is why it was essential that government stay out of the religion business. To "extinguish religious discord," he wrote in the "Remonstrance," the state had to refrain from choosing religious winners and losers. Any other policy would only encourage the sorts of "civil wars" seen in early modern Europe, during which "torrents of blood [had] been spilt."[23]

Finally, Madison argued that government subsidies such as the one Henry was proposing had a corrupting effect, both on the church and the government. The church would be the immediate casualty in Henry's arrangement, Madison argued. "During almost fifteen centuries has the legal establishment of Christianity been on trial. What have been its fruits?" He answered, "More or less in all places, pride and indolence in the clergy, ignorance and servility in the laity, in both, superstition, bigotry and persecution." Furthermore, Madison asserted, religious institutions tended to be props for tyrants and oligarchs, rather than free governments: "In some instances, they have been seen to erect a spiritual tyranny on the ruins of the civil authority; in many instances they have been seen upholding the thrones of political tyranny." Again, this was another basic Madisonian tenet, connecting unfair public policy benefits or burdens to the corruption of republican government.[24]

By the time the assembly reconvened in October 1785, the "Remonstrance" had done its work. The Presbyterian laity had been fully mobilized against the assessment and, when combined with the Baptists and Quakers, proved an insuperable alliance, especially against an Episcopalian laity that was lukewarm at best. Not only did the assessment fall to a decisive defeat, but the House of Delegates, under Madison's careful leadership, also enacted Virginia's Statute for Religious Freedom. Penned by Jefferson as part of the revisal, this landmark piece of legislation enshrined both the disestablishment of religion and tolerance for all believers, two principles that would eventually be established for the nation by the First Amendment.

If it had enacted nothing other than the Statute for Religious Freedom, the fall 1785 session of the House of Delegates would have been a consequential assembly. But Madison, building a head of steam, managed to push through a great number of Jefferson's proposed revisions. The powers of the governor and the executive council were expanded, the courts were reorganized, provisions were made to establish the Kentucky territory as an independent state, government spending was cut, the militia was reformed, and more. Madison declined to accept credit for his part in these accomplishments, focusing instead on what more could be done. In December 1785, near the end of the session, he wrote to Washington, informing him that "we have got through a great part of the Revisal." More could have been accomplished, he continued, if the delegates had not wasted so much time debating "whether it could be finished at this session" rather than "forwarding the work" to the next. "As it is, we must content ourselves with passing a few more of the important bills, leaving the residue for our successors of the next year."[25]

MADISON'S MANY SUCCESSES in the House of Delegates illustrate the sort of formidable politician he had become. Of all these, the Statute for Religious Freedom stands out as the signal achievement. Patrick Henry was no pushover. When he opposed something, there was often little left to do but "pray earnestly for his death," as Jefferson had sardonically noted. And yet Madison had won this battle, both by crafting persuasive arguments and by executing a superior political strategy. He knew that, if given an opportunity to consider the matter, the citizenry would oppose it fiercely, so he stalled for time until he could persuade the people. In the end, he succeeded not only in stopping the assessment but in finally getting the state government out of the chapel.

Much of Madison's success in the Virginia assembly was due to the tremendous professional growth he had undergone during his time in the Continental Congress. He had become an expert on matters of international affairs, public finance, commerce, the army, the western territory, and more. He had also honed his political skills, gaining insight into how deliberative bodies function on a day-to-day basis. More subtly, he had begun to appreciate that there was a kind of collective psychology to public assemblies such as Congress, and that a smart leader could bend it to his will. He was learning how to bargain with men of different views and interests, when to hold the line and when to compromise, when to push for a vote and when to keep talking, when to propose a measure and when to hold back. All of these skills were on full display in his triumph over Henry for the cause of religious freedom.

Though Madison was deeply engaged in Virginia politics during this time, national affairs were never far from his mind. His time in Congress had transformed his nationalistic disposition into a distinct political vision. The war may have been over, but the list of national problems was still long and imposing—massive public debts, runaway inflation, an army unpaid—yet the states, in their selfishness, refused to work together for the good of all. If the American experiment in self-government was going to succeed, the national authority had to be strengthened to force the states to behave themselves. Along with Washington, Hamilton, and other nationalists, Madison would renew the nationalist project starting around 1785. And when an opportunity for reforms came a few years later, James Madison—now a veteran of American politics—would make the most of it.

3

THE VIRGINIA PLAN

MADISON'S STINT IN the Virginia legislature would draw him into the orbit of George Washington. Now retired from the Continental Army and settled back at his Mount Vernon estate, the general's mind, like Madison's, was never far from politics. This would be a fateful alliance. Both men were deeply committed to strengthening the national government, and their talents perfectly complemented one another: Madison, the unassuming workaholic steeped in the classics of the republican political tradition, and Washington, the American Cincinnatus who had given every measure of his being to win the war. The one supplied the reasoning for a stronger national union; the other supplied his calm, dispassion, and, above all, authority to those arguments.

Washington, naturally, took the lead role, with Madison as a kind of prime minister. Always one to know where he fit in the grand scheme of things, Madison was careful to approach Washington with great deference. To Thomas Jefferson, by the mid-1780s he would close his letters as "your sincere friend" or "your affectionate friend," but to Washington he was "with perfect respect and sincere regard your Excellency's obedient and humble servant." Yet, though Madison treated Washington with reverence, he was never obsequious or cloying. He gave the general earnest advice, and he could be crafty and persistent in urging the great man to do that which he did not want to do. While his relationship with Jefferson was more personally satisfying—the two became best friends, while it would be a stretch to call Madison and Washington friends at all—Madison's professional association with Washington was nevertheless integral to the creation of the Constitution.[1]

The origins of their association began with a shared interest in expanding Virginia's commercial influence. In his previous life, Washington had been a surveyor, and he had come to appreciate the need to improve the transportation to and from the west; Virginia would have to dredge shallow rivers to make them passable for ships, dig canals, and build roads. Madison was of a similar mind. Both were also keen to form stronger ties between the western frontier and the eastern establishment, lest settlers past the Blue Ridge Mountains be drawn toward Spain or Great Britain, the two European powers that still held territory in North America. After resigning as commander in chief of the army in 1783, Washington spearheaded the move for the House of Delegates to charter the Potomac Company, created to improve navigation on the river. Madison served as his point man in the House of Delegates for the initiative.

Madison and Washington were also concerned about international trade. After the Treaty of Paris secured peace between Great Britain and the United States, trade relations with the former motherland resumed. This commerce could have been a source of tax revenue for America through duties on imported goods, but the Articles of Confederation did not give Congress the power to implement a uniform plan. Instead, commercial laws were left entirely to the individual states, which worked to Britain's advantage. If New York raised tariffs on British goods, merchants could merely redirect their ships to New Jersey, which was happy to receive the extra traffic, then transport their goods into New York by land. The only solution, in Madison's judgment, was to put Congress in charge. "If it be necessary to regulate trade at all," he wrote to James Monroe in the summer of 1785, "it has to be done through the federal government." The states, "acting in their separate capacities," can no more regulate trade "than they could separately carry on war." As Madison warned Jefferson the following spring, the states were turning on one another in ever growing numbers. "When Massachusetts set on foot a retaliation of the policy of Great Britain, Connecticut declared her ports free. New Jersey served New York in the same way. And Delaware I am told has lately followed the example in opposition to the commercial plans of Pennsylvania." In another missive to Jefferson, he mused darkly about the possibility that commercial rivalry could lead to disunion. "Without some such self-denying compact it will, I conceive, be impossible to preserve harmony among the contiguous states."[2]

Having failed to enact reforms through Congress, Madison and the nationalists turned their attention to hammering out agreements directly between the states. Surprisingly, the first breakthrough came with an agreement between Virginia and Maryland, the two states that had once fought so bitterly over the western territory. Washington's desire to develop the Potomac as a commercial waterway entangled the two states, as Maryland's royal charter had given it the right to traffic on the river. The two agreed to send delegates to a convention, held at Mount Vernon in the early spring of 1785. Madison was selected as one of the delegates, but Governor Patrick Henry did not inform him in time of the date or location of the meeting. With the former commander in chief serving as host, the delegates quickly came to an agreement to share the Potomac.[3]

The success of the Mount Vernon Conference, as it has come to be known, inspired Madison and Washington to push for a general convention on commerce. This flowed naturally from the agreement between Virginia and Maryland, for their ultimate goal was to extend the navigability of the Potomac River far enough west to connect commercial transport to the Ohio River, which would require the assent of Pennsylvania. The House of Delegates, now aware of the utility of interstate coordination on matters of commerce, made a call for a general convention of the states to be held at Annapolis in the fall of 1786. Ever the realist, Madison was not optimistic about the prospects of success. He had seen firsthand, as he wrote to Washington, "the difficulty . . . in obtaining a unanimous concurrence of the states in any measure whatever." The way national government worked in the 1780s, one bad apple—often Rhode Island—could spoil the bunch, and Madison doubted that all thirteen states could ever come together to craft a uniform commercial policy.[4]

He was right to be pessimistic. Several states did not appoint delegates, including Maryland, even though the meeting was within its borders. And though Massachusetts, New Hampshire, North Carolina, and Rhode Island appointed delegates, they failed to show. In the end, only five states—Delaware, New Jersey, New York, Pennsylvania, and Virginia—were represented, short of the quorum necessary to conduct any business. Fortunately, the delegates in attendance were strong nationalists, including Madison, Alexander Hamilton, Edmund Randolph of Virginia, Tench Coxe of Pennsylvania, and John Dickinson of Delaware. The assembly decided to use the meeting as an opportunity to rouse the states to action. Written by Hamilton, the "Address of the Annapolis Convention" encouraged the states "to effect a general meeting," to consider "other objects, than those of commerce," including "correspondent adjustment of other parts of the federal system."[5]

Firmly under Madison's influence, the House of Delegates ratified Hamilton's call for a general convention. Madison cleverly arranged for Washington to be nominated as one of the Old Dominion's delegates—a move that, he thought, would encourage other states to take the proposed meeting seriously. There was, after all, no greater American than Washington, and his participation would give the convention "a very solemn dress," as Madison told him. Yet Washington hesitated. The appointed time and place for the convention—May 1787 in Philadelphia— overlapped with a meeting of the Society of the Cincinnati, a veterans' organization that had elected Washington as its president. Washington had declined their invitation, citing personal business that could not be avoided. It would be a bad look for him to attend the Constitutional Convention having rebuffed his old comrades in arms.[6]

Washington's reticence was not the only problem. Virginia and the Carolinas had made appointments, and Madison wrote Jefferson in February 1787 that "Delaware, Pennsylvania, and New Jersey have made respectable appointments" too. Maryland was likewise expected to join. But Madison anticipated "an unpropitious aspect" from New York, whose governor, George Clinton, was intent on preserving his state's power. Connecticut's participation was likewise in doubt, as it "has a great aversion to conventions, and is otherwise habitually disinclined to abridge her state prerogatives." Massachusetts, he reckoned, "will concur," even though it is "not well inclined." Tiny New Hampshire "will probably do as [Massachusetts] does." As for Rhode Island, Madison dryly noted that it "can be relied on for nothing that is good."[7]

Regional squabbling was also a problem. A successful convention required the different sections to come together in a shared commitment to the national interest, but the South had grown deeply suspicious of late of the intentions of its northern neighbors. The bone of contention was the ongoing diplomatic outreach to Spain. The Spanish had dispatched Don Diego de Gardoqui as minister to the United States to secure a treaty of alliance and commerce between the two nations. His American counterpart was John Jay of New York, a negotiator of the treaty of peace with Great Britain. In July 1785, Congress instructed Jay that, while it was prepared to compromise on many points, its sine qua non was free navigation of the Mississippi River all the way down to New Orleans. Gardoqui countered with a generous commercial alliance, one that would guarantee American exports favorable rates but would still leave the Mississippi under Spain's jurisdiction. With negotiations at an impasse, Jay returned to Congress to see if he could get his instructions revised. The deal proposed by the Spanish was a very good one from a northern point of view. Spain wanted another quarter century of control over the Mississippi, a river that the United States seemingly had no use for yet. As Jay reasoned, it would be better to secure commercial and military advantages by cutting a deal to cede the Mississippi for the time being. But the southern states were eager to expand westward and feared that prohibiting American access to the Mississippi would cripple this endeavor. In the end, Congress voted seven states to five, along strictly regional lines, to rescind Jay's instructions regarding the Mississippi. This vote sent a stark message that the northern states were willing to vote against their southern neighbors if it benefitted their interests.[8]

Madison was aghast at these developments and immediately spearheaded passage of a resolution in the House of Delegates to contradict Congress's vote and reaffirm the importance of reserving navigation rights in any treaty with Spain. Granted, there was little chance of a bad treaty being adopted, since it required nine votes to ratify a treaty and no southern state would possibly agree. Even so, the timing of this could not have been more "ill chosen," as he told Edmund Pendleton, as it had occurred right when the nationalists were making a last-ditch effort to expand federal power. Pitting the northern and southern states against one another was bound to stir up the sorts of regional prejudices that could be "fatal . . . to an augmentation of the federal authority." Bad blood over the Jay-Gardoqui negotiations lingered for years thereafter, and as late as 1788 southern opponents of the new Constitution used the treaty as an example of how a stronger national government would endanger their regional interests.[9]

The list of challenges facing Madison and his allies seemed only to be growing. What was needed was a galvanizing moment that would induce the states to overcome their prejudices and bind themselves together. As it happened, the nationalists were in luck, for in Massachusetts, Daniel Shays and a band of down-and-out-farmers had been seizing courthouses in central and western parts of the state—an act of sedition that terrified the country's elites and finally forced them to acknowledge the necessity of reform.

———————

THE ORIGIN OF Shays's Rebellion, as the uprising became known, lay in the economic downturn that followed the Revolutionary War. The recession was widespread. Even Washington, one of the most prosperous planters in all of Virginia, felt the sting. But the hardest hit were the poorer farmers who were

deeply in debt. This was centuries before social welfare programs or aid to farmers, but the government did have one tool
at its disposal to ease their burdens: inflation. Printing money
would effectively cancel out the obligations of the deeply indebted, so that is what they demanded. Rhode Island, where the
poor farmers held a majority, passed aggressive debt-relief laws
that aggravated the wealthier creditors in nearby Boston who
had loaned the money. In Virginia, the wealthier planters were
firmly in control of Old Dominion politics; they naturally hated
the emission of paper money. At Madison's behest, the House
of Delegates in 1786 declared paper money to be "unjust, impolitic, destructive of public and private confidence, and of that
virtue which is the basis of republican governments."[10]

Like Virginia, Massachusetts rejected paper money. Dominated by the commercial men of Boston, the government refused to give the poor farmers of the central and western regions
any relief. Moreover, they had altered the state's tax structure,
shifting the burden of paying the government's bills onto land
and animals—good for the merchants of Boston, bad for the
farmers in Hatfield, which is where the trouble began. In the
summer of 1786, a convention representing local towns adopted
twenty-one articles, calling not only for inflationary policy but
for a wholesale revision to the tax system and the state government itself. When the state legislature ignored their pleas, the
protestors turned violent, taking over local courthouses. Shays,
who took part in this initial uprising, eventually emerged as the
de facto leader of this group of rebels, which between August
and December seized courthouses from the western edge of
Massachusetts all the way to Concord, just northwest of Boston.

The rest of the country—at least the propertied classes—
looked on in horror as the rebels seemed to run rampant while
the state government dithered. Rumors spread like wildfire.

Henry "Light-Horse Harry" Lee—one of the great cavalry officers of the Revolution, who had gone to the College of New Jersey with Madison—warned his old college friend that the rebels
were on the brink of taking over the state. By his math, the se-
ditious counties contained roughly half of the state's adult male
population. Major General Henry Knox wrote to Washington
that this was the revolt of an anti-government rabble. "The people who are the insurgents have never paid any, or but very little
taxes," he reported. "But they see the weakness of government;
they feel at once their own poverty, compared with the opulent,
and their own force, and they are determined to make use of the
latter, in order to remedy the former." While not as alarmist as
Lee, Knox saw this as a formidable body of discontents. One-
fifth of Massachusetts's counties were under siege, he estimated,
and the small farmers of Connecticut, New Hampshire, and
Rhode Island all seemed ready to rise up against their respective
governments. "They are chiefly of the young and active part of
the community. . . . They will probably commit overt acts of
treason. . . . Having proceeded to this length for which they are
now ripe, we shall have a formidable rebellion against reason,
the principles of all government, and the very name of liberty."[11]

By the fall, Washington was in a virtual panic. "We are fast
verging to anarchy and confusion!" he exclaimed to Madison in
November. The mob seemed to be proving the American experiment in republicanism a failure. The people could not actually
govern themselves. "How melancholy is the reflection," the general wrote Madison, "that in so short a space, we should have
made such large strides towards fulfilling the prediction of our
transatlantic foe!" Never one to overreact, Madison cleverly used
the Massachusetts uprising to encourage Washington to agree to
attend the Constitutional Convention as a delegate. Although
the general would feel some embarrassment from arriving in

Philadelphia at the same moment as the Society of the Cincinnati meeting, would not the present crisis serve as sufficient excuse? "I still am inclined to think," Madison wrote Washington in December, "that the posture of our affairs, if it should continue, would prevent every criticism on the situation which the contemporary meetings would place you in." Ultimately, Washington relented. The crisis was simply too grave. Likewise, the fear of Shays's Rebellion finally brought most of the states into agreement; it was time to reconsider the Articles of Confederation. In February 1787, Congress formally invited the states to a general convention, set for May, to "render the [federal government] adequate to the exigencies of government and the preservation of the union." The Constitutional Convention was set.[12]

The nationalists had worked diligently to bring about this kind of opportunity for seven years, yet for all their efforts, the Constitutional Convention ultimately took place thanks to forces outside of their control. A large swath of the country had finally decided that enough was enough. Many people had long intuited that the government as constituted was not fit to rule. Problems of territory, diplomacy, finance, taxation, currency— these had compounded upon one another since virtually the day independence was declared. But inertia is a powerful force. There was always a good reason for at least somebody to say no to change, some procedural objection, factional alliance, or personal grievance that prevented a critical mass of Americans from reorganizing government. If it did nothing else, Shays's Rebellion made it evident that the status quo was no longer tenable. Anarchy was afoot, and without a government to restore order, everything that the young nation had fought so hard to win could be lost forever. And while Shays and his band of hardscrabble rebels had given the nationalists a chance, they had given them only *one* chance. With the country at the point of crisis, a failed convention would surely doom any future reform efforts, and quite possibly scuttle the union altogether. This would be a make-or-break moment for the United States of America.

THE CONSTITUTIONAL CONVENTION would be Madison's finest hour. Everything in his life thus far had been leading to this. His adult life had been spent acquiring expertise in the history, theory, and practice of politics. In 1787, his skills, considerable though they were, were not enough to help him earn an independent living, but they were precisely the talents necessary to frame a new constitution for the young nation. Up to now, Madison had usually been the junior partner to some older colleague—a Washington, a Pendleton, a Jefferson, a Morris. But in Philadelphia in the summer of 1787, he would emerge as the indispensable man of American politics.

His triumph would not be because of his great oratory, impressive physical presence, or reputation for glory on the battlefield. Instead, Madison dominated the convention because he came prepared with a bracing new vision of republicanism. The Virginia Plan, as it has become known, drew on Madison's vast knowledge to offer a fundamental redesign of American government, one whose broad contours were acceptable to his fellow delegates.

He began with an ancient puzzle. As he wrote to Washington in the spring of 1787, "The great desideratum which has not yet been found for republican governments, seems to be some disinterested and dispassionate umpire in disputes between different passions and interests in the state." In a republic, he observed, the majority has the right to rule, but they can easily abuse their power, governing for themselves at the expense of the public good and the rights of the minority. In theory, a monarch might be able to check the excesses of the people, but too often in practice kings and queens have behaved as despots, putting themselves ahead of their subjects. Political philosophers since ancient Greece had struggled with this question, and Madison believed that nobody had yet found an answer.[13]

Madison had been thinking about this essential problem of government in one form or another since his days at the College of New Jersey under the tutelage of John Witherspoon. But he began a more disciplined and rigorous consideration of it around 1784 with a historical investigation into the nature of confederations, or loose associations of semi-independent sovereignties grouped together, like the United States was under the Articles of Confederation. He was aided in this endeavor by Jefferson, who by the winter of 1785 had sent Madison two trunks full of books from France. The product of Madison's scholarly exertions was his "Notes on Ancient and Modern Confederacies," completed sometime in the spring of 1786. This was not so much an essay as a recording of facts, impressions, and judgments he had gleaned from his investigation into European history. Madison's examination of confederacies such as those in ancient Greece and in Germany, the Netherlands, Poland, and Switzerland revealed a similar pattern: those that lack a strong central authority are doomed to fail. He would conclude that an imperium in imperio, or a government of governments, "is a solecism in theory" and in practice subverts the "order and ends of civil polity, by substituting violence in place of law, or the destructive coercion of the sword in place of the mild and salutary coercion of the magistracy."[14]

After his research into foreign confederations, Madison began thinking more deeply about the problems in America, and in the spring of 1787 finished an essay entitled the "Vices of the

Political System of the United States," which laid out how America was suffering from the same sorts of problems that afflicted confederacies like the Amphictyonic League of ancient Greece or the Holy Roman Empire in contemporary Germany. The biggest problem with the American system was the "failure of the states to comply with the constitutional requisitions" that were necessary to fund the national government. Likewise, the states had "encroach[ed]" upon the "federal authority," especially in violating treaties that Congress had entered into with the European powers. The states had abused the rights and seized the property of the loyalists who had sided with Great Britain, despite the fact that the United States had promised in the Treaty of Paris to leave them alone. The British used this mistreatment as a pretext to retain garrisons in the west, where they still hoped to reacquire complete control. Yet in other ways, Madison noted, Britain was glad for the parochialism of the states. Ever since the resumption of normal trade relations, Britain had been happy to play the commercial interests of American states off of one another, shipping goods to whatever state offered the lowest tariff rates. "How much," Madison bemoaned, "has the national dignity, interest, and revenue suffered from this cause?" How long would the public good "be defeated by the perverseness of particular states?" These kinds of interstate rivalries were undermining the sense of national unity forged during the Revolution, as was the proliferation of paper money in states like Rhode Island, which effectively defrauded the creditors in neighboring states. All of this was "adverse to the spirit of the Union" and "destructive of the general harmony."[15]

What Madison had hit upon in the "Vices" was a problem that modern economists call the collective action dilemma— namely, the challenge that individual agents (be they people or sovereign states) face when they try to work together to produce a good that will benefit them all. In many circumstances, it is in the interests of each agent to cheat, or not work for the public benefit, and instead let the others do the work. Since everybody has such an interest, the result is that nobody works to make things better. This is exactly what had happened among the thirteen states when it came to instituting commercial and financial regulations, enforcing international law, and supplying money for the national treasury. Collectively, the nation would be better off if the states did what they were supposed to do—pay their requisitions, abide by international treaties, and enact responsible monetary policy—but each individual state had an incentive to free ride, as today's economists would say, placing its own concerns above the national good.

Though Madison lived centuries before these terms would be invented, he nevertheless grasped the basic intuition. The Articles of Confederation were founded on the "mistaken confidence that the justice, the good faith, the honor, the sound policy, of the several legislative assemblies would" be enough to sustain it. People are simply too selfish for that to work. He believed that a central authority possessing the power to "sanction" the states was the only solution to the problem of collective action. Again, this is precisely the kind of idea that modern economists say is necessary. If the states intended to undermine the national interest, the national government had to set them straight.[16]

Accordingly, Madison called for a massive increase in federal power. He was not prepared to abolish the states altogether, which, he told Edmund Randolph, his longtime friend and political associate who had become governor of Virginia in December 1786, would be "unattainable" and "inexpedient," but he wanted to strip the states of most of their authority, to make them "subordinately useful" to the national government. In practice, Madison had two sweeping federal powers in mind.[17]

First, Madison proposed giving the Congress "positive and complete authority in all cases which require uniformity," as he wrote to George Washington in the spring of 1787. In the Virginia Plan, he recommended that Congress "legislate in all cases to which the separate states are incompetent, or in which the harmony of the United States may be interrupted by the exercise of individual legislation." Compared to the minimal powers endowed in the Continental Congress by the Articles of Confederation, this would be an extraordinary shift in the balance between the states and national government.[18]

Second, Madison believed that the national government should have a veto "in all cases whatsoever on the legislative acts of the states." Without this check, Madison warned that "every positive power" given to the national government "will be evaded and defeated. The states will continue to invade the national jurisdiction, to violate treaties and the law of nations, and to harass each other with rival and spiteful measures dictated by mistaken views of interest." The national government could dictate as it wished, but so long as the states could pass whatever laws they liked, they could still upend the public interest. He also suggested that, "in order to render the exercise of such a negative prerogative convenient," national officials "within the several states" should be on hand to "give a temporary sanction to laws of immediate necessity." Again, this was a massive expansion in national power, well beyond the Articles of Confederation or even what the Constitution would eventually endorse.[19]

All told, Madison advocated a complete inversion of the national-state relationship. Under his plan, the states would only retain power over strictly local matters, and Congress would have the final say on what constitutes a local matter and what is of national concern. Such a proposal would have been unthinkable just a few years earlier, but enough was enough. The states had proved themselves incompetent, selfish, even devious. They had to be brought to heel.

––––––––––

WHILE THE STATES had behaved atrociously, the Continental Congress had hardly been a model in probity. The business of government went far too slowly, negotiations over land cessions had been excessively divisive, and the Jay-Gardoqui debate had shown that sectional interests wielded too much power in the legislature. If the national government was to assume these expanded powers, its structure would need to be thoroughly revised.

Madison saw two major problems with the way Congress was organized. First, the principle of one state, one vote was an unreliable standard of justice. His experience with the Jay-Gardoqui negotiations illustrated that point. The North, which held a numerical majority in the Congress, allowed Jay to abandon his instructions in ways that were good for that region but bad for the South. That was unacceptable, so there had to be protections against numerical majorities that were merely looking out for themselves.

Second, Congress as organized could not properly exercise the powers Madison was looking to grant it. Under the Articles of Confederation, the laws of Congress created obligations only for the states, never the citizens themselves, who would only be affected by "the intervention of the legislatures" of the states. But investing taxing, regulatory, and other powers directly in Congress would enable it to operate directly on the citizenry, which meant that the people would have to have a direct say in its composition. If the old rule of one state, one vote remained in place, then a minority of the people could theoretically rule the majority—a standard inconsistent with republicanism.[20]

To solve these problems, Madison called for a total revolution in "the principle of representation in the federal system." If Congress was to govern the people directly, then it was only fair that representatives be apportioned by state population. That way, the more numerous people of the large states could never be governed by the minority of the population in the small states.[21]

But this still left the potential problem of the tyranny of the majority, a concern with republics going back to ancient Greece. If all authority is vested in the people, what was to stop a majority from using the government to enrich itself? Just as a king can turn into a despot, so, too, can the people turn into a mob. Indeed, this had been a problem with the internal politics of the thirteen states. They were exquisitely democratic by the standards of the age, and yet they had often behaved recklessly and unjustly. "Among the evils of our situation," Madison asserted, "was the multiplicity of laws" in the states. Laws are necessary to "mark with precision" the duties of citizens, but when they proliferate beyond the minimum necessary number, they transform into a "nuisance of the most pestilent kind," as it becomes impossible for citizens to know exactly what the government requires of them. Closely related to this problem was the "mutability of the laws" in all the states, whereby laws are "repealed or superseded before any trial can be made of their merits." Virtually every session of every state legislature, Madison complained, produces a "new volume" of rules and regulations. And just as quickly as new laws are added, they are altered or repealed altogether. Worst of all was the blatant "injustice of the laws of the states." Much like the states did violence against one another in their partiality to, say, debtors or creditors, they also mistreated minorities within their borders. Virginia had persecuted its minority Baptists, while Massachusetts's aggressive anti-inflationary policies came down especially hard on poor farmers in the west of the state.[22]

What, then, was to stop the national government, which Madison believed had to be founded on the republican principle of majority rule, from devolving into large-scale majoritarian tyranny? Here, Madison offered a novel innovation. The solution was to expand the polity. As he explained in the "Vices," people hail from "different interests and factions, as they happen to be creditors or debtors; rich or poor; husbandmen, merchants, or manufacturers; members of different religious sects; followers of different political leaders; inhabitants of different districts; others of different kinds of property, etc." If one group amounts to a numerical majority, its members can dominate government for themselves, but in an extended republic—one that includes a diverse array of economic, social, geographical, religious, and other groups—"society becomes broken into a greater variety of interests, of pursuits, of passions." With no single faction able to take total control, the factions will "check each other," forcing people to find common-ground solutions that work for the entire community.[23]

For Madison, the answer to the essential problem of government was *politics*. He would force all factions in society to argue, debate, broker, and compromise with one another until they found a solution that most of them could live with. This would secure justice for all groups and promote the general welfare.

———

If POLITICS WAS going to save the republic, then it had to be properly organized. An extended republic would be the foundation of what Madison would later call a "well constructed union," but he drew upon the Enlightenment thought of the last hundred years—what he and Hamilton would call the "science of politics" in the *Federalist Papers*—to add supplemental features that would organize factional conflict properly.

Naturally, something had to be done to check the greed, ignorance, and avarice of politicians. Having spent more than a decade in government, Madison knew firsthand how rotten so-called statesmen could be. In the "Vices," he noted that politicians seek office because of ambition, personal interest, or concern for the public good, and those who act upon the first two motives are the "most industrious and most successful in pursuing their object . . . in a perfidious sacrifice" of the public interest. Thus, Madison reasoned, republican government required "a process of elections as will most certainly extract from the mass of the society the purest and noblest characters it contains," those who "feel most strongly the proper motives" and are "most capable to devise the proper means of attaining it." Bicameralism— or the well-established practice of having a legislature with two chambers, elected in different ways—was an essential solution. In 1785, as Kentucky was mulling over its future constitution as an independent state, Madison suggested to Caleb Wallace, a lawyer and future appellate court judge for the state, that a state senate would provide the "wisdom and steadiness to legislation" needed to temper the impetuosity of the state house of representatives. This upper chamber, Madison believed, should "consist of a more select number" who hold "their appointments for a longer term and going out in rotation." In Madison's plan submitted to the Constitutional Convention, he proposed that senators be chosen by House members out of nominations submitted by the state legislatures. Such an institution, he reckoned, would still be founded on the people at large, as the senators were ultimately selected by the people's representatives. At the same time, the process of selection would yield a better class of leader than was to be found in the popularly elected House.[24]

Madison also embraced the popular idea of separated governmental powers. Following French philosopher Montesquieu, most Americans took it as an axiom that the legislative, executive, and judicial authority had to be divided into different branches, to keep leaders from abusing their authority. The Articles of Confederation, however, did not do this. Some executive functions—like the administration of finance and diplomacy—were retained by Congress, whose ample membership and committee style of governance meant too much debate and too little action. Meanwhile, the enforcement and adjudication of national laws was left entirely to the state governments, which were prone to disregard the national interest for parochial concerns. He therefore proposed a national executive and judiciary, both of which would be chosen by the Congress (the president for a single, fixed term and judges for life tenure on good behavior) and whose salaries would be set by law. He also called for joining the president and a select number of judges into a council of revision, akin to an institution that New York was using at the time. This body would have "authority to examine every act of the national legislature" and veto "fluctuating and indigested laws" that might violate "public interests" or "private rights." Ultimately, Madison's proposed Congress would have the right to overrule the council by a two-thirds majority.[25]

Altogether, Madison's design of government established the House of Representatives—which drew most directly upon all factions of society—as the center of American political life. The House would select the members of the Senate and, along with the upper chamber, select the president, organize the courts and confirm judges, enact whatever legislation was necessary for the common good, and veto the laws of the states. The president and the courts would act as a check upon this newly powerful Congress, but only up to a point. If a supermajority in Congress wanted something to happen, it was probably going to happen. And the ultimate check, Madison reasoned, was the extended republic. Congress would represent the diversity of this vast nation. Interest would be arrayed against interest, forcing the different factions to bargain with each other in search of compromises that would serve the public good.

What made the theory especially interesting is that it was not premised on any kind of faith in human nature. Since his youngest days, Madison had imbibed a Calvinism that took a dim view of humanity's ability to act according to selfless motives. It was here that he introduced an ironic twist: this very selfishness could make a large republic work. The small republics of the states had failed because interests were too homogenous, so one faction could acquire the mechanisms of government and ruin life for everybody else. But in a diverse republic, such a majority was less likely to exist. The various forces and factions would have to barter with each other, offering proposals and counterproposals through extensive negotiations. Whatever final compromise they agreed on would likely be amenable to the public interest and respectful of individual rights.

Thus, Madison became the first theorist of a truly national American politics, the idea that the strength of the union was in its diversity. Other thinkers called for a stronger union for the sake of economic prosperity and international prestige, but Madison's approach was predominantly political in its argument. Only by forging a stronger union among its disparate parts, he urged, could the United States actually secure the rights to life, liberty, and the pursuit of happiness proclaimed in the Declaration of Independence.

———————

WHEN THE CONVENTION opened at the end of May 1787, Madison had not only a plan of government but a strategy to get it implemented. He showed up in Philadelphia early, on May

3, eleven days before the proceedings were set to begin, and returned to Mrs. House's residence at Fifth and Market Streets. Because travel was difficult in those days, governing assemblies often struggled to achieve a quorum on time, which is what happened in this case; the convention did not have enough members to begin its business until May 25. The extra time gave Madison an opportunity to coordinate with like-minded delegates on how to proceed. Delegates from Pennsylvania, including Benjamin Franklin, were already in town, and they were generally disposed to a strengthening of the national government along the lines of Madison's proposed plan. The Virginia delegation was also in town, and it was settled upon that Randolph would submit the Virginia Plan at the start of the proceedings. That way, the nationalists could seize the agenda, pushing forward with a total revamp of the government. After all, Congress had called a convention to "render the constitution of the federal government adequate to the exigencies of the Union." This could have meant relatively modest changes, like granting Congress the powers to tax and regulate commerce. But Madison and his allies had something much more ambitious in mind, and by taking the first step, they oriented the convention toward their bold agenda.[26]

In many respects, the delegates were well disposed to this schema. Like Madison, they were men of the Enlightenment, and to a remarkable extent they were on the same page about the basics of government. Most of them were familiar with the classic tracts of republican political philosophy, which provided them with a shared set of ideas. The writings of William Blackstone, Viscount Bolingbroke, James Harrington, Thomas Hobbes, David Hume, John Locke, and Montesquieu were the lingua franca of the proceedings, and even if delegates had not read these authors, they certainly knew their views on government.

This meant the scope of disagreement was much narrower than one might expect, given the historic nature of the event. There was never any doubt, for instance, that the legislature would be bicameral. The "science of politics," as these men understood it, was quite clear that the legislature should be divided. Benjamin Franklin was a notable exception in that he supported a unicameral legislature, but—indicative of how out of step he was with the rest of the delegates—his proposal was politely but firmly rejected by the convention. So it went with many provisions. Though there were often exceptions to the consensus, delegates generally found common ground on the basics of governance. Instead, most of the main disagreements were second order. Not whether there should be a Senate, for example, but rather how to select senators. Not whether the House should be popularly elected, but how frequently those elections should be held. Not whether there should be an executive helmed by a single person, but how it should relate to Congress. A delegate here or there disagreed on the big picture, but most of the debates focused on hammering out the details or distributing political power among various factions in the country.

Shared experiences reinforced this intellectual consilience. Most of the delegates had been deeply worried by the events of the last decade, and not simply because they were patriots. While they differed in their professions—some merchants, some lawyers, some planters, some politicians—they were economically and socially established in life. They all had something to lose from a government that did nothing while Britain took advantage of the incoherent hodgepodge of state trade policies and down-on-their-luck rebels seized county courthouses in Massachusetts.

Plus, skeptics of central authority generally stayed away from the convention. Rhode Island, stubbornly committed to its own sovereignty, did not bother to send delegates at all. Patrick Henry, who would vehemently oppose the Constitution during the ratification debates, was invited but refused to attend. "I smelt a rat," he announced. Likewise, prominent radicals from the Revolutionary period like Samuel Adams and Richard Henry Lee did not attend and later would oppose ratification (although Adams was eventually persuaded). The New York delegation was dominated by loyalists of Governor George Clinton, who opposed a stronger national government, but they left the convention early.[27]

All told, delegates with nationalist sentiments outnumbered the opponents by more than three to one at the convention. The opponents were intellectually outmatched as well. If anything, the obstreperous Luther Martin of Maryland and the captious Elbridge Gerry of Massachusetts usually did their causes more harm than good. But the substantial numerical and rhetorical advantages for the nationalists did not mean that there was a majority in favor of Madison's Virginia Plan. While most delegates were generally supportive of strengthening the central government, there were widespread doubts about the proper scope of any such centralization.

Writing to his father a month before the opening of the convention, Madison predicted a "very full and respectable meeting," but he still had his doubts. "The probable diversity of opinions and prejudices, and of supposed or real interests among the states, renders the issue totally uncertain." Madison would offer an ingenious plan as an opening framework for discussion, but it would then be up to the convention as a whole to refashion it into an instrument of government they could agree upon.[28]

4

THE CONSTITUTIONAL CONVENTION

The Constitutional Convention, held at Independence Hall in Philadelphia from May 25 to September 17, 1787, has become the stuff of legend. A total of fifty-six men put aside their personal and parochial interests to frame a new government based on principles of reason, justice, and freedom. Or so the story goes.

This was a view that James Madison himself adopted later in life. Writing nearly half a century after the convention, he said of his fellow delegates, "Never was there an assembly of men, charged with a great and arduous trust, who were more pure in their motives, or more exclusively or anxiously devoted to the object committed to them than were the members of the Federal Convention of 1787." The "ability and intelligence" of the delegates was exemplified in the Constitution, "the offspring of their deliberations," which had been tested by the experiences of the "nearly half a century which has passed."[1]

But back in September 1787, at the conclusion of the convention, Madison had a much different judgment about the Constitution: he did not like it. The convention adopted a strict code of privacy, prohibiting delegates from talking about what it was up to, but Madison could not resist sending a coded message to Thomas Jefferson toward the end of the proceedings, in which he outlined the proposal and offered a barbed editorial. "The plan," Madison lamented on September 6, "will neither effectually answer its national object nor prevent the local mischiefs which everywhere excite disgusts against the state governments." This was not Madison's mature view of the Constitution, which would evolve over the subsequent months. It was, rather, his snap judgment—and it is not altogether unsurprising, given his experience in Philadelphia. He was prone to bitterness and hyperbole when he suffered a political setback, of which he had been dealt many during the prior three months. He had come with an innovative set of solutions to the problems plaguing the young nation, and the convention rejected what he thought were his best ideas.[2]

Madison could not convince the delegates to place their full trust in the idea of an extended republic. He ran into several problems. While most of them agreed that the power of the national government needed substantial expansion, delegates balked at the capacious view Madison adopted, especially the provisions that Congress should have the power to do whatever was in the national interest and veto state laws. There were also persistent demands for protections for minority interests against the will of the majority. The animating notion of the extended republic was that self-government practiced on a large enough scale would be safe for all factions. But the delegates did not buy that, at least not when they perceived that their own interests were at stake. The merchants of the northern states wanted protections for the wealthy in government, but their numbers were too few to effect any changes. Not so with the small states and the slave states, two factions that were numerous enough to secure exemptions for themselves. The small states secured equal representation in the Senate while the slave states won bonus representation in the House, as well as limits on how Congress could regulate both slavery and the export industries it facilitated.

None of this was consistent with the core logic, embedded in the Virginia Plan, that national majorities could safely govern. But Madison could not persuade his fellow delegates that they had nothing to fear. The whole affair was deeply exhausting and profoundly dispiriting. He believed he had come up with the great solution to the essential problem of government, a perfect mixture that would make republicanism work. Yet time and again, he watched his fellow delegates adulterate it. In due course, he would come to appreciate the Constitution as it is today—a work of monumental importance—but when he left Philadelphia in the fall of 1787, he was very disappointed indeed.

———————

THE CONVENTION MET in the Assembly Room on the first floor of the Pennsylvania statehouse, usually from Monday through Saturday. Tables were arranged in a semicircle, with members seated according to state delegation: New Hampshire on the left-hand side of the room, Georgia and South Carolina on the right, and the states organized geographically in between. On most days, thirty to forty delegates could be counted in attendance.

The delegates unanimously chose Washington as presiding officer, but most of the meetings would be overseen by Nathaniel Gorham. The effective leader of the Massachusetts delegation,

Gorham had been until a few months previous the president of the Continental Congress. Affable and widely admired, Gorham generally favored a stronger national government. He would preside over the "committee of the whole." This was the format the convention would use for most of its proceedings because it enabled the delegates to informally debate different proposals and take provisional votes. For the most part, Washington was seated with his fellow Virginians.

The great question at the Constitutional Convention was how to sustain a just and effective government. One common view held that polities had to be small, with an emphasis on civic virtue. That way, a citizenry grounded in a shared sense of the public good might keep a close eye on the government, ensuring that it worked for the community at large. Another view, embodied in the British system, envisioned a mixture of different classes, or estates, of society: the landed gentry represented in the House of Lords, the freeholders in the House of Commons, and a hereditary monarch above it all. This way, no faction could come to dominate the rest. From the American perspective in 1787, both of these approaches had proved unworkable. The Revolution was not just a break from Great Britain, it was a rejection of its system of self-appointed government. And seeing as how there was no class of nobles in the United States, this system was gone for good in the New World. Meanwhile, events since 1776 had demonstrated the fragility of the civic republican model. The states were a modern reincarnation of the classic civitates, yet they had behaved atrociously.

Madison's alternative was to shift the locus of political conflict from the states, where narrow-minded majorities governed in unjust and foolhardy ways, to the whole country, where no faction amounted to a majority. As he said during the debates at the convention, "This was the only defense against the inconveniences of democracy consistent with the democratic form of government." Republican politics, practiced on a large enough scale, could secure itself. If he was right, it followed that national majorities had to be invested with sweeping powers to govern on behalf of the public interest. He admitted that while he had a "strong bias in favor of . . . [a] definition of powers necessary to be exercised by the national legislature . . . he also brought doubts concerning its practicability." How could one possibly enumerate the powers necessary to "provide for the safety, liberty, and happiness of the community?"[3]

At first, Madison seemed to carry the day. Edmund Randolph introduced the Virginia Plan on May 30, and it drove the discussion for several weeks, as the delegates made adjustments to Madison's ideas rather than offering an alternative. While the convention had tentatively accepted Madison's proposal of a general grant of federal power early in its proceedings, the Committee of Detail—chaired by John Rutledge of South Carolina—chose instead to enumerate the specific powers of the government. One of the most successful lawyers in his state, Rutledge had participated in the Stamp Act Congress of 1765, served in the First Continental Congress, and been governor of his state when the British invaded. A moderate nationalist and unflinching advocate of slavery, he favored a stronger government but wanted to make sure South Carolina's interests were secure. The convention accepted this alteration without much fuss, and it subsequently rejected many additional enumerations: the powers to charter private corporations, to found a university and seminaries, to sponsor scientific research, and to promote agriculture and industry through rewards and immunities.

Worse, from Madison's perspective, the convention flatly rejected his recommendation of a congressional veto over state laws. This seemed to him like a killer blow at the time, for he judged such an authority "essential to the efficacy and security of the general government." He likened the congressional veto to the prerogative of the British Crown, whose veto over colonial laws helped "maintain the harmony and subordination of the various parts of the empire." Without the veto, Madison warned, the states "will continue to disturb the system." They would "violate national treaties . . . infringe the rights and interests of each other, [and] . . . oppress the weaker party within their respective jurisdictions."[4]

The rest of the convention disagreed. Most delegates thought this gave Congress too much power over the states. Luther Martin—the hard-drinking attorney general of Maryland who reviled centralization—called the power "improper and inadmissible." Roger Sherman, the moderate from Connecticut who had made a fortune as a merchant but had also served in public office for lengthy stints, considered it "unnecessary." Even Gouverneur Morris of Pennsylvania, who usually agreed with Madison on questions of federal authority, was dubious. He thought it would "be terrible to the states." As an alternative, the convention adopted what has come to be known as the Supremacy Clause, establishing the "Constitution and the laws of the United States" as the "supreme law of the land," and thus signifying congressional authority over the states but not going so far as to give Congress explicit power to strike against them.[5]

In retrospect, it is clear that the convention made a prudent choice in rejecting Madison's proposed veto power. While he had good philosophical reasons for his ideas, they were impractical. There was no doubt that the states were going to have to cede some power to the federal government, but he wanted them to give almost all of it away. They were never going to do that, which in due course he came to appreciate.

DATING ALL THE way back to ancient Greece, some thinkers had argued that good government requires a careful distribution of power between those with property and those without. The thinking was that if the rich were given all the authority, the government would devolve into oligarchy, but if the poor had all the power, it would devolve into mob rule. A balance had to be struck, and because the poor inevitably outnumbered the rich, there had to be some guarantee for property holders within government. This likewise had become a central theme in European governments.

Though the United States had ostensibly rejected this idea in the Declaration of Independence, which argued that the people alone are the legitimate fount of government sovereignty, many delegates believed that property owners had to be protected from the masses in some way. These men sampled heavily from the merchant community of the North, like Gouverneur Morris, Nathaniel Gorham, Alexander Hamilton, and Rufus King of Massachusetts—a young, articulate delegate who would go on to have a long career in the new government. They usually agreed with Madison on the need for a substantially stronger national government, and Madison was likewise sensitive to the dangers the masses might pose to property holders. Yet, whereas Madison believed that the diversity of the extended republic would protect the interests of the wealthy, the northern friends of the merchants had a more traditionally European view of property relations within civil society, with an explicit focus on carving out the rich and the poor as distinct factions in government.

Hamilton exemplified this view in his proposed plan of government, delivered to the convention on June 18. He called for the president and senators to be chosen for life tenures by electors, as opposed to the people or state governments. That way, they would be free from the back-and-forth of politics and better able to act on behalf of the whole nation. Part of his reasoning for this was because "in every community where industry is encouraged there will be a division of it into the few and the many. Hence separate interests will arise." The only way to protect the interests of the wealthy, Hamilton believed, was to separate certain institutions of government from direct control of the people. Morris, too, argued that senators should have life tenures, so that the upper chamber could act as an "aristocratic body . . . as independent and as firm as the democratic." Unlike Hamilton, Morris believed that the danger was not so much the aristocratic element being swamped by the democratic, but the opposite: "The rich will strive to establish their dominion and enslave the rest. They always did. They always will." Still, the implication for Morris was the same as it was for Hamilton: "The proper security . . . is to form them into a separate interest. The two forces will then control each other." All of this ran in stark contrast to Madison's idea of the extended republic.[6]

The views of Hamilton and Morris on the Senate were too elitist for most delegates to accept, and the convention never seriously considered such an aristocratic branch of government. Still, the idea of protecting the interests of the wealthy through some formal constitutional mechanism was periodically debated. Early in the proceedings, the Virginia Plan faced pushback from the generally nationalist South Carolina delegation, which opposed popular election to the House of Representatives for reasons similar to the logic of Hamilton and Morris. Filtering public opinion through some mediating body would refine it and thereby protect the interests of the wealthy. General Charles Cotesworth Pinckney—the son of a notable South Carolina planter whose reputation for bravery had earned him the rank of brevet brigadier general in the Continental Army—argued that this "would be a better guard against bad measures. . . . A majority of the people in South Carolina were notoriously for paper money as a legal tender; the legislature had refused to make it a legal tender. The reason was that the latter had some sense of character and were restrained by that consideration." Madison was willing to accept something like this for the Senate, but he "considered an election of one branch at least of the legislature by the people immediately" to be "a clear principle of free government." The South Carolina proposal went down to defeat, illustrating the general commitment of the convention that the people needed to play at least some direct role in the government.[7]

Later, in July, as the convention's attention turned to apportionment in the House of Representatives, the northern delegates began pushing for a resolution that would "vary . . . representation according to the principles of their wealth and population." Property, Morris contended, "was the main object of society," so "it ought to be one measure of the influence due to those who were to be affected by the government." Morris was particularly concerned about the "new states which would soon be formed in the [W]est" that would deny "the Atlantic States a prevalence in the national councils." Morris's anxiety was shared by South Carolinian John Rutledge, as well as the Massachusetts delegation. Elbridge Gerry—a wealthy merchant who had signed the Declaration of Independence and would go on to serve as vice president under Madison—warned that the West "will oppress commerce and drain our wealth," and called for limiting the number of western representatives to the same size as the Atlantic states.[8]

Madison and the Virginians wanted nothing to do with these limits. George Mason asserted that the western states "must . . . be treated as equals and subjected to no degrading discriminations." Madison agreed. "With regard to the western states," he averred that he "was clear and firm in opinion that no unfavorable distinctions were admissible either in point of justice or policy." Ultimately, Gerry's proposal fell on a four-five-one vote—with Connecticut, Delaware, Maryland, and Massachusetts in favor; the Carolinas, Georgia, New Jersey, and Virginia opposed; and Pennsylvania divided. The uniform opposition of the South was due in part to the widespread expectation that the first western states would come from the southwest. Kentucky was already clamoring for independence from Virginia, and Tennessee would be admitted at the end of President George Washington's first term. The South had nothing to fear from these states, so it voted confidently against protecting the wealthy.[9]

The problem that Hamilton, Gerry, King, and Morris faced was that they were defending the commercial interests of the North, which in 1787 was too small a faction to garner widespread sympathy in the convention. The slaveholding faction, on the other hand, was a different creature entirely. Like the northern merchants, the slave state delegates, too, had wealth that they wished to protect, but they had the numbers to secure carve outs in the Constitution.

The South's greatest victory was the "three-fifths rule," which counted an enslaved person as three-fifths of a free person for the purposes of apportionment. This metric was based on the old impost proposal, which would have apportioned taxes to the southern states on the same principle. This would have the same effect as Morris and Hamilton's proposed Senate, in that it created a bias in favor of property ownership—not in cash, debt holdings, or bills of exchange, but in human beings. In mid-July, nine states voted to approve the idea, much to the outrage of Morris. "There can be no end of demands for security if every particular interest is to be entitled to it. The northern states may claim it for their fishery, and for other objects, as the southern states claim it for their peculiar objects." The South demanded that the principle of majority rule be adulterated to accommodate its main source of wealth, even though northern demands for consideration against the rise of the West were rejected. What made the South so special? Morris demanded to know. The answer was simple: the South had more votes at the convention.[10]

Madison, who otherwise reliably opposed deviations from proportional representation, said nothing in response to Morris's impassioned and logically forceful argument. The logic of the Virginia Plan should have brought him into stark opposition to the three-fifths rule, for wealth should hold no basis for representation in the kind of republic he had envisioned. Yet he could not follow his own principles when they implicated the source of his family and region's wealth. Worse, his inaction came despite his clear understanding that the institution of slavery was incompatible with a free government. As he said at the Constitutional Convention, "We have seen the mere distinction of colour made in the most enlightened period of time, a ground of the most oppressive dominion ever exercised by man over men." Later, in the *Federalist Papers*, he would mount a rather anemic defense of the southern carve outs, a subtle indication that the contradiction of slavery in a republic was not lost on him. Yet he did nothing about it.[11]

The slave states got their way thanks to a combination of southern vehemence and northern indifference. The opening position of South Carolina was actually to apportion slaves on a one-to-one basis with free whites. Pierce Butler, the Irish-born son of a British nobleman, argued that "as wealth was the great means of defense and utility to the nation they are equally valuable to it with freemen," and thus "an equal representation ought to be allowed." In a not-so-subtle jab at the anti-slavery Morris, Butler explained that the South needed such a "security" so that "their negroes may not be taken from them which some gentlemen within or without doors have a very good mind to do." Charles Pinckney—the youngest member of the state's delegation, equal parts ambitious and intelligent—argued that "this . . . was nothing more than justice," for enslaved people are the "peasants of the southern states," adding "equally to the wealth" and "the strength of the nation." Southern delegates even threatened to scuttle the whole constitutional project if their interests were not secured. William Davie of North Carolina, who hardly ever bothered to speak at the convention, warned that "North Carolina would never confederate on any terms" less than three-fifths. Edmund Randolph of Virginia similarly demanded the "security" that would come from "including slaves in the ratio of representation."[12]

Northern delegates were simply not prepared to scuttle the union over slavery. Better to make concessions to the South, even if they were unfair to the North. James Wilson—the Scottish-born lawyer from Pennsylvania who was a fervent advocate of democracy—probably spoke for many in the North when, in one breath, he said he could "not well see on what principle the admission of blacks in the proportion of three fifths could be explained. Are they admitted as citizens? Then why are they not admitted on an equality with white citizens? Are they admitted as property? Then why is not other property admitted into the computation?" But in virtually the next breath, he offered, "These were difficulties however which he thought must be overruled by the necessity of compromise." Only Morris was prepared to suggest that the two regions "take a friendly leave of each other" rather than confederate on such manifestly unfair terms. A lawyer by training, Morris had made a vast fortune in business with Robert Morris (no relation). He had lost his leg below the knee in a carriage accident in 1780, requiring him to walk with a peg leg, whose distinctive rap could be used for emphasis during his lengthy speeches at the convention. Pierce Butler called him "one of those geniuses in whom every species of talents combine to render him conspicuous and flourishing in public debate." Morris's unflinching denunciation of slavery persuaded none of his colleagues in 1787 but has vindicated him in the pages of history as a farsighted man with a clear moral vision.[13]

The southern demands extended beyond House apportionment too. As chair of the Committee of Detail, Rutledge had overseen the insertion of shockingly pro-southern provisions into the rough draft of the Constitution presented to the delegates on August 6. If the South Carolinian had had his way, Congress would be forbidden from outlawing or taxing the slave trade, as well as exports like tobacco and indigo, and it would have to muster a two-thirds majority to pass navigation acts. All in all, this would be a boon for southern exporters who feared a trade war with European nations. Once again, the South defended this extreme position as a protection from northern threats. "If the Convention thinks that North Carolina, South Carolina, and Georgia will ever agree to the plan, unless their right to import slaves be untouched," Rutledge warned, "the expectation is vain." They would scuttle the whole deal before they "give up so important an interest." Abraham Baldwin of Georgia thundered about the imprudence of "purchas[ing]" the security of a stronger union "by yielding national powers" that "were of a local nature."[14]

Rutledge's proposal was too much for the northern delegates. It was one thing to accept the three-fifths clause to save the union, but to do that in conjunction with a potentially unlimited slave trade was appalling. How was it fair, Morris asked, for the slave masters of "Georgia and South Carolina . . . [who] in defiance of the most sacred laws of humanity tears away his fellow creatures from their dearest connections and damns them to the most cruel bondage" to be rewarded with "more votes in a government instituted for protection of the rights of mankind than the citizen of Pennsylvania and New Jersey, who views with laudable horror, so nefarious a practice"? Rufus King believed "there was so much inequality and unreasonableness in all this, that the people of the northern states could never be reconciled to it."[15]

Even some of the southern delegates balked at Rutledge's plan, especially regarding the slave trade, which had already been outlawed in Virginia. Mason denounced it as an "infernal traffic" and thought it essential that the "general government should have power to prevent the increase of slavery." Madison, who had seemingly caught a case of laryngitis when the three-fifths debate threatened the logic of the Virginia Plan, finally found his voice to object to Rutledge's restrictions on taxing and regulating the South. The power of taxing exports, he argued, "is proper in itself" and could be prudently used on "articles in which America was not rivalled in foreign markets," like tobacco. As the South's reliance on exports meant that it was most in need of "naval protection," it was only fair for Congress to have such an authority. As for navigation acts that regulated foreign trade, Madison thought it essential for the government to be able to strike back with "retaliating measures" against "foreign nations" that attempted to engage in a trade war. Moreover, the careful distribution of political power in the national government would ensure that "an abuse" of the power "was rendered improbable."[16]

Ultimately, the two sides cut a deal on these issues that was, in the main, extremely generous to southern interests: the slave trade could be regulated in twenty years' time, exports would not be taxed, and navigation acts could be enacted with a simple majority in Congress. These carve outs for the South were not justifiable according to Madison's logic of the extended republic. Under that theory, a national majority should not be restrained from enacting laws beneficial to the country at large. But southern delegates—who were otherwise generally amenable to a strong national government—were unwilling to take the risk when it came to their regional interests. Time and again, they demanded special treatment, and the North gave in.

THE OTHER MAJOR faction at the convention to successfully demand a carve out was, in Madison's view, not a real faction at all: the small states. Their delegates insisted that a purely national system of government, as embodied by the Virginia Plan, would be ruinous to their interests. Madison maintained that no such thing would be the case, because there was no discernible small-state or large-state interest. But the small states were relentless, and they had the numbers to get their way after a lengthy and weary struggle.

Madison's problem ultimately was a mathematical one. His idea for proportional representation in both chambers of Congress had, at its core, the support of six states: Massachusetts, Pennsylvania, Virginia, North and South Carolina, and Georgia. That was just a bare majority of the states in attendance when the debates were actually happening. If Rhode Island had agreed to participate, and if the New Hampshire delegation had not arrived so late, the large-state coalition would have been outvoted from the get-go.

Plus, the small states were much more vehement than the large states. Generally speaking, the small-state delegations were willing to agree to a proportional House of Representatives, but equal representation in the Senate was their sine qua non. They would never agree to anything less. On the other side of the spectrum, only three states—Massachusetts, Pennsylvania, and Virginia—were large enough to reap an immediate political benefit from the proportional distribution of senatorial power. The southern states were currently small in terms of population, but the vast territory to the southwest beckoned to them with assurances that they would someday be large. Of course, prospective advantages are never as great an inducement to action as calculations based on the here and now. Georgia above all needed protection from the national government against Spanish and Native threats. Its delegates were never going to allow the convention to fail over a proportional Senate. Even the large-state delegates were not altogether sold on proportionality in the Senate. Many members did not see proportional representation in such existential terms. It was not essential to the success of the republic, but rather a political advantage that would become useless if the convention failed. Benjamin Franklin spoke for many when he said that "both sides must part with some of their demands, in order that they may join in some accommodating proposition."[17]

In retrospect, the fate of the Virginia Plan on this issue was sealed before Randolph even submitted it to the convention. At the very beginning of the assembly, George Wythe of Virginia, chair of the rules committee, proposed that a quorum of "not less than seven states" was required for business, "and all questions shall be decided by the greater number of these which shall be fully represented." This rule, accepted without debate, guaranteed that tiny Delaware would have as much sway at the convention as mighty Virginia. And given that the small states outnumbered the large in the union, Madison would have to convince the small states to cede a large share of their power. This was never going to happen.[18]

Weakness in Madison's position was evident early on. On May 31, the delegates debated how the two houses should be chosen. Direct election of the House was approved, and then consideration turned to the Senate. The Virginia Plan called for the state legislatures to nominate candidates for the upper chamber, to be approved by the House. This was voted down three-seven, with only Massachusetts, South Carolina, and Virginia in support. Madison wrote in his notes that this vote had left "a chasm . . . in this part of the plan," as the Senate now had no mode of selection. On June 7, Delaware's John Dickinson proposed bridging the gap by having the state legislatures select senators. The convention overwhelmingly agreed to this, ten states in favor and zero opposed. This was doubly worrying to Madison. The legislatures had undermined the Continental Congress by appointing narrow-minded men who thwarted the long-term success of the nation for the short-term gain of their states. The new Senate was bound to carry over the same problems, he believed. Worse, he sensed that this vote was a stalking horse for equal representation in the Senate. The Virginia Plan implied (but did not state outright) that not every state would have senators. If Dickinson's method of selection prevailed, every state would have at least one—meaning that either the upper chamber would have to be very large to accommodate at least one senator from each state, undermining the virtue of the Senate as a venue to moderate the impetuosity of the larger House, or senators would be apportioned equally among the states rather than according to population. As Madison argued, "The more the representatives of the people . . . were multiplied, the more they partook of the infirmities of their constituents, the more liable they became to be divided among themselves either from their own indiscretions or the artifices of the opposite factions, and of course the less capable of fulfilling their trust." Under Dickinson's proposal, the convention either faced the choice of "depart[ing] from the

doctrine of proportional representation" or "admit[ting] into the
Senate" too many members. The test vote for proportionality in
the upper chamber occurred four days later, and Madison and
the nationalists carried it six-five. But by this point, there was
no workable plan for proportionality on the table. As it stood,
the Senate would be impractically large. Moreover, the five votes
opposed to a proportional senate were locked in and clearly unwilling to budge.[19]

The opposition of Dickinson in particular was a major
problem for the Virginia Plan, for he was one of the most distinguished leaders at the entire convention. The author of the
Letters from a Farmer in Pennsylvania, which had denounced the
Townshend duties in 1767 and 1768, Dickinson was already a
continental presence by 1769, when the then-teenage Madison
saw him receive a degree from the College of New Jersey. Since
then, Dickinson had held a variety of positions, in the Continental Congress as well as the state governments of Pennsylvania and Delaware (he owned property in both states). Delaware
had chosen him to represent its interests at both the Annapolis
Convention and the Constitutional Convention. He was widely
respected as a pragmatic, thoughtful statesman, and his intention was to strengthen the national government while preserving
Delaware's place within it.

Ever the moderate, Dickinson agreed that proportionality
was an appropriate standard for the House. Instead, he took his
stand over the Senate, where he did more than oppose Madison's
plan. He offered an alternative vision for the new Constitution,
one with antecedents in the British system. The British monarch,
he explained to his fellow delegates, enjoyed stability due to the
"attachments which the Crown draws to itself." America did not
have a monarch that garnered the kind of affection that gave
weight to the British government, but it did have the states. The

division of the country into thirteen states had been a historical accident, but a lucky one, for they could offer a "principal
source of stability" to the constitutional project. If the proposed
Constitution was the solar system, then the states should be the
"planets, and ought to be left to move freely in their proper or-
bits." Perhaps, then, a version of mixed estates was still possible
in the American context. Hereditary government was gone after
the Declaration of Independence. But the states remained—and
not, according to Dickinson, as some useless vestige of the old
system. People were loyal to their states. They respected state authority. Why not utilize that respect for framing the new government? Why not bring the states more fully into the national
system? Doing so, admittedly, would run contrary to the principle of majority rule, but then again everybody realized that
the excesses of majority rule had to be checked in some way.
Why not employ the states for that role, by establishing them as
a kind of nobility in the American system?[20]

This argument made no sense to Madison. It was, after all, the
state legislatures that had "run into schemes of paper money . . .
whenever solicited by the people, and sometimes without even
the sanction of the people." What kind of weight could they
possibly add to Congress? "Their influence . . . instead of checking a like propensity in the national legislature, may be expected
to promote it." Yet, as the vote to allow state legislatures to select
senators revealed, Dickinson's logic carried weight with the delegates. If nothing else, it had the advantage of familiarity. The
Virginia Plan was seeking to reduce dramatically the role that
the states played in government. Their irresponsibility demanded
nothing less, Madison argued. But still, this was a big request.
Dickinson, on the other hand, was proposing a more modest
course: supplement the governance of the states with the direct
involvement of the people. It was a middle ground between the

Virginia Plan and the status quo, and it was one the convention ultimately accepted.[21]

But not right away. The advocates of the Virginia Plan were stout in their defense, so the delegates from the small states spent many days in June threatening to blow up the convention if they did not get a guarantee. In so doing, they made ample use of the rhetoric of mixed estates. As a minority in this new system, the small states deserved guarantees against majoritarian threats; otherwise, they could be voted into oblivion. William Paterson of New Jersey asserted that proportional representation was "striking at the existence of the lesser states." Oliver Ellsworth of Connecticut asserted that it was hardly extraordinary that the few should have a check on the many, analogizing the states to the House of Lords, "who form so small a proportion of the nation" yet have "a negative on the laws as a necessary defense of their peculiar rights against the encroachments of the Commons." Just as with Dickinson, the warnings of Paterson and Ellsworth could not be brushed aside, for both had served the country with distinction and had come to the convention not to thwart reforms, but to make sure they were fair to their home states.[22]

Madison struggled in vain against their reasoning. The large-state-small-state divide, he noted, had no analogue in the typical cleavages of politics. If Massachusetts, Pennsylvania, and Virginia aligned against the small states, it would have to be out of some mutual interest. So, what was that interest? Madison could think of none. "In point of situation they could not have been more effectually separated from each other by the most jealous citizen of the most jealous state. In point of manners, religion and the other circumstances, which sometimes beget affection between different communities, they were not more assimilated than the other states. In point of the staple productions they were as dissimilar as any three other states in the Union." This must be why, he reasoned, "the journals of Congress did not present any peculiar association of these states in the votes recorded"—they had nothing in common except their large size. If anything, their size would drive them apart: "Among individuals of superior eminence and weight in society, rivalships were much more frequent than coalitions." Ditto among independent nations. England and France were the most preeminent nations in Europe, and they hated each other. The "great division of interests in the United States" was not regarding the size of the states, Madison noted, but between the North and South. This "resulted partly from climate, but principally from the effects of their having or not having slaves." Slavery at this point was legal in most states but had become essential to the southern economy, and because the small states were split between the South (Delaware and Maryland) and North (Connecticut, New Hampshire, New Jersey, and Rhode Island), Madison believed all this rhetoric was misplaced.[23]

The real danger, Madison argued, was to the majority of the people from this insistence on equal apportionment, for it was the wrong "foundation" upon which a durable "superstructure would be raised." Unlike the government established under the Articles of Confederation, this new government would operate directly upon the people. It was therefore inappropriate for it to be established as "partly federal, partly national"—in other words, partly derived from the people and partly derived from the states. In such a scheme, the "majority of states might injure the majority of the people" by obstructing necessary legislation, extorting "measures repugnant to the wishes and interests of the majority" in exchange for assenting to critical legislation, or using the special powers of the upper chamber to impose measures adverse to the majority.[24]

How, Madison asked time and again, was any of this fair to the people of Massachusetts, Pennsylvania, and Virginia? The Delaware delegates had told the convention that they could never agree to a Congress premised solely on proportional representation. How could the Virginia delegates agree to anything but? Did Virginia not have the force of republican logic behind its position, the idea that numerical majorities are the closest approximation to the public interest? As far as Madison was concerned, the choice before the convention was straightforward. It could either depart "from justice in order to conciliate the small states and the minority of the people of the United States or of displeasing these by justly gratifying the larger states and the majority of the people." This, in his view, was no choice at all. "The Convention, with justice and the majority of the people on their side, had nothing to fear. With injustice and the minority on their side, they had everything to fear."[25]

Back and forth the two sides went, neither persuading the other nor ceding an inch. As the debate dragged on through June, it grew more ominous. Gorham warned "that a rupture of the union would be an event unhappy for all," but the small states would be unhappiest of all. "What would be the situation of Delaware . . . in case of a separation of the states? Would she not lie at the mercy of Pennsylvania?" And what of New Jersey? "Should a separation of the states take place," its fate "would be worst of all. She has no foreign commerce and can have but little." She would be at the mercy of Pennsylvania and New York. Madison warned that the dissolution of the union and the attending interstate rivalries would usher in "vigorous and high toned governments" that would "introduce some regular military force," hand "great discretionary powers . . . to the executive magistrate," and destroy political liberty in the New World. In a comment that prompted outrage from many delegates, Gunning

Bedford of Delaware retorted that it was the large states who had more to fear from a dissolution, because the small ones "will find some foreign ally of more honor and good faith, who will take them by the hand and do them justice."[26]

By the end of the month, most delegates were exhausted by this impasse. A committee of eleven was chosen to fashion a compromise. Fatefully, the members appointed from the large states were those who sought compromise, like Franklin and Mason. From the small states, it drew upon hardliners like Bedford, Ellsworth, and Paterson. The compromise it proposed—a proportional House and a Senate with equal apportionment—had been suggested by Roger Sherman of Connecticut on June 11 and had subsequently been endorsed by Dickinson, Ellsworth, and others up to that point. It was exactly what the small states wanted. As a sop to the large states, the committee offered that all revenue bills originate in the House. Madison and his allies scoffed that this was useless—a prescient objection, since in practice the Senate has found all manner of ways to write its own tax legislation. Nevertheless, the compromise peeled enough delegates away to pass five to four on July 16, with Massachusetts divided and North Carolina voting in favor.

MADISON'S REPUBLICANISM WAS too nationalistic for most of his fellow delegates, even those who favored a dramatic increase in federal authority. Of those who contributed regularly to the debates, only James Wilson was consistently of a similar mind about how the new government should be structured. The reasoning behind Madison's theory of the extended republic may have been compelling, but it was still just a theory. It had not been tested by the rigors of experience. Delegates from the small states were simply not prepared to take it on faith that Madison's vision would be proved true. Most of them were willing to join together in a strong union, but they needed to hedge their bets. They were not the only ones either. Hamilton's plan of government, Morris's call for protections for northern financiers, and Rutledge's efforts to secure the interests of the South all illustrated broad-based hesitation regarding Madison's ideas about the extended republic and the potential for his new vision of politics to solve the essential problem of government. This is why the old British idea of mixed estates, with its protections for certain minorities, managed to find its way into the Constitution, albeit subtly. Fearing that a national majority might subsume their interests, delegates bargained for guaranteed protections for this or that faction against the dictates of the masses. Due to their numbers and their insistence, the small states and the slave states were able to carve out niches for themselves in the Constitution—a document that bears the stamp of Dickinson and Rutledge in addition to Madison.

Before the convention even finished its business, Madison was complaining bitterly to Jefferson about its failure. But, ironically enough, his frustration was proof of concept for his theory of the extended republic. He had come in with a brilliant plan that, from his perspective in the moment, was twisted all out of shape. But from another perspective, it is just as easy to say that the convention took the basics of the Madisonian system and, through a political process, bargained its way to a deal that satisfied a majority of delegates while still strengthening the national government and redesigning it along basically Madisonian lines. Politics could in fact work to fashion broad compromises that, while not logically airtight, served the public interest.

The convention finally finished its business in mid-September, and on the seventeenth the new Constitution received a warm encomium from Franklin, the most senior and, along with Washington, the most esteemed member of the body. He was "astonishe[d] . . . to find this system approaching so near to perfection as it does; and I think it will astonish our enemies, who are waiting with confidence to hear that our councils are confounded like those of the Builders of Babel. . . . Thus I consent, Sir, to this Constitution because I expect no better, and because I am not sure that it is not the best." He called upon the members to sign the Constitution to demonstrate the "unanimous consent of the states present."[27]

But Franklin's call for unanimity was rejected. In a sign of future trouble, Gerry, Mason, and Randolph refused to sign, despite having been energetic participants in the debates. Gerry was unpredictable and pertinacious, and so his unwillingness to compromise can be chalked up to his unique character. But the opposition of Mason and Randolph was another matter entirely. Mason was the convention's éminence grise on matters of republican probity, and Randolph was a major political figure in the Old Dominion. Though their participation had usually been constructive and their views moderate, their rhetoric had turned somewhat dark around the debate over slavery in the later sessions. Mason had wondered whether, since the southern states were in the minority in both chambers of Congress, "is it to be expected that they will deliver themselves bound hand and foot to the [northern] states, and enable them to exclaim, in the words of Cromwell on a certain occasion—'the Lord hath delivered them into our hands.'" Randolph had not been so poetic, but he complained about "features so odious in the Constitution as it now stands." Later, during a debate over presidential selection, he had warned that the convention had "in some revolutions of this plan made a bold stroke for monarchy." At the conclusion of the convention, he told his fellow delegates that his refusal to sign was not a rejection of the Constitution per se but was "meant only to keep himself free to be governed by his duty as it should be prescribed by his future judgment." This was his way of saying he was uncertain how Virginians would react, and he intended not to be on the wrong side of public opinion.[28]

On the evening they signed the Constitution, the delegates "adjourned to the City Tavern, dined together and took a cordial leave of each other," as Washington recorded in his diary. This was a time for relaxation and satisfaction at a job well done, but just provisionally. The delegates had bargained and bartered to find common ground with one another, but the Constitution would have to be approved by the people before it could become the law of the land.[29]

The coming fight over ratification would be the greatest democratic event in the history of the world up to that point in time. White male freeholders across all thirteen states would be tasked with electing delegates to special ratifying conventions that would determine whether the Constitution would be adopted. What would be the outcome? Nobody knew. As Madison wrote to Jefferson, "The Convention is . . . in the dark as to the reception which may be given to it on its publication." Having the support of such luminaries as Washington and Franklin was no doubt necessary for its success, but hardly sufficient. The opposition of Gerry and Mason, and the equivocation of Randolph, had cast a pall of uncertainty around the new instrument of government. Plus, the forces in opposition were already organizing. John Lansing and Robert Yates of New York had left the convention in July rather than carry on in fruitless opposition, and Luther Martin and John Francis Mercer of Maryland departed in early September after a bill of rights was rejected. And, Madison noted to Jefferson, "it may well be expected that certain characters will wage war against any reform whatever"—a not-so-subtle reference to the fearsome Patrick Henry.[30]

Like just about everybody else, Madison had his doubts about the new Constitution. It was far short of what he had initially envisioned in the Virginia Plan, and no doubt it stung him to see what he thought were his best ideas rejected. But as summer gave way to fall, he set those concerns aside. He prudently concluded that this was the best instrument of government that could practically have been produced, given the circumstances, so he would commit himself wholly to its defense. And he would have to give it everything he had.

5

THE *FEDERALIST PAPERS*

THE COUNTRY WAITED with bated breath through the summer of 1787, as the delegates to the Constitutional Convention debated behind closed doors, with nary a hint of their deliberations for the broader public. When their proposed instrument of government was signed on September 17, it was the delegates' turn to wait as people all across the country reacted to the fruits of their labors. James Madison wrote his father on September 30, "What reception this system will generally meet with cannot yet be pronounced." Similarly, Alexander Hamilton wrote privately that it was "essentially [a] matter of conjecture . . . whether the plan will be adopted or rejected."[1]

Madison mostly kept his negative opinions about the Constitution to himself. His best friend Thomas Jefferson was privy to his unvarnished thoughts, but otherwise Madison embraced the new instrument of government as a definite improvement over the status quo. After the end of the convention, he went to New York, where the Continental Congress was sitting, as he had again been selected as a delegate. The Congress did not have much business in the fall and winter of 1787–1788, which enabled him to spend most of his time working to get the new Constitution ratified—communicating political intelligence to allies and eventually writing dozens of essays in defense of the proposed government.

The early indications were positive, but not uniformly so. The Constitution received good reviews from the prominent citizens of Philadelphia, and Madison heard from allies in Virginia that the document had been well received. Yet it stumbled a bit at the Continental Congress. On September 23, Virginia delegate Edward Carrington warned Madison that "the same schism which unfortunately happened in our state in Philadelphia, threatens us here also." Richard Henry Lee—the famed Virginia revolutionary who had made the motion to declare independence back in 1776—was trying to thwart the Constitution. The delegates to the convention had sent the Constitution first to Congress, with the intention of having it ultimately approved or rejected by special ratifying conventions in the states. But Lee and a handful of other delegates were trying to amend it from within the national legislature. Advocates of the Constitution—who would come to call themselves Federalists—stopped these Anti-Federalist maneuvers, but Lee still managed to undercut any momentum coming out of Congress. The assembly voted unanimously to refer the Constitution to the states, but it did not offer any kind of approbation for the proposed plan of government, an "ambiguity," Madison worried to George Washington, that would undermine the Federalist cause in states "where stress will be laid on the agency of Congress."[2]

Granted, by the time the Constitution faced its toughest challenges—in the ratifying conventions of Massachusetts, New Hampshire, and Virginia in 1788—nobody would remember Lee's gambit. It is noteworthy not because it succeeded but because of who attempted it. As Hamilton noted in tallying up the plusses and minuses for the Constitution's prospects, it was important that the proposal enjoyed the "very great weight of influence of the persons who framed it, particularly in the universal popularity of General Washington." In general, this was probably the greatest asset of the Federalists. The men of esteem, of weight, who had led the country through the turbulent break with Great Britain generally fell in line behind the Constitution. But this was less true in Virginia. There, the weight would be more equally divided, as many notable statesmen opposed it: Lee, for starters, but also Patrick Henry and the two Virginia delegates who refused to sign, Edmund Randolph and George Mason.[3]

The ever-vacillating Randolph turned out not to be a huge problem for the Federalists. He kept his counsel until December, at which point he offered a lengthy, tedious explanation for his opposition to the Constitution at the convention. But he also sought to have his cake and eat it too. Declaring that the union was "the rock of our salvation," he prayed fervently for "the establishment of a firm, energetic government," and warned that "the most inveterate curse that can befall us is a dissolution of the Union." He promised that as "an individual citizen," he would "accept the Constitution." This was hardly the kind of political leadership the Federalists needed from the governor who was given the honor of proposing the Virginia Plan at the convention, but it would be good enough. Sensing the shift once more in the political winds, Randolph ultimately voted for ratification at the Virginia ratifying convention.[4]

Mason was a bigger problem. Madison reported to Jefferson that he "left Philadelphia in an exceeding[ly] ill humor indeed." There was no big break between him and his fellow delegates, but rather a "number of little circumstances," including "the impatience which prevailed towards the close of the business." Mason had jotted down at the convention a rough draft of his objections, which he shared in Philadelphia with the Anti-Federalists of the Maryland delegation. Now that the business was closed, he was allowing a more polished set of complaints to be widely circulated. He even sent a copy of his grievances to Washington on October 17, lamenting that "a little moderation and temper in the latter end of the convention might have removed" them.[5]

Of course, the biggest threat of all would be Henry, "the great adversary who will render the event precarious," as Madison wrote to Jefferson in December. Virginia Federalists expected him to oppose the Constitution for no other reason than it was a good idea, and Henry was congenitally adverse to good ideas. Past encounters with Henry had demonstrated that he could do enormous harm when his influence was united "with some pretty able auxiliaries," which was the case here.[6]

Outside the Old Dominion, the tentative view on the Constitution in the early fall was generally but not entirely positive for the Federalists. In a prescient letter to William Short, Jefferson's secretary in Paris, on October 24, Madison ran through the prospects. The "presumptive evidence" of support in New England was "pretty strong," with the obvious exception of Rhode Island, "whose folly and fraud have not yet finished their career." New Jersey looked solid. Delaware, whose delegates to the convention had struck a fantastic bargain for their state, "will fall in of course." Maryland looked "well disposed." Pennsylvania "is divided," but "the advocates of the Constitution at present are certainly the more numerous party." New York, meanwhile, remained a potential source of trouble. "The men of abilities are generally on the side of the Constitution," but Governor George Clinton was a "decided adversary to it." Moreover, New York was fast becoming the locus of a robust newspaper war between Federalists and Anti-Federalists.[7]

Stationed in New York, Madison grew alarmed in the early fall of 1787 by the proliferation of Anti-Federalist pamphlets and newspaper articles in that state. On October 21, he wrote to Randolph fretting that "the newspapers in the middle and northern states" had begun "to teem with controversial publications" that attacked "the organization of the government" and also the "omission" of a bill of rights. Madison was particularly anxious about a "new combatant," writing under the pseudonym Brutus, after the legendary defender of the Roman republic who conspired to murder Julius Caesar. Writing "with considerable address and plausibility," Brutus had struck "at the foundation" of the Constitution, arguing that any national government that "forms the states into one nation" was "improper and impracticable."[8]

Judged solely on the newspapers, Madison wrote to Randolph, one might "suppose that the adversaries" of the Constitution "were the most numerous and the most earnest." It seemed that there was a new Anti-Federalist writer emerging every week. The letters of Cato, possibly written by Governor Clinton himself, began appearing in September. Brutus—possibly authored by New York congressman Melancton Smith—first appeared in October. Ditto the writings of Centinel, written by Samuel Bryan, son of Pennsylvania judge George Bryan. The letters of the Federal Farmer, which may have been written by Smith or Richard Henry Lee, began appearing in November. These authors would together offer a formidable critique of the new Constitution.[9]

MADISON SCOFFED TO his brother Ambrose that "the adversaries" of the Constitution "differ as much in their objections as they do from the thing itself." At first blush, it certainly must have appeared that way. These Anti-Federalist critiques were almost certainly not coordinated among the authors, which gives the corpus of Anti-Federalist literature a slapdash, disorganized appearance. Collectively, they seemed to attack the Constitution from every angle, which made it look as though they were opposing it just for the sake of opposition. They also varied radically in terms of quality. Brutus was probably the best of the lot, while Centinel's essays were lackluster.[10]

Nevertheless, there was an intellectual coherence to Anti-Federalism that belies its scattershot origins, an ideology rooted as firmly in the principles of the American Revolution as Federalism and possessing a forceful appeal to both the theory and history of politics. Unlike the critics of the Virginia Plan at the Constitutional Convention—the small states, the northern creditors, and the slave interests—the Anti-Federalists were not looking for a carve out for their own clique. Their arguments were universal in scope. They had a strong view of how self-government was supposed to function, from which they derived their critiques of the Constitution.

Whereas Madison thought the only sustainable model for a republic was through a diverse, expansive polity, the Anti-Federalists held that republics had to be small in scope and uniform in population. In their letter of dissent to ratification, the minority delegates at the Pennsylvania ratifying convention wrote that history and theory confirmed "that a very extensive territory cannot be governed on the principles of freedom." Instead, according to Centinel, only "despotism" could "bind so great a country under one government."[11]

The Anti-Federalists concluded from this assumption that the only way to organize government was around states, for two main reasons. First, according to the Federal Farmer, "the state governments . . . possess the confidence of the people and be considered generally as their immediate guardians." Brutus noted that the leaders of state governments "mix with the people" and can "explain to them the motives which induced the adoption of any measure, point out its utility, and remove objections or silence unreasonable clamors to it." This sort of confidence was necessary for free government, which ultimately was based on the consent of the governed. In contrast, per Brutus, the people "will, probably, not know the characters" of the federal government, which will not enjoy "the good will of the people." Thus, its dictates "must be executed by force, or not executed at all."[12]

Second, state governments were the best way to keep republican government from degenerating into aristocracy. Brutus argued that the only way to have a true representation of the people—such that the various sentiments of all classes of the citizenry were accounted for—would require a legislative body "so numerous and unwieldy, as to be subject in great measure to the inconveniency of a democratic government." Obviously, an extended republic could not have a legislature that represented the people with sufficient granularity. Such an assembly would be too large to get anything done. The Anti-Federalists warned that as Congress became less representative, the influence of the wealthy would grow. Brutus predicted that "the natural aristocracy of the country will be elected," for "wealth always creates influence, and this is generally much increased by large family connections." So, in a country whose electorate was largely small landowners, only a "few of the merchants, and those the most opulent and ambitious, will have a representation from their body." The Anti-Federalists warned that the aristocratic flavor of the federal Congress would be compounded by the power of the president to appoint subordinate officers, which, as Brutus noted, in a country as large as the United States "must be various and of magnitude." These bounties would be pursued by "ambitious and designing men," who will use the power, once acquired, for "the purposes of gratifying their own interests."[13]

Some Anti-Federalists went so far as to warn that this was actually the intention of the Federalists. Centinel argued that they had taken advantage of the public reaction to Shays's Rebellion. "The people thus unsettled in their sentiments," he warned, "have been prepared to accede to any extreme of government." The Federal Farmer warned that the revolt of the "little insurgents, the levelers" of 1786, had given "encouragement to the other party, which, in 1787, has taken the political field, and with its fashionable dependents, and the tongue and the pen, is endeavoring to establish in great haste, a politer kind of government." Both sides—the very poor and the very rich—had agendas that ran contrary to the "solid, free, and independent part of the community." The plan of government created under the Constitution was not merely errant. It was a wolf in sheep's clothing, the way through which the wealthy and powerful could quietly steal the liberty of the people by destroying the sovereignty of the state governments.[14]

To these arguments, the Federalists responded that the Constitution was a federal system, one of dual sovereignty between the states and the national government. Not only were the powers of the Congress limited, but the state governments themselves had the right to select senators. The Anti-Federalists were unconvinced, holding instead that the Constitution would inevitably result in an aristocratically tinged national government overwhelming the states and destroying liberty. The minority delegation to the Pennsylvania ratifying convention called dual sovereignty a "solecism in politics"—a contradiction in terms. Inevitably, "one or the other would necessarily triumph in the fullness of dominion." And, the Anti-Federalists reckoned, all signs pointed to the national government prevailing in this great clash of sovereign wills. One need look no further than Article I, Section 8. It supposedly enumerated the powers of Congress, yet that last clause was the tell. There, the convention granted Congress the power to do what was "necessary and proper" to bring into effect the other powers. It seemed to the Anti-Federalists that the authors of the Constitution were actually trying to establish a federal government with unlimited power, while duping the public into believing that the grant of authority was limited. Why else would they put in a clause legitimizing virtually anything Congress did? Brutus even went so far as to wonder whether this "comprehensive and [in]definite" power could "be exercised . . . to abolish the state legislatures."[15]

The Anti-Federalists made a similar claim about the taxing authority. The Constitution granted Congress the right "to lay and collect Taxes, Duties, Imposts and Excises, to pay the Debts and provide for the common Defence and general Welfare of the United States." This, Brutus warned, amounted to a limitless taxing power, for the "common defense and general welfare" was such a vague phrase that it meant in practice that Congress could tax "at their pleasure." And if Congress had unlimited authority to tax, Centinel argued, it could "absorb the state legislatures and judicatories," for how were the latter to acquire any revenue for themselves if the former had already taxed it all? When combined with the power to maintain a standing army and call into service the state militias, the national government thus would have monopolistic power over "the purse and the sword," as the Pennsylvania minority delegation put it, making it "perfectly independent of, and supreme over, the state governments."[16]

And why, the Anti-Federalists asked, was there no bill of rights? Mason, the primary author of the Virginia Declaration of Rights, had asked for a bill of rights at multiple points during the convention, and it was probably the delegates' biggest mistake not to be more forceful in enumerating the limits of congressional authority. Nothing else animated Anti-Federalist sentiment quite so strongly. Brutus argued that it was "astonishing, that this grand security, to the rights of the people, is not to be found in this constitution." The Federal Farmer pointed out that the convention had inserted a miniature bill of rights into Article I, Section 9, which prohibited ex post facto laws and bills of attainder and which guaranteed writs of habeas corpus. "This bill of rights ought to be carried farther," he argued, in what was probably the most persuasive claim of the many Anti-Federalist assertions.[17]

If the powers of the new government were intended to destroy the states and threaten the liberties of the people, its structure must have a similar purpose. The House of Representatives, Mason warned, was not the "substance but the shadow only of representation." There would only be 65 members when Congress first assembled. How could that possibly represent the vast diversity of the United States? Federal Farmer noted that only 33 representatives will be required for a quorum, and of that only half would be necessary to pass legislation. "I have no idea," he exclaimed, "that the interests, feelings, and opinions of three or four millions of people, especially touching internal taxation, can be collected in such a house." Brutus scoffed that "the representation is merely nominal—a mere burlesque." He warned that "no free people on earth, who have elected persons to legislate for them, ever reposed that confidence in so small a number." Sooner or later, the government would either have to use force to impose its dictates or watch helplessly as its laws go unobserved.[18]

If the Anti-Federalists were wary of the House, they detested the Senate. It was an axiom of free government, popularized by Montesquieu—whose *The Spirit of the Laws* was one of the most widely read books among educated men in the 1780s— that the legislative, executive, and judicial authorities had to be separate from each other. Joining these powers into a single body or individual was a recipe for tyranny. And yet the Senate seemed to violate this principle. Its power to advise and consent on presidential appointments gave it a hand in executive power. The power to remove officials who have been impeached by the House gave it judicial power. Its ability to ratify treaties, independent of the House, gave it too big a share of the legislative power. Mason warned that this design "will destroy any balance in the government, and enable them to accomplish what usurpations they please, upon the rights and liberties of the people." Meanwhile, the president would become a "mere tool to the Senate." Centinel reached a similar conclusion. "The president, who would be a mere pageant of state, unless he coincides with the views of the Senate, would either become the head of the aristocratic junto in that body, or its minion, besides, their influence being the most predominant, could the best secure his re-election to office."[19]

The Anti-Federalists also directed their ire against the judicial branch, of which the Constitution only gave a bare outline. The convention had avoided specifying much about the judiciary, instead leaving it to Congress to fill in the details, including the size and appellate jurisdiction of the Supreme Court and the organization of the lower courts. That left quite a bit of ambiguity, which, when combined with the absence of a bill of rights, greatly troubled the Anti-Federalists. They warned that the Supreme Court would become a roving agent of republican doom, stripping citizens of their rights under the state constitutions and creating, in the words of Brutus, "an entire subversion of the legislative, executive and judicial powers of the individual states."[20]

History has mostly forgotten the Anti-Federalists, which is unfortunate. Their complaints were often overwrought, hyperbolic, and even paranoid, yet underlying them was a piercing and often prescient critique of the Constitution. For instance, in his sixth essay, Brutus made a very tortured argument for how the Necessary and Proper Clause would enable the federal government to obliterate the taxing power of the states. This obviously never came to pass. Yet Brutus was right that the limits on federal authority were actually less stringent than they first appeared, for the power of the central government would grow markedly over the centuries. And while the Anti-Federalists' warnings about the potential for oligarchy under the new Constitution hardly corresponded to the largely poor, rural, and roughly egalitarian America of the 1780s, a century later the government would indeed become dominated by the wealthy titans of the industrial revolution. And though the essays vary markedly in terms of style and quality of argument, the substance is the same. The Anti-Federalists were warning the country that an extended republic could never work and the only way to preserve self-government was to keep the locus of power within the states, where it could be jealously guarded by the people.

This presented Madison with a challenge as well as an opportunity to defend his novel vision of republican government. He had been disappointed in the Constitution, but he firmly believed that the Anti-Federalist critique was misguided. What was needed, Madison thought, was a systematic defense of the Constitution. There had to be an effort to go through the Constitution, clause by clause, to explain the logic behind each decision and to discuss the probable effects. Hamilton—the brilliant, loquacious, and peripatetic Federalist from New York—was of a similar mind. The two agreed on a joint project to rebut the errors of the Anti-Federalists and lay out the merits of the

Constitution. So, in October 1787, the two of them, with the occasional assistance of John Jay—the accomplished diplomat who helped negotiate the Treaty of Paris—began publishing a series of essays that would become the most important commentaries on the Constitution: the *Federalist Papers.*

ON NOVEMBER 18, Madison wrote George Washington a brief note updating him on the prospects of the Constitution, enclosing the first seven *Federalist Papers.* "If the whole plan should be executed," he told the future president, "it will present to the public a full discussion of the merits of the proposed Constitution in all its relations." In his characteristically roundabout way, he also told Washington that he and Hamilton were the authors. "I will not conceal from you," he wrote, partially in cipher, "that I am likely to have such a degree of connection with the publication here, as to afford a restraint of delicacy from interesting myself directly in the republication elsewhere. You will recognize one of the pens concerned in the task."[21]

For how important they would become, the *Federalist Papers* had virtually no impact on their immediate target: the politics of ratification in New York. When New York got around to selecting delegates for its ratifying convention in 1788, it elected a large majority that were dubious of the Constitution. It was only after the triumph of the Federalists in Virginia that the New York convention reconciled itself to the new plan of government. But as the essays spread throughout the country, they began to have an appreciable effect. Federalists in one state would mail them to their allies in other states to help the cause of ratification. The clarity of the prose and forcefulness of the reasoning made them handy tools in rebutting Anti-Federalist attacks up and down the continent. In later decades, politicians as well as judges would turn to the *Federalist Papers* to understand the reasoning of the Founders, and they remain today the single greatest commentary on the Constitution.

What makes the *Federalist Papers* especially interesting is that Madison and Hamilton were not always offering their own views, but rather channeling the consensus of the Constitutional Convention. The two of them had been very nationalistic at the convention and watched in dismay as their fellow delegates retained many aspects of the old system. Yet they put those objections aside and wrote effectively on behalf of the convention as a whole, even in circumstances when their personal preferences diverged from the consensus in Philadelphia. As such, Publius—the pseudonym employed for the *Federalist Papers*—was not merely the nom de plume for rhetorical purposes; it was the voice of the convention itself.

Hamilton would write the bulk of the essays, an extraordinary fifty-one of eighty-eight. His rhetorical style was swashbuckling, animated with passion and conviction. Madison, who had developed a strong working relationship with Hamilton from their years in Congress, lacked his colleague's exuberant style. He could not keep up with Hamilton's pace (nobody could), writing twenty-nine of eighty-eight essays. But whereas Hamilton was fast and slashing in his prose, Madison was careful and thorough, which made his contributions at least as persuasive, if not more so. Plus, Madison had attended every meeting of the Constitutional Convention and kept careful notes, which made him the greatest expert in the country on the intention behind every clause within the Constitution.

Not all of Madison's essays were entirely successful. His defense of the three-fifths clause in *Federalist* 54 was particularly limp. There, he noted that "government is instituted no less for protection of the property, than of the persons, of individuals. The one as well as the other, therefore, may be considered as represented by those who are charged with the government." However, he conveniently omitted the counterargument—offered at the convention by Elbridge Gerry, Gouverneur Morris, Rufus King, and other northerners—that if property is to be a basis for representation under the Constitution, southern as well as northern property should be included. At the end of his tortured reasoning, Madison refused to attribute the argument to Publius, a subtle indication that he could not adequately defend the special privilege accorded to the southern states. "Such is the reasoning which an advocate for the Southern interests might employ on this subject, and although it may appear to be a little strained in some points, yet, on the whole, I must confess that it fully reconciles me to the scale of representation which the convention have established." Admittedly, there was a certain level of delicacy on the issue for Publius, given the audience. New York permitted slavery in 1788, but the state was still bound to be a relative loser to the South on apportionment under the three-fifths rule. Still, Madison may have been better off omitting discussion of the clause altogether rather than offering this contrived justification, easily the most poorly argued public essay in his career.[22]

Madison's defense of the Senate was hardly his best work either. Regarding the compromise on apportionment, the most Madison could offer in *Federalist* 62 was that "the equality of representation in the Senate is another point, which, being evidently the result of compromise between the opposite pretensions of the large and the small States, does not call for much discussion." One imagines him writing this sentence through gritted teeth, mindful of the old adage that if you do not have anything nice to say, it is better to say nothing at all.[23]

Still, these were exceptions to the general rule. Sometimes Madison argued honestly, sometimes he hid his own opinions to make the best case for the Constitution as it had ended up, but he typically did a superlative job of explaining the thinking of the convention. A careful analysis of his essays reveals many of his own views on government during the ratification period.

Madison's first five entries in the *Federalist Papers* were a digest of the impressive political theory he began to build in 1784 regarding the insufficiency of the confederacy and the need for an extended republic. The history of European confederations, he demonstrated in *Federalist* 18 through 20, is a history of failure. "Experience is the oracle of truth," he pronounced in *Federalist* 20, "and where its responses are unequivocal, they ought to be conclusive and sacred." Madison argued that experience had demonstrated that a "sovereignty over sovereigns . . . is a solecism in theory," and in practice it substitutes "*violence* in place of *law*, or the destructive *coercion* of the *sword*, in place of the mild and salutary *coercion* of the *magistracy*."[24]

It followed, then, that the Articles of Confederation were doomed to fail, which left two options: either dissolve into thirteen separate nations or forge a stronger union, wherein the national government directly ruled over the citizen. *Federalist* 10—often praised as Madison's finest contribution and perhaps the greatest essay in the whole series—was where he offered the public a thorough recitation of the theory of the extended republic. He claimed that a large republic would be superior to a small one because it would "take in a greater variety of parties and interests," which would "make it less probable that a majority of the whole will have a common motive to invade the rights of other citizens," or at least "if such a common motive exists, it will be more difficult for all who feel it to discover their own strength, and to act in unison with each other." *Federalist* 14 dealt with the technical matter of whether a national union was practically possible. Madison's answer was yes because the "natural limit of a republic is that distance from the center, which will barely allow the representatives of the people to meet as often as may be necessary for the administration of public affairs."[25]

In *Federalist* 55 through 57, Madison used the extended republic theory to build his defense of the House of Representatives. Confident that self-government could span the entire territory of the nation, he rejected claims that the House would not represent the public interest, that it would be too small to understand the concerns and interests of the people, and that it would be susceptible to aristocracy. Admitting "that no political problem is less susceptible of a precise solution" than fixing the number of representatives—too small a chamber would make it easy for legislators to form "a combination for improper purposes," too large would produce the "confusion and intemperance of a multitude"—he nevertheless remained steadfast that the House of Representatives would be a bastion of "the public liberty."[26]

Of course, the House of Representatives was the only part of the new government to reflect fully Madison's original Virginia Plan. Was the theory of the extended republic really useful for a defense of the Constitution as a whole? Obviously, the public Madison said yes, otherwise he would not have introduced the argument in *Federalist* 10. And most of his private correspondence during this period was unequivocal in support of the Constitution, with a focus on how to secure enough votes for ratification. Most—but not all. Madison confided to Jefferson in early September that he thought the Constitution was deficient. He followed up that dour missive with a longer letter dated October 24, less than a month before *Federalist* 10 first appeared in print. His main frustration, he told Jefferson, was the absence of the federal veto over state laws. A lack of such power, he argued, "seems to have been mortal to the ancient confederacies, and to be the disease of the modern." Without the ability to check the fractious irresponsibility of the states, the Constitution embodied more "the aspect . . . of a feudal system of republics . . . than a confederacy of independent states." An improvement perhaps, but it still "involves the evil of imperia in imperio"—states within the state. So, even as he was defending the system of dual sovereignty in the *Federalist* essays, Madison had not yet reconciled himself to it. It is clear from this letter that he thought a proportional House was a necessary condition to secure the extended republic but not a sufficient one. No doubt, the people had to organize a national government to operate directly on the people, but this government also had to possess the power to strike down unjust or selfish laws created by the state governments. Otherwise, the states would eventually devour the national government.[27]

Madison's private criticism to Jefferson was essentially the opposite of the critique made by the Anti-Federalists. His opponents believed that the system of coordinate authority was a fiction—that two sovereignties could not rule side by side, that sooner or later one would dominate the other, and that the Constitution had rigged the competition in favor of the national government. Madison, in his letter to Jefferson, similarly predicted "a continual struggle between the head and the inferior members, until a final victory has been gained in some instances by one, in others, by the other of them." The difference was who was going to win that battle. Madison believed that the Anti-Federalists were exactly wrong. The Constitution had established too strong a "dependence of the general [government] on the local authorities," which "will be stimulated by ambition" to reclaim the power they lost under the Constitution.[28]

Ironically, this lack of faith in the Constitution enabled him to strike down many Anti-Federalist claims with rhetorical vigor. He believed that if the new government's rickety system of dual sovereignty was going to collapse, it would be to the benefit of the states. Thus, the Anti-Federalist prediction of a dominant national government was just paranoid fearmongering. *Federalist* 39 offered a particularly forceful rejection of this claim. Examining how the Constitution was to be ratified, how its officers would be chosen, the sources and scope of its power, and how it would be amended, Madison concluded that it "is, in strictness, neither a national nor a federal Constitution, but a combination of both." In clashes between the states and the federal government, he was confident that the states would have the upper hand. He argued in *Federalist* 44 that the states would be better able to check unconstitutional federal acts than vice versa because, "as every such act of [the federal government] will be an invasion of the rights of [the states], these will be ever ready to mark the innovation, to sound the alarm to the people, and to exert their local influence in effecting a change of federal representatives."[29]

Even in mundane instances, as Madison described in *Federalist* 45, he was confident that the state governments would have more influence on the people than the federal government, thanks to the fact that state governments would make up "constituent and essential parts" of the federal government, the "weight of personal influence" that state lawmakers would naturally possess from being in closer contact with their constituents, the greater scope of power invested in the state governments, and the states' ability to resist federal measures. In *Federalist* 46 he argued that the state governments would have an additional advantage on the basis of appointment. Senators, after all, would be chosen by state governments. If nothing else, "a local spirit will infallibly prevail" in Congress, more than a "national spirit will prevail in the legislatures."[30]

Madison's unvarnished opinion, judging from his private correspondence with Jefferson, was that these proclaimed virtues of the Constitution were actually its vices. Having spent years in the Continental Congress, he knew full well the pernicious ways that the states could undermine the national project. This was why his first choice at the convention was for a fully national government. But, having lost that battle, he would be damned if the Anti-Federalists were going to convince the people that even the half measures adopted by the convention would destroy the state governments. So, he cleverly turned his main criticism of the Constitution into a robust defense.

Madison was similarly aggressive in knocking down Anti-Federalist hyperbole about congressional power, once more turning a private complaint into public praise. He had initially proposed under the Virginia Plan a plenary grant of authority on all matters that involved the national interest. But he then watched as the Committee of Detail transformed that into enumerated powers and the convention voted down many proposed additions, like the power to charter corporations or establish a national university. In many respects, the main powers granted under Article I, Section 8—the power to tax, to regulate commerce and the currency, to provide for national defense—were pretty bare-bones, the "necessary means of attaining a necessary end," as he wrote in *Federalist* 41. In *Federalist* 45 he put the matter bluntly: "If . . . the Union be essential to the happiness of the people of America, is it not preposterous, to urge as an objection to a government, without which the objects of the Union cannot be attained, that such a government may derogate from the importance of the governments of the individual States?" In a callback to his career in the Continental Congress in the early

1780s, when he tried unsuccessfully to broaden the congressional power, he argued in *Federalist* 46 that the Constitution does not so much add "new powers to the Union" as it "invigorat[es] its original powers," which had steadily been eroded.[31]

In *Federalist* 41 through 45, he reviewed the specific powers to tax, regulate commerce and the currency, and provide for national defense under Article I, knocking down the charge that these amounted to a stalking horse for total federal control. Regarding the taxing power, which the Anti-Federalists had made so much hay of, he argued that the mistake of Brutus and others was to take the phrase "general welfare" in isolation from the rest of the section. Instead, it had to be understood in the context of the enumerated powers that followed. "For what purpose," he asked, "could the enumeration of particular powers be inserted, if these and all others were meant to be included in the preceding general power?" In *Federalist* 44 he applied the same logic to the Necessary and Proper Clause. Though "few parts of the Constitution have been assailed with more intemperance than this. . . . No part can appear more completely invulnerable." Once again, the substance of the clause had to be understood in the context of the previously enumerated powers. Its purpose was not to sneak a plenary grant of authority into the Constitution, but rather to enable Congress to attend to the innumerable smaller tasks necessary to effectuate the enumerated powers. If the Constitution had no such clause, "there can be no doubt that all the particular powers requisite as means of executing the general powers would have resulted to the government, by unavoidable implication," for "no axiom is more clearly established in law . . . than that wherever the end is required, the means are authorized."[32]

THE FIRST TWO-THIRDS or so of Madison's *Federalist* entries were not entirely forthright. Some, like *Federalist* 10, 14, and 18 through 20, were more vindications of his Virginia Plan than of the actual Constitution. In others, his defense of the Constitution, in an essay like *Federalist* 39, was a reflection of the convention's views rather than his own. All of this was by necessity—Madison the politician arguing unequivocally for something that, at the time, he merely judged as better than nothing. But one topic on which he was free to be himself was the extent to which the Constitution intermingled powers between the branches of government. The convention's compromises on this subject were not nearly as offensive to him, and he was able to craft an interesting justification for what had been done.

Building the presidency required the convention to delineate precisely the boundaries between the executive and legislative branches. On this matter, the Virginia Plan offered only the barest outline: a president chosen by Congress for a seven-year term, not eligible for reelection, and joined with the courts in a "council of revision" to reject congressional laws. The bulk of this scheme was rejected, and after lengthy debates the delegates settled upon a peculiar design for the executive branch, delegating its selection to an Electoral College and intermingling its powers with the Senate on matters of foreign affairs and judicial and executive appointments. This unconventional approach opened up the Constitution to the Anti-Federalist accusation that it was violating the most sacred maxim of free government: that the legislative, executive, and judicial functions had to be kept separate from one another. In response to these critiques, Madison constructed over the course of *Federalist* 47 through 51 an impressive defense of the constitutional system, drawn from his thorough grounding in the canon of Western political philosophy.

In *Federalist* 47, he began by stipulating the essential point of the Anti-Federalists, that "the accumulation of all powers . . . in the same hands . . . may justly be pronounced the very definition of tyranny." Montesquieu, Madison noted, was the modern-day herald of this idea, and he was particularly enamored of the British constitution. So, it was interesting, Madison continued, that "the legislative, executive, and judiciary departments" of the British system "are by no means totally separate and distinct from each other." They were, rather, intertwined, such that each has a measure of "partial agency" in the other. Thus, Madison concluded, Montesquieu must not have advocated a total separation of powers but instead a constitution under which the "whole power of one department is" not "exercised by the same hands which possess the whole power of another department." In the American context, Madison similarly found no state where "the several departments of power have been kept absolutely separate and distinct."[33]

So, the question that Madison thought Americans really should be asking was not how to keep the branches of government totally separate but how to stop them from acquiring the powers that should remain in the hands of the others. In *Federalist* 48, 49, and 50, he rejected a series of solutions, beginning with "parchment barriers": the idea that, as he wrote in *Federalist* 48, it would be "sufficient to mark, with precision, the boundaries of these departments, in the constitution of the government." Madison felt the "legislative department," which in a republican system founded on popular control was naturally going to be the most aggressive and enterprising branch, was unlikely to be checked by mere regulations and would instead be "everywhere extending the sphere of its activity, and drawing all power into its impetuous vortex."[34]

In *Federalist* 49 and 50, he raised a suggestion made by Jefferson to call a constitutional convention to reform the system when it had been abused. This, too, Madison rejected for the same reason: the power of the legislature would be overwhelming. If a convention was called to revise the Constitution in light of a dispute between the branches, the legislative branch would dominate the proceedings. More numerous than the president or the courts and more connected to their constituents, legislators would "be able to plead their cause most successfully with the people." On top of that, it was dangerous to disturb "the public tranquility by interesting too strongly the public passions." Granted, the Constitutional Convention had been successful, but such "experiments are too ticklish of a nature to be unnecessarily multiplied." Even if a convention could be pulled off successfully, regular revisions of the Constitution would "deprive the government of that veneration which time bestows on every thing, and without which perhaps the wisest and freest governments would not possess the requisite stability."[35]

So, if a constitutional separation of powers itself cannot be self-regulating, and the people cannot be tasked with policing the boundaries, how else might it be maintained? In *Federalist* 51, Madison argued that the responsibility must lie with the agents of government themselves, and that "the interior structure of the government" must be designed so "that its several constituent parts may, by their mutual relations, be the means of keeping each other in their proper places." This required, in practice, two features. First, "each department should have a will of its own," meaning that each branch "should have as little agency as possible in the appointment of the members of the others," and members of each branch should not have to depend on the others for the salaries of their offices. Second, each branch, having been given an independent will, should have the power to "resist encroachments of the others." In one of his most famous adages, Madison argued that "ambition must be made to counteract ambition. The interest of the man must be connected with the constitutional rights of the place." The president must have the power to defend the independence of his branch, as must the Congress and the courts to defend theirs. This was the only way, Madison suggested, that power would not accumulate in the hands of a single agent in government.[36]

Madison called this the "policy of supplying, by opposite and rival interests, the defect of better motives." He thus developed an analogue between the extended republic and the doctrine of checks and balances. In both instances, he was confronting the problem that individuals are selfish and inclined to pursue their own agendas over the good of the whole—be they voters electing demagogues rather than public-spirited statesmen or politicians snatching authority from one another. It would be wonderful if a virtuous regard for the national interest carried the day, but that expectation was fanciful. So, what did Madison suggest? In both cases, he proposed turning the selfish against one another in a robust political process where nobody could dominate anybody else. Factions in the extended republic cannot possibly hope to rule one another; so, ultimately, they would have to compromise. Similarly, agents of each governmental department would encounter resistance from other agents in other departments; nobody would be able to preponderate, and sooner or later they would have to make peace. Just as politics would keep popular majorities in check, so, too, could it rein in ambitious and unscrupulous politicians.[37]

In making this argument, Madison was drawing on very old ideas within the Western political tradition. The ancient historian Polybius, for instance, had praised the Roman Republic's intermingling of powers across its classes of society, "for when one part having grown out of proportion . . . and tends to become too predominant," it shall be "counterworked and thwarted by the others." This, Polybius noted in a line that anticipated *Federalist* 51, was a way for the state to provide "itself a remedy for the evil from which it suffers." But there was a Madisonian twist to Polybius's formulation. Whereas the ancient historian had praised the Roman state for a government that blended elements of monarchy, aristocracy, and democracy, Madison intuited that the same basic idea of checks and balances could be repurposed for a system based purely on the rule of the people.[38]

THE *FEDERALIST PAPERS* hold a mythical place in the annals of American constitutionalism. Two of the country's finest thinkers dedicated themselves to explaining, in engrossing detail, the real meaning of the nation's foundational charter. The essays have been read by lawyers, scholars, and laypeople ever since. Yet within the context of James Madison's story, they occupy a peculiar position. He did not entirely believe everything he was writing. Madison had accepted the Constitution the way one might accept half a loaf rather than none at all, but he had resolved to make the best case possible for it. He was, at his core, a pragmatic politician. He knew when to take a deal, and the Constitution was the best offer for a national government he was going to get.

Even though Madison's *Federalist Papers* are strategic in places, they nevertheless offer his most direct and forceful statement about how he believed well-ordered politics could address the essential problem of government. *Federalist* 10 recapitulated his idea of the extended republic, which he had developed in the "Vices of the Political System of the United States" and pitched to his colleagues at the Constitutional Convention. Madison's view, simply put, was that no single entity was needed to secure justice; instead, the diversity of the country would balance factions against one another through the political process, forcing them to find common ground. In *Federalist* 51, he employed the same basic concept to explain how checks and balances could keep avaricious or unwise politicians in their places: Each branch of government would be able to influence the proceedings of the others, which meant that selfish politicians could thwart the designs of one another. In the process of bargaining, something approaching the public interest would emerge.

While the Constitution did not introduce a fully national government as Madison envisioned, it was certainly more nationalistic than the Articles of Confederation. *Federalist* 10 and 51 offer an affirmative argument for this change. Self-government can only work on the national level, Madison asserted, because it was only there that a new type of politics could be designed to support justice and the general welfare. While Madison spent a great deal of his efforts rebutting Anti-Federalist critiques and attacking the idea of a confederated republic, he did his allies in the Federalist movement an enormous favor by giving them this positive case to make to their friends, neighbors, and relatives. And future generations of Americans would see in the Madisonian *Federalist* not only a vision of how this or that branch of government would function, but a justification for the entire project of a national union.

6

RATIFICATION

As JAMES MADISON and Alexander Hamilton churned out *Federalist* after *Federalist*, the Constitution rolled on toward ratification, aided by strong support from many small states. Recognizing that they had scored an impossibly good deal for their state, delegates to the Delaware convention ratified the Constitution with little debate on December 3. Georgia likewise ratified unanimously on December 31, followed by Connecticut on January 9. But there was trouble brewing. Pennsylvania's convention voted two-to-one to ratify on December 12, but it had only managed to do so by employing strong-arm tactics against Anti-Federalist opponents—even going so far as to forcibly return members of the state assembly to the chamber so that a quorum could be achieved to call a hasty convention. Opponents also complained of the lack of time between the calling and seating of the convention, which they said hindered the ability of the people in the western hinterlands to grasp the full implications of the Constitution. The convention itself rushed through its deliberations, as the Pennsylvania Federalists tried (unsuccessfully) to be the first state to ratify. The minority report of the delegates, which complained about the procedural shenanigans and also the problems of the Constitution, embarrassed the state's Federalists and gave a spur to the Anti-Federalist movement.

The first real test for the Constitution came in Massachusetts, where the elites were largely lined up in favor of it, but delegates from the central and western portions of the state—where the anger and passion of Shays's Rebellion had originated—were skeptical at best. Fortunately for the Federalists, Elbridge Gerry was not chosen as a delegate, which left the opponents without a stronger leader. Gerry's public statement regarding the Constitution praised the good faith of both sides and included only a short, terse paragraph outlining some basic Anti-Federalist themes that had prompted his opposition.

The success or failure of the Constitution in the Bay State would come down to the old radicals who had pushed for revolution in 1776, and these men had their doubts. Samuel Adams wrote to Richard Henry Lee that "as I enter the building I stumble at the threshold. I meet with a national government, instead of a federal union of sovereign states." John Hancock was similarly skeptical. He and Adams, recognizing the failure of the Articles of Confederation and the danger of doing nothing, accepted a compromise: Why not try recommendatory amendments? Anti-Federalists had been calling for another convention to revise the structure of the new government, a move that Federalists had said would destroy the project altogether. Adams and Hancock agreed to split the difference: Massachusetts would ratify the Constitution without condition but would also propose a series of amendments for the new government to consider. This was exactly the sort of middle ground that moderate Anti-Federalists had been searching for, and so the Constitution was narrowly adopted, 187 to 168, on February 6, 1788, with substantial opposition from the central and western parts of the state.[1]

In late winter, Federalists received unwelcome news of problems in New Hampshire, a state many assumed would easily support ratification. John Langdon, a delegate to the Constitutional Convention, wrote George Washington on February 28 to report that his state's ratifying convention had postponed its debates. Even though, per Langdon, the Granite State had "everything to gain and nothing to lose by the adoption of the government," a majority of the state's delegates were either themselves opposed to the Constitution or under explicit instructions by their constituents to oppose it. The good news was that after ten days of discussion, a number of their delegates "were convinced of their mistake and only wished an opportunity to lay the matter before their constituents." So, while Langdon remained confident that the Constitution would be accepted, the convention had postponed business until June, as delegates returned home to plead the case to their constituents.[2]

This left the Constitution with the support of six states by the start of the spring. Maryland ratified on April 28 by a vote of 68 to 11, demonstrating that Luther Martin's drunken harangues at the convention spoke only for himself, not his state. The South Carolina convention voted overwhelmingly to ratify in May, which increased the number to eight. Still, this was short of the necessary nine states for the Constitution to take effect. Meanwhile, prospects for ratification were nonexistent in Rhode Island—which had rejected the Constitution via a popular plebiscite in a vote of 2,708 to 237—and uncertain in North Carolina. Though Madison and Hamilton threw everything they had into the *Federalist Papers*, they could not move the needle in New York, which that spring elected a convention of delegates ill-disposed toward ratification.

The importance of the Virginia convention was growing by the day. With New Hampshire having delayed its ratification, there were still just eight states in approval. But regardless of how many states actually endorsed, the new government would be stillborn if it came into being without Virginia, at that point the most populous state in the union. As such, Federalists and Anti-Federalists in the Old Dominion girded for political war. Back in October, the state legislature had passed resolutions calling for a ratifying convention to be held the following June, much later than most of the other states. At the time, nobody was really sure what that would mean for the Constitution's prospects, but after the adjournment of the New Hampshire convention in February, it looked like the fate of the new document would be decided in Madison's home state.

———

VOTERS ACROSS VIRGINIA—white, male freeholders who either owned property or held long-term leases on land—held elections to the ratifying convention at the end of March 1788, with each county receiving two delegates to send. Madison stood for election in Orange County on March 24, giving, for the first time in his life, a political address to a large gathering of his fellow citizens. Initially, he had not wanted to participate at all. In November, he explained to his brother Ambrose that "the final decision" on the Constitution "should proceed from men who had no hand in preparing and proposing it." But, seeing as how this was a rule that others had not followed—delegates to the Philadelphia convention not only served in state ratifying conventions but had often led the charge for the Federalists—his resistance began to soften. And given that the "many objections in Virginia proceed from a misconception of the plan," there had to be experts on hand to "contribute some explanations and information which may be of use." And who was a better expert than James Madison? As such, he explained to his brother, he "shall not decline the representation of the county if I should be honored with the appointment."[3]

He was soon persuaded by his Virginia friends to actively campaign for the seat. Madison was still up in New York over the winter, attending to business with the Continental Congress, when he received letter after letter warning him about the uncertain politics of ratification in Virginia. Able and esteemed men like Patrick Henry and George Mason were lined up against it. Public opinion seemed divided and not at all settled. Even Orange County was not secure. Andrew Shepherd, a justice of the peace and local vestryman, warned Madison, "There is no guarding against artful persons from injecting their poison into the unwary." Madison's father confirmed the doubtful nature of local opinion, reporting "few that disapproved of it at first in this county," but when some planters had traveled to Richmond to sell their tobacco, they had heard "the many objections made to it, altered their opinions, and have influenced some others who are no better acquainted with the necessity of adopting it themselves."[4]

Virginia Federalists were quick to blame one person above all others: Patrick Henry. Edward Carrington wrote Madison in February that Henry's politics "have been so industriously propagated, that the people are much disposed to be his blind followers." Madison simply had to come back. Nothing could be left to chance so long as Henry was actively campaigning against the Constitution. So, Madison made the journey to Orange County. At the county courthouse on March 24, he "launch[ed] into a harangue of some length in the open air and on a very windy day," as he explained in a letter to his Philadelphia friend Eliza Trist. He was not sure if his speech had made a difference, but regardless he felt he had successfully corrected "the misconceptions" perpetuated by the Anti-Federalists. Madison earned 202 votes and Thomas Gordon 187. The two Anti-Federalists carried less than one hundred votes each.[5]

It was clear by April that Henry's game would not be to reject the Constitution outright—too many states had already agreed to it for that to be a feasible strategy—but rather to insist upon amendments prior to ratification. This was a crafty move. It may have seemed reasonable at first blush to marginal supporters or opponents of the Constitution—those who felt like it was basically sound but needed improvements—but in truth it was a way to kill the Constitution without having to be the trigger-man. "A conditional ratification or a second convention," Madison told Randolph in April, would "be either wholly abortive, or would end in something" much worse "than the plan now before the public." After all, he reasoned, how could Virginia basically demand to reconsider the judgments of the eight states that had already ratified?[6]

As the results of these countywide elections filtered across the state, it did not look like Henry would have the votes for this project, although it would be close one way or the other. Madison told George Washington that the returns "augur a flattering issue to the deliberations of June." It seemed "probable, though not absolutely certain," he wrote Jefferson, "that a majority of the members are friends to the Constitution." The Tidewater region had gone solidly for the Federalists, as had the western counties sandwiched between the Blue Ridge and Allegheny Mountains. The disposition of the Kentucky districts was still a mystery, while the Piedmont was a mixed bag. Jefferson's home county of Albemarle had elected Federalist delegates, as had Orange, but Amherst to the south and Culpeper to the north had not. Jefferson and Madison's mutual friend James Monroe had been elected from Spotsylvania County, whose voters "expressly required" their delegates to pursue amendments to fix the many

ways that the Constitution had "departed" from the concurrence of "the most approved writers on political liberty." Monroe
would eventually vote against ratification.[7]

The proceedings began in Richmond in early June, at first at
the recently completed Virginia statehouse, though the convention soon realized that the building was too small for the 170
delegates in attendance. It relocated to the New Academy on
Shockoe Hill, which had held concerts, dances, and even per-
formances of Shakespearean plays. Befitting his senior status in
Virginia politics, Edmund Pendleton was selected to be the presiding officer—fortunate for Madison and the Federalists, as he
favored ratification. Madison reckoned that the Federalist majority was roughly five or six delegates, a narrow margin in a such
a large assembly. Madison's back-of-the-envelope estimate would
basically stay the same throughout the proceedings, which ran
every day from June 2 to June 28, excepting Sundays.

Several years later, when he began battling Hamilton over the
scope of federal power granted under the Constitution, Madison would invest an almost mystical authority in the judgments
of the ratifying conventions. They spoke for the people of the
United States of America, he would claim, and their understand-
ings of the Constitution should be privileged. Yet Madison's own
experience at Virginia's ratifying convention was less than pleasant. He had told Washington back in February that the prospect
of battling the demagogic Henry and the obstreperous Mason
struck him as "very laborious and irksome." By June 9, he was
already complaining to Hamilton that "the business" of the convention was "wearisome beyond expression." Around the same
time, he filed reports with many of his Federalist allies about the
proceedings and included personal complaints about the flare-up
of another "bilious attack," perhaps a physical manifestation of
his mental weariness. Madison was not the only exasperated one

either. Even the usually exuberant Henry "Light-Horse Harry" Lee griped about the "desultory manner" of the convention's proceedings. Madison reported to Rufus King that the "impatience of the members" might mean the session would not last too long.[8]

Reading the transcripts more than two hundred years on, it is easy to see where Madison was coming from. Here were collected most of the titans of revolutionary Virginia for what should have been an exhilarating debate on this new instrument of government, with the very fate of the nation hanging in the balance. And yet the speeches were usually rambling, overlong, and tedious, and the general course of debate wandered from subject to subject without focus. Often, the convention would leave the Constitution aside to rehash parochial grievances over the Jay-Gardoqui Treaty, British debts, and claims to western territory.

In fairness, everything that could be said about the Constitution had already been said. The Constitutional Convention had finished its work some nine months before the Virginia ratifying convention was seated, giving everybody plenty of time to debate every dot and tittle. The Maryland convention had lasted less than a week for precisely this reason. Delegates already knew how their constituents felt and saw no need to debate more than the minimum necessary to keep up appearances. But Henry had to keep the debate going; he didn't have the votes. So, as Madison reckoned to Hamilton, his only move was to play for time, in the hopes that Virginia Anti-Federalists would "receive overtures" from their compatriots in New York—some bombshell announcement that might upend the proceedings. Madison also wondered if Henry's game was to wear out moderate Federalists, so that in their exhaustion they would vote for an adjournment. He told Washington that Henry might be exploiting issues like Jay-Gardoqui to manipulate "local prejudices" against the Constitution.[9]

Regardless of his motives, Henry's attack on the Constitution was scattershot and unpersuasive. Time and again, he would waste the convention's time giving long, unstructured stem-winders that jumped from subject to subject. He could still turn a good line, of course. He was still Patrick Henry. "Among other deformities," he would say of the Constitution, "it has an awful squinting; it squints towards monarchy." A classic Henry elocution, but there is an enormous difference between a catchy phrase and a reasoned argument. This he did not have.[10]

Henry was also a lackluster leader of the Anti-Federalists. He had on his side Mason, one of the finest republican theorists the commonwealth has ever produced. And yet it was clear from the outset that the two were not on the same page. On June 3, Mason moved that the Constitution be debated clause by clause, reckoning that he could best Madison in a detailed forensic contest. But Henry refused to follow the plan, instead launching into a harangue the next day that relitigated the question of whether the Constitutional Convention had the right to propose the Constitution in the first place. Next, Mason staked out his ground. "Candidly acknowledg[ing] the inefficacy of the Confederation," he warned that, without amendments, the Constitution was more dangerous. However, Mason would not find his erstwhile ally by his side. Henry claimed that prior to the disruptions of the Philadelphia convention, the country had been in a state of "general peace and a universal tranquility," and he questioned the need to scrap the Articles of Confederation, which "merit[ed] . . . the highest encomium" for guiding the nation through the war. How can, he asked, "a government which has been thus strong and vigorous be accused of imbecility, and abandoned for want of energy?" In a letter to Washington,

Madison snickered that "Henry and Mason made a lame figure and appeared to take different and awkward ground."[11]

The proceedings did seem to bring out the worst in the two men. Henry's paean to the Articles of Confederation illustrated the limits of his political appeal. Even a great rhetorician will struggle to convince a person of what he knows not to be true. The majority of the delegates realized that the country was in dire straits and that something had to be done to give the Congress more power. All the stentorian speechifying in the world was not going to change that. But that was what Henry proceeded to do, day after day. He dominated the proceedings with a slash-and-burn approach, denying that the Constitution had any virtues and discovering vices in every clause. Mason hardly covered himself in glory either. Basic features of the Constitution seemed to elude him at times. At one point he contended that a "majority of the whole number" of electoral votes "was required" to be chosen as president. Madison pointed out that this was not true. In the original scheme, each elector would cast two votes apiece, and a candidate had to win "a majority of the electors appointed." But Mason continued to insist, and Madison could only express his "astonishment" at the spectacle. As the debate wound down, Mason took to fearmongering. He warned of the "alarming consequences" if the Constitution was ratified and expounded on the "dreadful effects which must ensue, should the people resist." After the convention was finished, Mason refused to admit defeat. He called a meeting of Anti-Federalist delegates, where he made an intemperate call to whip up opposition back home. Several delegates left in disgust, and Mason was finally rebuked by Benjamin Harrison, a signer of the Declaration of Independence.[12]

Perhaps the only time the Anti-Federalists had the Federalists on the ropes was when Henry revealed the contents of a letter Thomas Jefferson had written to Alexander Donald, a prominent

Richmond merchant, in which Jefferson hoped that nine states would ratify the Constitution and four others would "refuse to accede to it till a declaration of rights be annexed." Though they had long been rivals in Virginia politics, Henry was happy to appropriate Jefferson's moral authority for the cause, praising him as "an illustrious citizen," a "worthy citizen," a "servant of the republic," and "our common friend"—who just so happened to support Henry's efforts. As Henry pointed out, New Hampshire seemed on track to accept the Constitution, so was it not incumbent upon Virginia to reject it? "Whatever be the opinion of that illustrious citizen," Madison responded feebly, "considerations of personal delicacy should dissuade us from introducing it here." The truth was that Jefferson had been sending mixed signals about the Constitution from France, where he was serving as American minister, and it was probably a lucky break for the Federalists that he was an ocean away, for his chronic indiscretion, if not his lifelong skepticism of a strong central government, probably would have been helpful to the Anti-Federalists.[13]

Finally, on June 25, the delegates grew tired of Henry's dilatory tactics and voted eighty-eight to eighty against insisting on amendments to the Constitution before ratification. They then voted eighty-nine to seventy-nine to ratify, while also proposing recommendatory amendments, the same position that had carried the day in closely divided Massachusetts. The final margin was slightly better than what Madison had been guessing all along. So if conventional opinion budged at all, it had probably moved toward Madison, whose eminent reasonableness revealed the jeremiads of Henry and Mason to be so much bluster.

Though the debates in the Virginia convention were not particularly illuminating, Madison's contributions were impressive.

He hardly broke any ground that had not been covered in the *Federalist Papers*, but instead mounted regular, careful defenses of the Constitution that drew upon his extensive knowledge. Perhaps the most revelatory speech from Madison was his last address to the convention, delivered on June 24. Read alongside *Federalist* 37 and 38—essays Madison had written in praise of the work of the delegates at the Constitutional Convention—it showed how he had undergone a change of heart from the bitter disappointment he felt in September 1787 to the vigorous, unyielding defense he offered in June 1788.

The American experiment, he argued to the Virginia convention, was unique in the history of the world. Never had a people "been seen deliberating on a form of government," as had happened in the United States since the Revolution. On the contrary, most ancient and modern confederacies had been formed either on "the wisdom of some eminent sage" or from "dangers" that "stimulated [them] to unite." Instead, the Americans were endeavoring to remake their government on the basis of common ground. This was a project "liable to be frustrated by so many accidents." There were, for starters, many philosophical questions upon which people of good faith could disagree. How to balance respect for individual liberty with the need for a vigorous government? How to find the proper demarcation between the states and the national government? How to reconcile the power of the people to change their leadership with the need for stability in public administration? History could serve as a guide on some of these questions but only to a point. And what of more parochial concerns? In *Federalist* 10, Madison had argued that a diversity of interests could help sustain a republic by promoting compromise, but in *Federalist* 37 he pointed out those same differences made "the task of forming" a republic that much harder. The large states versus the small states, the northern states versus the southern states, the commercial states versus the agrarian states—each jockeying for its own position, each threatening to bring the convention to a halt.[14]

And yet, despite the odds, the delegates to the Constitutional Convention had produced a reasonably good instrument of government. Did it conform to an "abstract view of the subject" that some "ingenious theorist" (like himself) might have insisted on? Of course not. Was everybody going to be happy? Again, no. Compromises had to be made, with sacrifices all around. Many similar deliberations had fallen apart when some faction felt as though it had made one compromise too many and stormed out. It amazed Madison that this had not happened at the convention. The delegates had hung together, ironed out their differences, and achieved something close to unanimity on a general system of government. They placed their commitment "to the public good" above "private opinions and partial interests" and steered clear of "the pestilential influence" of factional rivalries, which so often undermined deliberative bodies. How, Madison wondered, could one look upon that and not see "a finger of that Almighty Hand which has been so frequently and signally extended to our relief in the critical stages of the revolution?"[15]

Now, here stood Virginia, faced with the decision of affirming or rejecting the convention's hard work. It was a "most awful thing" that depended on their decision, "no less than whether the thirteen states shall unite freely, peaceably, and unanimously, for the security of their common happiness and liberty, or whether every thing is to be put in confusion and disorder!" The Anti-Federalists wanted to go back to the drawing board because they were unhappy with this or that provision. Madison urged his colleagues to ask themselves: Could they reasonably expect ever to be back at this point again? A rejection by Virginia— be it outright or indirectly by demanding amendments prior to ratification—might force either a new federal convention or another round of state conventions. Even though New Hampshire was expected to ratify (and technically had by the time Madison gave this speech, although the Virginians did not know this), equivocation by the largest state in the union would have been a potentially fatal blow to the project. How, Madison wanted to know, would this not yield chaos? "Will not every state think herself equally entitled to propose as many amendments?" he asked.[16]

Bear in mind, Madison warned the delegates, that the opponents to the Constitution could not even themselves agree on amendments. Some thought it had "too much state influence," some too little. Some complained about the "equality in the senate"; others celebrated it. Just as Virginia Anti-Federalists were divided on how to approach the Virginia convention—with Henry praising the Articles of Confederation and Mason admitting the need for reform—so, too, was "there . . . no sort of uniformity in the grounds of the opposition" in the other states. The choice facing the country, Madison therefore argued, was between the Constitution, which was admittedly imperfect, and the status quo, which was totally unacceptable. Henry and Mason were either fooling themselves or trying to fool the convention when they argued that the Constitution could be rejected at this late date and an alternative devised that would be satisfactory to all.[17]

In *Federalist* 38, Madison had analogized the situation of the United States to a very sick patient visited by a group of capable doctors. They carefully and coolly examine the situation, then recommend a course of treatment. But then "a number of persons interpose," warning that, while the patient's condition is very dire and something must be done, the recommended treatment is dangerous. Yet they cannot "agree among themselves on some other remedy to be substituted." What, then, is the prudent patient to do? Of course, he must follow the first set of doctors;

some treatment must be applied, after all, and theirs is the only option. And so it was for the United States. The only sensible choice was the Constitution, despite its defects.[18]

This was a message not only for the Virginia delegates but for Madison himself. He had built the Virginia Plan upon a brilliant new theory of republican government, only to see the Constitutional Convention gut it. At first he was bitterly disappointed, as he had every right to be. Yet over the course of the next nine months, he let these frustrations go. Maybe if he had been like some ancient sage, imbued with the power to hand down an instrument of government from on high, he could have gotten everything he wanted into the founding document. But that was not his role. The United States was building a new government through consensus. The Constitution was an imperfect compromise, but it clearly was the only compromise available. It was either the Constitution or failure and all of its attending consequences: a crippled government, a divided and angry people, and perhaps eventually disunion. Madison's previous misgivings notwithstanding, accepting the Constitution was the only sensible choice. And, in a way, the compromises hammered out during and after the convention—over the Senate, over slavery, even over recommendatory amendments—mimicked his vision of politics: nobody dominates anybody else, so everybody has to bargain to find common ground. Seen in this light, it was little wonder that Madison had committed himself fully to its defense. Its very existence was proof that his idea of the extended republic could work.

SHORTLY AFTER THE conclusion of the Virginia convention, Madison returned to New York City. The soon-to-be defunct Continental Congress busied itself with setting dates for the new federal elections and debating where the new government would be seated, deciding to locate it temporarily in Manhattan. The Federalist victory in Virginia had the intended effect on New York. Even though the latter's convention was stocked with Anti-Federalists, it agreed narrowly to ratification. That meant eleven states had agreed to the Constitution, two more than necessary for it to go into effect. But there the number would stay for the time being. Rhode Island had already rejected the Constitution and would not join the new government until the spring of 1790. Meanwhile, Anti-Federalists outnumbered Federalists by a two-to-one margin at the North Carolina convention, which met in Hillsborough from late July until early August. Delegates voted overwhelmingly neither to accept nor to reject the Constitution.

Though the New York convention had acceded to the new government, its Anti-Federalist majority had laid something of a trap. While agreeing to an unconditional ratification, the convention also urged the calling of a second convention at a time "not far remote" from the seating of the new government. New York Federalists were obliged to agree to this recommendation as the price for getting the Constitution adopted. John Jay, John Lansing, and Alexander Hamilton wrote a letter, signed by Governor George Clinton and circulated among the thirteen states, urging other state governments to do likewise.[19]

The ever-uncertain Randolph suggested to Madison that maybe this was a good idea. "I believe the assembly of Virginia perhaps ought . . . [to] concur in urging it" as a way to "incorporate the theory of the people with the theory of the convention; and each of these theories is entitled to equal respect." But Madison knew better: the Anti-Federalists were once more trying to defeat the Constitution by indirect means. "It is pretty clear that a majority of the people . . . are in favor of the Constitution as it stands," he told Randolph. The Anti-Federalists simply did not have the numbers to defeat the Constitution, but at another convention superior "management" or "extorted . . . menaces" might stir up feelings "of party and passion" to sacrifice "the public will as well as of the public good" to the "views of individuals and perhaps the ambition of the state legislatures." The real danger, of course, was the scheming of Henry, who still wielded enormous power in the state government and would no doubt put forth every effort to dominate Virginia's delegation to any second meeting.[20]

True to form, Henry wholeheartedly embraced the idea. He had been outnumbered and outshone at the Virginia ratifying convention, but he was firmly in control of the House of Delegates when it met in the fall of 1788. Richard Bland Lee warned Madison that "the assembly is weak." Its Federalist members were too "young and inexperienced" to be anything but a "feeble band" against Henry, who was the "only orator . . . amongst us." By October 30, Henry had secured passage of a resolution calling for a second convention, which warned that "all the great essential and unalienable rights, liberties and privileges of freemen" had been "rendered insecure" by the Constitution as written. Henry also made sure that Virginia selected two Anti-Federalists to the US Senate. He refused to take one of the seats because, as Randolph told Madison, he was "unwilling to submit to the oath" of office to support and defend the Constitution. Instead, he endorsed William Grayson and Richard Henry Lee, who were chosen on November 8 with ninety-eight and eighty-six votes, respectively. Madison finished third, with seventy-seven votes. Madison was instead chosen to return to the Continental Congress, a dubious honor indeed—considering that it was soon to be defunct—and perhaps a way for Henry to keep Madison out of the state during the upcoming elections.[21]

Madison was unperturbed by his defeat for the Senate seat, having told his friends he would rather serve in the House of Representatives anyway. This might sound strange to modern ears, since today a seat in the Senate is more prestigious than one in the House. But it is worth bearing in mind that the House was only going to be slightly larger than the Senate (sixty-five members to twenty-six members, when all states had ratified), and as the body chosen directly by the people it would presumably wield vast authority in the new government.

Madison hoped that Orange County would be placed in a district friendly to him, so that he would not have to engage in "electioneering, which I despise," but instead enjoy the "spontaneous suffrage of the constituents." Unfortunately for Madison, Henry crushed his hope of an easy election. "The Anti's have levelled every effort at you," Carrington wrote glumly on November 15, telling his friend that Henry and his allies had designed a district specifically to defeat Madison. His home county of Orange was included in the Fifth District, whose voting population—at least judged against the elections for the ratifying convention—ran roughly three to one Anti-Federalist. And though the Constitution stipulated that one only need to be a resident of a state to run in any district, the election law enacted by the House of Delegates mandated that candidates had to be residents of their districts as well. Madison's cousin, the Reverend James Madison, suggested he might acquire a freehold in Williamsburg, for "lots in this town may be had at a very low rate," but Madison did not take his namesake up on the suggestion. He would stay in Orange and he would fight.[22]

Henry added insult to injury when the Anti-Federalists convinced Madison and Jefferson's friend Monroe—who lived in neighboring Fredericksburg—into running as the Anti-Federalist candidate in the Fifth. After the election, Monroe would write

Jefferson that though he was concerned by the prospect of keeping Madison out of Congress, he had been "pressed . . . to come forward in this government on its commencement." Ever the pessimist, Madison figured defeat was a foregone conclusion. He told Jefferson in early December that he had little hope of victory, given the "prevailing temper of the district."[23]

But as it turned out, Madison proved to be an adroit campaigner. He wagered, correctly, that most Americans, including those of the Fifth District, basically accepted the Constitution. They wanted some tweaks, especially the inclusion of a bill of rights and reassurance that they would not be burdened by new federal taxes, but they had no interest in the sorts of schemes Henry was plotting. As such, Madison did not need to abandon his Federalism. Rather, in a series of letters released to the public, he endeavored to reassure the voters on these two issues.

Taxation was a dicey subject in eighteenth-century America. The colonists had, after all, fought a war over taxes imposed by a distant and high-handed sovereign. Voters were especially dubious of the new government's power to impose taxes directly on the citizenry, like a head tax. So, Madison emphasized the virtues of the national taxing authority. First, he argued, it would ensure justice between the states. Gone would be the days of states like Rhode Island failing to pay their "just share of the public burdens." Now, everybody would be obliged to give exactly what they owed. Madison also promised that direct taxes would "prevent contests among the states," like when New York imposed tariffs on goods entering the harbor at New York City, an expense ultimately borne by residents in Connecticut and New Jersey. Second, Madison urged that direct taxes would help secure the country "against danger abroad." The failure of the states to pay requisitions had made the United States look weak and quarrelsome to the European powers. Eventually, state malfeasance was bound to "invite foreign attacks by showing the inability of the union to repel them." With a stable source of revenue, the national government would be able to provide "security against danger from foreign nations," which now would no doubt think twice before attacking.[24]

Voters were even more anxious over a bill of rights, and Madison staked out a basically unassailable position on the issue, assuring people that he had no opposition to amendments in principle and admitting that the Constitution "might be improved in several points," as he wrote Thomas Mann Randolph, a young Virginia planter who would soon wed Jefferson's daughter Martha, in a letter later published in the *Virginia Independent Chronicle*. Privately, he wrote to Jefferson that he had "always been in favor of a bill of rights." It was just that he did not think it would add much to the Constitution, in part because "parchment barriers" tend to be ineffective exactly "on those occasions when its control is most needed." At Virginia's ratifying convention, he had opposed making ratification contingent on the passage of amendments, telling Thomas Mann Randolph that this would be "a dangerous road to public confusion." But, as he explained to Baptist minister George Eve, "circumstances are now changed." With the Constitution ratified, amendments, so long as they were "pursued with a proper moderation," would "not only be safe," they would satisfy "the minds of well-meaning opponents" and provide "additional guards in favor of liberty."[25]

Madison then attacked the Anti-Federalists for insisting on a second convention. Elections for such an assembly would cause too much "agitation" for the public mind by engaging "the most violent partisans on both sides," and the members of the convention would be "the most heterogeneous characters," as well as "individuals of insidious views" who were looking to use a convention not to improve the Constitution but to destroy it. Better to leave amendments to Congress, "the most expeditious, most certain . . . most safe, and most economical" way to add a bill of rights.[26]

Anti-Federalists were outraged by Madison's apparent flip-flop. Later that summer, George Mason complained to his son that it was a "farce" for Madison to act like "the ostensible patron of amendments." Maybe so, but it was politically brilliant, for he had snatched the Anti-Federalists' best issue away from them. And if Madison was overstating how much he valued a bill of rights, many Anti-Federalists were downright lying about their intentions. Monroe earnestly believed that a second convention might improve the Constitution, but Henry's true motive was to destroy it altogether.[27]

To the modern political junkie, the idea of seeing two future presidents campaign seems like a most thrilling prospect. Yet to hear Madison tell it, the residents of the Fifth District received the two of them with respect, if sometimes slight bemusement. The campaign itself would be short, with Madison arriving toward the end of December and the election being held on February 2. On Election Day, voters supported Madison overwhelmingly: 1,308 votes to 972 for Monroe. The respectful tone of the campaign persisted in its aftermath. Late in life, Madison would recall that there was "never an atom of ill will between" Monroe and him. For Monroe's part, he had written to Jefferson shortly after the election that his defeat had given him "no private concern," as he had no "private object to gratify" in pursuing the seat in the first place. Rather, he had only done it for the sake of the public good. By the spring, Madison and Monroe had resumed their friendly correspondence.[28]

Madison's victory was part of a larger story. Federalists dominated the House elections in Virginia, carrying seven of the ten seats. Nationwide, the Anti-Federalists' effort to turn the first election into a referendum on the Constitution backfired on them as the Federalist faction won a sweeping majority in both the House and Senate. Whatever doubts citizens may have had about the Constitution, the elections that year revealed a widespread consensus that the work of drafting a new government had gone reasonably well, and that it was time to bring this fractious phase of American politics to a close.

IF THE FIRST half of the 1780s was a disastrous time for the cause of American nationalism, the second half had been a triumph. From the Mount Vernon Conference onward, the advocates of a stronger national government had outmatched their opponents at almost every turn. This had never been more the case than during ratification, when the Federalists proved themselves superior operatives. The best argument the Anti-Federalists had against the Constitution was that it lacked a bill of rights, so the Federalists simply adopted the idea for themselves. Madison's triumph over Monroe in Virginia's Fifth District, and Federalist candidates' similar victories all across the country, demonstrated their political virtuosity. It also proved the old adage that you cannot beat something with nothing. The truth is that the "anti" in Anti-Federalism was its most important descriptor. The Anti-Federalists no doubt had been guided by an honest vision of self-government, grounded in the idea of a small republic populated by virtuous citizens. But they had no specific plan upon which they could all agree to realize this vision while dealing with the crisis of the moment. The Federalists, on the other hand, had the Constitution. For all the Anti-Federalists thundered against this proposal, it was at least a plan to deal with the problems facing the country.

The triumph of the Federalists brings an end to Madison's career as the architect of American politics. Though it was not everything he wanted, the Constitution generally embodied his system of the extended republic and the belief that a diverse polity could find common ground that advanced the public interest without endangering the rights of the citizenry. In fact, many of Madison's most cherished ideas were compromised away in precisely the kind of process he was looking to create. The Constitution was not perfect; it was the product of bargaining between different self-interested factions from all across the country. But it was much better than the status quo, and most everybody could live with it. This was exactly what Madison hoped politics in the extended republic would look like.

As Madison left Montpelier for New York in the late winter of 1789 to take his seat in the First Congress, he knew that, to secure their triumph, the Federalists would have to make good on their promises. The Constitutional Convention had begun the task of framing a new government, and the state conventions had approved their work, but it would be during the first session of the First Congress that this process would be finished. Congress would have to enact a system of taxation to deal with the public debt. It would have to establish executive departments and courts to fill in the gaps of the Constitution. And it would have to follow through on the Federalists' pledge to the ratifying conventions to propose a series of amendments.

Madison would take a leading role in many of these deliberations, and though he was shifting from framing a government to being an operative within it, he maintained the same basic commitments. Benefits and burdens had to be distributed evenly and individual rights respected. The people held ultimate sovereignty, and their judgments had to be honored. These ideas had informed his design of the Virginia Plan, and they would guide his career in the new government. He would continue searching for common ground, pursuing his understanding of the national interest, and vehemently opposing policies he thought picked favorites among the citizenry.

7

LAUNCHING THE
GOVERNMENT

WEDNESDAY, MARCH 4, 1789, was the day prescribed by the
old Continental Congress for the new US Congress to begin its
business in Federal Hall in New York City. Built at the turn of
the century on Wall Street, Federal Hall had a colorful history.
John Peter Zenger had been tried there for libel against the royal
governor in 1735 and had been acquitted by a jury of his peers.
They believed he had the freedom to print what he liked, a right
that would be enshrined by this new Congress with the First
Amendment. In 1765, the Stamp Act Congress met there to
complain about British taxation without representation. And the
Continental Congress had been meeting there since 1785. The
year before the new government met, Federal Hall had been re-
modeled by Pierre Charles L'Enfant, the French engineer whom
Washington would select to design the city that would become
Washington, DC.

During his time in New York, Madison stayed at the boarding house of Dorothy Elsworth, located at 19 Maiden Lane in
today's Financial District, just three blocks north of Federal
Hall and a short walk from Trinity Church, which had been
rebuilt after burning in 1776. Prior to the Revolution, the city
had been growing rapidly as a center of trade and commerce, a
development that had been halted when the British occupied it
in August 1776, a post they would hold until the peace treaty in
1783. Free from British rule, New York had once again continued its expansion, aided by the presence of the Congress there
beginning in 1785. Though it lacked the refinement of a Boston
or Philadelphia, New York was by this point the largest city in
the nation.

As had been the case for more than a decade in public life,
Madison was virtually consumed with the business of politics.
He had no love interests during his time in the First Congress,
although he did enjoy socializing with New York's French vis-
itors and residents. His affection for the people of France went
hand in glove with his disdain for the English, and after the
French Revolution began in May 1789, he would find in the new
French Republic an ideological kinship.

Only fourteen House members showed up on time for the
new session of Congress, far short of a quorum. The next day,
another five members arrived, but so dismal were the prospects
for a quorum that the House adjourned for another week. Madison, who anticipated that the session was unlikely to begin on
time, had not rushed getting to New York, staying for a few
days at Mount Vernon to help the soon to be president, George
Washington, draft his inaugural address. By March 5, a day after the Congress had been set to convene, Madison was stuck in
Baltimore, where he wrote to Washington complaining of the
"badness of the roads and the weather." He was in New York by

the time Congress reconvened on the fourteenth, but the House once more failed to muster a quorum. It was not for another two and a half weeks—on April 1—that the House had enough members to get down to business. The Senate followed suit on April 5.[1]

Finally, the new government was underway.

As was his wont, Madison was a tad downbeat about the prospects of success in Congress. Writing to Edmund Randolph on his way from Virginia to New York, he fretted that "a very scanty proportion" of House members would "share in the drudgery of business." He also predicted "contentions first between federal and antifederal parties, and then between northern and southern parties." He need not have been so worried. Though the second and third sessions of the First Congress would be hotly contentious, the first session—lasting from April until September 1789—was one of the most agreeable and constructive in all of American history.[2]

Much of this success had to do with the electoral wipeout of the Anti-Federalists. Supporters of the national government could claim forty-six of fifty-nine House seats and a whopping twenty of twenty-two Senate seats, reflecting broad-based Federalist strength in the state legislatures. The voters, it seemed, had sent a clear message: After eighteen months of contentious debate over the Constitution, the matter was settled. It was time to get to work.

The members of the First Congress were an impressive lot, committed to the project of nationalism and intent on getting the new government off to a fast start. Many members had served at the Constitutional Convention, among them Roger Sherman of Connecticut, James Jackson and Abraham Baldwin of Georgia, Elbridge Gerry of Massachusetts, Nicholas Gilman of New Hampshire, Hugh Williamson of North Carolina, and

Thomas Fitzsimons of Pennsylvania. George Clymer of Pennsylvania had signed both the Declaration of Independence and the Constitution. Fisher Ames of Massachusetts, a young up-and-comer who had defeated Samuel Adams for his House seat, would go on to be a key advocate of Alexander Hamilton's economic policies and perhaps Madison's most formidable opponent in the House.

The Senate was likewise stocked with a veritable who's who of statesmen from the early republic. Richard Henry Lee, who had edged out Madison for a Senate seat, represented Virginia. He was one of just a handful of opponents of the new Constitution in the upper chamber and would thus be able to exercise little sway. Instead, it was strong Federalists like Oliver Ellsworth and William Johnson of Connecticut—both signers of the Constitution—who would dominate proceedings. Other senators who had served at the Constitutional Convention included John Langdon of New Hampshire, William Paterson of New Jersey, Robert Morris of Pennsylvania, and Pierce Butler of South Carolina. Rufus King, who had represented Massachusetts in the Constitutional Convention, had moved to New York and won election to the Senate. Joining him would be General Philip Schuyler, who had served in the victorious Battle of Saratoga, which had stopped the British advance in the East and persuaded the French to join an alliance with the United States. Schuyler's daughter Eliza was the young wife of Alexander Hamilton, and both General Schuyler and King would be steady supporters of Hamilton's financial program. Capping off this impressive group was John Adams, the famed patriot leader who had been overseas serving as a minister for the United States. As vice president, it was his duty under the Constitution to serve as the presiding officer of the Senate, an insignificant role that he felt was beneath his formidable talents.

Aside from stipulating that the vice president serve as the president of the Senate and that the House elect a Speaker, the Constitution offered but the vaguest outline of each chamber, leaving the specifics of how they were to run to the members themselves. So, when Congress first assembled, there were no parties, no leaders, no organization—nothing. In the House, Frederick Muhlenberg of Pennsylvania was elected Speaker, but it was Madison who filled the power vacuum. He seized the legislative agenda, just as he had done at the Constitutional Convention two years prior, able to run the show because he worked harder and knew more than anybody else who might claim the mantle of congressional leadership.

The first order of business was money—or, more specifically, the government's desperate lack thereof. The confederation government was badly in arrears, overwhelmed by debt, and totally incapable of raising the needed revenue. With the Constitution giving Congress the power to tax, it was time to put the nation's finances back in order by enacting an impost on imported goods. Madison took the lead. On April 8—just one week after the House had achieved a quorum—he proposed a sweeping tax plan, built largely on the remnants of the old impost from 1783. Madison called for a 5 percent tax on all imports, plus additional levels on luxury goods like rum, wine, molasses, pepper, and silk. He also proposed a tax on the amount of goods carried by ships, according to their country of origin. American-owned ships would be taxed at 6 cents per ton. Ships from nations with which the United States had a commercial treaty would be taxed at 30 cents per ton, and those with which it had no treaty were taxed at 50 cents per ton.

In the main, the purpose of the bill was to raise revenue. But Madison's discriminatory taxes on tonnage were different and would come to define his approach to foreign policy from 1789 until the War of 1812. The main target of the measure was Great Britain, which—unlike France—had no commercial treaty with the United States. So, in effect, Madison was proposing a kind of commercial warfare with the British. In a speech the following day, he acknowledged that he was "the friend to a very free system of commerce, and hold it as a truth, that commercial shackles are generally unjust, oppressive and impolitic," while leaving "industry and commerce . . . to take their own course" will result in greater productivity. But he believed in exceptions. For instance, he supported protective tariffs on domestic goods necessary for national defense and on goods with inelastic demand, like alcohol and sugar, as they could fetch a very large amount of revenue for the government. Ditto his proposed discrimination against the British—additional tonnage duties were a way to force them to negotiate a commercial treaty with the United States.[3]

Great Britain was far and away the number one supplier of foreign goods to the United States, and Madison thought it held too great a share of American commerce. He argued that "the long possession of our trade, their commercial regulations calculated to retain it, their similarity of language and manners, their conformity of laws, and other circumstances" had all conspired to channel American commerce unnaturally into British ports. For too long the British had used this to their advantage. Counting on the continuation of American trade, they had stubbornly refused to allow Americans to trade directly with the Crown's West Indian colonies. This was a trade that the colonies had enjoyed when they were part of the British Empire, but now that they were an independent nation, they were excluded from it.

It was Madison's strong belief that the United States now had the power to remedy the unfair restrictions placed on them by the British by "wag[ing] a commercial warfare with that nation."

The United States provided food and other necessities of life to Great Britain, while Great Britain provided manufactured luxuries that the United States could either make itself or do without. "If we were disposed to hazard the experiment of interdicting the intercourse and the powers not in alliance," Great Britain would be forced to yield sooner or later. Britain needed trade with the United States more than the United States needed trade with it. Ultimately, Madison convinced the House to agree to his discrimination plan, but it failed in the Senate. The merchants of the North would be the big losers in Madison's system—as it was their firms that engaged Great Britain in commerce—and though they were relatively weak in the southern-dominated House, they held a decisive advantage in the upper chamber.[4]

Frustrated by this defeat, Madison was also disappointed by the tediousness of the debate. He had hoped for a quick, temporary bill to be enacted prior to the arrival of much of the spring commerce, so that the government could tax the goods that would soon be arriving in the eastern harbors. But other members had different ideas. Thomas Fitzsimons of Pennsylvania suggested expanding the scope of Madison's proposal so that it would help "encourage the productions of our country, and protect our infant manufactures." He called for additional duties on dozens of items: everything from beef and pork, raisins and figs, and tacks and brads to gloves and hats. Thomas Hartley, his colleague from the Keystone State, concurred, calling on Congress to lend the "fostering hand of the general government" to industrialization.[5]

Although the final version of the impost did enact protective tariffs in some cases—such as shielding industries that had received statewide protection during the confederation period— the protectionist push largely failed. America at this point was dominated by farmers, who had little to gain from protection.

They would have to pay higher prices for imported goods and potentially suffer retaliatory tariffs on the staple crops they exported to other nations. Meanwhile, domestic industry was still too insignificant to demand much of anything through the political process, and the northern merchants had no interest in following Madison's suggestion of using taxes as an instrument of foreign policy. Nevertheless, the proposal from the Pennsylvanians opened up a lengthy back-and-forth between representatives from the major regions—North, South, and West—over how various regional goods would be taxed. New England, with its distillery industry, fought for reductions in duties on molasses, which it used to make rum. The South lobbied for reductions in duties on sugars and imported spirits, which—if not essential to life itself—certainly enhanced the enjoyment thereof. The West demanded reductions in the duties on salt, which it depended heavily on for preserving food.

Madison endeavored to play the role of conciliator. The failure of the impost in the Continental Congress had taught him that every region in the country had to be confident that it was getting a fair deal, otherwise the negotiations would fall apart. Amid all of these conflicting interests, Madison called again and again for moderation in duties and tried to cultivate a spirit of nationalism. He encouraged his colleagues "to weight and regard the sentiments of the gentlemen from the different parts of the United States; but on the other hand . . . we must consider the general interests of the union." He reminded New Englanders that the South was paying a sizeable duty on sugar, and that it was not too much to ask them to do likewise on molasses. To the westerners agitating for easing the salt duty, he explained that it was the only major tax they would have to pay, so that overall they were not being unduly burdened. To the southerners who wanted a reduction in the rates on imported spirits, Madison warned that giving them a carve out would prompt demands from every economic interest, and "we shall be reduced to a system inadequate to our wants, and thereby defeat the chief object of our appointment." Again and again, his argument was that, while some particular tax may fall more heavily on one interest or another, on balance the system was fair.[6]

While it took longer than Madison wanted to hammer out a tax deal, the House and Senate finally came to an agreement on an impost in early July—too late to tax the spring traffic, but still an extraordinary accomplishment, considering nearly a decade's worth of failed attempts to levy a national tax. Its passage was in fact a vindication of Madison's theory of the extended republic. No regional or economic faction preponderated in Congress, so they had to bargain with one another. The final result, while not perfect, was reasonably fair. As Madison wrote to Jefferson, the impost debate "called forth in some degree our local feelings. But the experiment has been favorable to our character for moderation, and in general the temper of the Congress seems to be propitious."[7]

The passage of the impost demonstrated a Madison near the peak of his political powers. Representative Fisher Ames, who would later clash with Madison over Alexander Hamilton's financial program, wrote during the impost debate that Madison was "a studious man, devoted to public business, and a thorough master of almost every public question that can arise, or he will spare no pains to become so, if he happens to be in want of information." Madison knew the various rate schedules of the thirteen states, how much revenue they had collected, and the effect of these taxes on commerce. Moreover, his approach to the impost was a practical application of his constitutional theory, and it demonstrated his core principles of self-government. Just as he wanted to build a government that would balance factions against one another, so did he seek to be such a balancing force within it. Though the task of writing the Constitution had been completed, he was the same Madison: always with an emphasis on finding the compromise that could appeal to the greatest number of factions while still promoting the national interest.[8]

———

IF THE HOUSE'S pace on the impost was deliberate, its speed on the Bill of Rights was downright glacial. Members were decidedly uninterested in engaging on the matter, and Madison had to badger the lower chamber into taking the issue up. Its reluctance was due mainly to the fact that the Federalists had swept the field in the congressional elections; the sorts of Anti-Federalists who had been adamant in calling for amendments were in short supply. So it fell upon Madison—who himself had been a somewhat hesitant champion of amendments—to take the lead. He wrote the initial drafts of the amendments and essentially hectored the House into agreeing to them.

Madison's motivations for introducing a bill of rights were a combination of high-minded republicanism and Machiavellian realpolitik. He believed that the people, acting through the state ratifying conventions, expected Congress to propose amendments to the Constitution. Massachusetts, New Hampshire, New York, South Carolina, and Virginia had all put together a wish list of proposals. It was thus the duty of the people's representatives in Congress "to satisfy the public that we do not disregard their wishes," as he explained to the House. Moreover, a gesture of good faith on the part of the Federalists might soften the Anti-Federalists in their opposition and hopefully induce North Carolina and Rhode Island—the two states that had so far refused to ratify the Constitution—to end their holdout.[9]

Madison had also come to see some virtues in a bill of rights. As he had noted to Jefferson the previous winter, "parchment barriers" never stopped "repeated violations" by "overbearing majorities in every state." But maybe, he now admitted, they can "impress some degree of respect" for liberty on the people, "to establish the public opinion in their favor, and rouse the attention of the whole community" so that the majority may be taught to constrain itself. That was especially true in states with either no bills of rights or "defective ones." Additionally, a bill of rights would delineate the limits of the Necessary and Proper Clause, ensuring that the government never pursue illegitimate means, like denying due process, to achieve necessary ends, like collecting tax revenues. More than anything else, a bill of rights—if it was written with care and consideration—would do no harm.[10]

But Madison had some craftier notions in mind as well. The Constitutional Convention had rejected his plan to invest Congress with a veto over state laws. Over his strenuous objections, the delegates had decided that it was sufficient for the Constitution to declare that federal laws would reign supreme. Madison had never been satisfied with that and sought to remedy this defect with the Bill of Rights. His fifth proposal declared, "No state shall violate the equal rights of conscience, or the freedom of the press, or the trial by jury in criminal cases"—quite different from the final text of what became the First Amendment, which explicitly enjoined Congress from regulating religion, speech, press, or assembly. This was yet another Madisonian strategy to establish limits on the bad behavior of the states. Most of the rest of his proposed amendments did by implication what this one did explicitly; they did not delineate which government— the states, the federal, or both—was to be restrained.[11]

Madison was also seeking to box out the staunch Anti-Federalists, who still wanted to sharply curtail the power of government. Enacting a bill of rights that protected civil liberties while retaining all of the Constitution's delegated powers would bring moderate Anti-Federalists into the coalition while leaving extremists like Patrick Henry on the outside looking in. On the House floor, he was unequivocal in his motives: "I should be unwilling to see a door opened for a re-consideration of the whole structure of the government, for a re-consideration of the principles and the substance of the powers given; because I doubt, if such a door was opened, if we should be very likely to stop at that point which would be safe to the government itself." So for instance, while several states had called for an amendment to restrict the imposition of direct taxes, Madison would have none of this, and he refused to include it in his proposal. On the other hand, he gladly accepted Virginia's call to outlaw cruel and unusual punishment.[12]

Of course, nobody in the House bothered to attack the Constitution, so dominant was the Federalist majority. Indeed, Madison's colleagues were mostly uninterested in the project altogether. When he first proposed his amendments on June 8, he was met with a collective shrug of the shoulders. "I am of opinion we ought not to be in a hurry," responded James Jackson of Georgia. "Our constitution . . . is like a vessel just launched, and lying at the wharf, she is untried, you can hardly discover one of her properties." To amend it without giving it a "fair trial . . . is doing it at a risk, which is certainly imprudent." Others were open to the idea of amendments, but not yet. William Smith of South Carolina reminded Madison of the "important and pressing business of the government," which should come first. Likewise, Elbridge Gerry called the amendment debate "improper," so long as "our attention is occupied by other important subjects."[13]

Madison found himself in the strange position of pleading the case of the Anti-Federalists. He warned his colleagues that continued postponements "may occasion suspicions" and "may tend to inflame or prejudice the public mind against our decisions." There were many skeptics of the Constitution who nevertheless supported ratification on the good faith of its advocates in pursuing a bill of rights. "They may think we are not sincere in our desire to . . . secure those rights." Alas, his Federalist colleagues were unpersuaded. The matter was eventually sent off to a select committee, rather than an open discussion on the floor, which reported a set of amendments at the end of July. But still the House dragged its feet. There was "more important business requiring immediate attention," argued Theodore Sedgwick of Massachusetts, a view shared by many colleagues. Madison warned once more that these delays could foster a "spirit of jealousy," which may not "be allayed without great inconvenience."[14]

Finally, the House approved a draft of amendments on August 24, after a languid and uninspired debate. Most of the conversation involved issues of form rather than substance. The House eventually rejected Madison's proposal to integrate the amendments into the original Constitution but left most of his substantive suggestions intact. The Senate made a few meaningful alterations—striking out Madison's prohibition against the states infringing on the rights of conscience—but again, most of the original text was retained. The final package of amendments approved by both chambers was remarkably similar to Madison's initial draft—a notable contrast from his impost, which was heavily revised during the course of legislative debate.

But where Congress was indifferent, Madison was dogged, even though he did not originally think the Bill of Rights was an essential addition to the Constitution. A lot of this was strategic. He was looking to secure the Constitution against further Anti-Federalist threats and maybe find another way to restrain state assaults on freedom of conscience. But he also believed that it was necessary to secure broad public support of the

Constitution, a document whose preamble claims it emanates from "we the people of the United States." For that, it needed amendments. Madison, with his insistence on finding common ground, was willing to champion the project. As he told his colleagues, "I believe that the great mass of the people who opposed [the Constitution], disliked it because it did not contain effectual provision against encroachments on particular rights." As far as he was concerned, conciliation was not just a good strategic move; it was what should happen in a republic that tried to be fair and just to everybody.[15]

WHILE SERVING AS de facto leader of House Federalists, Madison also did double duty as a senior advisor to George Washington. The president had a similar institutional problem as Congress; there was really nothing to the executive branch when he took over. John Jay was a holdover as secretary of foreign affairs from the confederation. Henry Knox was secretary of war, overseeing a bare-bones fighting force. Thomas Jefferson was minister to France. Moreover, there was no structure of presidential governance for Washington to inherit regarding congressional relations, deliberations among advisors, or even rules of protocol. In time, Washington would use his cabinet as a forum to deliberate questions of foreign and domestic policy, and he would generally fill in the details of how the executive branch was to operate. But there was no cabinet for most of 1789. The State Department would not be established until July, the War and Treasury Departments until August. So, Washington turned to Madison for advice on selecting officers, interacting with the public and Congress, and issuing proclamations.

It was Madison, for instance, who helped scuttle a proposal by Vice President John Adams to give the president a dandified title.

The vice president's suggested nomenclature was "His Highness the President of the United States and Protector of Their Liberties." This mostly embarrassed Washington, and Madison made sure that the House instead referred to him simply as "Mister President," arguing that copying the "pompous sovereigns of the east, or follow[ing] the inferior potentates of Europe" by adorning the plain, republican office with "splendid tinsel or gorgeous robe would disgrace the manly shoulders of our Chief."[16]

It is remarkable in a way that Madison would take on this dual role, leading the House and serving as Washington's top advisor. After all, Madison was the author of *Federalist* 51, which famously detailed how rivalries for power between the branches would secure republican government. And yet it was this alliance between the leader of the House and the president that helped secure the government in its early days. The most amazing illustration of this interbranch coordination was Washington's inaugural address, delivered on April 30, 1789. It had been composed largely by Madison, after Washington had rejected an initial draft written by his secretary, David Humphreys. Madison also drafted the official response from the House of Representatives to the inaugural address, meaning that he was effectively corresponding with himself.

No doubt, Madison's deep regard and profound respect for Washington obliged him to assist the president. Yet he also wanted to establish the executive branch as an independent bulwark against legislative encroachments. The Constitution had more or less left the executive branch and the courts undefined. The design of the court system was mainly handled in the Senate by Connecticut senator Oliver Ellsworth, who had been integral in hammering out the compromise over congressional apportionment in the Constitutional Convention. But it was Madison in the House who helped liberate the president from legislative micromanagement.

The main point of controversy had to do with staffing. There was no doubt that executive offices would be created, and it was generally agreed that departments of state, treasury, and war had to be established, so that the basic tasks of government could be accomplished. Similarly, there was widespread agreement on the fact that the officers of these departments would be answerable to the president, who would appoint them with the advice and consent of the Senate. But after that, the Constitution was silent. As members of Congress sat down in June to create the State Department, they confronted a tricky question: Who should have the power to remove executive officers?

There were several answers to this question. One, offered by William Smith of South Carolina, held that executive officials could "only be removed by an impeachment before the Senate." Hardly anybody shared this view, for, as Madison rightly replied, if this was the constitutional standard for the secretary of state, it would likewise have to apply to all executive officers, rather than just the senior ones. If that was the intention of the framers, it was a "fatal error interwove[n] in the system" that "would ultimately prove its destruction." A more plausible interpretation, and one that certainly appealed to senators, was that the removal power should mimic the appointment power. So, the president could only dismiss an executive officer with the advice and consent of the Senate. Theodorick Bland of Virginia argued that, if the Senate lacked power to consent to removals, its appointment authority would be "rendered almost nugatory." A related theory, offered by Roger Sherman of Connecticut, held that it was up to the discretion of Congress in creating the law. Members of Congress, Sherman contended, "may say he shall hold his office during good behavior, or that he shall be annually elected. We may say he shall be displaced for neglect of duty, and point out how he shall be convicted of it; without calling upon the President or Senate."[17]

Privately, Madison complained to Pendleton that Sherman and Bland's theories "could not possibly have been intended by the Constitution." The Constitution, he argued, primarily vested the executive power in the office of the president. "Are there exceptions to this proposition? Yes, there are." But the removal power was not one of them. "Have we a right to extend this exception? I believe not." Instead, Madison asserted, we should take the silence on the removal power as a sign that it is vested fully in the president. The advantage of this interpretation was that it rendered the president uniquely responsible for the conduct of executive officials, which would ultimately help secure the republican form of the government. "The lowest officers, the middle grade, and the highest," Madison argued, "will depend, as they ought, on the president, and the president on the community. The chain of dependence therefore terminates in the supreme body, namely, in the people."[18]

This would also help stop the legislative branch from growing beyond its intended functions. Madison believed that, as the branch most dependent upon the people, the legislative branch should naturally be the dominant force in a republic. His concern was it extending beyond its proper sphere and drawing the other branches into its "vortex," as he called it at the Constitutional Convention. This was one reason why he originally wanted the Council of Revision to be made up of the judiciary and the executive. He reckoned that only together could they withstand the "encroachments" of Congress. So it was with the removal power. During the legislative debate, Madison wrote to Randolph, "I see, and politically feel, that [the executive] will be the weak branch of the government." If the president were to depend on the Senate for removing officers, he told Edmund Pendleton, "the federal government should lose its proper equilibrium within itself."[19]

Fortunately for Madison, the strongly Federalist character of the First Congress enabled him to carry the day. In carefully chosen language, the House bill creating the State Department did not formally invest the removal power in the president, but instead implied that he already possessed it under the Constitution by outlining the procedures for filling a vacancy "whenever the [secretary] shall be removed from office by the President of the United States." The measure passed easily through the House, although the Senate—jealous of its prerogatives—split equally on the bill. Vice President John Adams broke the tie by voting in favor of sole executive discretion, perhaps anticipating that he might someday hold the executive office and would like to have the power to fire his subordinates.[20]

FOR THE MOST part, the first session of the First Congress was free of factional strife. There had been squabbling here and there, especially over the impost, but otherwise it was a time of harmony and shared purpose. Yet this unity was strained as summer changed to fall, when Congress turned its attention to the permanent location of the capital city. The Continental Congress had set New York City as the temporary capital and left the final determination to the new Congress. Unlike the impost, there was little hope for a compromise built on shared sacrifice. Every section had an incentive to have the capitol placed as close to itself as it could, and a victory for one region would surely mean a loss for some other. New Yorkers and New Englanders were interested in a permanent seat on the Susquehanna River, near present-day Harrisburg, Pennsylvania. Madison, like the rest of the Virginia delegation, favored a permanent location on the Potomac River. But that was not the only contender, and in a bid to draw support from Pennsylvania, Madison backed temporarily placing the capitol in Philadelphia. Meanwhile, the Philadelphians hoped that temporarily moving the seat of government to their city might evolve into a permanent placement.

Madison's motives on the issue were a mixture of high-minded republicanism and parochial politics. In early September, Thomas Scott of Pennsylvania proposed that the capitol be fixed "near the centre of wealth, population, and extent of territory." Madison agreed that population and extent of territory were good standards for placing the capitol, but not wealth. "Government is intended for the accommodation of the citizens at large," he argued. "An equal facility to communicate with government is due to all ranks; whether to transmit their grievances or requests, or to receive those blessings which the government is intended to dispense." Moreover, placing the capitol on the Potomac would better connect the West to the national government, especially if Washington and Madison's long-standing dreams of internal improvements extended the navigability of the Potomac watershed into the Ohio River valley. This was another classic Madisonian statement on the importance of balance between factions in society. The government should not play favorites between the rich and the poor, and in a country lacking good networks of transportation, placing the capitol near the rich would make it easier for them to influence the government. Yet it just so happened that the Potomac River was in roughly the middle of the country, right along the border of Virginia. Placing the capitol there would be good for his home state, so he worked diligently behind the scenes to make that happen.[21]

It was not to be—at least not yet. After a series of backroom bargains, which Madison told Edmund Pendleton would be "tedious to explain," the New Englanders and New Yorkers struck a deal with the Pennsylvanians: a permanent capitol on the Susquehanna and the temporary one to remain in New York City. The Virginians had lost, but only for the time being. Madison employed a series of dilatory tactics to put off the vote until the end of the session, which adjourned on September 29. The Senate would have to take the matter up after Christmas, giving the southerners time to strike a better bargain with the Pennsylvanians.[22]

THE FIRST SESSION of the First Congress was the culmination of Madison's Federalist period, which had begun nearly a decade before. From the moment he entered the Continental Congress, he worked tirelessly to strengthen the powers of the national government. After years of failure, he and his fellow nationalists had achieved a great deal through the Constitution—not everything they had hoped, but quite a bit and, given the political power of the state governments, about everything they could have attained. Madison's three big legislative accomplishments in 1789—the impost, the Bill of Rights, and the executive departments—were a capstone to this effort. For years, he had fought to fund the government through a dedicated tax; now, he had done it. He had worked to separate the executive functions of government from congressional politics under the Articles of Confederation; now, he had established the president as the sole authority for the removal of government officers. And he had dreamed of national unity, a country brought together not by shared ethnicity or religion, but by a sense of shared fate; the Bill of Rights helped accomplish this by satisfying moderate Anti-Federalists. If Madison had suddenly dropped dead on September 29, 1789, he would still be remembered as one of the greatest Founding Fathers in the history of the United States, so substantial were his accomplishments in that fateful decade.

But of course he lived on, and his career took a seemingly surprising turn. He would dissociate himself from many of his former Federalist allies, especially Alexander Hamilton, appointed secretary of treasury under Washington. Instead, he would join in an alliance with Thomas Jefferson and many former Anti-Federalists to check the growth of federal authority. This apparent flip-flop has puzzled people ever since it happened. Hamilton was himself caught unawares in 1790, when he discovered his old friend working behind the scenes to squash his proposal for the federal government to assume the debts of the states and charter the Bank of the United States. Biographers from succeeding generations have long struggled to reconcile the seemingly two-faced nature of Madison's politics.

But Madison's dispute with Hamilton has been widely misunderstood. His break from his former ally was not a rejection of his beliefs but an affirmation of them. Madison's vision of republicanism was premised on the idea that the government served as a neutral judge, arbitrating among all factions of society, regardless of economic or social status. Hamilton, on the other hand, saw government as an agent of national economic development. This required it to play favorites, especially with the moneyed elites in the large cities, whom he thought were essential to the country's political success. These contrasting visions of self-government also included different views of who should actually rule. Madison thought Congress should be the dominant force in government because it reflected the people. This meant, in turn, that its members should be free from conflicts of interest, so that they could vote for what was good for the people they represented. On the other hand, Hamilton emphasized the role of "energy in the executive," as he termed in it *Federalist* 70, as a way to guide the fractious members of the legislature to an end that was good for the whole country. This meant Hamilton was comfortable with an executive branch that rained patronage upon legislators to get them to vote the "right" way.[23]

Ironically, Madison had helped create the institutions Hamilton used to promote his financial proposals. During the debate on the Treasury Department, Elbridge Gerry had suggested that, rather than a single treasurer, the powers of the department should be held by a three-person board. Gerry made explicit reference to the rumors about the corruption of Robert Morris, which had caused such a "noise and commotion" among the public that the Continental Congress had felt obliged to create a three-member Treasury Board to manage the public finances. Madison disagreed, and Gerry's measure went down to overwhelming defeat, which gave Hamilton a perch from which he could influence public policy.[24]

Also of lasting importance was a seemingly insignificant debate over whether the secretary of the Treasury should have the power to submit plans directly to Congress. Skeptics of executive power worried that the secretary might use that ability to set the legislative agenda and thus control Congress indirectly. At the time of the debate, Madison waved off these concerns. He admitted there was a "small probability" that the secretary "may have some degree of influence upon the deliberations of the legislature," but the threat of that was much less than the danger of "not having well formed and digested plans." Again, Madison carried the day, and the secretary won the power to submit reports directly to Congress. Hamilton would use this allowance to great success, producing a flurry of detailed, lengthy reports that set the legislative agenda on economic policy—much to Madison's initial surprise and, later, regret.[25]

For Madison, his opposition to Hamilton was anchored by a single question, which he kept asking himself throughout the

1790s: Who should rule in a republic? He had given his answer in the proposed (but ultimately rejected) preamble he had written as one of his amendments. In language reminiscent of the Declaration of Independence, Madison wanted the preamble to declare that "all power is . . . derived from the people," that government exists only "for the benefit of the people," and that the people have an "indubitable, unalienable, and indefeasible right" to change their government whenever it is "found adverse or inadequate to this purpose." The people possessed ultimate sovereignty in a republic, and as its representative Congress should be the guiding force of the government. Madison's break with his former Federalist allies was, to his mind, about who should really be in charge. In Hamilton, he saw an alternative vision: one of economic and political elites using a strong executive department to dominate Congress through patronage and favors, to manage public opinion, and perhaps, Madison wondered darkly, even to bring about a monarchy.[26]

8

PARTY POLITICS

THE COMITY OF the first session of the First Congress ended shortly after the second session began, when, in early January, Alexander Hamilton submitted his *First Report on Public Credit* to Congress. This document proposed a revolution in American public finance and would lead to a sea change in politics too. During the 1780s, the plantation gentry of the South and the merchants of the North had joined together in an alliance because both sides needed a stronger government to protect their interests. Hence, a Gouverneur Morris and a James Madison would vote virtually in lockstep at the Constitutional Convention. But now that the new government had been instituted, the question stopped being whether it would acquire additional powers and became how—or, more specifically, *on whose behalf*—those powers should be exercised. Hamilton was a friend to the commercial interests. He believed that strengthening their situation would eventually redound to the benefit of the whole country, and he pursued a system of public finance that would do just that. There was little, if anything, for the son of a Piedmont planter such as Madison to gain from such a plan. So, the old large-state axis of Massachusetts, Pennsylvania, and Virginia was bound to fall apart. After Hamilton published his first report, a new division between economic and ideological interests would open up, factions whose first leaders would be James Madison and Alexander Hamilton.

Madison and Hamilton had followed remarkably different trajectories to come together in the *Federalist Papers* to defend the Constitution. Hamilton had been born into a hardscrabble life on the Caribbean island of Nevis and later traveled to New York. There, he had pulled himself up by his bootstraps. Falling in with the Revolutionary cause, he joined the army, became aide-de-camp to George Washington, and rose to be one of the leaders of the nationalist movement. Confident, unabashed, and teeming with barely controlled passion, he saw himself as a man of destiny but often struck others as vain and abrasive. Madison, on the other hand, was born into relative luxury and immediate social status on Montpelier. He was the eldest son of the most prosperous planter in all of Orange County and was due to inherit that position just for being who he was. He was modest and reserved in his manners and cautious in his dealings with others. Often underwhelming on first impression, he would win people over slowly, as they came to appreciate his integrity and his intellect.

What brought these men together in the 1780s was their shared commitment to a firmer union, the belief that the nation needed a stronger central government or else the whole country would fall apart. But they had different visions for how this union would actually function. A hint of their competing views can be found in the *Federalist Papers*. Madison's *Federalist* 10 was his basic treatise on how an extended republic can mitigate the "violence of faction" by bringing into the body politic a diverse variety of competing interests, forcing each to bargain with the others. In this way, Madison reasoned, the government would behave like a neutral judge, distributing the benefits and burdens of government equally across society. But flip the page to *Federalist* 11, written by Hamilton, and one will see a vastly different ideal. There, he focused on "the importance of the Union, in a commercial light," arguing that "a vigorous national government" could direct "the natural strength and resources of the country" to make America a rival to the European powers. In *Federalist* 12, he expanded upon this theme by arguing that a government that focused on commercial development could blend and merge the interests of the various factions in society. "The assiduous merchant, the laborious husbandman, the active mechanic, and the industrious manufacturer" could all be induced to coordinate their economic endeavors for the good of all, and the greatness of the nation.[1]

The implied purpose of government here is slightly different, with Madison elevating justice among competing factions while Hamilton celebrates the capacity of economic integration to achieve social harmony. It might, of course, be possible to achieve both of these visions at the same time, but they could also easily clash. A Madisonian government that is studiously fair among all factions of society may not be able to promote economic growth, and a Hamiltonian emphasis on economic integration might favor some factions over others, at least in the short term. *Federalist* 10, 11, and 12 also point to competing views of how government should be managed. Hamilton's approach was top-down, while Madison's bottom-up. Madison saw the Constitution as a structure to negotiate mutually agreeable compromises between various groups in society, while Hamilton saw it as a vehicle for visionary policy experts such as himself to direct the natural resources and intrepid character of America to national greatness.

These sorts of disagreements were mainly academic in the 1780s because the Continental Congress had so little power. But that all changed when Hamilton released to Congress his *First Report on Public Credit*. The competing visions of government he and Madison held would become suddenly consequential, and the rift that opened up would ultimately lead to the creation of the first political parties in the United States.

———————

THE *FIRST REPORT on Public Credit* was an ambitious program for salvaging the nation's public finances, and it included several key provisions. First, Hamilton called for the repayment of the national debt virtually at its full face value. Foreign creditors would be paid in full, while domestic creditors would receive western land claims in exchange for a small reduction on the interest rate, from 6 to 4 percent. In addition to securing the creditworthiness of the new government, Hamilton argued, a "properly funded debt . . . answers most of the purposes of money." If consumers and merchants believed that the government would pay back everything it had borrowed, debt certificates could be used as a uniform, stable, and truly national currency, which the country had sorely lacked since the Revolution. This is why, Hamilton believed, "the proper funding of the present debt will render it a national blessing."[2]

All else being equal, this was a proposal Madison could get behind. He had supported a plan similar to this when he served in the Continental Congress. But everything was not equal, at least not anymore. Madison's problem was not what the government had to pay, but who was going to get the money. Many veterans had been paid after the war in government bonds, when confidence in the government was at an all-time low. The vets had sold their bonds at 10 to 15 cents on the dollar to northern speculators, who were betting that someday the government might redeem a portion of them. As late as November 1788, these bonds were still trading for as little as 18 cents on the dollar, but just a few weeks before Hamilton's report was submitted, the prices shot up to 50 cents, indicating that investors anticipated windfall profits from the government. Sure enough, Hamilton was proposing to pay them back at their full face value. Madison did not like this at all. In his view, republican government had to model itself as a courtroom, treating all citizens equitably. How was it fair, he asked in several speeches in the House in February 1790, that the veterans received nothing while the speculators got everything? Instead, Madison proposed splitting payments equally between the original holders of the debt (the veterans) and the current holders (the speculators). He believed this "will do more real justice and perform more of the public faith than any other expedient proposed." The speculators "will have a profit that cannot be reasonably complained of," while the veterans "will receive . . . a tribute due to their merits."[3]

Madison's alternative was voted down overwhelmingly on February 11, and rightly so. This proposal may have been equitable on its face, but it was not a good idea. Madison was in effect calling for a 50 percent haircut for current bondholders, a massive reduction from the pledged amount to the actual payment. The fact that he would have used the proceeds to remunerate the veterans was irrelevant from the perspective of the bond markets, both domestic and international. They would have lost faith in the United States' willingness to pay back its debts, which would have had calamitous effects. The cost of borrowing for the government would have skyrocketed. Worse, the value of existing bonds would have plummeted, leading to the destruction of wealth in the young nation. And without faith in the trustworthiness of the government, bonds would inevitably have traded at varying discounts across the country, undermining Hamilton's purpose of creating a uniform national currency. If Madison had gotten his way, the public credit would have been utterly eviscerated and the economy profoundly damaged.

The real action in Congress was over the second half of Hamilton's plan, which would assume the debts of the states, estimated to be around $30 million. This was in part a simple matter of equity. After all, certain states had racked up huge bills fighting the Revolution, and it was only fair that this burden be shared equally by all Americans through the new national government. But Hamilton—ever the visionary—had another idea in mind. Shifting the public debt from the states to the federal government would also shift the loyalty of the public creditors in the same way. State bondholders in Georgia or Massachusetts or New Hampshire or South Carolina would become federal bondholders and would accordingly have a financial stake in the success of the national government. Hamilton believed that "if all the public creditors receive their dues from one source their interest will be the same," united "in the support of the fiscal arrangements of the government."[4]

All told, the *First Report on Public Credit* was quintessential Hamilton in its shaping of economic means toward political ends. Like many northern politicians with ties to the merchant community—Robert and Gouverneur Morris, Rufus King, Philip Schuyler, and others—Hamilton understood the importance of public finance to the commercial interests and, ultimately, the prosperity of the whole nation. But he also appreciated how a good system of public and private credit could secure a mighty civic purpose. A strong central government with good credit could promote national development, thereby binding all the diverse regional, social, and economic factions of society together in a shared quest for prosperity.

Madison had long been an advocate of economic development when it meant building roads and improving waterways, but Hamilton's vision of a commercial republic was anathema to him. Those merchants in the northern cities struck him as greedy. Madison and other southern planters often derided investors—in private stock, government debt, or land—as "jobbers" looking to maximize their gains for the sake of the public good. Banks, he believed, were downright dangerous to free government, as a handful of monied elites located therein could dictate policy to the nation.

This is not to say Madison saw no merit at all in Hamilton's plans. He had supported an assumption of state debts and could do so again under certain circumstances. Rather, he simply could not fully appreciate Hamilton's nationalism, for it was too different from his own. Still, Madison understood something Hamilton did not: the nature of fairness in a republican government. Madison's complaint about the repayment plan was that it was inequitable. Those who had fought for the nation's freedom received very little, while wealthy speculators received a lot. He had a similar complaint about Hamilton's debt-assumption plan, for its benefits were also distributed unfairly. Back in the early 1780s, Madison had supported a version of assumption as part of a logroll to get the impost passed, but in the intervening years several states, including Virginia, had begun paying off their debts. In fact, only three states—Connecticut, Massachusetts, and South Carolina—lagged behind the others, and they would receive a disproportionately large bounty from Hamilton's assumption. Madison did not think that was right. He favored assumption in principle, but he thought it had to come after a final settlement of accounts between the states and the federal government, whereby each state tabulated the costs it had incurred for the war, and those states that had paid back some of their debts would receive a corresponding credit from Congress.

This, Madison believed, was consistent with "the object of doing full justice," rather than favoring some states over others,
while Hamilton's plan would "work . . . injustice to a majority of
the states."[5]

Thanks to Madison's efforts, Hamilton's assumption plan
went down to a narrow defeat in the House on April 16, by a
margin of twenty-nine to thirty-two. Madison brought together
the handful of House Anti-Federalists, who thought assumption
was a handmaiden for consolidation; members who feared that
it would raise the national debt; and those who, like himself,
supported assumption in principle but not until a final settlement of accounts. Madison hoped that would be the end of the
discussion, but he was wrong. After assumption was defeated,
many of the public creditors—including a few who were actually serving in government—adopted desperate tactics to sal-
vage their investments, even if it risked ruining the credit of the
new government.

Like the repayment plan, Hamilton's assumption plan was an
easy opportunity for those in the know to make windfall profits,
thanks to the asymmetry of information that persisted in the
eighteenth century. The bond market clearly knew something
was up in the fall of 1788, when the price of national debt certificates increased markedly. Something similar happened with
the assumption plan but on a much more pernicious scale. News
of congressional debates could take weeks, sometimes months,
to trickle out to the hinterlands, which gave insiders an opportunity to dispatch agents across the country to purchase state
debts on the cheap. Unsuspecting state creditors in far-flung
places like the Carolinas or New Hampshire had no idea what
was happening in New York and were persuaded to sell their
debt certificates for much less than their true value.

Many government officials participated in such schemes. This
being the start of a new government—an age when it was not

unheard of for a gentleman to mix public service with private profit—there were hardly any legal boundaries to keep officials from enriching themselves. Indeed, some of the most daring and audacious debt schemes were hatched by public officials. Pennsylvania senator William Maclay believed that many members had used their advance knowledge of Hamilton's plan to build a "system of speculation," and mentioned in his diary that Connecticut representative Jeremiah Wadsworth was likely involved in such schemes. He also reported that Senator Benjamin Hawkins of North Carolina had told him that, on his way to New York, he had "passed two expresses with very large sums of money . . . for purposes of speculation in certifications." When Maclay met with Charles Pettit—a signer of the Declaration of Independence who had been appointed by Pennsylvania to settle final wartime accounts with Congress—Maclay found him totally uninterested in the public business but rather obsessed with meeting other speculators from Boston and New York to maximize their gains. Andrew Craigie—the former apothecary general for the army and now a major speculator—recorded in his diary that Congress had suspended debate on the assumption plan "because their private arrangements are not in readiness for speculation." Perhaps the most audacious speculator of all was William Duer—a former member of the Treasury Board and now Hamilton's assistant at the Treasury Department. Along with Gouverneur Morris, Jeremiah Wadsworth, and a few others, Duer used his inside information about Hamilton's plans to try to build the first American-based international banking syndicate, whereby his friends would purchase large quantities of domestic debt to be resold to the major financial houses in the Netherlands.[6]

Madison did a number on all these machinations when he defeated assumption. Many of the speculators had been borrowing large sums to buy up state debts, expecting Hamilton's measure to be enacted quickly. Now, facing immense losses—and possibly debtors' prison—they responded by hijacking the funding of the national debt. Either Congress would vote both to pay off the national debt and to assume state debts, or neither would pass. Madison had heard rumblings of this strategy back in the winter. As far as he was concerned, it was pure deviousness, for the two issues had no necessary connection. Provisions had to be made immediately for the national debt, but the assumption of the state debts, though important, was not as urgent. It could wait until the states settled their war accounts with the national government.[7]

But the speculators and their allies insisted, so as the spring rolled into summer, the House ground its gears. Madison explained why to Edmund Randolph in May. "The zealots for the assumption of the state debts," he wrote, "keep back in hope of alarming the zealots for the federal debt. . . . Motives are felt I suspect which will account for the perseverance." This was Madison's characteristically roundabout way of blaming the speculators, for what public-spirited motive could possibly induce these advocates to hold up funding the national debt? Writing to Monroe in July, Madison lamented, "It seems, indeed, as if the friends of the measure were determined to risk everything rather than suffer that finally to fail." Even Hamilton found himself struggling against the speculators. In the *First Report on Public Credit*, he had called for reducing the interest paid on domestic debt from 6 percent to 4 percent, but this faced pushback in the Senate. Robert Morris, Philip Schuyler, and Rufus King—all heavily invested in public securities—demanded full repayment. Ultimately, Hamilton had to fashion a compromise that included 6 percent interest on the principal and 3 percent on overdue interest. Thomas Fitzsimons, a close Hamilton ally, privately "condemn[ed] the supporters of the measure," who had "pressed it without discretion and really so as to disgust" those moderate nationalists who may have been willing to compromise.[8]

These sorts of maneuvers set the context for the so-called Compromise of 1790, whereby assumption and funding were passed in exchange for placing the capitol on the Potomac River and special credits to states like Virginia that had paid back some of their old debts. The public memory of that deal has largely been set by Jefferson's later reminiscences. To hear him tell it, he sat down with Madison and Hamilton just a few weeks after he had been sworn in as secretary of state, and they were said to have hammered out an agreement. But this narrative has problems. Madison never endorsed this version of events, and he was completely disgusted by the whole affair, telling Monroe that giving in on assumption had been an "unavoidable evil," even with the sweetener of the capitol added to the deal.[9]

Regardless of the specifics, a compromise of some sort was hashed out. As a parochial matter, it was a victory for Madison the Virginia politician. As he told his father, "In a pecuniary light, the assumption is no longer of much consequence to Virginia." But for Madison the republican statesman, it was a crushing defeat. He sensed—not unreasonably—that the only reason assumption had passed the way it did was that members of Congress had a personal stake in the outcome. Too many members had voted their wallets rather than the interests of the people. He believed this was simply not how self-government was supposed to function. Representatives were supposed to refine and enlarge the views of their constituents. They should not be using their inside knowledge of government business to enrich themselves, let alone to threaten the national credit when their payday was delayed.[10]

To Madison, this was an existential threat to the republic, for it pointed to a potential weak spoke in the very structure of representative government. Members of Congress were not monks, cloistered from the rest of society. The First Congress was full to bursting with southern planters and northern merchants who might use the sweeping new authority of government either for the public interest or to line their own pockets. During the confederation era, this was not that big of a problem, as the old Congress lacked the power to do much of anything. But now under the Constitution, the new Congress had vast powers to tax, to regulate, and to spend.

The real question for Madison was never whether conflicts of interests were present in legislators. That was inevitable. Even Madison himself could be said to be guilty of such mixed motives. With his friend Light-Horse Harry Lee, Madison had made a small investment in land near the Great Falls of the Potomac. So, he had a personal incentive in seeing the capitol moved to that region. It was a modest interest, to be sure—ranking far behind his solicitation for Virginia's interest as well as his goal of unifying the Atlantic with the West. But it was no doubt there.

It was better to ask whether these motives held sway. Were members of Congress voting against their constituents and for themselves? It might be tolerable if a handful did so, but if the difference between the success and failure of a measure was corrupted motives, then the republican quality of the government would come into question. This was what Madison observed in the vote over the assumption of state debts. Members of Congress voted their personal interests, rather than the interests of their constituents. This, for Madison, looked more like the corrupted rule of a pseudo-republic, something closer to Great Britain, where the king's ministers were said to use royal patronage to buy votes in Parliament.

And who sat behind the scenes, ostensibly directing these affairs? To Madison, the answer was obvious: Hamilton. Madison thought back to those debates at the Constitutional Convention and began connecting dots he perhaps had not noticed before. Behind closed doors, Hamilton had suggested that the people were unfit to rule and needed a large cadre of natural aristocrats looking over them. He had praised the British constitution and especially admired the king's ability to use patronage to buy the votes of members of Parliament. He had proposed establishing a life tenure for the president and the Senate. His politics, in a word, were decidedly elitist by American standards. It seemed to Madison that he was trying to bring that Old World ethos to the New World, employing the debt as a kind of patronage to buy votes in Congress and maybe ensconce himself permanently in the government. Hamilton, Madison increasingly came to reckon, had become a threat to the republic. He had to be stopped.

IN DECEMBER 1790, Hamilton submitted *The Second Report on Public Credit*, today known as *The Report on a National Bank*, which called for Congress to charter a national bank. Located in Philadelphia, Hamilton's bank would hold public tax revenues but be owned mainly by private investors and free to lend like any bank. The Bank of the United States, as it would come to be known, was another Hamiltonian masterstroke, a sign he knew his financial history well. Established in the late Stuart era, the Bank of England had helped Great Britain transform itself into a European dynamo. It not only facilitated the flow of private credit through the nation's burgeoning economy, but it also was there to lend cash to the government in a pinch, a feature that Hamilton knew the young United States desperately needed too.

Jefferson took the leading role in opposing the bank, writing a memorandum to President George Washington that the power to charter such an institution "[has] not, in my opinion, been delegated to the United States, by the Constitution." Madison believed likewise, and he held this view for the rest of his days, explaining late in life that "the divergence between" Hamilton and Madison occurred because Hamilton desired "to administer the government . . . into what he thought it ought to be; while, on my part, I endeavored to make it conform to the Constitution as understood by the Convention that produced and recommended it, and particularly by the State conventions that adopted it."[11]

Madison was hardly consistent on the scope of federal power. In April 1789, he had urged Congress to support John Churchman's scientific expedition to Baffin Bay to study magnetism, on the basis that doing so "comport[ed] with the honor and dignity of government." That was not a power invested in the Constitution under a strict reading. In December 1796, he would present to the House a testimonial in favor of chartering a national university, even though he opposed chartering a bank. As for Madison's reverence for the ratifying conventions, it must be noted that he systematically excluded all of their recommendations for limiting congressional power, so he can hardly claim to have considered their judgments final in every case.[12]

Ironically, the Father of the Constitution had a muddled view of exactly what the Constitution allowed and what it prohibited. If Madison supported a measure, he could usually discover legal sanction for it, and if he opposed it, he was wont to uncover constitutional grounds for doing so. He had never liked the idea of the government getting itself entangled with banks, for he believed they tended to concentrate public wealth and power in the hands of an elite few.

The details of Hamilton's plan hardly made Madison more amenable. The secretary of the Treasury proposed selling shares of Bank of the United States stock for $400, but only 25 percent had to be paid in cash. The remainder was deliverable in government debts. This meant that the bank was yet another boon to northern speculators, who had hoarded public certificates in 1788 because they had known Hamilton's plan before the rest of the country did. Meanwhile, the subscription window for bank stock would open in July 1791, just a few months after Congress enacted the law. Madison believed that this, too, favored the speculators in the northern cities, who would get word earlier and thus be better able to get their finances in order to purchase stock. In Madison's judgment, the balance of power in the new bank between the public and private sectors was tilted too far toward the private. By holding the tax revenues of the new government, the bank would enjoy an implicit federal guarantee, meaning that it was virtually assured to make money. Madison believed that the government should get something more direct out of this arrangement—like a bonus from the bank for chartering it—but Hamilton called for no such payout.

Madison was also worried about the bank acquiring political power from the people. He warned his colleagues in the House that "the power of granting charters is a great and important power," which cannot be taken lightly. Such institutions in Europe had become "powerful machine[s] . . . competent to effect objects on principles, in a great measure independent of the people." He was not wrong about this. England had become a commercial powerhouse because of its public-private institutions, like the Bank of England and the British East India Company, but those corporations had come to wield tremendous power in political matters. The Tea Act of 1773, which led to the Boston Tea Party, was enacted in part because Prime Minister Lord

North had felt pressured by the "nabobs" in Parliament—those who had grown rich from the East India Company—to bail out the struggling corporation. Most infamously, the South Sea Company was originally chartered in 1711 with a monopoly on British trade to South America. A few years later, the company struck a deal with the British government to help manage the public debt. This caused a speculative mania that led to the "South Sea Bubble" of 1720, wherein the price of the stock became inflated very quickly then collapsed, ruining many investors and wreaking widespread havoc upon the British financial system. Madison worried that the bank could likewise give American "stockjobbers," as he derisively called them, leverage over government policy.[13]

Madison's constitutional theory may have been scattershot, but he had a keen understanding of the use and abuse of political power. Some of his worries about the bank were soon realized. The charter passed easily through the House and Senate, and Washington—persuaded more by Hamilton's case that it was constitutional than Jefferson's that it was not—signed it into law. Subscriptions opened in the summer of 1791 for bank "scrip," guaranteed options for bank stock sold for $100 apiece, or 25 percent of the total price. The demand for bank scrip quickly exceeded the supply, and a robust secondary market developed. As Madison told Jefferson, "It seems admitted on all hands now that the plan of the institution gives a moral certainty of gain to the subscribers with scarce a physical possibility of loss."[14]

The problem was that there seemed to be no end to the rise in scrip price. In August 1791, Light-Horse Harry Lee wrote to Madison bemoaning the mania: "One continued scene of stock gambling; agriculture, commerce, and even the fair sex relinquished, to make way for unremitted exertion in this favorite pursuit." Hamilton's old chum William Duer was in the eye of this hurricane. He had left the Treasury Department in the spring to pursue his various speculative endeavors and helped bid the price of scrip up to $300 apiece by August, three times its face value, fueled in part by rumors (likely started by Duer himself) about what Hamilton thought the real value of scrip was. But then the upward surge abated, and the price began to fall. Hamilton, worried about the effect of a collapse on the stability of the markets, tipped his hand to Rufus King, now a senator from New York, telling him he felt that scrip was worth about $195 apiece. He then reached out to Duer with similar information, asking him to help support the price of scrip at that level. He also sent word to William Seton at the Bank of New York with instructions to use tax funds to purchase $150,000 worth of government debt, in the hopes of stabilizing the markets, privately instructing him to purchase from the bulls and not the bears.[15]

Hamilton's quick action stopped a larger financial panic, but it was in essence a government bailout of the markets, particularly of irresponsible investors like Duer. Hamilton had implicitly established a signal to the market of when the government would involve itself to keep prices from falling below a certain level. Accordingly, Duer plunged back in by the early winter, intent on cornering the market on public securities. He borrowed from anybody he could, including local New York shopkeepers and even widows. Once again, a bubble began to form, much to Hamilton's dismay. "These extravagant sallies of speculation," he complained, "do injury to the government and to the whole system of public credit, by disgusting all sober citizens and giving a wild air to everything." Once again, the bubble inevitably popped, in what became known as the Panic of 1792. Hamilton again had to employ government revenue to shore up the market, which prevented a broader recession. Fortunately for the country, Duer was permanently ruined by this failure. He would spend the rest of his life in debtors' prison, where he could not threaten the financial solvency of the new government ever again.[16]

Madison could only look on in horror as these events unfolded. Was this, he asked himself in anger and frustration, why he had labored so hard to improve the government? So that a narrow clique of commercial interests and speculators could seize public policy for their own benefit and almost bring down the country in the process? In August 1791, writing to Jefferson from New York, he lamented how the "stockjobbers" were becoming "the praetorian band of the government—at once its tool and its tyrant; bribed by its largesses, and overawing it, by clamors and combinations." Seemingly at the helm of this faction was Hamilton, who in Madison's judgment had exploited conflicts of interest within Congress to deliver to the northern financiers a huge payday and then nearly brought the nation to financial ruin. This, for Madison, was no mere policy disagreement between former allies. This was a threat to self-government itself. Who was supposed to rule? The Constitution gave that power to the people, but it seemed like Hamilton had handed that authority to speculators like Duer.[17]

If the year of 1789 was a triumph for Madison, 1790 and 1791 were terrible defeats that left him reeling. It seemed as though the republic was slipping away. But he and Jefferson would not go down without a fight. They would dig in their heels and strike back by establishing the first American political party.

MADISON WAS AN unlikely inventor of American party politics. After all, this was the same person who had authored

Federalist 10, which praised the capacity of a "well-constructed union" to "break and control the violence of faction." Were parties not a specific type of faction? Madison himself used the terms "faction" and "party" interchangeably in the essay. When combined with his sudden opposition to big, expansive government, his apparent flip-flop on the question of partisanship made him look terribly inconstant, as if the Madison of 1787 was different from the Madison of 1792.[18]

But he was the same Madison. The difference was that he believed the republic was facing a different threat. In 1787, the problem was majority factions—embodied in the state governments—that mistreated political minorities and undermined the national good. The solution then, he believed, was a stronger central government built upon an extended body politic. In 1792, Madison believed the problem was a minority faction: a wealthy and well-positioned group of insiders who had used Hamilton's system of public finance to enrich themselves to the detriment, and perhaps ultimate destruction, of the republic. That required a different solution, an entity to represent the public interest: a political party.

Madison and Jefferson did not see their party as a faction, but rather the avatar of a broad majority, anchored on the general principles of self-government in pursuit of the common interest. This is why they chose the name Republican Party (the contemporary moniker, Democratic-Republican Party, was mainly used by later generations). Madison and Jefferson saw themselves not as one faction among many, but as an antidote to the factionalism of Hamilton and his "Federalist" allies, as they would become known. In modern parlance, we might say that Madison and Jefferson saw themselves as leaders of a would-be unity government of the sorts that parliamentary systems often elevate during times of great crisis, or that Abraham Lincoln briefly established for the 1864 presidential election. There were a diversity of factions and interests in society, no doubt, but the purpose of the Republican Party was to represent the common interest that most people had in stopping Hamilton's seemingly corrupt approach to governance and his one-sided policy agenda. Their plan was to sound a general alarm among the people so that they might be aware of the Federalist threat and exercise their authority before the Hamiltonians took total control of the government.

In other words, their response to what they considered Hamilton's anti-republican designs was to advance the art of American politics, drawing the broader public more fully into the debate about the future of government. Far from being inconsistent with the *Federalist Papers*, Madison's embrace of party politics was an extension of his earlier ideas applied to a new problem.

This is why the first great partisan action in the United States of America was the creation of a newspaper: the *National Gazette*. Its purpose would be to warn the people about the schemes of Hamilton and the Federalists, and encourage them to participate more intently in the political process. To edit their paper, Jefferson and Madison tapped Philip Freneau, an old college friend of Madison's from the College of New Jersey. In February 1791, Jefferson offered Freneau the "clerkship for foreign languages" in the State Department, perhaps the first ever use of party patronage in American history. "The salary indeed is very low, being but two hundred and fifty dollars a year," Jefferson explained, "but also it gives so little to do as not to interfere with any other calling the person may choose, which would not absent him from the seat of government." Freneau initially rebuffed him, but after some persuading by Madison and Lee, he wrote back in August that he had changed his mind.[19]

Madison, for his part, encouraged family and friends to subscribe, and even secured passage in the House of a bill to lower postage rates to make it easier for Freneau to do business, though it was defeated in the Senate. He also lent his pen, writing nineteen anonymous essays for the *National Gazette* between November 1791 and December 1792 that laid out his view of the Federalist-Republican divide. This was Madison at his most polemical, as his essays served as commentaries on contemporary politics. But, Madison being Madison, he still drew on deeper themes of republican self-government. When the layers of partisan bombast are peeled away, his *National Gazette* essays reveal a counterbalance to his *Federalist Papers*. If the Madisonian *Federalist* explained how a republican government may be inoculated against the excesses of popular majorities, the *National Gazette* endeavored to rouse the majority to use the political process to throw off a minority faction that was growing dangerously strong.

For this task, Madison drew deeply on the ideology of the "Country Whigs" of early eighteenth-century Britain, when polemicists like Viscount Bolingbroke and "Cato" (the pseudonym used by John Trenchard and Thomas Gordon) had blasted the economic policies of British prime minister Robert Walpole, whose government, they claimed, had systematically employed royal patronage to bribe Parliament to institute a system of finance and speculation. This undermined the simple, agrarian values that had long been the backbone of British republicanism. Unsurprisingly, the American colonists found the political tracts of the Country Whigs highly useful during the lead-up to the Revolution, as they seemed to explain why their pleas to the king for redress had gone unheeded. Now, Madison found value in them once more, as they supplied not only an explanation of what Hamilton was seemingly up to but a dire prophecy of what would happen to American republicanism should he succeed.

Madison's *National Gazette* essays offered his answer to the question of the day: Who should rule in a republic? Madison returned to this query again and again to juxtapose the competing visions of government offered by the Federalists and the Republicans. The Republican view, Madison argued, was simple. The people should rule, with a watchful eye for an assault on their liberty. "Public opinion . . . is the real sovereign in every free" government, which naturally derives "its energy from the will of the society" and operates "by the reason of its measures . . . on the understanding and interest of the society" rather than by bribery or military force. The task of this new Republican Party lay in bringing the people together for this purpose, "banishing every other distinction" between social, religious, and economic groups, uniting the true "friends to republican government," and "promoting a general harmony" among the great mass of people in common defense against the threats to freedom. The Federalist alternative, meanwhile, could not rely upon the consent of the people, for its measures were designed to enrich a handful of speculators over the great agricultural masses. It was "weaker in point of numbers" but strong with "men of influence, particularly of moneyed." Thus, it had to "operat[e] by corrupt influence, substituting the motive of private interest in place of public duty, converting its pecuniary dispensations into bounties to favorites, or bribes to opponents, accommodating its measures to the avidity of a part of the nation instead of the benefit of the whole." The Federalists, Madison believed, could not win in a fair fight. Instead, they had to enlist "an army of interested partizans, whose tongues, whose pens, whose intrigues, and whose active combinations" to "support a real domination of the few, under an apparent liberty of the many." In so doing, the Federalists had "avow[ed] or betray[ed] principles of monarchy and aristocracy."[20]

This was a hyperbolic, and in many respects unfair, caricature of Hamilton, inadvertently revealing the deep geographic and economic roots of the partisan divide. The basic truth was that the most zealous Republicans tended to be farmers or planters whose wealth was mainly tied up in land and enslaved people, so they did not have access to sufficient liquid capital to take advantage of his proposals. They also lacked Hamilton's sophisticated understanding of public finance. They could not appreciate the long-term benefits of an economically integrated union and how an unreserved promotion of commerce and industry were essential to bringing this about. That they immediately reached back to the Country Whigs, and indeed went so far as to accuse Hamilton of favoring a "monarchy bottomed on corruption," in Jefferson's later description, spoke to their relative ignorance on the matters on which Hamilton could rightly claim preeminent subject expertise.[21]

Nevertheless, Madison's incendiary description of Hamilton's views was not without merit, highlighting three essential elements of the divide between Republicans and Federalists. First, there were skeptics on the Federalist side of the aisle who questioned the extent to which the people should rule. Hamilton was chief among them—his speeches at the Constitutional Convention illustrated that plainly enough—but he was far from alone. There was a sense among many that natural aristocrats should be able to make crucial decisions in government and that the people should play a modest role—if not quite as diminished as in Britain's system, then something pointing in that direction. Vice President John Adams's efforts to institute a fancy title for President Washington seem patently ridiculous in historical retrospect, but he wanted to establish a "high tone" to inculcate in the people a sense of reverence and awe for their rulers. So, the Federalist-Republican divide, for all its overwrought rhetoric, did get to that crucial question of how involved the people would be in government. Madison, along with many Republicans, was certainly not a democrat by contemporary standards, but there was still a significant gap between him and many Federalists.

Second, there was the question of fairness. Indisputably, Hamilton was a visionary, foreseeing an economically integrated United States that could "baffle all the combinations of European jealousy to restrain our growth," as he put it in *Federalist* 11. This plan was of long-term benefit to the entire country, but the short-term benefits were one-sided, favoring the merchants and speculators of the cities and, yes, Hamilton's friends. Not only that, the benefits compounded on one another: Hamilton offered full redemption of public debts, then magnified the bounty by accepting public debts as payment for bank scrip. What a boon this was for the select few who had money and access in 1790. But it was not much of anything for the overwhelming majority of the country, which was predominantly agricultural and certainly in no position to take advantage of Hamilton's programs. If a republic was supposed to distribute the benefits and burdens of government in a neutral fashion, Hamilton was clearly biased toward the commercial class.[22]

Third, there was the matter of how Hamilton had managed to get all of this enacted. Admittedly, the Federalist triumph in the 1789 elections swept into office those who were likely to adhere to Hamilton's way of things. Madison's struggles to get the Bill of Rights passed illustrated the somewhat high-toned disposition of the First Congress, as members of the House seemed uninterested in following through on promises made during the ratifying conventions. Both the Bank of the United States and the plan to fund the national debt had passed overwhelmingly, implying that the personal interests of individual congressmen were not a decisive factor. But the same could not be said for the assumption of state debts. The final vote on that measure was exceedingly close. While the bill was primarily of short-term interest to the three most indebted states—Connecticut, Massachusetts, and South Carolina—it received sweeping support from the New Jersey, New York, and Pennsylvania congressional delegations, whose constituents would gain little from the measure but whose representatives were among the significant holders of government debt. Even worse was the manner in which it was passed, whereby certain members—rather than delaying assumption until the final settlement of accounts—threatened to hold up the funding of the national debt. It was reasonable for Madison and Jefferson to infer that the self-interest of members of Congress had made a difference in the passage of assumption.

While Madison was certainly wrong to ascribe monarchical intentions to Hamilton, it was clear that these events ran contrary to Madison's deeply held beliefs about how self-government should function. Though public opinion had to be elevated and refined through the representative process, the people should rule the government, not the other way around. Policy had to be fair and neutral, and the speculative ventures of politicians should not make the difference between success or failure. That Hamilton was not only comfortable with this approach, but that he encouraged it (after all, he had named Duer, a notorious speculator well before 1789, number two at the Treasury Department), was enough to end their working relationship for good.

UNFORTUNATELY, GEORGE WASHINGTON found himself caught in the middle of this fight—literally, for he had brought both Jefferson and Hamilton into his cabinet. The president saw himself as a symbol of American resolve and a tribune of national unity, and it grieved him tremendously to see partisanship grow during the second half of his first term.

Yet this partisanship was an inevitable result of the evolution of normal politics, which the country had so sorely lacked since its founding. Men of goodwill of all different socioeconomic and ideological stripes had come together to frame an effective government; now that they had succeeded, they had the luxury of disagreeing, as the debate shifted from how to build a government that could do things to what things such a government should do. And while Washington lamented the collapse of unity, there was still an underlying thread of commonality, a shared commitment by Madison and Hamilton, Republicans and Federalists, to the Constitution as a framework for resolving policy disputes. Politics in the 1790s was no doubt played with rough elbows, but neither side ever contemplated breaking the oath of loyalty to the Constitution, a fact that was quite extraordinary considering how untested the new government was.

Over the rest of the decade, partisan differences would become especially sharp. Britain and France returned to war with one another in 1793, and the United States would find itself caught between these two powers, with no obvious way to extricate itself from the dilemma. The foreign tumult only made the squabbling worse, as Republicans and Federalists accused each other of betraying the country, and Madison would find himself in a rhetorical battle against Hamilton in the newspapers.

9

BRITAIN AND FRANCE

In the summer of 1792, George Washington reached out to the men in government he respected most—Thomas Jefferson, Alexander Hamilton, and James Madison—with shocking news. He intended to retire when his presidential term was over. He was tired. His age was getting to him. He missed Mount Vernon. He hated the partisan backbiting. To a man, they all gave him the same answer: You have to stay. The fate of the republic depends on it.

This was a telling response. Madison and Jefferson differed greatly from Hamilton on many matters, but all three were men of the Enlightenment, devotees to what Madison and Hamilton had called the "science of politics" in the *Federalist Papers*. Madison in particular had envisioned the extended republic as some kind of Newtonian system for politics, balancing the forces of factionalism against each other in predictable ways. "Enlightened statesmen will not always be at the helm," Madison warned in *Federalist* 10. What really mattered was the structure of politics. And yet here he was, urging the president to stay on. As he recorded the conversation later on, he explained, "That in the present unsettled condition of our young government, it was to be feared that no successor would answer all the purposes to be expected from the continuance of the present chief magistrate." A typically circuitous Madisonian formulation, which, when unpacked, reveals his dark truth of 1792: he was scared this government was not going to make it. It seemed like only the universal esteem of Washington was holding the United States together.[1]

The heady days of 1789—when Madison led a broad coalition in the House to give shape and meaning to the constitutional structure of the government—were long gone. Everything had changed with the release of the *First Report on Public Credit*. Hamilton had taken effective control of the government, and his administration was a challenge not only to Madison's policy preferences but also to some of his most cherished ideas on republicanism: that government should operate according to public opinion rather than conflicts of interests, that it should not play favorites, and that it should rule for the good of all rather than a few. Another surprise was the strength of the executive. Madison had long been convinced that the legislature would be the most dangerous branch of government. This was the main reason he was so keen in 1789 to ensure the president had the authority to fire government officials; the executive had to have a means of self-defense. But now it seemed that the executive, or at least the Treasury Department, was the dominant player in the government, setting the agenda in Congress, whipping votes, and spreading its largesse.

For Madison, these two trains of thought arrived at the same destination. What government had a strong executive where an energetic minority could use wealth to buy the political power it did not derive from the people? The British system. Hamilton and his friends, Madison deduced, were looking to transform the republicanism of the United States into a mixed system that balanced democracy, aristocracy, and monarchy. And so far, they had been shockingly successful.

This is why Washington had to stay on, for his replacement would likely be a member of the "British party," as Madison would derisively refer to his opponents. Who would the top contenders be? John Adams, who had praised the mixed system of the British in his various written works, and whose effort to give the president a fancy title suggested he held high-toned views of government? John Jay, who had already demonstrated his partiality to the commercial interests of the North with the Jay-Gardoqui Treaty? The only Republican of sufficient stature was Jefferson, but he had made it clear that he intended to retire to Monticello as soon as he could. No, it was Washington or bust.

There was, of course, a fatal flaw in Madison's line of thought. After all, it was Washington who had empowered Hamilton. He could resolve the danger in an instant by firing Hamilton once and for all. But he had not. This left one of two possibilities: either Washington himself was a "monocrat," or he was a dupe. Madison rejected the former out of hand; Washington was a tried-and-true republican. And though Madison would never consciously adopt the latter idea, it began to seep into his correspondence with Jefferson from 1792 onward—the old man did not understand the stakes of the game that was being played. But of course, Washington was no fool. If anything, he understood the utility of Hamilton's system better than Madison. The Republicans were inadvertently giving Washington a choice: he was either with them, or against them. When the Republicans pushed him, Washington chose Hamilton.

AFTER A STRING of Hamiltonian victories—on debt repayment, assumption of the state debts, and chartering the Bank of the United States—the battle between Hamilton and Madison had reached a kind of stalemate by early 1792. Submitted to Congress in December 1791, Hamilton's *Report on Manufactures* proposed an elaborate system to patronize domestic industries that emphasized cash subsidies to privileged manufacturers, but the plan was basically dead on arrival. Madison once more pressed a constitutional objection. Congress only had the power to tax for the general welfare, so how was giving cash bounties to favored industries possibly legitimate? As he wrote Light-Horse Harry Lee, if Hamilton's doctrine was taken as professed, "the fundamental and characteristic principle of the government," namely the principle of enumerated powers, would be "subverted." Here was another constitutional hypocrisy on Madison's part, for he had already supported payments to New England cod fishermen, as well as public subsidies for scientific expeditions. His critics, as well as subsequent historians, saw these as politically convenient contradictions. But to Madison, the difference was that Hamilton's proposal was just another way to attach the wealthy permanently to government, and he would not abide that.[2]

Having battled themselves to a draw inside Congress, the Federalists and Republicans took their fight to the president. In May 1792, Jefferson warned Washington that Hamilton was looking to transform "the present republican form of government to that of a monarchy, of which the English constitution is to be the model." Hamilton, of course, denied the charge outright, and similarly accused his opponents of having malicious intentions. He told Edward Carrington that he had been wrong to once think Madison's character was one of "candor and simplicity;" he was now of the "decided opinion that it was one of a particularly artificial and complicated kind." That summer, Hamilton publicly outed Jefferson and Madison as the patrons of Philip Freneau's *National Gazette*. In a series of anonymous letters for the *Gazette of the United States*, Hamilton revealed that Freneau was on the payroll of the State Department and intimated that he had been placed there by Jefferson and "a particular friend of that officer" as a form of "patronage and encouragement" for the *National Gazette*. Though unnamed, there was no doubt among anybody in the know that this "particular friend" was Madison. This seemingly petty maneuver by Hamilton was the first step in a bigger game he was playing. Washington hated the *National Gazette* and took criticism of his administration personally. By identifying Jefferson and Madison with Freneau, Hamilton sowed doubts in the president's mind about the Republicans he had long trusted.[3]

The fall of 1792 saw the first stirrings of modern presidential politics. Washington was universally acclaimed as the only man for the presidency, but what about the second seat? Vice President John Adams, possessed of what Madison called "monarchical principles," was "unpardonable by the republican zeal." To excise him from office, Republicans from Virginia and New York began coordinating their efforts. A crucial node in this connection was John Beckley, the clerk of the House of Representatives, a zealous Republican, and a formidable gatherer of political intelligence. Beckley helped bring the Virginia Republicans together with the old Anti-Federalist faction in New York, especially George Clinton and Melancton Smith. The alliance was formalized in October when Madison and James Monroe wrote to Smith to endorse Clinton, whom New York Republicans had nominated for the vice presidency. A leader of the Anti-Federalist forces during the ratification period, Clinton was far from an ideal choice, but the Constitution prohibited Virginia electors from voting for two Virginians, so Jefferson could not

be run as Washington's vice president. Ultimately, Adams won
the vice presidency, but Clinton carried votes from Georgia,
New York, North Carolina, and Virginia, while Jefferson carried
Kentucky.[4]

The Republicans' assault grew nastier in the winter of 1792–
1793. Convinced that Hamilton was enriching himself at the
public expense, they sought to have him removed from office.
There was no real evidence of malfeasance—if anything, the
Republicans merely betrayed how little they understood about
how the government books were managed—but in the heat of
that partisan moment, it was an explosive charge. In February,
William Branch Giles of Virginia, with the backing of Madison
and Jefferson, introduced a series of resolutions censuring Hamilton for the misapplication of government funds—supposedly
to shore up the Bank of the United States, and by implication
himself and his cronies. In one of the lowest moments of his
career, Madison spoke in favor of the resolutions in a lengthy
speech on March 1, 1793. Not only was this a petty shot at a former colleague and friend, but it also backfired badly. For when
Hamilton unveiled all the requested details, it was evident that
he had been acting in good faith all along. The censure motions
were overwhelmingly defeated.[5]

The purpose of the Giles resolutions was not actually to drive
Hamilton from office, at least not in the short term. The Federalist House majority in the Second Congress numbered about
nine seats (although party loyalties still being inchoate, both
sides always had to be wary of defections), and the resolutions
were introduced at the end of the Congress when there was no
hope of passage. It was, rather, part of the broader war to lower
the estimation of the secretary in preparation for a more direct
attack during the Third Congress, when the Republicans expected to have stronger control of the House. The true audience

for these partisan shenanigans was ultimately the president himself. The Republicans figured that once Washington came to appreciate Hamilton's true designs, and saw strong opposition to his leadership in Congress, he would push the secretary out.

But then in March news arrived in Philadelphia that the French revolutionaries had lopped off the head of Louis XVI. In that instant, everything changed.

WHEN IT BEGAN in 1789, the French Revolution was greeted with broad acclaim in America. It seemed as though France was following in the footsteps of the United States, embracing the principles of free government. When word came in early 1792 that Louis XVI had accepted the constitution of 1791, which reduced the monarchy mainly to a figurehead and empowered the French National Assembly, Madison spoke on the House floor in favor of a resolution praising the new government. But events took a dramatic turn in 1792, as Louis XVI denounced the constitution, attempted to escape, and was captured and eventually executed on January 21, 1793—a regicide that united the European powers against the revolutionary government. The Republic of France, already at war with Austria, declared war against Spain, the Netherlands, and Great Britain shortly thereafter.[6]

Americans were at first excited by the war. They wanted the French to stick it to those high-handed Brits, who had refused to abandon their posts in the northwest territory, despite their promise to do so in the Treaty of Paris of 1783. The British had even been arming Native Americans with an eye toward creating a Native buffer state in the region; their ultimate hope was to keep the region's lucrative fur trade for themselves. Jefferson had lobbied the British minister George Hammond relentlessly to leave the area, but he always gave the secretary of state the run-around, citing the failure of Americans to repay debts to British merchants as justification for his government's continued non-compliance with the treaty.

Madison hated the British with a passion and, like most Republicans, was to be counted as an ardent enthusiast for the cause of *liberté, égalité, fraternité*—to the point of excusing the bad behavior of the revolutionary government. On March 15, Madison wrote his friend George Nichols to report that France's conduct in the war had been "great both as free and a martial nation," and he hoped that it would "baffle all her enemies, who are in fact the enemies of human nature." In April, when he learned that the French Republic had made him an honorary citizen, Madison wrote a formal response that praised the Revolution for having played "a part towards banishing prejudices from the world and reclaiming the lost rights of mankind."[7]

But the Federalists were dubious. If the American Revolution had been a necessary fight to preserve and protect ancient rights, the events in France looked to be a radical and increasingly bloody upending of society. They were also profoundly concerned with the prospect of the United States being caught in the middle. Despite America's political independence from Great Britain, it was still closely entangled economically with its old motherland, which remained its number one trading partner by a large margin. Hamilton had repurposed this trade to build his elaborate system of public finance, which—thanks to the Bank of the United States—was helping proliferate private credit too. The whole architecture hinged upon the confidence of the federal government to pay its debts, which in turn required a steady stream of import duties, mainly on products from Great Britain. As Hamilton would later warn the president in 1794, interfering with this trade "would cut up credit by the roots."[8]

On April 18, Washington circulated to the cabinet a series of questions concerning what the United States should do about this war. When the cabinet met the next day, Hamilton suggested the president issue a proclamation of neutrality, despite the fact that the 1778 Treaty of Alliance pledged that the Americans would assist the French should their territories in the Americas come under threat. Jefferson, greatly sympathetic to the French cause, did not like this idea at all. He certainly did not want war, but he doubted the prudence of Hamilton's idea. He suggested that the United States drive a hard bargain. American neutrality was something that the administration should make the British and the French bid for.

Jefferson had constitutional qualms as well. The treaty-making power was shared jointly between the president and the Senate, while the authority to declare war belonged exclusively to Congress. How could the president unilaterally make such a decision? On the other hand, Congress was out of session until December, and the administration could not wait that long. Ultimately, the cabinet struck a bargain. The president would issue a proclamation that effectively declared neutrality without actually using the word. On April 22, the president proclaimed not that the United States was "neutral," but that the country would "with sincerity and good faith adopt and pursue a conduct friendly and impartial towards the belligerent powers."[9]

Back in Orange County for the congressional recess, Madison was intensely displeased. He wrote to Jefferson that he could "offer no bona fide explanations" to the questions critics were asking about the proclamation. What about the legal obligations of the United States to France? What about the moral duty of one republic to another? And why should the executive issue such a proclamation? It was the last one that irritated him the most. "The right to decide the question whether the duty and interest of the [United States] require war or peace under any given circumstances," he argued, "seems to be essentially and exclusively involved in the right vested in the legislature." Washington, he fretted, was unaware "of the snares" being laid "by men whose politics at bottom are very different from his own." In a subsequent letter to Jefferson, Madison wrote that he was "mortif[ied] . . . that [the president's] fame and influence should have been unnecessarily made to depend in any degree on political events in a foreign quarter of the globe." It was to be lamented that he had been tricked into issuing the proclamation, which "was in truth a most unfortunate error." Madison would never say it outright, but he believed Washington was being played for a fool.[10]

If Madison could never bring himself to criticize the president directly, the Republican press was hardly so indulgent. In June, the *National Gazette* printed a series of letters, penned by "Veritas," that laid into the Washington administration for the proclamation. Jefferson was horrified by these polemics. Given that Hamilton had already identified Jefferson and Madison as the patrons of the *National Gazette*, any criticism in that paper of Washington might damage their standing with the president. John Beckley suspected that William Irvine, a Hamilton clerk, had actually written the letters to push Washington further into the Federalist camp. Either way, the *National Gazette* had transformed from an asset into a liability for Madison and Jefferson. Once a forum to get the Republican message to the people, it had become a source of tension with the president. Mercifully, Philip Freneau shut down the paper during Philadelphia's yellow fever epidemic in September 1793 and never restarted it. Moving forward, the *Aurora General Advertiser*, edited by Benjamin Franklin Bache (grandson of Benjamin Franklin and a committed Republican), would become the main Republican newspaper. Madison and Jefferson would henceforth keep the press at arm's length, lest they run the risk of being identified with incendiary rhetoric.[11]

Hamilton, meanwhile, was eager to use the press to further his aims. On June 29, the Federalist *Gazette of the United States* published the first in a series of essays defending the proclamation, written by Hamilton under the pseudonym Pacificus. Rather than offer the cabinet's consensus view of the matter, Hamilton instead justified the "Proclamation of Neutrality," as he pointedly called it, on the broadest possible grounds, the very ones that had drawn Jefferson's ire. Conceding that executing the terms of the "treaty of alliance with France would be contrary to the sense and spirit of the proclamation," Hamilton argued instead that "*under the circumstances of the case*" the United States is "*not bound*" by the treaty to intervene. Moreover, Hamilton asserted that "though treaties can only be made by the president and Senate, their activity may be continued or suspended by the president alone." Jefferson was apoplectic. He wrote the next day to Madison complaining that Hamilton had transformed the "real . . . milk and water . . . views of the Proclamation" into "the sum of his arguments"—the ones Hamilton had made but the cabinet had rejected. A week later, Jefferson wrote Madison in a state of panic. "Nobody answers him," he lamented, "and his doctrine therefore will be taken for confessed. For God's sake, my dear sir, take up your pen, select the most striking heresies, and cut him to pieces in the face of the public. There is nobody else who can and will enter the lists with him."[12]

Madison, hundreds of miles away, was hesitant to jump into the fray. He wrote to Jefferson that since he was not privy to private discussions, the state of diplomatic negotiations, or the mind of the president on this matter, he should probably not engage with Hamilton. "None but intelligent readers will enter into such a controversy," he explained, so it was better he write nothing than something ill-informed. Ever accommodating to his best friend, he nevertheless expressed a willingness to try if nobody else would and asked Jefferson to send along any documents that might illuminate "the real object of the proclamation." Jefferson persisted with his entreaties, and by the end of July Madison relented. He had "forced" himself "into the task of a reply," even though responding to Hamilton was "the most grating one I ever experienced." He felt keenly "the want of counsel on some points of delicacy as well as of information as to sundry matters of fact," and he anticipated that the "prolixity and pertinacity" of Hamilton would ensure "that the business will not be terminated by a single fire."[13]

On August 24, the *Gazette of the United States* published the first of Madison's five essays under the pseudonym Helvidius. In it, he offered a detailed analysis on the nature of treaty making and treaty suspending, concluding, contrary to Hamilton, that these actions "can never fall within a proper definition of executive powers." The executive was merely "a convenient organ of preliminary communications with foreign governments . . . and the proper agent for carrying into execution the final determinations of the competent authority." Since treaties have "the force and operation of laws," their creation and suspension belong properly to the legislature. In other words, Hamilton had it exactly wrong. The joint responsibility of treaty making between the executive and Senate was not an exception to executive authority; it was a check on legislative authority. Where the Constitution was silent (as in the case of suspending a treaty), the power should be assumed to reside with Congress, not the president.[14]

The Pacificus and Helvidius essays were the first time Madison and Hamilton engaged in a war of letters in the press, but given the partisan buildup over the last three years, it made for a disappointing forensic contest. The two were basically talking past one another. Hamilton asserted early on a sweeping power for the executive on the matter of treaties but hardly demonstrated such an authority with any careful reasoning. Instead, he spent the bulk of his efforts justifying why Washington was right to set aside the Franco-American treaty of 1778. His main political agenda was to shift public opinion away from the French Republic. Madison, on the other hand, was telescopic in his analysis. He avoided the broader foreign policy crisis, since neither he nor Jefferson actually wanted war. He was also at pains to denounce Hamilton's view of executive-legislative relationships without actually criticizing the proclamation (even though he did not like it), lest he offend Washington. Instead, Madison tried to reframe the debate along existing Republican-Federalist lines, suggesting that Hamilton was looking to swap American republicanism for a British-style monarchy. "The power of making treaties and the power of declaring war," Madison warned in Helvidius 1, "are royal prerogatives in the British government, and are accordingly treated as Executive prerogatives by British commentators." In Helvidius 4, Madison argued that the sweeping powers Hamilton argued the president had could only be safe in the hands of a hereditary monarch. An "*elective and temporary* magistrate" cannot be trusted with such vast authority. Thus, Hamilton's doctrine was actually "an *argument* and *advance* towards the security afforded by the personal interests of an *hereditary* magistrate."[15]

The Helvidius-Pacificus exchange had an ethereal quality, as Hamilton and Madison were debating over theories that had no real-world analogues. The proclamation was a carefully worded, narrow statement of American nonintervention that anybody with sense knew was the only viable course. Hamilton's pontificating in the Pacificus essays was spin, with no force of law behind it. Jefferson overreacted to their publication, and Madison probably should have told Jefferson not to panic. Instead, he indulged his friend, writing essays in response that were labored, pedantic, and repetitive. The only thing they illuminated was how intensely Madison had come to detest Hamilton.

———————

SHORTLY AFTER IT executed Louis XVI, the French Republic set the stage for a diplomatic crisis with America by sending Edmond-Charles Genêt to the United States as its minister. Citizen Genêt, as he was styled by the French Republic, landed in Charleston on April 8, 1793, and began a leisurely tour of the country. At every point along the way, he was greeted rapturously by Americans celebrating the freedom of the French people. By early May, he finally arrived in Philadelphia and made a good initial impression upon Jefferson. "It is impossible for anything to be more affectionate, more magnanimous than the purpose of his mission," he raved to Madison. "He offers everything and asks for nothing." But in fact Genêt asked for quite a bit. He wanted the president to accept France's interpretation of the 1778 treaty and allow it to set up a base of operations in the United States for the purposes of defending its colonies in the West Indies. He also wanted immediate repayment of the loans that France had made to the United States. These were extravagant demands, and even the most accomplished diplomat would have struggled to extract anything approaching them from the Washington administration. But Genêt was a fool. Against the explicit instructions of the Washington administration, he outfitted a ship called the *Little Democrat* and dispatched it on raids against British ships. He had mistaken his adoring crowds as the true voice of the nation. Believing that the country was with him and not the president, he threatened to take his case directly to the people.[16]

By July, he had exhausted Washington's patience. "Is the minister of the French Republic to set the acts of this government at defiance—with impunity?" Washington incredulously asked Jefferson. "What must the world think of such conduct, and of the government of the U[nited] States in submitting to it?" Jefferson, already in a state of agitation over Hamilton's Pacificus essays, was beside himself over Genêt. "Never in my opinion," he wrote to Madison, "was so calamitous an appointment made, as that of the present minister of F[rance]. . . . Hotheaded, all imagination, no judgment, passionate, disrespectful and even indecent towards the [president] in his written as well as verbal communications, talking of appeals from him to Congress, from them to the people, urging the most unreasonable and groundless propositions, and in the most dictatorial style." Back in Orange County, Madison reported to Monroe that Genêt's "conduct has been that of a madman."[17]

The Genêt fiasco played right into the hands of the Federalists, who encouraged communities to enact proclamations that contrasted the antics of Genêt with the steady prudence of the Neutrality Proclamation. The Federalists also attacked the "democratic societies" that had sprung up on the diplomat's arrival. These spontaneous civic organizations were on the fringe of Republican politics in their calls for democracy and equality. The Federalists saw in them the same kind of French radicalism that had wrought so much havoc in Europe and used them to tarnish the entire Republican Party. Madison speculated to Archibald Stuart, a Virginia politician who had studied law under Jefferson, that the Federalists were trying "to turn the public sensation with respect to Genêt against the French nation," "produce . . . an animosity between America and France," and forge "a consequent connection with Great Britain, and under her auspices, of a gradual approximation towards her form of government."[18]

By midsummer, enough was enough. Jefferson reported to Madison on August 3 that the cabinet unanimously voted to "require the recall of Genêt," whom Jefferson feared would "sink the Republican interest." While Genêt was embarrassing himself in the United States, the French government was undergoing another revolution. The moderate Girondist faction, of which Genêt was a part, had been removed from power by the radical Jacobins, who ordered Genêt to return to France, where he likely would be executed. Genêt requested asylum in the United States, and—at the urging of Hamilton—Washington granted it. Genêt married the daughter of George Clinton and lived the rest of his days quietly in upstate New York.[19]

If the French (or at least Genêt) were a nuisance, the British were becoming a menace. Their refusal to vacate the northwest territory had long been a source of frustration, and their actions in 1793 only heightened the tensions. They negotiated a peace treaty between the Portuguese and the Algerian corsairs, which freed the Algerian pirates to begin raiding American merchants in the Mediterranean. More ominously, the British reinstated what was commonly called the Rule of 1756. Unable to maintain the food supply to its West Indian colonies, France had opened its colonial ports up to American merchants, a privilege not enjoyed during peacetime. The Rule of 1756—named after the commercial policy the British had employed during the French and Indian War—sought to squash this trade by declaring that ports that had been closed during peacetime could not be opened during war. An order in council issued by the British government in June authorized the Royal Navy to redirect any foreign vessels traveling to French ports with foodstuffs to British ports, where the provisions would be purchased. The United States did not recognize the legitimacy of the Rule of 1756 and saw it as a violation of the commercial rights of neutral nations. Jefferson formally protested these actions to British minister George Hammond, but he was rebuffed. The British were intent upon pressing every advantage against the French that they could, even if that meant antagonizing the Americans.[20]

When Congress reconvened in the fall of 1793, the time seemed ripe to Madison to push once more for commercial discrimination. If the British were going to be high-handed on the high seas, the Americans should respond in kind by raising the cost for them to trade with the United States. On December 16, Jefferson released his *Report on Commerce*, which proposed higher taxes on imports from Great Britain in response to its refusal to sign a commercial treaty. Congress had commissioned Jefferson to write the report back in 1791, but he had withheld it until the political moment was right. In the House, Madison used Jefferson's report as the basis for a new round of discriminatory measures against Great Britain.[21]

Ultimately, however, this was a battle Madison would have to wage without his closest friend and ally, for Jefferson left the State Department on December 31. The departure had been a long time coming. Indeed, Jefferson had never really wanted the job in the first place. After his stint as French minister, he had longed to return to Monticello—his estate in the Virginia Piedmont—and had taken the post mainly out of a sense of duty. Since then, he had grown tired of dealing with Hamilton. It was not just the pointed debates in the cabinet, but the treasury secretary refused to limit his portfolio to matters of finance. Instead, Hamilton meddled freely in matters of foreign policy. The Pacificus essays substituted his judgment for the consensus of the cabinet, and he long had been engaging in shadow diplomacy with Hammond, whose interactions with Jefferson were accordingly stiff and unproductive, for he knew Hamilton would be more sympathetic to the British interest.

Washington told Jefferson that Madison was his first choice as replacement, but the latter wanted no part of the cabinet. Years later, Madison explained to Light-Horse Harry Lee that he had refused Washington's offer to remain true to his original decision to serve in the House. That may very well have been the case, but there is no doubt that Madison, having seen how Hamilton dabbled in diplomacy, did not want the hassle either. Either way, it was a fateful refusal. Washington, looking to maintain balance in the cabinet, tapped for the job Attorney General Edmund Randolph, Madison's old friend and a moderate Republican. But the ever-indecisive Randolph was not up to the task. Jefferson was not far from the mark when he complained to Madison that Randolph was "the poorest chameleon I ever saw, having no color of his own and reflecting that nearest him." He stood no chance against Hamilton.[22]

Jefferson's departure coincided with the first crisis in Anglo-American relations since the end of the Revolutionary War. On November 6, the British government issued a new order in council, which authorized the seizure of all ships coming from or going to the French West Indies. Deviously, the British kept the order secret from the world until late December, when the trading lanes would be packed with American merchants. About 150 American ships were captured in the British dragnet. Then, in February 1794, Lord Dorchester, the governor of British North America, delivered a fiery address to the Natives in which he declared, "I shall not be surprised if we are at war with [the United States] in the course of the present year."[23]

News of these events reached the American government by late winter 1794. If nothing else, this new British aggressiveness made the plan for commercial retaliation seem like a half measure, though Madison still believed in it. He wrote to Horatio Gates, the famed Revolutionary War general, that he did not see "a design to make war" in these British aggressions. Doing so would turn American trade against Britain and into the waiting arms of the French. "I conclude therefore," he wrote, "that she will push her aggressions so far and no farther, than she imagines we will tolerate." He was relieved to learn in April that Great Britain had rescinded the November 6 order. Madison believed this was an illustration of the potential commercial influence the Americans had to leverage.[24]

The center of action remained Washington's cabinet—and with Jefferson gone, Hamilton held the whip hand. Enraged by British effrontery, he encouraged Washington to enact a temporary embargo and begin a military buildup. Hamilton also read the riot act to Hammond, who reported to his superiors back in London that the secretary had "entered into a pretty copious recital of the injuries which the commerce of this country had suffered from British cruisers, and into a defense of the consequent claim which the American citizens had on their government to vindicate their rights." Though Hamilton wanted to prepare for war with Great Britain, he still had every interest in avoiding one if he could, and he prevailed upon Washington to appoint a special minister to travel to Great Britain to negotiate a treaty. His Federalists allies wanted the post to go to Hamilton, but he was too controversial to win nomination in the Senate. Instead, Washington appointed Chief Justice John Jay, a nomination that suited Hamilton just fine, as the two were basically in agreement on the central importance of good Anglo-American relations.[25]

Jay was commissioned on April 19, which effectively paused the crisis for nearly a year, as overseas diplomatic negotiations moved at a snail's pace in the eighteenth century. In the interim,

US politics ground to a bitter standstill, with neither the Federalists nor the Republicans able to enact their agenda through
Congress. That summer, whiskey distillers and disaffected settlers in western Pennsylvania revolted against the federal government, complaining about a new excise tax on spirits as well
as a lack of representation in Congress. Washington assembled
a militia force that quickly put an end to the rebellion. In his
annual address to Congress in November, the president blamed
the democratic societies for stirring up the rebellion—a not-so-
subtle shot at the Republicans. Once more, Madison suspected
the influence of Hamilton. "The game," he speculated to Monroe, "was to connect the democratic societies with the odium of
the insurrection, to connect the Republicans in Congress with
those societies, [and] to put the [president] ostensibly at the head
of the other party, in opposition to both." By this point, Madison
no longer had any influence over the president. The two would
maintain a cordial relationship for the rest of Washington's life,
but their days of close collaboration were gone for good.[26]

DURING THIS EXTENDED break in the political action, Madison finally found time for a personal life. Or perhaps better put,
he found the right woman with whom to build one. In the late
summer of 1794, he wed a beautiful young widow named Dolley Payne Todd. The groom was forty-three years old and the
bride twenty-six. It was a little peculiar that Madison had never
before married, but then again there was very little that was typical of James Madison. Shy and reserved in large gatherings, he
had never been one to charm a room, leaving him at a distinct
disadvantage at the kind of soirees in Philadelphia that might
have found him a wife. Moreover, his dedication to politics was

so thorough that he never seemed to spare a thought for anything else. And Madison was, in his own way, a romantic. He was looking to marry not for social status or wealth, but for love. Since the Kitty Floyd fiasco back in 1783, he had not found anybody who had sparked his interest, until he laid eyes on Dolley.

Dolley Payne was born in the Quaker community of New Garden, North Carolina, on May 20, 1768, to John Payne and Mary Coles, who hailed from two of Virginia's more prominent families. Shortly after Dolley's birth, her parents moved back to Hanover County, Virginia. Her mother was born into the Quaker faith, but her father was a convert, possessed of all the attending zeal. When Dolley was fifteen years old, John Payne freed his slaves and moved the family to Philadelphia, where he opened a laundry-starch manufacturing business. John struggled with debts, and his business shut down in 1789. Believing spiritual rectitude and business acumen went hand in hand, the Quakers booted John Payne from the Pine Street Meeting for failing to pay his debts, and he died a few years later—but not before securing Dolley's hand in marriage to John Todd, a successful lawyer and Quaker. The two were married in the winter of 1790, when Dolley was twenty-one years old.

The Todds moved into a fine home at the corner of Fourth and Walnut in Philadelphia, and the family set about filling it with luxury furniture, contrary to the simple pietism of the Quaker lifestyle. Dolley had always struggled under those strictures. When she was a young girl, her grandmother had given her a gold broach, which she had to hide secretly under her dress. As a young wife, she was not a particularly "good" Quaker; she liked pretty dresses and fine home goods.

She bore John two sons: John Payne, nicknamed Payne, born in the winter of 1792, and William, born in the summer of 1793. But a few months later, tragedy struck the family, as a yellow fever epidemic swept across Philadelphia. John and William both succumbed to the disease. Dolley moved young Payne and herself back into her mother's home, which had been converted into a boardinghouse for politicians like Aaron Burr, and where her younger sister Anna lived. Many families had to endure tragedies such as that which befell Dolley. Some five thousand people died in the city's outbreak. Like so many others who had to bury loved ones, she picked herself up and moved on, because she had to.

She soon became the most eligible bachelorette in all of Philadelphia. Her niece, Martha Cutts, wrote that she had a "beauty, loveliness of character and perfect freedom from vanity" that "soon became celebrated." At five feet seven and "well proportioned, her features were pleasing," with porcelain skin, black hair, blue eyes, and a mouth that was especially "beautiful in shape and expression." It was said that men would stare at her dumbstruck as she walked down the street, prompting a friend to say, "Really, Dolley, you must hide your face." She quickly accumulated a large number of suitors, one of whom was Madison. In the spring of 1794, Burr (who perhaps had his advances rebuffed, on account of his being married) played matchmaker between Dolley and "the great little Madison," as she is reported to have called him.[27]

Madison worked his charms quickly on Dolley. He asked Catherine Coles, the wife of her uncle, to tell Dolley he "thinks so much of you in the day that he has lost his tongue; at night he dreams of you and starts in his sleep a calling on you to relieve his flame for he burns to such an excess that he will shortly be consumed and he hopes that your heart will be callous to every other swain but himself." While he lacked the traditional physical qualities of masculinity—being unusually short and slim and often sickly—he was still quite the catch. He was gentlemanly, warmhearted, extremely funny in intimate gatherings, and very successful. When Madison asked for her hand in marriage that summer, Dolley said yes, and on September 16, 1794, the two were married at Harewood, the estate of George Steptoe Washington, the nephew of President George Washington and brother-in-law to Dolley. Madison's younger sister Frances was in attendance.[28]

For Madison, it was no doubt a love match. Dolley's charm, grace, and beauty were virtually beyond compare, and he was smitten. But Dolley seemed to have had a more pragmatic view of the nuptials, at least at first. No doubt, over the next forty years she would fall deeply in love with him, but it seems as though in the summer of 1794 she was driven by common sense. She wrote her friend Eliza Collins Lee, the wife of Virginia politician Richard Bland Lee, that she had married "the man who of all others I most admire," joining in a union that "is soothing and grateful in prospect—and my little Payne will have a generous and tender protector." These were hardly the words of a woman who was head over heels, but the love she would eventually share with "the great little Madison" would nevertheless be profound.[29]

Having wed Madison less than a year after the death of John, Dolley had violated Quaker rules regarding appropriate mourning periods, and she was unceremoniously booted from the Society of Friends. This seems to have suited her just fine. Absent their regulations of dress and furnishing, she could truly come into her own. She became one of the most charming hostesses of Philadelphia society, and her wit, glamour, and beauty made an invitation to dine with the Madisons one of the most sought-after social engagements. Dolley loosened up the otherwise stiff Madison, and he would evolve into an amiable, engaging cohost of his wife's fashionable events.

THE INTERLUDE IN foreign troubles was never going to last forever. Finally, the president received the details of the Jay Treaty on March 7, 1795. Washington was not pleased, and for good reason. Jay had gained precious little by way of concessions from Great Britain: a pledge to leave the northwest territory (which it had already promised to do back in 1783), an allowance for small American ships to trade directly with the British West Indies (although this was attached to so many commercial restrictions that the Senate ultimately rejected the provision), and a more generous allowance to trade with British colonies in the East Indies. For these minimal concessions, Jay pledged that the United States would not discriminate against British trade, acceded to a very expansive definition of what constituted contraband that could be seized from American vessels, and agreed to send disputes over past seizures to third-party mediation. Great Britain did not renounce the Rule of 1756 and made no pledge to do so.

Washington knew the treaty was a dog, but he nevertheless handed it off to the Senate for its consideration. The Senate debated the treaty in secret, and it was not until a copy was leaked to the *Aurora General Advertiser* that the public discovered what Jay had actually negotiated. The country was incensed. The newspapers lit into him with an unyielding ferocity, and the diplomat was even burned in effigy in Lexington, Kentucky. Washington was not spared from criticism, either, with an article in the *Aurora* calling him the "omnipotent director of a seraglio, instead of the first magistrate of a free people. He thunders disdain upon the people." Madison likewise hated the treaty. In August 1795 he complained to Robert Livingston, the chancellor of New York who would later serve as minister to France under Jefferson, that it was a "ruinous bargain" that disregarded the rules of "justice and equality" and lashed the United States to the mast of Great Britain, just as the Federalists wanted. "The treaty from one end to the other," he wrote, "must be regarded as a demonstration that the party to which the envoy belongs . . . is a British party, systematically aiming at an exclusive connection with the British government, and ready to sacrifice to that object as well the dearest interests of our commerce, as the most sacred dictates of national honor."[30]

Hamilton was generally happy with the treaty. It secured peace with Great Britain, foreclosed Madison's plan to enact commercial discrimination, brought a resolution to the lingering tensions in the northwest, and, most important of all, protected Hamilton's system of finance. The secretary once more took to the newspapers to unleash a torrent of words in defense of the treaty, writing a remarkable twenty-four essays under the pseudonym Camillus, plus another four as Philo Camillus. Back at Monticello, Jefferson implored Madison to respond: "For God's sake take up your pen, and give a fundamental reply." But Madison demurred. He was dissatisfied with his Helvidius letters and did not want to enter public debate with Hamilton once more.[31]

The Senate ratified the treaty by the bare minimum of two-thirds necessary to approve all foreign agreements. Congress went into recess, public passions began to cool, and the matter seemed to be over. But the Republicans still held a sizeable majority in the House, and the treaty's most vehement critics were intent on stopping it there by any means necessary. On March 2, 1796, Congressman Edward Livingston of New York, the younger brother of Robert, proposed resolutions calling on Washington to submit a copy of Jay's instructions as well as any correspondence and documents related to the treaty. This was merely a fishing expedition to unveil information that might embarrass the administration. Still, Madison supported it, although he admitted that interpreting the Constitution to include the House in treaty-making powers was hardly "free from difficulties," and he privately told Jefferson that it was such a "questionable" idea that Livingston "will probably let it sleep or withdraw it." But Livingston pressed on, and his resolution passed the House on March 25 by a twenty-five-vote margin. In an uncharacteristically blunt retort, Washington categorically refused the House's request. Invoking what today is known as executive privilege, the president explained that the "nature of foreign negotiations requires caution, and their success must often depend on secrecy." In a not-so-subtle rebuke of Madison, the president went on to remind the House that he had "been a member of the general convention" that framed the Constitution, and it was his strong impression from that conclave that the "power of making treaties is exclusively vested in the president, by and with the advice and consent of the Senate."[32]

The Republicans persisted, hatching a scheme to deny funding for the commissions that the treaty had established to resolve outstanding disputes. This was, at best, a dubious exercise of the House's authority, since Washington was right that the Founders had excluded the House from treaty making. Madison, in one of the least considered moments of his career, supported this move, so incensed was he over the terms of the Jay Treaty. Fisher Ames, a leading Federalist from Massachusetts, wrote that Madison had been "irrevocably disgraced, as a man void of sincerity and fairness." That was an overstatement from a partisan opponent, but it is still hard to deny that Madison once more had allowed his policy preferences to dictate his understanding of the Constitution. In two lengthy but uncompelling speeches on the House floor, he was at pains to defend himself from the charge of inconsistency, an accusation that wounded him deeply.[33]

Republican headcounters in the House were confident that they had the numbers to defund the commissions, but they were wildly overoptimistic. It was one thing to ask Washington for papers, quite another to interfere with the implementation of a duly enacted treaty. And public opinion in the North had begun to swing in favor of the Jay Treaty, as the merchant community celebrated the maintenance of peace and the prospect of commercial prosperity. Republican support evaporated in the mid-Atlantic delegations, and the twenty-five-vote margin to compel Washington to hand over the documents in March collapsed into a tie vote to deny funding in April, which Speaker of the House Frederick Muhlenberg broke in favor of the administration. Madison was bitter in defeat, blaming the loss, in a letter to Jefferson, on "the unsteadiness, the follies, the perverseness, and the defections among our friends," whom he derided as "wrongheads."[34]

The Republican failure was complete. Hamilton and the Federalists had extracted everything they could possibly have wanted from the war between Britain and France. The country had brokered a tighter connection with Great Britain, as the Jay Treaty foreclosed the possibility of commercial discrimination. Washington had been totally alienated from the Republicans. Even Randolph, the last Republican in the cabinet, was embarrassed into resigning in the summer of 1795 due to indiscreet communications with the French. The British had intercepted a packet from French minister Joseph Fauchet to his government in Paris, which contained the report of a candid conversation between Randolph and Fauchet. Randolph posited to Fauchet that British agents were trying to use the Whiskey Rebellion to start an insurrection, and he suggested that French bribes to a few indebted agents might help the French position. Read through a Federalist lens, it looked as though Randolph was soliciting a bribe; in truth, he was just in over his head. Washington revealed the information to Randolph in front of the entire cabinet, and the secretary resigned the following day. The president replaced him with Timothy Pickering, a stalwart ally of Hamilton. Madison, who had once enjoyed the close confidence of Washington, was now totally on the outside looking in.

10

THE VIRGINIA RESOLUTIONS

IF NOTHING ELSE, the Jay Treaty demonstrated that the Federalist Party was firmly in control of the government by the summer of 1796. Washington's original cabinet was long gone, replaced exclusively by Federalists: Timothy Pickering at the State Department, Oliver Wolcott at Treasury, James McHenry at the War Department, and Charles Lee as attorney general. Hamilton had retired from the Treasury Department in 1795 and returned to New York to start a private practice in the law, but he still exercised enormous influence. Pickering and McHenry were especially loyal to him, and Washington still regularly counted on his counsel.

The Republicans, meanwhile, had been cut out of decision-making in the administration. Washington removed the last major Republican official, James Monroe, from his post as minister to France in the summer. Monroe caught the blame for France's bad disposition toward the Jay Treaty, and Washington suspected he had been undermining the administration's agenda. The president tapped Charles Cotesworth Pinckney to replace Monroe, explaining that he needed a minister who could be a "faithful organ" for the administration, "well attached to the government of his own country." Madison was taken totally by surprise by the move, and blamed Monroe's ouster on the machinations of the "British faction."[1]

Exhausted and frustrated by a difficult eight years in office, Washington formally announced his departure from public life in September 1796, but political insiders had known for about a year that he planned to retire, meaning there would be a presidential election, the first in which the two parties would be competing with one another. On the Republican side, Jefferson was the only option for president. No other national figure could unite the Republicans across the country. The problem was that Jefferson appeared to be done with politics for good. He had returned to Monticello in 1795 and seemed to be enjoying his life as a country gentleman. So, the campaign for his election was waged entirely by others, via the newspapers, pamphlets, circular letters, and endorsements by state legislative caucuses. Madison figured that Jefferson would take whatever job was thrust upon him, but he was careful not "to push him," as he wrote Monroe, lest he "mar the project . . . by a peremptory and public protest." So careful was Madison that he even avoided visiting Monticello, so as not to present his friend with "an opportunity of protesting . . . against being embarked in the contest."[2]

Republicans were divided on their options for vice president. Senator Aaron Burr of New York was an obvious standout. He had distinguished himself among Republicans in his opposition to the Jay Treaty, and better yet he would provide the Republican ticket with regional balance. But there were doubts about Burr's character. He was a known womanizer, and he had defied the conventions of eighteenth-century statesmanship by actively campaigning for himself as vice president in New England. One simply did not pursue office, at least not openly; rather, one was to accept with ostensible humility when the office was offered by the people. John Beckley suggested to Madison it might be "prudent to vote one half" of Virginia's electoral votes "for [George] Clinton," which is ultimately what happened.[3]

The Federalists, meanwhile, were not as cohesive as their present national standing might have suggested. Hamilton was the intellectual leader of the party and its most forceful personality, but he was far too polarizing to be a candidate for public office. John Jay had certainly distinguished himself as a diplomat, and he had the confidence of the Hamiltonians. However, the treaty with Great Britain had been a political disaster, and the South was still nursing bruised feelings over the aborted Jay-Gardoqui Treaty of 1786. So, almost by default, the Federalist choice for president went to John Adams, much to Hamilton's disappointment. Adams was certainly a Federalist by disposition, but he had expressed skepticism about Hamilton's economic system in general and the bank in particular. Above all, Adams was his own man, not to be cowed by the likes of Hamilton.

So, Hamilton hatched a convoluted scheme to deny Adams the presidency by pairing him on the Federalist ticket with Thomas Pinckney of South Carolina. In the original design of the Electoral College, presidential electors cast two votes for president, without specifying whom they preferred for the presidency or vice presidency. Whoever won the majority of the electors became president, and the second-place finisher became vice president. Hamilton's plan was to encourage electors in the northern states to vote a straight Federalist ticket, then hope that a few southern Republicans might be inclined to cast a vote for Pinckney out of regional solidarity, thereby placing him ahead of Adams.[4]

Ultimately, Hamilton's plotting came to nothing. Southern Republicans figured out what he was doing and held the line. Adams won a narrow victory—seventy-three votes to sixty-eight for

Jefferson—in the wake of a very nasty contest. Though the two contenders demurred from campaigning and still regarded each other as friends, their surrogates engaged in a vicious pamphlet war that saw Jefferson castigated as an atheist and Jacobin, and Adams as a pig-headed monarchist. Moreover, the French minister, Pierre-Auguste Adet, inserted himself into the campaign by publishing a series of dispatches in the *Aurora General Advertiser* warning that the French government was reconsidering its relationship with the United States in light of the Jay Treaty. This was a very obvious effort to tip the scales in favor of the Republicans, who were known as the pro-French party, but it backfired. It did not sway any electoral votes toward Jefferson and solidified an impression among Federalists that their opponents were aligned with a foreign power to undermine American interests.

For how vitriolic the campaign was, Jefferson was perfectly content to serve as vice president under Adams. "He has always been my senior from the commencement of our public life," Jefferson wrote to Madison in December, "and the expression of the public will being equal, this circumstance ought to give him the preference." Jefferson even drafted a letter to Adams congratulating him on his victory and commiserating with him on the scheming of his "archfriend of New York." But Madison warned Jefferson that the missive was too indiscreet to send, for it could give the false impression that Jefferson "might wish to make [Adams's] resentment an instrument for avenging that of others." Jefferson wisely refrained from sending it along.[5]

If Jefferson was content with the election of Adams, Madison was dyspeptic. He had never much cared for the curmudgeonly New Englander, despite Jefferson's warm recommendations. Like many of Adams's contemporaries, Madison found him vain, irascible, and self-righteous. Worse, in Madison's judgment, his commitment to republican government was dubious. Madison never forgave Adams for the "sin" of writing *A Defense of the Constitutions of Government of the United States of America* in 1787, a sweeping and at times shambolic discussion of the proper organization of government. Adams wrote that disparate "advantages of birth, fortune, and fame" inevitably created inequality, and that government had to manage these distinctions between the haves and the have-nots. He argued that the wealthy and wellborn should have a branch of government all to themselves, and he defended the American state governments partially on the basis that their senates tended to draw upon these better sorts. As far as eighteenth-century political theory was concerned, this was a perfectly mainstream idea. Unlike Hamilton, Adams did not place particular trust in the aristocrats or oligarchs; rather, he wanted them quarantined in the Senate so they did not infect the rest of the government. Nevertheless, Madison had marked Adams as a man "unfriendly to republicanism" back in 1787, and it was a view he still held a decade later.[6]

LUCKILY FOR ADAMS, he would not have to square off directly against Madison during his turbulent administration. Madison's term in the Fourth Congress, which adjourned in early 1797, would be his last. His departure from the House had been a long time coming. Fifteen months earlier, Jefferson had expressed a "fear of your retirement" and urged him to "hold on . . . my dear friend." But Madison was done. He had told his father in the late winter of 1796 that he was "extremely anxious" for his "liberation from this place," and with the adjournment of Congress, he was ready to come home to Montpelier. He rebuffed the entreaties of John Taylor of Caroline—Jefferson's friend and a leader of the Virginia Republicans—that he run for governor. Madison told his father that he had no desire to be drafted as a candidate for the House of Delegates either, and that "if Mr. Jefferson should call and say anything to counteract my determination, I hope it will be regarded as merely expressive of his own wishes on the subject, and that it will not be allowed to have the least effect."[7]

Madison had been in politics in one way or another for twenty years, starting in his midtwenties. Now in his midforties, he needed a break. He needed a real home. He had been little more than an occasional sojourner at Montpelier since he had left for the College of New Jersey a quarter century early. His father needed him too. Madison's younger brother Ambrose, who had helped his father in managing the family's sprawling estate, had died in the fall of 1793. The elder James Madison, now seventy-six years old, was in declining health.

In the spring of 1797, Madison returned to Montpelier to live the life of a country squire. With Dolley, his new stepson Payne, and teenage sister-in-law Anna in tow, he brought with him a sizeable new family of his own and set about overseeing a massive expansion to the main house. A thirty-foot extension on the north end of Montpelier added four rooms: a parlor and dining room downstairs and two bedrooms upstairs. It also transformed Montpelier into a duplex, framed by a Tuscan portico that Madison had built. Madison's mother and father continued to live in the original house, while James, Dolley, Payne, and Anna occupied the new half. Madison would make later additions in the nineteenth century, after his father died, merging the duplexes, adding wings to the north and south ends, and enlarging the windows. The remodel in the 1790s would transform it basically into the form it has today, with an emphasis on the symmetrical Georgian style popular in the late colonial period and in contrast to Jefferson's Monticello, which emphasized Italian and French motifs.

Monroe shipped back from Europe assorted luxuries to fill out the home: serving dishes and fine china, furniture, a master bedroom set. Madison also had slowly built up an art collection, including a bust of George Washington that could serve as a conversation prompt for visitors. The interior, combined with the stately yet straightforward architecture of the building, left visitors with a distinct impression that the owner was a well-to-do but essentially republican planter. Over the next several years, Madison settled comfortably into his new life. His correspondence was briefer than it had been before, dealt less with politics (although it was still a subject of discussion), and more and more involved matters of home improvements and plantation affairs. For the rest of his life, tending to Montpelier would be a source of joy, comfort, and satisfaction.

This was a time of happiness for the recently married James and Dolley. Though the two never had children of their own, Madison was for all intents and purposes father to Payne, and Anna was just fifteen years old when they met. So, Madison's home life was suddenly full and happy. The family hosted friends and extended family frequently. Members of the Taylor clan from all across the area would stop by to dine and talk about politics. Jefferson would visit on his way from Philadelphia to Monticello, and the Madisons would begin their regular habit of going to his home twice a year. When Monroe returned from his service in Europe, he settled into an estate of his own near Monticello, and the Madisons would call on him as well. With his marriage to Dolley and return to Montpelier, Madison had transformed himself from an itinerant, professional politician into a republican gentleman.

MADISON'S RETIREMENT TO Montpelier marked the start of a new era in his personal life. The days of lengthy travels across the country and extended absences from Orange County were mostly over. He would instead stay firmly rooted in his family's estate and try to return home as often as he could. And so he would take control of the large community of enslaved people living at Montpelier. He was by all accounts not a strict master over them, but he expressed little interest in their freedom. Though he viewed human bondage as being incompatible with free government, this was not much more than an intellectual judgment. Slavery for him never seemed to have been a moral dilemma over which he lost sleep.

This divide between his heart and his head runs throughout his career in politics, whereby time and again he would acknowledge the injustices done to nonwhites yet never feel bestirred to action. At the Constitutional Convention, he bemoaned "the mere distinction of color made in the most enlightened period of time, a ground of the most oppressive dominion ever exercised by man over man." In *Federalist* 54 he referred to enslaved Africans as an "unfortunate race." He wrote to the Marquis de Lafayette in 1821 that slavery was a "sad blot on our free country." Madison thought that the slaves might someday be capable of a life of freedom. In 1789, he wrote a private memorandum on the logistics of a colony in Africa for freed slaves, "a benevolent experiment" which might encourage voluntary manumission for the "600,000 unhappy negroes . . . now involved." On a trip to the New York countryside in 1791, he made note of a "free negro" near Lake George who owned "a good farm of about 250 acres, which he cultivates with 6 white hirelings." Madison observed that "he is intelligent; reads, writes, and understands accounts, and is dexterous in his affairs." All in all, "by his industry and good management" his farm had turned "to good account."[8]

Yet Madison never did anything of substance to help African Americans realize this kind of life. Even his apparent gestures could have mixed motives. In 1783, while serving in the Continental Congress, Madison wrote his father regarding Billey, a slave who accompanied him on his trip to Philadelphia. Billey's trek northward had a profound effect on him, as Madison explained to his father, for he had begun to covet "the liberty for which we have paid the price of so much blood, and have proclaimed so often to be the right, and worthy the pursuit, of every human being." So, Madison decided not to bring him back to Virginia. But his intentions were not purely selfless, for he also warned that a liberty-loving Billey was too "thoroughly tainted to be a fit companion for fellow slaves in Virginia." Better for Montpelier to let Billey go than for him to spread the idea of freedom around to his fellow slaves. Indeed, Madison had at one point considered selling Billey to purchase philosophy books, a sobering juxtaposition of his intellectual acuity and moral blindness. Madison eventually sold Billey into indentured servitude; the young man changed his name to William Gardner, married and had a family, and worked in the mercantile trade.[9]

Madison tended to view the Native Americans with greater fear and disgust, at least in his youth when they were still warring with white settlers west of the Blue Ridge Mountains. In a 1774 letter to his college friend William Bradford, he noted the "unusual cruelty of the Indians," who sought the "extirpations" of the colonists during conflicts in territories in present-day Kentucky, Pennsylvania, and West Virginia. As he grew older, Madison's views would soften as the Native American threat receded. In 1822, he wrote that Native Americans "have special claims on our endeavors" to save them "from the vices" of the "savage mind" and "savage manners." The United States, Madison believed, should encourage the Native Americans to substitute "the torpid indolence of the Wigwam and the precarious supplies of the chase" with the "comforts and habits of civilized life," which will eventually make them capable of "moral and intellectual improvement."[10]

Madison's long-standing interest in civilizing the Native Americans and freeing the slaves illustrated that he did not believe they were hopelessly benighted, nor did he think that the natural state of the world was one of perpetual white supremacy. He was also keenly aware of the contradictions between the revolutionary language of liberty and republicanism on the one hand, and the chauvinism of the whites on the other. Still, this tension did not weigh heavily on his soul, and he never employed his vast political powers to bring about a plan of integration or colonization for the slaves or a civilizing program for the Natives. Indeed, his view of nonwhites was awfully convenient, seeing as how it reinforced the economic imperatives of the South without explicitly contradicting the radicalism of the American founding. The Natives had to be pacified, ultimately for their own good, and the slaves could not yet thrive under conditions of freedom. In its way, the gentry class of the Piedmont thought of itself as doing nonwhites a kindness.

Madison's late-in-life correspondence with Frances Wright was illustrative of his lifelong tendency to acknowledge intellectually the problem of white supremacy in a free society while simultaneously denying the moral imperative of finding a remedy. A Scottish-born social reformer, Wright began the Nashoba commune in Tennessee in 1825, a utopian-style community whose stated purpose was to prepare slaves for emancipation. That year, she wrote both Jefferson and Madison asking for public memorials in support. Neither would oblige her, but Jefferson at least encouraged her endeavor, arguing that "every plan should be adopted, every experiment tried, which may do something towards the ultimate object" of abolition. Madison, on the other hand, went out of his way to pour cold water on her scheme in a lengthy response. While admitting "the magnitude of this evil" of slavery, he noted that the "physical peculiarities" of the slaves precluded "their incorporation with the white population." Even if slave owners voluntarily freed their slaves, he did not think a communal mode of living—as then practiced by religious groups like the Shakers—would help prepare them for freedom. Moreover, exiling them would leave a "blank in the general field of labor" that would be "distressing in prospect to the proprietors of the soil"—namely, men like himself.[11]

Such was the contradictory nature of a liberty-loving republican who kept more than one hundred human beings in bondage. The unfortunate truth is that Madison's views on nonwhites were entirely typical for his day and age. There was a general, diffuse, and abstract sense of embarrassment among Virginia republicans who had been the most ardent backers of liberty and a widespread consensus that slavery was a problem to be solved by later generations. Madison was more than content to share this view. While he had a farsighted vision of the human potential for freedom, he never really tried to move beyond the racial and cultural chauvinism of his age.

———

WITH MADISON SETTLED in at Montpelier by the summer of 1797, the duty to spearhead the opposition to Federalism fell primarily upon Jefferson. He had been the informal leader of the Republican Party for several years. Though Madison had begun the fight against Hamilton and the Federalists, Jefferson was older in years and more prominent in reputation than Madison, who had long shown professional deference toward him. But Madison had been the party's intellectual workhorse, and with him now in semiretirement, Jefferson relied increasingly upon the formidable talents of Albert Gallatin, the Swiss-born Pennsylvania congressman. Gallatin was devoted in his Republicanism and probably the only one on the Republican side of the aisle who could go head-to-head against Hamilton in matters of public finance. In 1795, Gallatin helped organize the Ways and Means Committee, the first permanent committee in the House of Representatives, as a counterbalance to the influence of the Treasury Department on matters of congressional spending. With Madison gone, Gallatin would become the de facto leader of the Republicans in the House.

Meanwhile, the Adams administration was nothing but unending misery for the new chief magistrate. John Adams was perhaps the last true independent elected to the presidency, which placed him perpetually between a rock and a hard place. Congressional Republicans remained forever suspicious of him, and Federalist backers of Hamilton (often termed "High Federalists") still hoped to replace him with one of their own. Fatefully, Adams decided to retain Washington's cabinet, the most influential members of which—Timothy Pickering at the State Department, James McHenry at the War Department, and Oliver Wolcott at the Treasury—were allies of Hamilton. Pickering in particular took every opportunity to undermine the president in favor of Hamilton, until Adams finally fired him in the spring of 1800.[12]

The problem for Adams was the truculence of the French in the wake of the Jay Treaty. As Monroe had written from France to Madison, the French would rather "have an open enemy than a perfidious friend." With the defeat of Jefferson in the presidential election, the French took a substantially more aggressive posture toward the United States. Adams's fervent desire was for peace, while many High Federalists were eager for war with France to solidify the nation's relationship with Great Britain and secure the power of the Federalist Party at home. Meanwhile, the Republicans had not reconciled themselves to the Jay Treaty and were inclined to excuse French aggression.[13]

The flashpoint was the so-called XYZ Affair. The French government had refused to receive Charles Cotesworth Pinckney, whom Washington had appointed to replace Monroe as minister to France, and between the summer of 1796 and 1797 the French seized more than three hundred American ships. Their attitude was that if the Americans were going to excuse British aggressiveness in the Atlantic, as they seemingly had under the Jay Treaty, then the French would take the same liberties. Adams initially sought Jefferson or Madison as a replacement for Pinckney, though both rebuffed his entreaties. So Adams reappointed Pinckney along with John Marshall and Elbridge Gerry to serve as special envoys to reach an agreement with France. This was an act of bipartisanship on Adams's part—Pinckney and Marshall were Federalists, while Gerry was not—but it was not a particularly adroit move by the president. Gerry was independent minded to the point of cantankerous, and his personal vanity was a weak spot that the French could manipulate. And though Marshall was a rising star within the Federalist Party, he had not served in a diplomatic post, leaving him ill prepared for such a consequential appointment.

The mission was a disaster. Foreign Minister Charles Maurice de Talleyrand-Périgord (or Talleyrand for short) refused to meet with the American diplomats and sent agents—labeled "X, Y, and Z" in diplomatic communications—to ask for loans for the French government as well as a bribe for himself. When Adams got word of the insult, he made public the diplomatic communications to show the country how badly the French had behaved. This was a bold move to rally public opinion behind the president, and it worked—at least for a while. When

Adams asked Congress to strengthen America's coastal defenses
and create the Department of the Navy, the legislature obliged,
and the president even managed to garner a few Republican
votes. Congress also authorized the creation of a larger army,
up to twenty-two thousand soldiers. Soon, American naval vessels as well as privateers—legally authorized to outfit themselves
with armaments—were engaged in an undeclared conflict, or
the "Quasi-War" as it came to be called, with the French on the
high seas.

Meanwhile, Republicans faced a public-relations nightmare.
They had lashed themselves to the mast of a country that now
seemed intent to go to war with the United States. Madison
could not believe the Republicans' misfortune. In the spring
of 1798, he wrote Jefferson, "The conduct of Talleyrand is so
extraordinary as to be scarcely credible. I do not allude to its
depravity, which however heinous, is not without examples. Its
unparalleled stupidity is what fills one with astonishment." Just
as they had with the Genêt fiasco of 1794, the Republicans were
on the hook defending a government that, while it might have
had some ideological overlap with the Americans, was unreliable, capricious, and erratic.[14]

Luckily for the Republicans, the Federalists overplayed their
hand. They called for the creation of a standing army, which
made political sense in the spring of 1798 when war fever had
hit its peak, but the substantial cost of the internal taxes to pay
for it would alienate the country by the election of 1800. Moreover, Hamilton, though ostensibly a private citizen in New York,
was scheming to use the army as a pathway back to power. Adams named George Washington lieutenant general of the new
force, but the former president made it clear that he would only
be called into active service if a national emergency was truly
upon the country. So, the real power would be housed with

Washington's second in command. At Hamilton's urging, Secretary of State Pickering and even Washington himself insisted to Adams that Hamilton be named number two. Ever the visionary, in both brilliant and foolish ways, Hamilton speculated to his friends about using this army to conquer the interior of the continent and suppress domestic insurrections. This was sheer madness as far as Adams was concerned, and in his retirement he would compare Hamilton to Caesar and Octavius, "schem[ing] to get rid of Washington, Adams, Jay, and Jefferson, and monopolize all power to himself."[15]

But it was President Adams, not Hamilton, who made the fateful decision to sign into law the Alien and Sedition Acts of 1798. The Alien Acts restricted immigration into the United States and gave the president sweeping powers to deport immigrants. The Sedition Act made it a crime to "write, print, utter or publish . . . any false, scandalous and malicious writing or writings against the government of the United States, or either house of the Congress of the United States, or the President of the United States, with intent to defame the said government." This blatantly unconstitutional law was enacted supposedly to quell a rising Jacobin movement within the country. But anybody with an ounce of independent judgment saw it as a brazen Federalist attempt to rig the next election, for it expired on March 3, 1801, which happened to be the day before the next presidential inauguration. The contest against Jefferson and the Republicans had been very narrow in 1796. With Jefferson widely expected to be renominated, the Federalists wanted every advantage they could get in the rematch, even if it undermined the free character of the government.[16]

By enacting the Sedition Act, the Federalists inadvertently revived the fortunes of the Republicans. Many party newspapers were so tied to the French interest that they had been losing subscriptions. Jefferson worried to Madison in the spring of 1798 that Benjamin Franklin Bache's *Aurora General Advertiser*, the flagship of the Republican press, was "totter[ing] for want of subscriptions." Responding to his friend, Madison predicted that the Federalists were overreaching. "The sanguinary faction ought not," he wrote, "adopt the spirit of Robespierre without recollecting the shortness of his triumphs and the perpetuity of his infamy." Madison was right. Bache was arrested but died before he could stand trial. His successor at the *Aurora*, William Duane, was likewise charged under the Sedition Act, as were Republican printers across the country. But the Republicans responded to this assault by redoubling their efforts, and the number of party newspapers across the country increased dramatically. Often run by immigrants and artisans, these newspapers' ideological commitment to Republicanism was unwavering, and they denounced the Adams administration and the Federalist-controlled Congress in strident terms. By the time of the 1800 election, Connecticut senator Uriah Tracy complained that there seemed to be a Republican newspaper "in almost every town and county in the country."[17]

The political danger for the Republicans was for themselves to overreact to the Federalist assault on civil liberty. Some High Federalists no doubt hoped that the Republicans would take the bait—that they would take up arms against the government, prove themselves traitors, and allow the new, Federalist-dominated army to smash the rebels to pieces. Jefferson was supremely worried about this. Time and again in 1798 and 1799, he urged his allies to remain calm. "A little patience," he wrote to John Taylor of Caroline in June 1798, "and we shall see the reign of witches pass over, their spells dissolve, and the people, recovering their true sight, restore their government to its true principles." On January 30, 1799, he dashed off three letters, to Madison, Nicholas Lewis (Jefferson's friend and a prominent Piedmont planter), and Jefferson's son-in-law Thomas Mann Randolph, all on the same general theme. He wrote Lewis that "peace is ours unless we throw it away." To Madison, he advocated "firmness on our part, but a passive firmness." To Randolph, he explained that it was crucial that Virginia not do anything that would "occasion the middle states to rally round the measures which are ruining us."[18]

Madison was worried too, so much so that he put aside his life as a country gentleman to return to public affairs. He won election to the House of Delegates in 1799, with the intention of serving as a counterweight to Patrick Henry, who had abandoned his old principles and since become an ardent Federalist. But Henry died suddenly in July, and Madison would have a free hand in the state legislature, where he would pen one of most important yet least understood tracts of his career, the Virginia Resolutions.

MADISON'S VIRGINIA RESOLUTIONS seem to pair naturally with the Kentucky Resolutions, a series of declarations against the Alien and Sedition Acts that Jefferson wrote on behalf of the Kentucky legislature around the same time. Presumably, the two worked on these petitions in tandem, although the details of their collaboration remain mysterious. There is little surviving written correspondence between the two of them on the subject. It is likely they fleshed out the specifics during two face-to-face meetings in July at Montpelier and October at Monticello. However exactly they came into being, both the Kentucky and Virginia Resolutions were unequivocal denunciations of the Federalist-backed Alien and Sedition Acts, a defense of civil liberty, and a call to action for the other states. Yet the differences between them were substantial.

Jefferson's Kentucky Resolutions declared that the noxious laws were unconstitutional and thus "altogether void and of no force, and that the power to create, define, and punish such other crimes is reserved, and of right appertains solely and exclusively to the respective states, each within its own territory." This was a radical solution that would implicitly result in each state having a veto over national policy, for the act of nullifying the Sedition Act would establish the right of the states to strike down federal laws they think are unconstitutional. Not only was this a clear violation of the Constitution's Supremacy Clause, which established federal laws above state laws, but it would take the country back to the days of the Articles of Confederation, when the minority could thwart the majority. Nowhere does the Constitution give the states judicial authority over federal legislation, and insofar as that might be read into the Constitution (a dubious interpretation), such power certainly is not housed in the state legislatures. This is a point that Madison himself made to Jefferson in the winter, after the Kentucky Resolutions were published. "Have you ever considered thoroughly," he asked his friend, "the distinction between the power of the *state*, and that of *the legislature*, on questions relating to the federal pact?"[19]

While Jefferson's doctrine of nullification was as big a danger to the union as the Sedition Act, Madison offered an eminently reasonable alternative in the Virginia Resolutions. He declared that the states had the right "to interpose for arresting the pro[gress] of the evil, and for maintaining within their respective limits, the authorities, rights and liberties appertaining to them." In the "Report of 1800," which Madison wrote to defend the Virginia Resolution against the criticism it had received from other state governments, he elaborated on what interposition meant. It was not in any way intended as a judicial action. Rather, it was strictly political. "Where can be the impropriety of communicating the declaration to other states, and inviting their concurrence in a like declaration?" he asked. "What is allowable for one, must be allowable for all; and a free communication among the states, where the constitution imposes no restraint, is as allowable among the state governments, as among other public bodies, or private citizens." In other words, the purpose of Madisonian interposition was to rally the states to use their political influence—upon members of Congress from their states as well as their citizens—to persuade the federal government to rescind the law. Not only was there nothing inherently unconstitutional about this, but Hamilton of all people had made a similar argument. In *Federalist* 26, he argued that the "the state Legislatures, who will always be not only vigilant but suspicious and jealous guardians of the rights of the citizens, against encroachments from the federal government, will constantly have their attention awake to the conduct of the national rulers and will be ready enough, if any thing improper appears, to sound the alarm to the people and not only to be the VOICE but if necessary the ARM of their discontent." This was exactly what Madison was proposing.[20]

Though the Virginia Resolutions made no similar claims about state authority, their association with the Kentucky Resolutions damaged Madison's reputation as a resolute nationalist. Even John Quincy Adams, the son of President John Adams who would become a strong admirer of Madison, would write in 1836 that though Madison's arguments "have none of the deadly venom of Jefferson's nullification," he nevertheless "admitted rather too many of his premises." This was not a fair characterization. Admittedly, when viewed without consideration of the dramatic events of 1798, the Virginia Resolutions appear to depart from Madison's otherwise consistent nationalism. But the context is crucial for understanding what Madison's true project was.[21]

Madisonian republicanism was premised on the belief that wise and fair policy could emerge only when no faction was large enough to dictate terms to the rest. That was when each faction must begin to bargain, negotiate, and ultimately compromise with one another. Politics would save the republic, and for politics to work, the people must be free to think, speak, write, and organize without prior restraint from the government. As Madison wrote in the *National Gazette*, "Public opinion is the real sovereign in every free [government]." By criminalizing dissent, the Sedition Act struck right at the heart of self-government. Its passage was, for Madison, a national crisis of the first order.[22]

And how else was Madison supposed to defend the freedom of the press, now that the Federalists had criminalized dissent? He could not employ the newspapers, at least not without worrying about his publisher being arrested. Today, the courts defend the people's First Amendment rights, but in 1798 the courts were stocked with Federalist judges, many of whom were eagerly pushing for prosecutions under the Sedition Act. The Virginia House of Delegates, if nothing else, could not be jailed by the federal government. Madison could employ it to safely denounce the anti-republicanism of the Federalists in appropriately strident terms.

Madison has also drawn criticism for declaring that the Constitution was a compact to which the states were a party. Once more, if one reads the Virginia Resolutions as an analogue to the Kentucky Resolutions, this sounds problematic, perhaps admitting by implication the Jeffersonian idea of nullification. But given Madison's rejection of nullification, and indeed any judicial authority of the states over federal laws, Madison's position in 1798 is basically identical to the one he held about the Constitution for his whole life. As Madison wrote in *Federalist* 39 about ratification, it was an act by the people, "not as individuals composing one entire nation; but as composing the distinct and independent states to which they respectively belong." Likewise, in a letter in 1830 to Daniel Webster, a leading opponent of nullification, Madison affirmed that the American system "constitute[d] the people of the several states one people for certain purposes, with a government competent to the effectuation of them." It was exactly this understanding of a compact that informed the Virginia Resolutions.[23]

In sum, there were no controversial doctrines contained in the Virginia Resolutions, neither explicit nor implicit. To argue otherwise is to confuse Jefferson's thinking with Madison's. Still, there was a notable shift in emphasis for Madison between 1787 and 1798, one that requires some consideration. At the Constitutional Convention, he called for stripping most political power from the states. In 1798, he saw the states as a bulwark against anti-republicanism on the federal level. Why the change?

Again, the context is of signal importance. In 1787, Madison was looking to check dangerous majorities that dominated the state governments. In 1798, he was trying to rebut what he took to be a tyrannical minority in control of the federal government. The Virginia House of Delegates was solidly Republican, and absent viable alternatives, it made sense for Madison to employ it to attack the Federalists, whom he believed were a danger to the republic. In his view, the Federalists' crimes against the country were numerous: They had wrongly expanded the scope of power afforded the federal government to reward Hamilton's friends and allies with unmerited public policy benefits. They had negotiated a treaty that yoked the fate of the nation to its former colonial master Great Britain, led the nation on the path to war with France, and stifled those who dissented to this agenda. The High Federalists longed for the rule of elites and wished to turn "the Republican system of the United States into a monarchy," as Madison wrote in the "Report of 1800." There was a lot of hyperbole in this analysis, but there was no doubt that Madison's vision of self-government differed radically from the Federalist alternative.[24]

The Virginia Resolutions signified a change in Madison's defense of his philosophy, rather than a change in that philosophy itself. He was committed to the sovereign rule of the people of the United States, in accordance with the principles of justice and equity. The people alone were to govern, and properly organized they could generally be counted on to respect individual rights and promote the welfare of the whole country, as opposed to a handful of factions. This was the through line of his career to date, the consistent view he had expressed when he allied with the nationalists at the Continental Congress between 1780 and 1783, when he worked with the Federalists to adopt and ratify the Constitution between 1786 and 1788, when he backed the Bill of Rights and fought for the impost in 1789, when he opposed the financial policies and constitutionalism of Alexander Hamilton between 1790 and 1792, when he fought against increased presidential prerogatives during the foreign policy crises from 1793 to 1796, and finally when he authored the Virginia Resolutions. The strategies no doubt had changed given the circumstances, but the essential beliefs remained consistent.

––––––––––

THE VIRGINIA RESOLUTIONS may have been consistent with Madison's views of politics, but they were still a political disaster. Seven states replied in negative terms, none positively. And when Madison, as a member of the House of Delegates, penned the

"Report of 1800" to defend Virginia's stand, no states bothered even to reply.

Nevertheless, the year 1800 was a complete triumph for the Republican Party. Not only did Jefferson win more electoral votes than Adams, seventy-three to sixty-five, but the Republicans took the House of Representatives sixty-eight to fifty-three and held seventeen of thirty-four Senate seats. The main reason for this sweeping victory was that the Federalists had overextended themselves. The tax increases required for the military buildup led to violence in the countryside, as a band of armed men under the leadership of John Fries resisted the tax assessments in the German parts of eastern Pennsylvania. Fries's Rebellion, as it became known, was limited to Pennsylvania, but it was an illustration of popular discontent with Federalist policy. If any single factor drove the Republicans to victory, it was probably widespread public opposition to the Federalist tax increases.

The Federalists were again racked by internal divisions. Hamilton had wanted to beef up national defenses ultimately for the purpose of war against France. Though Adams favored the measures, what he really wanted was peace. So, too, did the French. Talleyrand recognized that he had misjudged the Americans and reached out to Gerry, who of the three ministers alone remained in France. Sensing an opportunity, Adams appointed William Vans Murray, minister to the Netherlands, Chief Justice Oliver Ellsworth, and North Carolina governor William Davie as new ministers to France. They negotiated the Convention of 1800, which ended the Quasi-War with the French. The High Federalists, especially Hamilton, were apoplectic. Peace would skunk their grand designs for the army and undermine their efforts to strengthen the alliance with Great Britain.

Once more, Hamilton schemed behind the scenes to use the party's vice-presidential nominee to boot Adams from the presidency. Once more, he used a Pinckney, this time Charles Cotesworth Pinckney. And once more, people saw it for the transparent ploy it was. Whatever political acumen Hamilton had possessed, he seemed to have lost it by the end of the decade. In one of the foolhardiest moves of his career, he published under his own name in October 1800 a vitriolic denunciation of President Adams. Running about fourteen thousand words, the "Letter from Alexander Hamilton, Concerning the Public Conduct and Character of John Adams" was a rambling screed that inadvertently helped the Republicans. It frustrated Hamilton's allies, further divided his party, and made him look like a fool. Decades later, Adams would assert that Hamilton had gone "stark mad"—a judgment that, though harsh, was hard to deny.[25]

If the Federalists were divided, the Republicans were more united than ever. A cross-regional alliance, anchored by strong party organizations in Virginia and New York, helped sweep Jefferson to victory. In New York, the choice of presidential electors was determined by a joint vote of both chambers of the state legislature, and New York City's at-large state Senate elections would be decisive in tipping the state one way or another. Burr took the lead in organizing the Republican interest in the city, swept the Jeffersonian slate to victory, and was rewarded with a spot as the vice-presidential candidate. Meanwhile, in Virginia, Republicans in the state legislature, led by Madison, changed the election law so that all electors would be chosen in a statewide vote, eliminating the opportunity for the Federalists to win a spare elector or two in their strongholds in the Tidewater region of the state, where the wealthiest traders and planters were more amenable to the party's financial policies.[26]

As it turned out, the Republicans were a little too disciplined for their own good, as their electors uniformly voted for Jefferson and Burr. In the end, the two carried seventy-three Electoral

College votes apiece, meaning that it was up to the House of Representatives to break the tie, with each state delegation getting one vote apiece. In January of 1801, when the prospect of a tie was certain, Madison wrote optimistically to Jefferson, "I can scarcely allow myself to believe that enough will not be found to frustrate the attempt to strangle the election of the people, and smuggle into the chief magistracy the creature of a faction." But the scarcely believable almost came true. The ever-ambitious Burr made overtures to frustrated Federalists in the House, inducing them to vote for him. Between February 11 and 17, 1801, the lower chamber deadlocked across thirty-five ballots: Jefferson winning eight states, Burr six, and two states split. Finally, on the thirty-sixth ballot, Jefferson won, as enough Federalist delegations backed down to provide him a ten-to-four victory.[27]

WHEN JEFFERSON GAVE his inaugural address on March 4, 1801, he could not possibly have known that the occasion would mark the political death of the Federalist Party, which would never again seriously contest the presidency or come close to winning either chamber of Congress. In 1804, Aaron Burr killed Hamilton in a duel, depriving the party of its half-brilliant, half-mad leader and instigator. By 1820, the party would basically cease to exist.

Federalism had wrung itself out for reasons that Madison had been highlighting all along in his critiques. The largely egalitarian, largely agricultural people of the United States had no interest in the "high tone" of Federalist rhetoric, the party's preference for strong executive government, its systematic favoritism to the commercial elites of the northern cities, its standing army and the taxes needed to afford it, or its suppression of a free press. Madison was wrong to see in these principles an incipient monarchy, but he was right to suspect that they were deeply inconsistent not only with his view of republican politics but with the spirit of the age. In the long run, a moderate variety of Federalism would be vindicated. John Marshall would establish the supremacy of the federal government over the states from his perch as chief justice of the Supreme Court, and Madison himself would charter the Second Bank of the United States. Still the party's core political conceit—that an aristocratic elite had to guide and manage public affairs—was rejected by the American people.

This was both a blessing and a curse for the Republicans. It was a blessing because, absent a viable political opposition, they were basically free to remake the body politic in their own image. Jefferson, backed by Madison at the State Department and Gallatin at the Treasury Department, believed that the bulk of the nation could be unified around Republican principles implemented in a moderate, careful, and prudent way. In this, he was essentially correct; the partisan strife of the 1790s would not return again until the 1820s. But the Federalists always had a much more realistic view of America's place in the world, and the party's collapse would expose the naivete of Republican foreign policy. Madison, Jefferson, and the Republicans clung to a fanciful notion that the virtuous, agrarian republic of the United States was more powerful than Britain, and that it could drive a hard bargain in diplomatic negotiations. Whenever Madison or Jefferson had brought up this idea in the 1790s, the Federalists were quick to strike it down. With the collapse of the party, the Republicans had a free hand to act. The results would be disastrous.

11

SECRETARY OF STATE

THERE WAS NEVER any question that Thomas Jefferson would ask James Madison to be his secretary of state. Even if the two had not been best friends and the closest of political confidants, Madison was the most qualified Republican in the nation. He had been immersed in national politics and international affairs at that point for twenty years, organized the party in the House at its very origins, and led it against the Federalists in most of the early skirmishes. He was Jefferson's obvious choice for the job. Likewise, there was no doubt that Madison would answer the call of his dear friend to return to national office once more.

Madison was delayed in this transition back into government by the death of his father in early 1801. Unwinding James Madison Sr.'s massive estate among his children and grandchildren was a time-consuming process, made worse by the fact that his father had not updated his will in quite some time. Madison did not arrive in Washington until May and soon turned around to leave, for the heat of the summer led to another attack of "bilious fever." For the next sixteen years, between his time at the State Department and the White House, he and his family would generally depart Washington for the summer months, abandoning the swampy DC climate for the cooler weather of the Virginia Piedmont between May and October.

Madison's labor as secretary of state was monumental, the best evidence of which is the voluminous record that his tenure left behind. His main duties were to assist the president in formulating foreign policy and then see to its implementation. He also advised the president on domestic matters, although implementation was usually handled by the Treasury Department, which Albert Gallatin helmed. The two of them along with the president worked as a kind of Republican triumvirate during Jefferson's administration. No doubt, the president was in charge, but he encouraged free-ranging discussion in cabinet meetings, which included Madison, Gallatin, Henry Dearborn as secretary of war, Robert Smith as secretary of the navy, and Levi Lincoln as attorney general. Usually, the president acted only after a consensus was reached. As such, Jefferson's cabinet was much more harmonious than those of his predecessors.

Implementing foreign policy required regular correspondence with American diplomats serving abroad. Madison would receive communication from half a dozen or so foreign ministers and was required to keep them abreast of the thinking of the Jefferson administration, events in Congress, and larger happenings on the world stage. He also was tasked with writing detailed instructions to each minister. Because transatlantic communication was painfully slow, ministers basically worked in isolation from their home governments, so Madison had to outline at length what American interests were, how to parlay potential offers or demands from foreign governments, and what kind of treaties or settlements would be acceptable.

The State Department also doubled as a kind of home office for the young government. Madison had to respond to congressional requests for information and to correspond with governors, judicial officials, marshals, and US attorneys. His office was tasked with preserving public papers, publishing the laws, overseeing weights and measures, supervising patents and the census (although the latter duty never fell during his tenure), and more. And Madison had to do all of this with a staff that by today's standards would be skeletal—really just a handful of clerks and a messenger. It was, to say the least, a burden. In March 1806, he wrote to James Monroe that "for the last year, especially the last five or six months, the weight of business has almost broken me down, and robbed me of every leisure for writing to my friends."[1]

The heavy crush of executive duties inevitably meant that Madison's role in the Republican Party waned. He had been the first organizer of the Republican interest, but Jefferson had claimed the mantle of leadership after becoming vice president in 1797 and continued in that capacity as president. In Congress, a new crop of party leaders was coming into its own. Nathaniel Macon of North Carolina became Speaker of the House in 1801 and named his friend John Randolph of Virginia (commonly referred to as John Randolph of Roanoke) chair of the House Ways and Means Committee. Macon had served with Madison in the House, but the two had not been close, and the conservative Randolph was downright suspicious of Madison, believing him to be insufficiently committed to Republican purity. Randolph even doubted Jefferson's commitment to party orthodoxy, observing that both he and Madison "advocated the leading measures of their party until they were nearly ripe for execution, when they hung back, condemned the step after it was taken, and on most occasions affected a glorious neutrality."[2]

While Madison was no longer in the thick of Republican politics within Congress, he was still an important figure on the Washington scene. Life in the capital city in the first decade of the nineteenth century was dreary. Laid out by Pierre Charles L'Enfant on a plot of land selected by George Washington, the city mostly still existed on paper. There were just a handful of boardinghouses and a few shops. The terrain was swampy, cold in the winter, and hot in the summer. Opportunities for socializing were few and far between, a grim prospect made worse by the president's aversion to formal entertaining. Both Washington and Adams had hosted formal levees, but Jefferson disdained such events and preferred small, intimate dinners where conversation could flow freely and he could "cultivate personal intercourse with the members of the legislature," as he wrote in 1806.[3]

With Jefferson mostly retired from the party circuit, it was up to the Madisons, especially Dolley, to fill the void. They settled into a four-bedroom house on F Street, just a few blocks east of the White House, where James and Dolley lived with Payne and Dolley's younger sister Anna. In keeping with the Republican scruples of the commander in chief, the Madisons furnished the house simply, but Dolley nevertheless turned their residence into the top destination for DC socialites. Between tea parties and dinners, she and James hosted foreign diplomats, members of Congress, and the local gentry. It was a welcome respite from life in the congressional boardinghouses, which were full of men whose talk inevitably turned to grim disagreements about politics, diplomacy, or society. The Madison events, on the other hand, were a mix of men and women, keeping the mood lighter and enjoyable. Card games (Brag for the men and Loo for the ladies), alcohol, and even snuff were common staples of their social life.

Madison, who as a young delegate to the Continental Congress had been derided as a stick-in-the-mud, had transformed into a gracious and entertaining host, becoming known throughout the city for his witty conversation and grace on the dance floor. Of course, he was still James Madison, and so he socialized in his own sort of way. Samuel Harrison Smith—the founder of the Republican newspaper the *National Intelligencer*—once wrote to his wife, Margaret Bayard Smith, about a party at the Madisons' where the champagne had been flowing freely, and after everybody was tipsy Madison proposed a scientific experiment to see how much the attendees could drink without being hungover. As it turned out, the guests drank and drank and drank, but the "only effects were animated good humor and uninterrupted conversation."[4]

These parties were not simply about whiling away the hours between government business in the quiet little village of Washington, DC. Dolley had tremendous instincts for politics and knew that such events helped her husband's career prospects. Diplomats and foreign visitors were frequently invited to Madison parties, and, just as important, Dolley would regularly call on the ladies of Washington, whose husbands often occupied important positions in the government. Likewise, political allies of Madison would be similarly cultivated, as would his potential foes. So, while Madison's direct role in congressional politics waned, his stature in the Republican Party did not. In this way, Dolley fit seamlessly into a long-standing political tradition where wives, in managing the social engagements of the family and community, facilitated their husbands' public careers. Indeed, she was one of the great female politicians of the nineteenth century, so capable was she at managing the social levers of political power.

JEFFERSON'S FIRST TERM as president was a triumph for the Republican agenda of pacificism, low taxes, and economical government. The administration slashed military spending to the bone, reducing the army to just 3,300 men by 1802. Similarly, the navy was radically downsized. By the end of 1801, there were only six frigates, eight smaller vessels, and sixty gunboats in service. These drastic reductions enabled Jefferson to lower taxes, to great popular acclaim. Meanwhile, as the foreign crises faded away, robust international trade kept federal coffers full of impost duties, so even as it cut taxes, the administration substantially paid down the federal debt. George Washington and John Adams sacrificed much of their political capital to make this peace dividend possible through the Jay Treaty and the Convention of 1800, and Jefferson reaped the political benefits.

About the only survivor of the Federalist economic program was the Bank of the United States. Jefferson still hated it on an instinctive level, but the bank found a champion in Gallatin. The only Republican who understood public finance as well as Hamilton, Jefferson's financier grasped what the president could not: a well-run financial institution could be a boon to both the government and the economy. Whenever Jefferson complained to Gallatin about the bank, the latter was polite but firm in his argument that it was a positive good.

Politically, Jefferson pursued a centrist course. He believed that the party spoke for the broad majority of the nation, hence the name "Republican," and that it was his duty to bring moderate Federalists into the fold. So, he did not go measure for measure: When the Sedition Act expired in March 1801, he did not call for its renewal to be used against the Federalists. He also left the bulk of Federalist officeholders in their jobs, although he did undo last-minute Federalist attempts to stuff government offices with their partisans. The most outrageous such measure was the Judiciary Act of 1801. Passed after the Federalist Congress learned that Adams lost the election of 1800, this law dramatically expanded the courts, and thus the number of judicial vacancies, which Adams scrambled to fill. The Republicans duly repealed the act, and Jefferson did whatever he could to deny the last-minute Federalist appointees their positions.

Still, the Federalist domination of the judiciary was a problem for the Republicans. In 1801, Adams named John Marshall chief justice of the Supreme Court. A moderate Federalist along the lines of George Washington, Marshall did more to advance the Federalist view of government than anybody except, arguably, Hamilton. But while Hamilton's life would be cut short in 1804, Marshall would helm the high court until 1835, advancing the ideal of a strong national government that constrained the states.

Marshall was not only a great jurist; he was also a clear-eyed politician who grasped the potential power of the Supreme Court. He used the controversy over Adams's last-minute appointments to establish the power of judicial review in *Marbury v. Madison*. William Marbury had been appointed and confirmed as a justice of the peace in Washington, DC, but Madison's State Department refused to deliver his commission. Marbury asked the Supreme Court to force Madison to turn it over, but Marshall ruled against him, declaring that a portion of the Judiciary Act of 1789 had unconstitutionally expanded the jurisdiction of the Supreme Court. In so doing, he established the precedent of judicial review, or the right of the court to strike down laws that it judges are inconsistent with the Constitution. After delivering this bombshell, Marshall never again struck down another federal law, but rather used this power mainly to prevent states from impeding federal authority, thus achieving through the bench what Hamilton had endeavored to do through the Treasury Department.

In principle, Madison agreed that the Supreme Court should be an arbiter of the meaning of the Constitution, but Marshall's approach to jurisprudence rankled him. The chief had a habit of writing lengthy opinions full of dicta that injected Hamiltonian views of the Constitution into the law. There was precious little the Republicans could do about it. The only remedy—apart from waiting for Federalist judges to retire or die—was impeachment and removal, which requires a majority in the House and two-thirds support in the Senate.

The Republicans did pursue this strategy, but with very limited effect. In 1803, the House impeached New Hampshire district judge John Pickering, and the Senate convicted him. But Pickering was low-hanging fruit for the Republicans; he had been exhibiting signs of dementia and had refused even his son's entreaties to resign. The next year, the Republicans focused their ire upon the hyper-partisan justice Samuel Chase, who had broken no laws, but had denounced Republican printers from the bench and had harangued a grand jury about the repeal of the Judiciary Act of 1801. The House overwhelmingly voted to impeach him in March 1804. When the Senate took up the matter the following winter, Chase argued that his actions did not rise to the level of impeachment. Meanwhile, the fiery John Randolph of Roanoke—who argued on behalf of the House—generated more heat than light with his rambling, unpersuasive arguments. The Senate fell five votes short of conviction, effectively ending the Republican war against the Federalist judiciary.

On the foreign policy front, Jefferson and Madison scored their greatest diplomatic coup in 1804, when they purchased the Louisiana Territory from France for just $15 million. Spain had acquired the title to Louisiana in 1762, but by the end of the century it was clear that it could not stop land-hungry Americans from pouring in. Talleyrand prevailed upon Spain, a French ally, to trade Louisiana for present-day Tuscany. This, he suggested, would create a "wall of brass" in the West, "forever impenetrable to the combined efforts of England and America."

The deal was brokered via a secret treaty in October 1800. Napoleon Bonaparte, who had taken control of France in 1799 and would crown himself emperor in 1804, would thus have an opportunity to rebuild New France, with the Louisiana Territory serving as the breadbasket for his future West Indian conquests.[5]

Jefferson and Madison heard rumors of the deal but did not confirm it until the spring of 1802. They were alarmed. It was not so much the western lands that they craved but rather access to New Orleans. By that point, three thousand ships passed through its port every year, half of which were American. Spain had long been a paper tiger in the West, but with France now in charge, continued access through this crucial waterway seemed in doubt. In October, the Spanish intendant of New Orleans closed the port to all foreign shipping. Both sides quickly wrote the event off as a diplomatic misunderstanding; nevertheless, the prospect of losing access to New Orleans suddenly seemed very real. Acquiring the port city became the top diplomatic priority of the administration.

The problem was that Napoleon was notoriously difficult to deal with. Robert Livingston, the American minister to France, complained to Madison that "there never was a government in which less could be done by negotiation than here. . . . One man is everything—he seldom asks advice and never hears it unasked." To back Livingston up, Jefferson appointed James Monroe as a special envoy in January 1803. Monroe had just finished a stint as Virginia governor and was eager to return to private life to get his personal finances back in order, but Jefferson begged him to serve his country once again. There was nobody, apart from Madison and Gallatin, he trusted more. "The fever into which the western mind is thrown by the affair at New Orleans," he wrote his old friend, "threatens to overbear our peace. In this situation we are obliged to call on you for a temporary sacrifice of yourself, to prevent this greatest of evils in the present prosperous tide of our affairs."[6]

The administration's goal was to purchase New Orleans and as much as possible of west Florida, which at that point included the coastal regions of present-day Alabama and Mississippi. Congress secretly appropriated $2 million for the purchase and was prepared to forgive $4 million in outstanding French debt, for a total offer of $6 million. The argument the Americans would make depended on years of careful Republican cultivation of good relations with France. First, they would assure France that it had nothing to fear from American control of New Orleans. The United States was pacifistic and committed to neutrality. As Madison wrote to Livingston in March 1803, France could "be sure" that the United States would provide "whatever supplies her islands may want . . . in times of general peace." Second, they would suggest that French control of New Orleans might force a change in American posture. As Jefferson wrote his French friend Pierre Samuel du Pont de Nemours (who served as an informal go-between for the president and the French government), Louisiana seemed like "nothing" to Europe, but it was everything to America. French control of the port was "the embryo of a tornado which will burst on the countries on both shores of the Atlantic and involve in its effects their highest destinies." If America could not control New Orleans for itself, Jefferson warned, the country might have to align with Great Britain in preparation for war someday. Similarly, Madison explained to Livingston that French control of Louisiana "could not be friendly to the harmony which both countries have so much an interest in cherishing, but if the possession" of New Orleans "is to be added to other causes of discord, the worst events are to be apprehended."[7]

By the time Monroe arrived in Paris to make this case, Napoleon had already instructed his finance minister to float the sale of the whole territory, for he had soured on his New France project. His efforts to retake the island of Santo Domingo from the insurgency of Toussaint L'Ouverture and his liberated slaves had gone horribly awry. The French force had been decimated by the guerilla tactics of the Haitians as well as a yellow fever epidemic, which also killed Napoleon's brother-in-law General Charles Leclerc. Napoleon abruptly cut his losses and offered all of the Louisiana Territory. Monroe and Livingston jumped at the opportunity. In most modern retellings, the administration does not receive much credit, for Napoleon decided to sell his vast claims without any American pressure applied. While this is no doubt true in part, it understates the extent to which Jefferson and Madison successfully parlayed their well-known sympathies for France. It is hard to believe that the wily Napoleon would ever have sold his North American holdings to the United States if the pro-British Federalists were still in power.

By accepting Napoleon's terms, Livingston and Monroe had vastly exceeded their diplomatic mandate, but this was no problem. As Madison wrote Monroe in June 1803, the administration reacted to the news with "much pleasure and much expectation"; the cabinet had not suggested such a purchase only "because it was not deemed at this time within the pale of probability." Still, the president had a constitutional objection. The "difficulty" was not "the acquisition of territory," he had told Gallatin in January 1803, but whether it may be "taken into the union." There was no explicit provision in the Constitution for Congress to incorporate a foreign people—particularly, the residents of New Orleans—into the country. Initially, Jefferson preferred that the treaty be ratified and the money paid, then an amendment enacted to transform Louisianans into Americans. To that end, the president sent a draft of an amendment to Madison in July, but the secretary of state did not think this was a prudent course. Any uncertainty around the incorporation might prompt the French to back out. Instead, he told John Quincy Adams that though the Constitution "had not provided for such a case as this," the "magnitude of the object" was such that the government should act and "rely upon the candor of their country for justification." In other words, if the people judged it unconstitutional, they could render their verdict at the ballot box. Eventually, Jefferson came around to this view, admitting to Madison in August that "the less we say about constitutional difficulties . . . the better" and that whatever challenges existed should be dealt with "sub silentio."[8]

By the time of the purchase of Louisiana, then, Madison had positioned himself on both sides of virtually every major constitutional controversy. He had advocated for vast executive discretion in 1789 during debates over who had authority to remove officers from the government, but tried to force the president's hand by denying funding for the Jay Treaty in the House in 1796. He had denounced Hamilton's system of protective bounties as a tortured misreading of Congress's power to levy taxes for the general welfare in 1792, but had already advocated spending on scientific expeditions in 1789. He had opposed the Federalist's capacious view of the Necessary and Proper Clause in the fight over the Bank of the United States in 1791, but waved away the problems his strict constructionism obviously created for the acquisition of Louisiana in 1803. And that he never seriously pursued Jefferson to eliminate the Bank of the United States demonstrated that he was not terribly troubled by it, either, so long as it was in the right hands.

As a legal doctrine, Madisonian constitutionalism had become a complete mess. The only way to reconcile these contradictions is to understand it through the prism not of the law but of politics, and in particular how he viewed the Republican battle against Federalism. The High Federalists were not republicans, their pretensions notwithstanding. Deep down, Madison believed, they were aristocrats and monarchists. They did not trust the people to rule and were looking to ensconce themselves permanently in power. Surely the Constitution, which established a republican form of government, did not allow for them to snatch power away from the people and use it to reward their friends and allies. The Republicans, on the other hand, were republicans, looking to govern according to the will of the people and for their benefit. How could the Constitution possibly prohibit that? Madison's belief was no doubt self-serving, but it was earnestly held. Regardless, in the process of opposing Federalism and then governing as a Republican, he offered a confused and arbitrary constitutional hermeneutic.

THE EARLY 1800S was a period of enormous prosperity for the United States, but not in ways that conformed to the agrarian republic Madison and Jefferson had long idealized. The nation was quickly becoming a merchant power. Ship tonnage tripled between 1790 and 1810, and the export trade that the United States enjoyed up until the War of 1812 would not be equaled for another century. This exchange was not simply between the United States and Europe, but a "carrying trade" that ferried goods to and from European colonies in the West Indies. Americans kept the Spanish and French West Indies afloat, as their home nations were engulfed in war with Great Britain.

The carrying trade was in part an indulgence granted by the British. Even as Great Britain imposed tight commercial restrictions on the French West Indies in 1794, it dialed them back before the Jay Treaty was ratified. Though that agreement granted few formal concessions to the Americans, it did encourage further British conciliation on the Rule of 1756. In the *Polly* decision of 1800, the British admiralty court decreed that, so long as trade with the Spanish and French Indies was imported first into American ports, it was allowable. American merchants quickly exploited British forbearance of the "broken voyage," initiating a massive reexport trade that by 1805 would be worth some $60 million. They did this with the tacit sanction of American officials, who often did not even require that goods be unloaded at American ports before they were redirected to foreign destinations.

With the resumption of hostilities against France in 1803, the British attitude toward the United States began to harden once more. The most immediate shift was in the stepping up of impressments. In the spring of 1803, British vessels began lurking just out of American territorial waters, stopping merchant vessels to check for deserters. Life in the Royal Navy was extremely hard, and servicemen took any chance they could to abandon their posts to enlist on an American merchant vessel. On top of that, the British ships were often desperately undermanned, so they were not above forcing bona fide American citizens into service. Nothing wounded American pride more than the practice of impressment—but, then again, were it not for British deserters, the lucrative carry trade of the last decade would have been impossible. Consequently, American officials had been decidedly lax in checking the citizenship of its merchant marine.[9]

The admiralty court also began rolling back the exemptions allowed under *Polly*. In 1801, the Royal Navy had seized the *Aurora*, an American merchant ship bound for Barcelona with cargo from Havana, Cuba. In April 1804, the admiralty court ruled the *Aurora* was in violation of the Rule of 1756, despite the fact that it had broken its voyage with a stop in Charleston,

South Carolina. In May 1805, the court formally revoked the *Polly* precedent by closing the broken-voyage loophole and essentially declaring the American reexport trade illegal. The British justification for this was straightforward: their country was at war with a tyrant, its strongest asset was the Royal Navy, and it need not tolerate America's provisioning of its enemies via the high seas. In a widely read pamphlet that reflected the views of the British ministry, lawyer James Stephens argued, "The commercial and colonial interests of our enemies are now ruined in appearance only, not in reality. They have, in effect . . . only changed their flags, chartered many vessels really neutral, and altered a little the former routes of their trade."[10]

But, the Americans objected, the Rule of 1756 was no rule whatsoever. It was a decree by the British, in blatant defiance of American rights as a neutral nation. Nobody advocated this position more vociferously or exhaustively than Madison. In fact, the longest essay of his career was on this very subject. Published in the winter of 1805–1806 in the *National Intelligencer,* Madison's "An Examination of the British Doctrine Which Subjects to Capture a Neutral Trade Not Open in Time of Peace" ran on for an astonishing seventy thousand words and was about as readable as the prolix title suggested. Madison's argument boiled down to the fact that no historical precedents justified the Rule of 1756, many contradicted it, and that Britain was motivated at least in part by a desire for "usurpation and monopoly" of maritime commerce.[11]

Madison's insistence on American rights to the carry trade dispelled the old Federalist claim that he had shrunk from his nationalism after the Constitution was ratified. The carry trade was of relatively little economic benefit to the South and its plantation gentry. Rather, it was the merchants and shippers in the mid-Atlantic and New England—Madison's political rivals in the 1790s—who reaped the greatest rewards. His defense of this trade was, for him, a defense of the United States.

Still, his argument in favor of American commercial rights was more reminiscent of Helvidius than Publius, precisely made with an impressive attention to detail, but somehow less than the sum of its parts. Even some members of his own party believed Madison was missing the forest for the trees. Thomas Cooper, an English émigré, chemist, and longtime friend of Jefferson, wrote the president that while "it certainly does credit even to Mr. Madison's pen," "the doctrines defended in it, are carried to their very utmost bounds." Cooper worried that in failing to "deprecate commercial wars," Madison's arguments could lead to hostilities to advance "the mercantile interest." John Randolph of Roanoke was acerbic in his denunciation. Deriding the pamphlet's "tangled cobwebs of contradictions," he suggested that Madison's moral compass had been inverted. From the House floor, he pointed out that the United States was profiting off European wars. "It is not for the honest carrying trade of America, but for this mushroom, this fungus, of war—for a trade which as soon as the nations of Europe are at peace will no longer exist." Madison's critics had a point. By elevating the carrying trade to a national right, he was creating a pretext for war, even if it was a war that he was not courting. And this was a trade enriching Napoleon, the same tyrant whose acquisition of Louisiana had terrified Jefferson and Madison not too long ago. If they were right to fear Napoleon gaining a foothold in the New World, how could they defend a trade that worked overwhelmingly to his interests in Europe?[12]

Having established the continuation of the carry trade and a ban on impressment as essential rights of the United States, the Republicans had to formulate a strategy to bring Britain to terms. This would be easier said than done. Congress took a tentative step in this direction in the spring of 1806, when it passed a bill prohibiting importation of British goods that could be acquired from other nations or purchased from domestic manufacturers. Such a weak measure was hardly a gauntlet thrown down, and Congress even delayed its implementation until 1807. Randolph was not far from the mark when he dismissed it as a "milk-and-water bill, a dose of chicken broth to be taken nine months hence."[13]

The administration initially tried diplomacy, hoping that British setbacks in the continental theater of war might soften the hard stance against American shipping. Since Jefferson had sent Monroe to France to settle the New Orleans dispute, the latter had become the administration's top European diplomat, toggling between France, Spain, and England over the next eighteen months. When he returned to London in the summer of 1805, he received the runaround from the British ministry. At Congress's insistence, Jefferson appointed Federalist attorney William Pinkney to back Monroe up in London in 1806, an appointment that wounded Monroe's pride deeply. He took this as a vote of no confidence in his abilities, and he broke protocol by writing Jefferson directly (rather than through Madison) to complain about the "inquietude" he felt for having been "placed in a situation . . . altogether unexpected, and in consideration of the parties to it equally novel."[14]

One diplomat, two diplomats, ten, twenty—it did not matter. The British were uninterested in making any significant concessions, at least on paper. They had a war to fight. Monroe had sensed this months earlier, when he wrote Madison in 1804 that it was unlikely that they would sign a "treaty which trenches accommodation on . . . what they call their maritime rights." A better bet was to persuade them to offer "an accommodation precisely the same in effect, by their own orders to the admiralty." Nothing had changed by 1806. If anything, the British had become more intransigent. Lord Horatio Nelson had scored a smashing naval victory for Great Britain at the Battle of Trafalgar in October 1805, effectively eliminating the Spanish and French maritime threat. Two months later, Napoleon's victory at the Battle of Austerlitz had made him the master of continental Europe. By the time Monroe got down to business in London, France and Britain were committed to commercial warfare against each other. Napoleon's Continental System had made it illegal for European nations to trade with Britain, while Britain clung to its naval restrictions all the more tightly.[15]

The best Monroe and Pinkney could get from the British was not much at all. Signed on December 31, 1806, the Monroe-Pinkney Treaty secured from the British a concession to return to the *Polly* decision, but in exchange the Americans were prohibited from engaging in commercial restrictions for a decade, meaning that there was little the United States could do should the British again harass its ships. Monroe and Pinkney also conceded to restrictions on American trade with the British West Indies, as well as the East Indies (one of the few victories from the Jay Treaty back in 1795). Moreover, the diplomats could get the British to agree to nothing on impressment, despite the fact that Madison had made it the sine qua non of the negotiations. Worst of all, Great Britain insisted that America had to defy Napoleon's Continental System as a prerequisite for the treaty to go into effect.[16]

Jefferson was so disappointed with the treaty that he did not bother even to submit it to the Senate. Madison tried to let Monroe down gently. "The President," he wrote, "has seen in your exertions . . . ample proofs of that zeal and patriotism in which he confided; and feels deep regret that your success has not corresponded with the reasonableness of your propositions, and the ability with which they were supported." Monroe was profoundly wounded by the whole ordeal. He had never wanted to go to Europe in the first place, and indeed had petitioned several times to go home. Throughout his time as a diplomat, he had warned that Great Britain would never make formal concessions, and that the better strategy was to work through informal means. He suspected that Madison had intentionally undermined him to secure his own succession to the presidency. Monroe was wrong about this, but the botched treaty effort opened a breach between the two friends that would not be closed until 1811.[17]

Ultimately, the Republicans fundamentally misunderstood the British. The island nation was at war with the most powerful country on the Continent, helmed by a cunning and ambitious tyrant. Great Britain was only going to give the United States as much as it believed it had to. It was not scared of commercial retaliation, and it certainly did not fear American use of force. Faced with a similar crisis with the French after the XYZ Affair, the Federalists had committed themselves to a military buildup. But the Republicans could hardly contemplate such an idea in 1806. The ancient prejudice against standing armies ran deep among the Republicans; they believed that historically the main purpose of a standing army had been to frighten the citizenry into obeying despots. And the fiscally prudent Gallatin primarily viewed the Navy Department as an easy mark for budget cuts. Jefferson had become enamored with gunboats—small vessels with a cannon or two—which he believed could secure coastal defenses. So, insofar as the administration spent money on defense, it invested disproportionately in these, which turned out to be of no use when Britain and America finally went to war in 1812.

The Republicans also feared that a larger naval presence risked misunderstandings that could turn into international incidents. They were right to worry about this. On June 22, 1807, the HMS *Leopard* stopped the USS *Chesapeake* off the coast of Norfolk, Virginia. The British commander demanded to search the *Chesapeake* for British deserters. When the commander of the *Chesapeake* was slow to respond, the *Leopard* opened fire, killing several crewmen. It forced the Americans to surrender and ultimately seized four British deserters. The American public was outraged, but the British refused to make formal amends.

Nations have gone to war for much less than the offense America suffered in the *Chesapeake* incident, and the Jefferson administration began mulling the prospect of open hostilities. The president called Congress into a special session in anticipation of such an event. Seemingly as a prewar measure, Congress quickly enacted a full trade embargo on December 22, 1807, which, combined with a beefed-up nonimportation law, effectively shut down American commerce with the rest of the world. The initial motivation was to remove American merchant vessels and sailors from the high seas, so that if war was declared they would not be caught outside territorial waters. It would also ensure that the United States could pick the time at which war might begin, rather than leaving it up to a random incident. As Madison explained, the embargo was "effectual security for our mercantile property and mariners" that "at the same time neither a measure, nor just cause of war."[18]

As time wore on, the desire for war began to wane, yet the embargo remained in place for more than a year. It evolved, in fits and starts, from a prewar precaution into the kind of commercial retaliation that the Republicans had been promoting for almost twenty years. Nobody advocated for this shift in policy more than Madison. Just a few days after the passage of the embargo, he was already touting its potential as an instrument of commercial war. In an unsigned editorial for the *National Intelligencer* on December 23, Madison argued that the embargo would have the "collateral effect of making it the interest of all nations to change the system which has driven our commerce from the ocean." In a December 28 editorial, he outlined the reason why. "It is not denied that an embargo imposes on us privations," he admitted, "but what are these compared with its effects on those who have driven us into the measure? We shall be deprived of market for our superfluities. They will feel the want of necessaries. The profits of our labor will be diminished. The supplies that feed theirs will fail. Which of the parties will suffer most? Which will first be tired of the trial?" This was exactly the sort of argument he had long made, fitting snugly into his ideal of an agrarian republic. The United States supplied Great Britain with food, and in return Britain provided manufactured goods. The latter the hearty yeomen farmers of America could do without, but Britain needed the United States to feed it. And so, just as he had argued in the 1780s and 1790s, Madison claimed that it was actually America that had power over Great Britain, which it should exploit for maximum benefit.[19]

The embargo became for Madison the grand experiment in commercial policy that he had always wanted, but it was hardly calibrated for this larger purpose. Madison's proposal to discriminate against British ships during the debate over the impost of 1789, as well as Jefferson's *Report on Commerce* from 1793, did not suggest restrictions on American exports but taxes on imports. So, the best strategy for commercial war in 1807 would have been a tough nonimportation law, which would have maximized pressure on foreign manufacturing while minimizing pressure on American farmers. But the embargo would have to do. From the winter of 1807–1808 until the fall of 1808, Madison became the faithful apostle of administration policy.[20]

Despite Madison's ardent proselytizing, the embargo simply did not work. It failed to convince the British ministry to alleviate its restrictions on American commerce, it did enormous damage to the US economy, and it created out of whole cloth an elaborate, nationwide black market, whereby American goods were surreptitiously traded with the British, often by sneaking them across the US-Canadian border or ferrying them quietly from New England to Newfoundland. This, in turn, required the administration to implement draconian enforcement measures, with the president issuing exemptions on a case-by-case basis. Eventually, Jefferson even issued a proclamation that upstate New York was in a state of insurrection. Such measures were an order of magnitude more oppressive than anything ever proposed by the Federalists, and they absolutely exhausted the president, who by the end of his tenure had mentally checked out. He wrote to Attorney General Levi Lincoln in November 1808 that he was content to "be myself but a spectator" and to leave decisions about diplomacy "to the wisdom of Congress." This was a sad decline from the beginning of his first term, when he had exerted great influence to bend Congress to his will.[21]

Rather than reevaluate the wisdom of the embargo based on this widespread disobedience, Madison instead blamed the greed of merchants. In July 1808, he warned Pinkney that "partisans are . . . promoting every effort to render the embargo unpopular and ineffectual." In September, he blamed the embargo's "enemies" in New England for "artifices and the petitions" that had "pervert[ed]" its success. Even years later, in retirement, he was still bitter about the bad faith of the New England mercantile community. The problem with the embargo was that he and Jefferson "did not sufficiently distrust those in a certain quarter whose successful violations of the law led to the general discontent which called for its repeal."[22]

Despite the economic ruin created by the Embargo Act, the Republicans were well-placed to win the presidency against the

Federalist Party in 1808. The Federalists by that point had become a moribund coalition, thanks to the rapid growth of the South and West, which accounted for nearly half of all electoral votes that year. The Federalists, with their partiality toward merchants and industrialists, held little appeal in those regions. Madison, as the most senior Republican in the party after Jefferson, was the obvious successor. He easily won the presidency over Federalist Charles Cotesworth Pinckney. The Eleventh Congress was likewise firmly Republican, with just one-third of House members belonging to the Federalist Party, and only seven of thirty-four senators.

Yet there were portents of trouble for the new president. Madison lost Massachusetts and New Hampshire to Pinckney, both of which had gone for Jefferson in 1804. Federalists also made gains in the House at the expense of New England Republicans, picking up a total of twenty-four seats over their showing in the 1806 midterm.

More worrisome for Madison were the multiple fractures within the Republican coalition. After Aaron Burr's unsuccessful bid to snatch the presidency from Jefferson, Republicans in the state legislatures ratified the Twelfth Amendment in 1804, which required members of the electoral college to cast separate ballots for president and vice president. As a sop to the New York wing of the party, the Republicans nominated former governor George Clinton for the vice presidency in 1804. They did likewise in 1808, despite Clinton's advanced age and frail health— once again as a token for the New Yorkers, but also to keep his ambitious nephew, New York City mayor DeWitt Clinton, from challenging the Virginia faction for the presidency. Many New York Republicans had grown tired of playing second fiddle to the Virginians, so the Clintonite forces protested by fusing with the state's Federalists to back George Clinton for the presidency, leading to the historical curiosity of Clinton being the only candidate to win electoral votes for president *and* vice president in the same state.

A different threat came from inside Virginia, where a combination of ideological disputes and clashing ambitions momentarily seemed to threaten Madison's election. Conservative Republicans—known as "Old Republicans" or "Tertium Quids" (the "third force")—had greeted Jefferson's election in 1800 with unalloyed joy, anticipating a triumph over Federalism. But as his tenure wore on, they grew tired of his moderation. Men like John Randolph of Roanoke and John Taylor of Caroline hated Jefferson's tolerance of the Bank of the United States, objected to his retention of Federalist officeholders, griped that he did not back amendments to further limit federal power, and especially despised the prospect of war over the carrying trade.

The Old Republicans viewed Madison with special skepticism. He was not a true Republican, they thought, for he had once been an ally of Hamilton. As Taylor wrote to Virginia congressman Wilson Cary Nicholas in 1808, Madison was a "trimmer," and that "book called the *Federalist* is full of federalism, if I understand what federalism is." It reminded Taylor of the "obnoxious doctrines" of the supposedly monarchical John Adams. Meanwhile, Randolph had been Madison's sworn enemy ever since Madison had backed federal involvement to resolve the Yazoo land scandal, which had taken place years earlier in Georgia. In 1794, Georgia had granted land companies thirty-five million acres for $500,000. When it came to light that the companies had bribed several officials, the Georgia government revoked the sale. But the companies had already resold a portion of the lands, and some of the new buyers did not want to give up their claims. To arbitrate the dispute, Madison was placed on a commission that recommended Georgia cede the land to the United

States government for $1.25 million. Randolph was aghast at this egregious expansion of federal authority, killed the deal in the House, and blamed Madison for the heresy.[23]

The Quids worried that the 1808 election might be the last chance to arrest the Republican Party's slouch into Federalism, and they found in Monroe a champion for the old orthodoxy. There was a lot to like about Monroe as the anti-Madison. He had a strong personal following in Virginia. He had served in the Revolutionary War. He had been an Anti-Federalist during ratification. Best of all, he had been on the outs with Madison since the Jefferson administration rejected his British peace treaty in 1807. Randolph had taken up correspondence with Monroe while the latter was still in London and had been feeding him information about supposed conspiracies to thwart his ambitions.

Jefferson had warned Monroe in March 1806 that he was being manipulated. "Some of your new friends are attacking your old ones [not] out of friendship to you, but in a way to render you great injury." But Monroe, his sense of honor deeply wounded by the rejection of his treaty, went along with Randolph's scheme. He did not explicitly endorse the candidacy, but he did not reject it either. In a letter to Representative Walter Jones in early 1808, Monroe wrote that, though he had "not offered [himself] a candidate" for the presidency, it was his "opinion that the nation should be left perfectly at liberty to make its own election." Given the norms of the age, which made it indecent to seek the presidency actively, this was as close to a declaration of a campaign as was practical.[24]

Madison's backers responded with an aggressive strategy to pop the Monroe bubble before it could get off the ground. On January 21, 1808, his Virginia allies in the House of Delegates met at the Bell Tavern in Richmond, where they endorsed his

candidacy by a vote of 124 to 0, opponents of Madison not having been invited to participate. Two days later, his congressional
supporters rammed through his nomination in the party caucus, eighty-three to eight, with both the Quids and the Clintonites abstaining in protest of the hurried process. The unity and
vigor of the regular Republicans, combined with the failure of
the Clintonites and Quids to join forces, was enough to secure
victory for Madison, who easily defeated Monroe in Virginia.
But this political victory came at a dear personal cost for the new
president, for Madison and Monroe were alienated for the next
two years, a difficult time for Madison when his friend's sage
counsel would be sorely needed.

Madison played only an indirect role in these events. The
norms of the day prohibited him from actively campaigning for
the office, so these endeavors were managed by his close political associates. Still, he was not entirely idle. Presidential politics
in the early nineteenth century depended a great deal on the
sentiments of members of Congress and other political elites,
whose endorsements were necessary to wage a serious campaign.
James and Dolley hosted an array of members of Congress and
other prominent officials at their house on F Street, as well as
lavish dinners back in Montpelier. Though the campaign was
never actually discussed, the couple's charming ways helped
sway the country's leaders to their side. Dolley in particular was
a skilled campaigner. Consciously taking on a more reserved
persona for the purposes of wooing voters, she even wrote to
Margaret Bayard Smith about the evils of card games. After the
election, Pinckney complained that he "was beaten by Mr. and
Mrs. Madison. I might have had a better chance had I faced
Mr. Madison alone."[25]

MADISON MAY HAVE been "inclined to hug the embargo, and die in its embrace," as Congressman Orchard Cook wrote to Senator John Quincy Adams—who had initially entered Congress as a Federalist but had slowly evolved into a Republican during Jefferson's tenure—but it was clear by the fall of 1808 that his was a minority opinion. When Congress reconvened, a critical mass of Republicans from New England and the mid-Atlantic joined with the Federalists, as well as anti-war Republicans like Randolph, to repeal the embargo in early February 1809. The vote was not even close: seventy-six to forty, a stunning rebuke of the administration's foreign policy. As a way to save face and hold on to the hope that commercial warfare might yet work, Madison and his allies prevailed upon Congress to pass the Nonintercourse Act, prohibiting trade only with Britain and France. Madison hoped that nonintercourse would "show that it is not meant as an acquiescence in those edicts, but as an appeal to the interest of the aggressors, in a mode less inconvenient to our own interest." Yet in truth it was a paper tiger, for once merchant vessels left an American port, they were practically free to travel wherever they liked. Jefferson signed the Nonintercourse Act on March 1, three days before the end of his term, at which point Madison would rise to the presidential office and inherit the country's many problems.[26]

Madison had been one of the longest serving secretaries of state in American history, yet his service in the State Department usually ranks low in critical assessments of his achievements, and often it does not rate at all. Much of this is because his earlier efforts to establish the government were so monumental that little else could possibly compare. But it also must be said that Madison was not a very good secretary of state.

To be sure, he was quite skilled at the detail work required in the job. As he did with everything else, Madison brought an unparalleled work ethic to the executive branch. He was never asleep at the switch. He was reasonable and moderate in his conduct, typically hallmarks of diplomatic success. His correspondence with American ministers overseas and representatives of foreign governments was always precise and exacting in its attention to protocol. He also did not lack for experience. He had little direct role in foreign affairs in the House of Representatives, but his stint in the Continental Congress had certainly educated him on the subject, and he had kept up with it in the intervening years.

Madison's troubled tenure was due to his misunderstanding of America's place on the world stage in that moment, in two important respects. First, he fundamentally misjudged the diplomatic situation. He was outraged by the British seizure of American vessels and saw it as an assault on national rights. But while his arguments against British depredations may have been technically persuasive, they were offered in defense of a morally dubious trade. The United States was turning an enormous profit in the Napoleonic Wars because France and its Spanish ally could not overcome British dominance of the high seas, leaving it to American vessels to ferry goods to and from their West Indian colonies. This carry trade had helped the French in their wars of conquest, a calamity that Madison's Jesuitical arguments about international law could not account for. And the British were never going to allow America to supply the Napoleonic war machine unless it was forced to.

Second, Madison misjudged the economic might of the United States. He believed that America could use commercial means to force the British to negotiate because the former produced the necessities of life while the latter produced manufactured goods that the United States could do without. But the United States was not nearly strong enough for an embargo to be effective. Instead, it damaged the American economy, undermined the rule of law in the United States, divided the Republican Party, and worst of all had no effect on the British ministry.

On March 2, Jefferson wrote his French friend de Nemours that "within a few days I retire to my family, my books, and farms. . . . Having gained the harbor myself, I shall look on my friends still buffeting the storm, with anxiety indeed, but not with envy." On the day he took the oath of office, James Madison was certainly in the midst of a storm, a crisis more dire than any since the ratification of the Constitution, and he really had nobody to blame but himself.[27]

12

THE FAILURE OF DIPLOMACY

JAMES AND DOLLEY Madison, as well as Dolley's sister Anna, her husband Richard Cutts, and their children, moved into the White House about a week after Madison was sworn in as the fourth president on March 4, 1809. Dolley's son Payne was off at boarding school in Baltimore, and by the end of the year the Cuttses would have a house of their own in Washington. Dolley took over the tasks of managing domestic life at the presidential mansion, including overseeing slaves such as Paul Jennings, whom the Madisons brought with them from Montpelier. She was at this point "the queen" of Washington, DC, as diplomat Joel Barlow called her, and the White House became the center of social life in the city.[1]

One of Dolley's most significant contributions was remodeling the White House. John Adams was the first chief executive to occupy the new presidential mansion, although it was still not entirely finished when he moved in. For all the love and care he poured into Monticello, Jefferson had little regard for making the White House a residence fit for the nation's chief magistrate. When the Madisons moved in, the White House was drafty and drab, with a leaking roof, and was not yet totally furnished. Moreover, Jefferson hated hosting formal events, instead preferring small gatherings of intimates. Dolley set about remedying that, and in so doing she created the style that the White House still employs today: refined but tasteful, befitting the leader of a republican nation rather than a European prince. Whereas the furnishings of Montpelier were French, Dolley emphasized American designers when and as she could. The centerpiece of the White House, unveiled on New Year's Day in 1810, was the "yellow oval room," a reception room that typified Dolley's sense of style, conveying that the White House was a center of power, but not in a way that suggested an overawing authority that emanated from the president himself.

Life during the Madison years in the White House was exactly the opposite of the time under Jefferson. There were always people around. Anna and Richard Cutts visited often, and there was a burgeoning extended family never far away. Dolley's sister Lucy regularly came with her children, and nieces and nephews were often bouncing about. As for the social life, Dolley was the greatest hostess the executive office had yet seen. Not only did she restore the soirees that had been abandoned during the Jefferson years, but she livened them up. They had been formal events under Martha Washington and Abigail Adams, where guests usually stood in one place—not at all pleasant, and presidents Washington and Adams did not especially care for them either. Parties under Dolley, by contrast, were free-flowing affairs, where people mingled and interacted freely, enjoying a wide variety of drinks, wine, cakes, and ice cream. This, too, had a subtle republican effect, for President Madison was just a man who temporarily held the executive office and did not require such stiffness from his guests.

Dolley's changes to the social life of the White House have set the standard for "first ladies" ever since. In fact, it is her tenure there that inspired the term: she was eulogized by President Zachary Taylor as "America's first lady" when she died in 1849. But more important for her husband, she offered the president a welcome respite from what was an extremely difficult administration. Madison could enjoy these parties as he pleased, largely leaving the burdens of hosting to his wife. Indeed, the first six years of his administration were utterly exhausting, as the diplomatic crisis with Great Britain eventually devolved into war.

———————

Madison's inaugural address on March 4, 1809, delivered before a joint session of Congress, set the tone for the administration. Admittedly, it was not a speech for the ages. Contemporaneous reports say he seemed nervous at first, although he gained confidence as he continued, and his voice as usual was soft. The text itself exemplified the typical Madisonian approach: intricate sentences that seem to swirl around arguments without making them directly.

Yet it was a significant address, for Madison hinted at what he believed was the deep malevolence of Great Britain. Describing how Britain and France had assaulted American naval rights, he declared, "In their rage against each other, or impelled by more direct motives, principles of retaliation have been introduced equally contrary to universal reason and acknowledged law." The president was careful to use the passive voice—"have been introduced"—and did not mention the specific countries violating the norms of justice, for he still hoped that he might come to an agreement with Britain and France. But there was an insinuation in the phrase "impelled by more direct motives," one that would eventually become the central justification for war. Great Britain was jealous of the United States. It envied America's growth as a commercial nation. It hated the fact that, over the last decade, American shipping had become a prime mover of goods to and from European colonies in the West Indies. The British imposition of the Rule of 1756 was not simply a consequence of its "rage" against Napoleon but an effort to clip the wings of a rising United States of America.[2]

Unfortunately, Madison was forced to admit—again in an elliptical fashion—that he was at a loss about how to respond: "How long their arbitrary edicts will be continued in spite of the demonstrations that not even a pretext for them has been given by the United States, and of the fair and liberal attempt to induce a revocation of them, cannot be anticipated." In other words, the commercial policy of the Jefferson administration— the policy for which he had been a great champion—had failed. Maybe it could have succeeded if given enough time, but the political will in the United States to continue the program had evaporated. Either way, Madison was not prepared to go to war, at least not yet. He pledged to "maintain sincere neutrality toward belligerent nations" and to "prefer . . . reasonable accommodation of difference" over "an appeal to arms."[3]

Judged against the diplomatic course laid out in his inaugural address, Madison's first term—often criticized for being wobbly and incoherent—looks firm and precise. He used every opportunity presented to him to prevail upon Britain and France to forebear upon the Americans. Simultaneously, he shifted as much blame as possible to Britain instead of France, so that if war came, it would come against the nation he believed to be America's true enemy. By the time Madison recommended a declaration of war to Congress in June 1812, he could make a very persuasive argument. As Albert Gallatin wrote to former

Maryland congressman Joseph Nicholson in December 1808, "Mr. Madison is, as I always knew him, slow in taking his ground, but firm when the storm arises."[4]

The real problem with Madison's first term was his management not of foreign diplomacy but of political factions in Congress. As leader of the congressional Republicans in the 1790s, he was intimately involved in the formulation of legislative policy and strategy. As president from 1809 through 1817, he was basically absent from those decisions. This was a consequence of his views about how republican government should function. He believed that Congress spoke for the people and that it should make decisions without executive interference.

He even went so far as to let congressional politics influence executive decision-making. The most significant instance of this was Madison's choice to name Robert Smith rather than Albert Gallatin as secretary of state. Smith was an amiable enough fellow who had served as Jefferson's secretary of the navy. He and Madison had worked well together in the cabinet. But he was not up to the job of secretary of state, which required giving clear direction to American ministers abroad and having sensitive discussions with foreign ministers in America. Gallatin, on the other hand, was a gifted statesman, and with Monroe having aligned himself with the Quids, Gallatin was the obvious choice. Yet Gallatin had accumulated many congressional enemies during Jefferson's tenure, chief among them senators William Branch Giles of Virginia and Samuel Smith (Robert's brother) of Maryland. The Malcontents, as they are often known, hated Gallatin for his relentless commitment to economy in government, especially when it came to keeping military spending in check. Robert Smith had been, after all, secretary of the navy under Jefferson, and his department was particularly subject to the rigors of Gallatin's frugality. They were also suspicious of his loyalties because he had been born in Switzerland, and they were undoubtedly jealous of his talents.

In February 1809, Giles wrote Madison a rambling letter warning against nominating Gallatin. Some of his advice was merely political intelligence—information from a Senate leader about the feelings of other senators—intimating that Gallatin was a politically risky choice. But Giles also leveled personal attacks against Gallatin. He had "no confidence in the sincerity of his professions either in favor of yourself or Mr. Jefferson." He doubted Gallatin's fitness for the job. He may have been an adequate secretary of the Treasury, Giles admitted, but "the distinction between the application of his talents to internal and external objects, is more general than you seem to imagine." Giles warned that installing Gallatin would "extend these distrusts" throughout the Senate toward the new administration, including upon Giles himself. This was not political intelligence; it was political intimidation.[5]

The bark of the Malcontents was likely greater than their bite, as even Giles had to admit that it was "probable the nomination" of Gallatin "would succeed in the Senate." But rather than fight for the best man for the job, Madison allowed himself to be cowed. He named Smith to the State Department and retained Gallatin at Treasury. Such surrender was notably different from the Madison of the 1780s and 1790s, who had never shrunk from a fight. Why would he back down now? Perhaps his instincts for legislative politics had been dulled over the years. He had been out of Congress since 1797, and for the previous eight years had been primarily concerned with foreign affairs. He also overestimated the good faith of Giles and Samuel Smith. He reckoned that keeping them happy was in his long-term interests, only to learn later on that nothing could appease them. And, of course, he still could make use of Gallatin's talents while he was at the Treasury Department. As for Robert Smith, Madison knew he was not up to the job, so the president—ever the workaholic—would just pick up the slack, serving for all intents and purposes as his own secretary of state.[6]

This was a terrible insult to Gallatin. He was not an especially vain man, and unlike Monroe he harbored no presidential ambitions. But it grated on him to see his performance in the Jefferson administration rewarded by Madison surrendering to his enemies. In a letter to Jefferson in November 1809, Gallatin expressed appreciation for the confidence that the former president had reposed in him, but still had to note his "extreme apprehensions" about the current situation. The Malcontents were "disposed to destroy" his reputation, and Gallatin worried "that they were sufficiently skillful and formidable to effect their object." If taking Gallatin down would threaten the Jeffersonian program, then his continuance in the cabinet "would be neither useful to the public or honorable to myself." Fortunately for Madison, Gallatin swallowed his pride, remained in office, and served admirably in the face of unrelenting and often dishonest criticism. Still, the whole affair reflected poorly on the new president, who let congressional pettiness debilitate his cabinet and insult his most trusted advisor.[7]

—————

THE ELEVENTH CONGRESS would not be seated in regular session until November 1809, eight months after Madison was inaugurated, so the new administration had some time to test whether the newly passed Nonintercourse Act might bring the European powers to the bargaining table. The law placed Great Britain and France on the same technical footing—as direct trade from the United States to either was prohibited—but in practice it strongly favored the British. The power of the Royal Navy was so vast that Great Britain could easily scoop up American vessels trading with the French, but the French naval presence in the Atlantic was so insignificant that it could not do the same for vessels trading with the British.

So it came as quite a surprise that spring when David Erskine, British minister to the United States, told Smith that he wanted to make a deal. Erskine was a pleasant fellow who was well-liked among Americans. Importantly, he was a Whig, the British political party that drew support from the London merchants who desperately wanted trade relations normalized. He had been named to the American post by Foreign Secretary Charles Fox, another Whig who had long been warmly disposed to the United States. But Fox had died suddenly in 1806, replaced in 1807 by George Canning, a Tory who wanted to drive a harder bargain. Erskine had managed to keep the American post despite the political shift in Britain, and he told the administration that Canning was willing to finally settle the *Chesapeake* affair and come to terms on their larger commercial dispute.

On the *Chesapeake* affair, Erskine and Smith easily found common ground. Great Britain agreed to disavow the assault on the *Chesapeake*, return the men forcibly taken from the American ship, and pay reparations to the families of those killed. Madison, who had long hated King George III, could not help but toss in an insult at the king via the instructions to his secretary of state. Smith told Erskine that while it was acceptable for the commander of the *Chesapeake* to not be further punished, the president would leave it to the "honor" of the king to do what he thought best.[8]

Canning's instructions to his minister on the trade war were much tougher than Erskine let on to the Americans. First, he told Erskine that Great Britain was willing to lift the orders in council that had so harassed American shipping in exchange for the United States withdrawing "the interdiction of its harbors to ships of war, and all non-intercourse and non-importation acts" for Great Britain—but not for France. Second, he wanted the United States to acknowledge the legitimacy of the Rule of 1756 and "renounce . . . the pretension of carrying on in time of war all trade with the enemy's colonies, from which was excluded during time of peace." Third, Canning wanted the United States to authorize Great Britain "to capture all such American vessels as may be found attempting to trade" with France.[9]

Sometimes the wish is the father of the thought, and Erskine thought Canning was offering him more flexibility than the foreign secretary actually was. In a lengthy back-and-forth between Erskine and Smith (who was carefully overseen by Madison), Erskine substantially watered down Canning's demands. The first condition was easy enough. The Americans were willing to reauthorize trade with Britain (but not France) in exchange for the repeal of the orders in council. It was the second and third terms that got Erskine into trouble. The Madison administration argued that a policy of nonintercourse with France but not with Britain would create the same effective condition as the Rule of 1756. Erskine concurred, and so the Americans did not have to agree to the rule's legitimacy. As for Canning's demand that British vessels be allowed to police American merchants, the administration rejected it out of hand but countered that, under the Nonintercourse Act, American merchants caught trading with France would have no recourse under American law, so there could be no basis of complaint from the United States against British captures. Again, Erskine agreed, and so the deal was done.

On April 19, Madison issued a proclamation announcing the resumption of trade with Great Britain, effective June 10. This was a diplomatic triumph for the administration, one that the president hoped to use as leverage to induce Napoleon to bargain. Scores of American merchant ships flooded British ports over the summer. If France wanted a piece of American commerce, it would have to cut a deal too. "If France be not bereft of common sense," Madison wrote to Jefferson just a few days later, "she will certainly not play into the hand of her enemy. . . . She cannot be insensible of the dangerous tendency of prolonging the commercial sufferings of her allies." In July, Madison followed up to Jefferson that "great inconveniences are felt in France, from the want of her external commerce," and that a "continuance of the blockading system" around Europe had become "peculiarly grating everywhere."[10]

But it was not to be. On April 30, Erskine wrote Canning that he believed it was "in conformity of the views of His Majesty's Government" for him to follow "the spirit of your instructions," by "my obtaining an official recognition" on nonintercourse, "and an understanding" on the Rule of 1756 and British action against American merchants. But Erskine had judged wrong. He learned in late July that Canning rejected the trade deal outright. As for the agreement on the *Chesapeake*, rumors filtered back to America that George III was so offended by Madison's dig at his honor that he rejected the settlement. Triumph turned into disaster. Madison complained to Gallatin of "Canning's insidiousness, as he must have known . . . that so degrading an idea" of British enforcement of American treaty obligations "would be received with disgust and indignation." Even more obnoxious was that the administration had suspended nonintercourse with Great Britain just long enough for London merchants to replenish their stocks. Britain seemed to be negotiating in bad faith.[11]

Adding insult to injury, Canning sent Francis Jackson to replace Erskine. A loyal Tory, Jackson was not a diplomat known for delicate negotiating. The president told Gallatin that he was "arrogant in his temper and manners, and that he has been the instrument for certain offensive transactions." This was likely a reference to an event that had occurred just a few years earlier, in 1807, in which the British government had dispatched Jackson to Copenhagen to give the Danes an ultimatum right before the British began a bombing campaign against the city. Jackson arrived in Washington, DC, at the end of the summer while Madison was still at Montpelier, but the new minister told Secretary of State Smith that he was in no hurry. "Delay suits him," Smith wrote to Madison on September 11. Four days later, Madison wrote back expressing disappointment that Jackson was unwilling even to speak "informal[ly]" about "his authorized communications" from the foreign secretary. It suggested to the president that Jackson had not been dispatched to "produce a conciliatory effect, and much less to change the present commercial relations of the two countries."[12]

He was right to be suspicious. When formal talks began in late summer, Smith asked Jackson for more information on why Canning had rejected the Erskine agreement, but Jackson waved the request off. He had nothing more to add beyond what Canning had told William Pinkney, the American minister in Great Britain, back in London. Realizing that Jackson was not there to bargain, Madison and Smith requested that future negotiations be conducted in writing. It was better for the administration to have a paper trail demonstrating British truculence to show Congress if the negotiations faltered. Jackson bristled at what he judged an inappropriate request, but Madison's instincts were right. As the talks continued, Jackson accused the Americans of negotiating with Erskine in bad faith. He claimed that Canning's instructions to Erskine "were in substance made known to you"—in other words, that Madison should have known the previous deal was illegitimate. When the administration rejected that accusation, Jackson doubled down on it. Finally, Madison and Smith told Jackson that "no further communication will be received from you," and they instructed Pinkney to ask Canning to recall him.[13]

If the collapse of the Erskine agreement and the breakdown of relations with Jackson accomplished anything, it was to disabuse the president of the hope that Britain wanted a real settlement. In the winter of 1810, Madison wrote former Pennsylvania senator George Logan that while he "devoutly" wished for "peace by means of justice," Britain had no such interest. Great Britain "persists in proceedings, which comprise the essence of hostility," and "she violates towards us rules, which she enforces against us in her own favor." Madison pointed out that the Erskine agreement offered in substance everything Britain wanted. So why take the "extraordinary" step of disavowing it? "We are compelled," Madison concluded, "to look to other motives for an explanation, and to include among these, a disinclination to put an end to differences from which such advantages are extracted by British commerce and British cruisers." In other words, Britain was jealous of the United States and was using the Napoleonic Wars as a pretext to suppress its rising commercial power.[14]

Madison was slowly setting the stage to establish Great Britain as the greater threat to American interests. The truth was that Napoleon was little better in his treatment of American merchants during this moment of crisis. As Madison wrote Jefferson in the spring of 1810, "The late confiscations by Bonaparte, comprise robbery, theft, and breach of trust, and exceed in turpitude any of his enormities, not wasting human blood." But Great Britain had assaulted American commerce for so much longer, and had proved itself so hostile to any reasonable conciliation, that its actual motive must have been to keep the United

States in its place. If war was to come, Madison would wage it against Great Britain, America's true rival.[15]

MADISON SUBMITTED HIS first State of the Union message to Congress in November 1809. Jefferson had established the tradition of written messages, rather than in-person addresses (which George Washington and John Adams had done), and the soft-spoken president was more than happy to follow in his friend's footsteps. In his message, he recounted the rejection of the Erskine agreement as well as the insults of Jackson, who had "[forgotten] the respect due to all governments." Meanwhile, France, "the other belligerent," had ignored "our just remonstrances," and the administration had been unable "to effect a favorable change" in Napoleon's Continental System. Yet Madison's address offered Congress no clear suggestion on how to respond to these indignities, and Congress itself had no particular course of action in view when it settled into business that fall. As Madison told Pinkney the following January, the Eleventh Congress was marked by a "diversity of opinions and prolixity of discussion"—lots of talk, but little else.[16]

One thing, at least, was clear to most: war at that time would be a bad idea. A decade of Jeffersonian frugality had cut the military to the bone. In Adams's last full year as president, the government spent $2.5 million on the army. Five years later, Jefferson and Gallatin had cut that figure down to a measly $700,000. After the attack on the *Chesapeake*, expenditures had increased, back to $3.3 million in 1809, but the armed forces were still in pitiful shape. By January 1810, the War Department reported a fighting force of just under 2,800 men. The navy was no better. A target of Jeffersonian economy, it, too, had been built up after

1805, but Jefferson's emphasis on small gunboats would do little good in a war against the greatest naval power on the face of the earth. Gallatin warned Congress that war would require substantial loans as well as heavy tax increases, two policies that had been anathema to the Republicans since the 1790s.[17]

Still, something, anything, had to be done. The Nonintercourse Act was a stopgap measure that was nearing its expiration. Representative Nathaniel Macon, in conjunction with Gallatin, proposed a new round of nonintercourse. "Macon's Bill Number 1," as their plan came to be styled, would have prohibited French and British ships from entering American ports, while giving the president the option to repeal the restrictions if either country began respecting American neutrality. The bill passed the House in late January, but Samuel Smith and the Malcontents gutted it in the Senate. After a month of back-and-forth between the two chambers, Congress passed what came to be known as "Macon's Bill Number 2." This law reversed the tack of Macon's first proposal by immediately opening trade with both Britain and France. That was the carrot. The stick was that the United States would impose commercial restrictions on the enemy of whatever nation agreed to end its depredations against US commerce.

This was truly the lowest common denominator, the bare minimum that Republicans who opposed both war and submission could agree to. Nobody supported it with any passion, perhaps because it made little sense: How was giving both sides exactly what they wanted up front going to convince them to change their behavior? If Madison had been a different type of president—willing to intervene actively in legislative affairs—he might have been able to provide some guidance. No doubt, Representative Madison would have been in the thick of the battle, working hard to guide public policy down a sensible path. But President Madison remained aloof.

The British saw Macon's Bill Number 2 as a total triumph, and rightly so. After swatting away the Erskine agreement, they were rewarded with the reopening of trade. And while the French technically enjoyed the same privileges, the Royal Navy dominated the Atlantic Ocean, ready to interdict American vessels bound for France or its colonies. In May 1810, Madison wrote to Jefferson that Great Britain "has every earthly motive to continue her restrictions against us. She has our trade in spite of France, as far as she can make it suit her interest, and our acquiescence in cutting it off from the rest of the world, as far as she may wish to distress her adversaries, to cramp our growth as rivals, or to prevent our interference with her smuggling monopoly." Yet the president sensed a potential diplomatic angle to pursue. Perhaps France may be induced to open up trade with the United States. Granted, Britain dominated the high seas by that point in the war, but the Royal Navy could not be everywhere at once. There was only so much naval traffic between America, France, and its colonial possessions that Britain could interdict. Would it not be in the interests of the French, Madison wrote to Pinkney, "to turn the tables on Great Britain by compelling her either to revoke her orders, or to lose the commerce of this country"?[18]

Napoleon took the bait, or so it seemed. In August 1810, the Duke of Cadore, French minister of foreign affairs, wrote to General John Armstrong, American minister to France, that effective November 1, Napoleon would revoke the Berlin and Milan Decrees, which had restricted American trade on the Continent. But Cadore's letter was tricky. He added, "It being understood that, in consequence of this declaration, the English shall revoke their orders in council, and renounce the new principles of the blockade . . . or that the United States, comfortably to the act you have just communicated, shall cause their rights to be respected by the English." What exactly did that mean?

Were the decrees repealed, or *would* they be repealed after the English acted? Compounding the ambiguity, Napoleon refused to release American ships seized before Cadore wrote the letter and continued to seize ships up until the effective date of November 1. The French emperor was trying to have his cake and eat it too. He wanted to induce the Americans to resume commercial warfare against Great Britain without actually granting substantive concessions on his own part.[19]

It would have been better for the United States if Napoleon had been an honest broker, but this was good enough for the president. On November 2, Madison issued a proclamation declaring that the Berlin and Milan Decrees were revoked, and that "all restrictions imposed" by Macon's Bill Number 2 "shall cease and be discontinued in relation to France and their dependencies." A new nonintercourse bill against Great Britain was enacted in the winter of 1811.[20]

Madison was no fool. He knew how much diplomatic wiggle room the Cadore letter left for Napoleon, and he knew that the crafty emperor played by his own rules. The president wrote Armstrong in October 1810 that it was "to be hoped that France will do what she is understood to be pledged for"—the implication being that, when it came to Napoleon, it was always better to hope for good faith than to expect it. Indeed, Napoleon continued to disappoint. As Madison reported to Congress in December 1810, France had so far failed to make "restoration . . . of the property of our citizens." The French seized the American vessels *Friendship* and the *New Orleans Packet* after the revocation was supposed to have gone into effect. Still, Madison's hope was either that Napoleon would begin to behave or that the president could bluff the British into thinking the emperor was behaving.[21]

The British were not deceived. In their read of the Cadore letter, it was clear that Napoleon was only offering to act secondarily. Richard Wellesley, the new British foreign secretary, told Pinkney that Napoleon was going to revoke Berlin and Milan Decrees, "*provided* that Great Britain . . . in consequence of *this declaration*, should revoke the orders in council, *and* should renounce those principles of blockade which the French Government alleged to be new." So, the British offered a similar bargain: they would repeal their orders, provided that Napoleon would actually repeal his. *Plus ça change, plus c'est la même chose.*[22]

The Cadore gambit had failed, but it was a clarifying failure. As the president told Attorney General Caesar Rodney in September 1810, while Napoleon may not really open trade with the United States, he at least offered the United States "an extrication from the dilemma, of a mortifying peace, or a war with both the great belligerents." By indulging in the Napoleonic fiction that the oppressive decrees had been lifted, Madison narrowed the potential outcomes to just two: a negotiated settlement with Great Britain or war with it alone.[23]

ON TOP OF doing the work of the presidency, Madison had to micromanage the State Department's delicate negotiations, for Smith simply lacked the capacity to handle them himself. Worse, it was becoming increasingly clear that the secretary of state was aligned with the Malcontents in Congress to undermine Madison's administration.

In the Senate, Smith's brother Samuel was still plotting to humiliate Gallatin, and he found an opportunity with the Bank of the United States. Chartered in 1791 for twenty years, it would need a new federal charter in 1811. Gallatin strongly advocated for renewal. In his judgment, the bank had been an unequivocal success. Not only had it served all the purposes Alexander Hamilton had originally envisioned, but the branch in New Orleans

had aided the Jeffersonian project of territorial expansion by pro-
liferating credit in the West and facilitating timely payments for
land purchases. Plus, under a Republican administration, there
was no need to fear it becoming a kind of political machine for
Federalism. Much of the party's old opposition to the bank had
softened, as the mainstream of the party had come to see it as
Gallatin did.

But the bank still had formidable opponents. The conservative Republicans remained steadfast in their opposition to it.
And the Malcontents were happy to sacrifice the bank to make
Gallatin look bad. The bank also had a new group of rivals. The
number of state banks had increased from less than ten in 1791
to more than one hundred in 1811. The Bank of the United
States regularly collected state bank notes as payment for taxes
or outstanding debts. This enabled it to act as a kind of primitive
central bank. By calling in the notes of the state banks, it could
contract their credit issuances, much to the state banks' dismay.

All told, Congress was evenly divided on the matter, and a
nudge from the president could have made the difference. But
Madison, who had been one of the harshest critics of the bank
when Hamilton first proposed it, refused to intervene, keeping
with his hands-off approach to legislative matters. Gallatin lobbied hard, but the anti-bank coalition prevailed and the recharter fell to a narrow defeat.

Robert Smith was not directly entangled in these congressional machinations against the administration's program, but
Samuel Smith certainly was—and it was nonsense to think that
the two were not working together. A congressional delegation
including Nathaniel Macon visited the president in early March
to warn that the ultimate aim of the Smiths was not just the removal of Gallatin but the defeat of Madison in the 1812 election.
When their entreaties had no effect on the president, Gallatin

took action himself. In March 1811, he offered Madison his resignation. He told the president that a successful cabinet required "not only capacity and talents in the administration, but also a perfect heart-felt cordiality amongst its members." In a pointed jab at Robert Smith, Gallatin continued, "in at least one of those points your administration is defective." He warned the president that "subdivisions and personal factions equally hostile to yourself and to the general welfare daily acquire additional strength." As for Gallatin, he felt that continuing at Treasury was "no longer of any public utility."[24]

This was the shot in the arm Madison needed. If it came down to a choice between Smith and Gallatin, that was no choice at all. Madison fired Smith by the end of the month. As a face-saving measure, Madison offered to appoint Smith minister to Russia, but Smith declined. A few weeks later, the *National Intelligencer* published a lengthy essay by Smith denouncing the administration. It had little political effect, except to confirm for the president that Smith was indeed the enemy his friends had warned him he was.

There really was just one option to replace Smith: Monroe. Though he had allowed John Randolph of Roanoke to run him against Madison during the 1808 election, Monroe had since returned to the party mainstream, thanks in large part to Jefferson. It grieved the former president enormously to see his closest friends become rivals, and he began working to heal the wounds as soon as Madison's term began. He wrote to Madison in March 1809 that Monroe had "separated himself from the junto which had got possession of him, and is quite sensible that they had used him for purposes not respecting himself always." Monroe visited Washington, DC, in the spring of 1810 and had a good meeting with Madison. Jefferson was "delighted to see the effect of Monroe's late visit . . . on his mind. There appears to

be the most perfect reconciliation and cordiality established towards yourself. I think him now inclined to rejoin us with zeal."
That summer, Madison and Monroe began corresponding with
one another for the first time in years.[25]

With the support of Madison's allies in Virginia, Monroe had
easily won the governorship in early 1811. This paved the way
for his return to prominence in the national party. In a series
of delicate letters written in a flurry at the end of March 1811,
Madison asked Monroe to helm the State Department. The two
were careful neither to assign nor accept blame for the kerfuffle
over the Monroe-Pinkney Treaty. They also mutually acknowledged that though they had differences of opinion in the past,
they could once again work together for the national interest. By
April 6, Monroe was secretary of state.

Meanwhile, Congress was finally growing a backbone. The
Twelfth Congress, seated in November 1811, was notably different from the wobbly Eleventh Congress. As always, there were
a multiplicity of factions within the body: the Federalists and
Old Republicans who opposed war, as well as the trimmers in
the middle who were unsure how to extricate the United States
from these foreign assaults on its commerce. But there was also
a rising group of pro-war members, dubbed the War Hawks.
While not necessarily more numerous than the other factions,
this group had the talent and drive to take control of Congress.
The War Hawks of the Twelfth Congress were a veritable who's
who of future political all-stars, including John C. Calhoun and
Henry Clay.

Clay had served briefly in the Senate during the Eleventh
Congress, but won election to the House for the Twelfth, recognizing that the real political action was in the lower chamber.
Handsome, charming, and politically astute, he quickly built up
an enormous following among the pro-war Republicans, who

elected him Speaker of the House. Clay transformed this previously ceremonial role into a position of real power, stacking the key committees with his War Hawk allies. He also stared down the imperious Randolph, who was used to intimidating the House into letting him rant and rave on the floor for hours on end. Clay used the Speaker's gavel without hesitation to keep him in line.

A brilliant orator, Clay gave forceful expression to the Republican view that Britain was motivated by jealousy. He told the House in December 1811, "The real cause of British aggression was not to distress an enemy but to destroy a rival." The trade that the United States had enjoyed before the embargo "was not of very vital consequence to the enemy of England." So, why would she "relinquish her valuable trade with this country . . . nay, more, hazard the peace of the country?" Clay answered that Great Britain "sickens at your prosperity, and beholds in your growth—your sails spread on every ocean, and your numerous seamen—the foundations of a power which, at no very distant day, is to make her tremble for her naval superiority."[26]

War sentiment was particularly strong on the western frontier, where settlers were convinced the British were encouraging Native assaults on their settlements. This was not precisely true. In point of fact, the British were lining up Native support to rebut a potential invasion of Canada, but it was hard to arm the Natives and lobby them against the Americans without inadvertently prompting a few attacks. After all, the Native tribes in the region had their own interests to advance, which only tangentially aligned with the British in this circumstance; they would fight the stream of white settlers pouring into their homelands regardless of how doing so affected Britain's international agenda. Angry Natives had found a natural-born leader in Tecumseh, a Shawnee warrior and chief who tried to forge a pan-tribal alliance against the United States. His forces clashed with those of territorial governor William Henry Harrison at the Battle of Tippecanoe in November 1811, which the Americans won despite heavy casualties. The victory turned Harrison into a national hero and seemingly confirmed the fears that the Natives had become the cat's-paw of the British.

Two days before Tippecanoe, Madison submitted his third State of the Union address to Congress. It expressed nary a trace of hope for diplomatic success with Great Britain, and instead conveyed the president's "deep sense of the crisis in which you are assembled." He called on Congress to make haste in expanding the army and navy and suggested in his ever so delicate manner the need for a tax increase. "I recommend to your consideration," he wrote, "the propriety of insuring a sufficiency of annual revenue at least to defray the ordinary expenses of Government, and to pay the interest on the public debt, including that on new loans which may be authorized." Gallatin followed up in January with a specific plan to raise $5 million through higher duties on several items, including sugar and spirits, as well as a stamp tax—an idea that he admitted had some "odium" thanks to the Revolutionary War, but was no "more inconvenient than any other internal tax." Gallatin also called for a $10 million loan to support government operations.[27]

The War Hawks might have imbued the Twelfth Congress with a more warlike spirit, but these proposals were still anathema to most Republicans. A larger army and navy, internal taxes, and an increase in the national debt were bound to be a hard sell for even the most vigorous administration—and executive vigor was not Madison's hallmark. Congress dithered on the tax issue for months, and the House did not pass a revenue bill until March. The Malcontents played politics on the army expansion; the administration called for an extra force for the army, but William Branch Giles took this as an opportunity to up the target number, as a way to make the president look weak. As for the navy, Congress refused an expansion outright, despite the fact that the United States was preparing to fight the most powerful navy in world history.[28]

As the winter turned to spring, the final hope for peace vanished. Day after day, the president waited for word that the British had softened their position, but no good news came. Enough was enough. On June 1, 1812, Madison submitted a war message to Congress that catalogued the various abuses the country had faced at the hands of the British since 1803. "In vain," Madison complained, the United States had "exhausted remonstrances and expostulations," yet there was "no proof" of "conciliatory dispositions" from Great Britain. The reason for that, Madison ultimately concluded, was the one he had hinted at in his inaugural address three years earlier and that Clay had stated outright: British jealousy of American commerce. Britain was looking to monopolize the Atlantic trade "which she covets for her own commerce and navigation. She carries on a war against the lawful commerce of a friend that she may the better carry on a commerce with an enemy." The House supported Madison's declaration of war by a seventy-nine-to-forty-nine vote, while the Senate agreed by a narrower nineteen-thirteen margin. New England was much stronger in the Senate than the House, and the region had no interest in going to war against its main trading partner.[29]

Sudden political and economic shifts in Great Britain forced a change in the country's posture, but too late to avert war. On June 23, 1812, just weeks after Madison had sent his war message, Britain revoked the orders in council. The mercantile and industrial interests, represented by the Whig Party, had long opposed commercial war with the United States, but the Tories enjoyed the backing of George III. By 1810, the king had gone insane, overwrought by the untimely death of his beloved daughter Amelia, and the prince regent (who would one day be crowned George IV) was more amenable to the Whigs. Meanwhile, a glut of paper money, combined with diminished trade with continental Europe and the United States, had tanked the British economy. With the prince regent now in charge, and the clamor from the Whigs overwhelming, the British government gave way. Alas, it was too late. War had already arrived.[30]

THE FIRST TERM of Madison's presidency has come in for a good deal of historical criticism over the years. The conventional narrative sees Madison as an uncertain leader who was ultimately outfoxed by Napoleon. In light of new evidence—especially a continuous stream of Madison's papers that have been unearthed, organized, and released to the public—that is not entirely a fair characterization, for they show a president with a clear-eyed view of the French dictator, determined to extricate his country from a war against both Britain and France. To be sure, it was particularly Madison's fault that the United States got itself stuck in that position during his time as secretary of state, but given the circumstances, the president made the best of a bad diplomatic situation.

This is not to say that Madison's first term was not without mistakes. Many of them were political in nature. Above all, he could not appreciate what Alexander Hamilton meant when, in *Federalist* 70, he argued that a "a vigorous Executive" is not only not "inconsistent with the genius of republican government" but is in fact a "leading character in the definition of good government." A strong executive, Hamilton noted, was "essential to the protection of the community against foreign attacks . . . to the steady administration of the laws . . . [and] to the security of liberty against the enterprises and assaults of ambition, of faction, and of anarchy." Madison did not see the presidency in these terms. In his political universe, the proper vehicle for republican politics was the legislature, and the task of the president was to offer Congress gentle guidance. So where Hamilton would have encouraged active intervention in congressional affairs, Madison demurred—even when legislative schemers kept Gallatin out of the State Department, indecisive moderates refused to give Madison a hard-nosed commercial policy he could use as a real bargaining tool against the British or French, and War Hawks demanded battle while refusing to prepare the country for all that war would entail.[31]

Nevertheless, it would be wrong to suppose Madison a passive spectator to his presidency or a simple executive clerk. He steadfastly refused to bend the knee to Great Britain. He would not accept the Rule of 1756 or impressments. When it was clear that a strategy of commercial restrictions would not be successful, he purposefully pushed Napoleon out of the way. The French had assaulted American commerce, often just as aggressively as the British, but the president believed Great Britain was the bigger threat. That country was still trying to keep the United States in its place, just as it had done during the colonial era and just as it had done with the Jay Treaty. America had to stand up for itself, and if commercial warfare would not achieve this object, then it would have to be by a military contest. It is to Madison's credit that he methodically and systematically narrowed the range of options so that, by June 1812, war with England alone was the only remaining choice. Madisonian diplomacy did not achieve an honorable peace, but it avoided the choice between, as the president put it, "a mortifying peace, or a war with both the great belligerents."[32]

As the nation girded itself for war in the summer of 1812, a great irony hung over the administration. Madison had always believed deep in his bones that the institutions typically required to wage war—heavy taxes, standing armies, strong navies—were anathema to self-government. These were tools for elites to burden the people, cowing them into obeying a government out of fear rather than consent. Madison had tried for nearly a decade to resolve the conflict with Great Britain peacefully, but to no avail. There was no other choice but for the United States to take up arms for itself against the British once more. The peace-loving Madison was now the nation's first wartime president.

13

THE WAR OF 1812

FROM A MILITARY standpoint, the United States was totally incapable of waging an effective campaign against Great Britain when it declared war in June 1812. The problems were wide-ranging, each of them serious in and of themselves, catastrophic when taken together. For starters, years of Republican policies had reduced the regular army to a bare minimum. In 1811, there were but seven infantry regiments, plus one regiment each of rifles, artillery, and light artillery, though the government had sold the horses belonging to the light artillery regiment. Congress approved a massive expansion of the army, but by November, the War Department estimated that only 9,800 new recruits had signed up. One problem was the puny benefit package for enlistees: a bonus of $15 for a five-year term, which was less generous than what many state militias offered.

If the army was too small at the bottom, it was incompetent at the top. Many of the generals put in command at the beginning of the war were holdovers from the Revolution. In the words of Winfield Scott, a young officer who would distinguish

himself during the conflict and would become the Whig nominee for president in 1852, a number of them were "very generally
sunk into either sloth, ignorance, or habits of intemperate drinking." The junior officer corps was hardly better. The Jefferson administration had established the military academy at West Point
in 1802, but by the time of the war it had produced only 120
graduates. The junior officers who commanded most forces on
the field were, per Scott, "coarse and ignorant . . . swaggerers."
Politics made this problem worse. Scott recollected, "Party spirit
of that day knew no bounds. . . . Federalists were almost entirely excluded from selection, though great numbers were eager
for the field, and in New England and some other states, there
were but very few educated Republicans. Hence the selections
from those communities consisted mostly of coarse and ignorant
men." Madison took steps to correct that, searching for qualified
Federalists to give commands, but was usually met with pushback from politicians within his party. In March 1812, Henry
Dearborn, Jefferson's secretary of war, warned Madison that the
"the active supporters of the government, and the Republicans
generally" might "feel very unpleasantly, and be less active in the
necessary preparations for war" if the president offered too many
positions to Federalists.[1]

The military also struggled on basic matters of logistics.
When the war began, Secretary of War William Eustis—whose
primary qualification for the job had been his loyalty to the Republican cause—had just eight clerks working under him. In
1812, Congress expanded the department to include a quar-
termaster general, a commissary general, and an ordnance department. But there still was no rational system in place, and
military planners would often find themselves in competition
with one another for the same supplies.

Meanwhile, the navy was so small as to be an afterthought
in strategic calculations. Jefferson's obsession with gunboats as

coastal defenders turned out to have been useless for this conflict. The British patrolled American high coasts at their leisure.
The country only had a few frigates that could go up against the
Royal Navy. They were mainly tasked with picking and choosing
battles against the British on the high seas. This their young and
intrepid commanders did to enormous effect, winning victories
against the British that Napoleon's fleets had never managed.
As small as it was, the American fleet was easy for the mighty
Royal Navy to underestimate, and the Americans exploited this
seeming weakness to their advantage, selecting battles that maximized the opportunity for success. While the navy's triumphs
yielded relatively few strategic gains, they were enormously important in boosting public morale.

The great hope of the Republican cause was the militia,
whose existence had been essential to the party's orthodoxy since
its founding in the 1790s. Republicans believed that the rule
of a free government was premised on the consent of the governed rather than the force of its arms, so it had no need for
a large standing army. Thus, military establishments should be
kept to a minimum, while militias—or state-regulated bodies of
private, arms-bearing citizens—could defend the republic. This
fear of standing armies informed the Second Amendment's right
to "keep and bear arms," as well as the stipulation in Article 1,
Section 8 of the Constitution that "no Appropriation of Money"
for the army "shall be for a longer Term than two Years." The
additional army sanctioned by the Federalists during the Quasi-
War of 1798 against France had prompted a widespread public backlash that brought the Republicans into power two years
later. Ever since, Republican leaders had touted the militia as the
backbone of American defense.

This aspiration was illusory. By 1812, the War Department
estimated there were more than seven hundred thousand militiamen available, but they were badly trained, poorly equipped,

and wedded to parochial interests rather than national objectives. Former congressman Walter Jones complained to Madison in the fall of 1813 that the Virginia militia was "undisciplined, indifferently armed, worse clad and still worse commanded. . . . The appointment of militia officers has long dwindled, into an affair of favor, intrigue and relationship. No military feeling in those who canvas for commissions, no military judgment in those who bestow them."[2]

Once again, politics was a confounding factor. New England states persistently refused to comply with presidential requests for militia support. The war was unpopular there, and governors were not going to put their men in harm's way for it. In July 1812, Elbridge Gerry—the former governor of Massachusetts who would soon be elected vice president—wrote Madison that the state's current governor, Caleb Strong, was not going to help raise needed soldiers, and that Gerry had "urged Republicans in their private capacities" to search for "every man in the state who will enroll himself for supporting at all hazards the national government." Writing from Boston around the same time, Henry Dearborn warned the president that leaders both in and out of the state government were "endeavoring to inspire as general an opposition to the measures of the general government as possible." Madison himself complained privately that the "rancorous opposition in some of the eastern states to the war is peculiarly unfortunate, as it has the double effect of crippling its operations, and encouraging the enemy to withhold any pacific advances otherwise likely to be made."[3]

Despite these problems, the government was supremely confident of success in the summer of 1812. News of the repeal of the orders in council came in August, but it was too little, too late. Madison recollected in retirement that if word had come a little sooner, the declaration "would have been stayed," so that "negotiations on the subject of impressments" could have commenced. But the government did not receive the announcement until a month after the war had begun, when British forces seized Fort Mackinac between Lakes Michigan and Huron, and the Americans were already preparing for their assault.[4]

The administration's first target was Canada—specifically, the Niagara Peninsula, which would put the Americans in place to attack Montreal. The United States set its sights on its northern neighbor for several reasons. First and foremost, the administration and its allies believed that it could be easily acquired. Jefferson boasted that conquest of the region "will be a mere matter of marching." There were not that many British regulars in the territory, and Americans placed little stock in the threat posed by the Canadian militia or the Native tribes who had allied with the British. Contrasted against the seeming invincibility of the British Royal Navy on the Atlantic Ocean, a land war against Canada seemed like a good idea.[5]

Victory in Canada could serve American ambitions in many ways. For some, it scratched the itch of Manifest Destiny that had begun to flare after the Louisiana Purchase, as Americans, particularly westerners, grew convinced that North America belonged to them by divine right. From Madison's point of view, the acquisition of Canada might revive the prospects of commercial discrimination, since the British West Indies had relied on Canadian staples to feed itself during the trade war of the last five years. Canada could also be used as a bargaining chip. If the British wanted the territory back, they would have to grant the concessions that America had demanded in its declaration of war.[6]

Canada was sparsely populated, with the great bulk of the population living in "Lower Canada," today known as the province of Quebec. The American assault would begin against

"Upper Canada," or present-day Ontario, which had many fewer residents. The administration planned a three-pronged attack for the summer of 1812. William Hull would march a force eastward across the Detroit River, while Stephen Van Rensselaer would attack westward from the Niagara River. Henry Dearborn would then march northward to Montreal. Combined, these assaults would secure Lower Canada for the United States and put it in a better position to assault the well-fortified city of Quebec.

The plan was a total failure, perhaps the most embarrassing series of military campaigns in all of American history. Hull took a squad of a couple hundred regulars, veterans of the Battle of Tippecanoe, and over a thousand badly disciplined militiamen across the Detroit River in July, but was pushed back to Fort Detroit on the American side in early August by a British force under the intrepid leadership of Isaac Brock, who then tricked Hull into surrendering. Brock dressed Canadian militiamen as British regulars, while his Native allies, under the command of Tecumseh, marched around the fort to make it look like their numbers were greater than reality. Hull, who was drinking heavily, feared an impending slaughter, panicked, and gave up Fort Detroit without firing a shot. Eventually, he was court-martialed for cowardice and sentenced to death, though President Madison spared his life.

The Niagara expedition was just as disastrous. Van Rensselaer, a wealthy New York merchant, arrived in August to find a ragtag assortment of badly trained militiamen, whose leaders were squabbling with the officers of the regular army over who should command. The Americans attacked in early October, but their assault across the Niagara River was hampered by a limited number of boats, which kept them from bringing their full complement into Canada. Worse, New York militiamen, frightened by the sounds of Native war cries, refused to cross into a foreign country. The Americans who did make it over fought bravely under the command of Winfield Scott. Though the battle went well at first, the Americans were overwhelmed, and some one thousand surrendered to the British.

As for the Montreal campaign, it did not end in disaster like Detroit or Niagara, but only because it never happened. Dearborn struggled to raise sufficient troops, prompting Madison to complain to Monroe in August that "the enlistments for the regular army fall short of the most moderate calculation," while "the militia detachments are either obstructed by the disaffected governors, or chilled by the Federal spirit diffused throughout the region most convenient to the theater." Finally, in November, Dearborn was ready to march—or so it seemed. When he reached the Canadian border, some two-thirds of his soldiers refused to cross, forcing him to call off the whole assault.[7]

It was only the navy, so long ignored by the Republicans, that kept the nation from total humiliation that year. In August, the USS *Constitution* defeated the HMS *Guerriere* southeast of Halifax. It was a fantastic moral victory for the Americans, who captured the *Guerriere*'s crew and liberated ten impressed American seamen. The *Constitution* became the stuff of legends, earning the nickname Old Ironsides for its ability to withstand cannon fire from the *Guerriere*. In October, the USS *United States* defeated the HMS *Macedonian* several hundred miles south of the Azores, claiming the British frigate as a prize of war. The *Constitution* followed this up with another victory against the HMS *Java* in late December, off the coast of Brazil. For the British to suffer three defeats like this was virtually unheard of and gave a needed boost to American morale. Even the defeat of the USS *Chesapeake* in June at the hands of the HMS *Shannon* became a rallying cry for the American cause, as the mortally wounded

American captain James Lawrence urged his sailors, "Don't give up the ship!"[8]

THE VICTORIES OF the *Constitution* and the *United States*, along with the valor of the *Chesapeake*, may have been good for public relations, but they did little to advance the American cause. The Canadian invasion was a complete failure, a national embarrassment, and a spur to resistance for a large portion of the country—especially New England, which had long warned that such a war would be disastrous. The grim fact was that by the time Congress reassembled in the fall of 1812, President Madison had little but bad news to report.

In fact, it was not entirely certain that he would be president for much longer. The presidential contest of that year was the closest since 1800, and it was not clear that Madison had won until December. Madison had easily been renominated by the Republican congressional caucus, and Elbridge Gerry had joined the ticket to prop up the party position in New England. Madison's opponent, the ever-ambitious DeWitt Clinton of New York, had built a coalition between New York Republicans disaffected over Virginia's domination of the presidency and northern Federalists upset about the war. But this had required the Clintonites to temporize about the conflict. To northern War Hawks they promised a more vigorous campaign, and to the Federalists they talked of peace. Madison swept the South and the West, and carried Pennsylvania comfortably, albeit with ten thousand fewer votes than he had four years earlier. But the Federalists won more northern votes for Congress than the Republicans, the first time this had happened since 1798. The Republican congressional majority, while still secure, had shrunk—a clear signal of public disaffection with the administration, especially in the North. It was hardly a ringing endorsement of the president's performance in his first term.

In his State of the Union message in November 1812, written before his reelection was certain, Madison felt it his "first duty" to remind Americans of "the providential favors which our country has experienced": the health of its citizens, the bounty of its harvests, and the development of its natural resources. But "these blessings" were "necessarily mingled" with "the pressures and vicissitudes incident to the state of war into which the United States have been forced by the perseverance of a foreign power in its system of injustice and aggression." With that prologue, the president retold the sorry events of Detroit and Niagara, making sure to rebuke New England for its refusal to provide militia support. "It is obvious," he warned, "that if the authority of the United States to call into service and command the militia for the public defense can be thus frustrated . . . they are not one nation for the purpose most of all requiring it." He alluded to that old Republican bugaboo of standing armies: should states continue not to do their part, "the public safety may have no other resource than in those large and permanent military establishments which are forbidden by the principles of our free government."[9]

It was an unhappy address for an unhappy moment. Indeed, Republican faith was flagging—if not in the martial vigor of the country itself, then in the capacity of Madison to bring it fully to bear. In a letter to Caesar Rodney in December, Henry Clay said that he did "not despair. The justness of our cause— the adequacy of our means to bring it to a successful issue—the spirit and patriotism of our county . . . will at last I think bring us honorably out." But he had his doubts about "Mr. Madison," whom he believed was "wholly unfit for the storms of war.

Nature has cast him in too benevolent a mold. . . . He is not fit for the rough and rude blasts which the conflicts of nations create." But Gallatin was closer to the mark than Clay in sizing up Madison's character. As the secretary of the treasury had remarked back in 1808, the president was "slow in taking his ground, but firm when the storm arises." Madison may have been short, slightly built, and soft-spoken, but his spirit would not flag during the three years of this brutal contest.[10]

His first move in the fall of 1812 was the most obvious: a change of personnel in the cabinet. Secretary of War William Eustis and Secretary of the Navy Paul Hamilton had to go. The failure of the land campaign demonstrated that Eustis was not up for the job, which the secretary all but admitted when he tendered his resignation. The department, he wrote, needed "some other citizen . . . possessing greater military knowledge and commanding in a higher degree the public confidence." As for Hamilton, the naval victories that year provided him no cover. He was widely thought to have mismanaged the department, and he had a reputation for heavy drinking.[11]

Of course, it was easier to fire incompetent administrators than to find good replacements. At the Navy Department, Madison settled upon William Jones, a Philadelphia merchant who had some experience in maritime commerce. The War Department was a more difficult matter. The obvious choice was Monroe, who agreed to take the position only on a temporary basis. Presidential ambitions were never far from his mind, and if he was to leave the State Department, it would have to be for something that set him up for 1816, like a lieutenant generalship. That left two alternatives: New York governor Daniel Tompkins or John Armstrong, former minister to France. Gallatin recommended Armstrong, who had more experience in military affairs and who had a public "standing . . . as both a military man and as a man of talents." Anyway, Tompkins was needed "in the present political situation of New York," lest the Federalists get control of the state and further undermine the war effort. But Armstrong had his downsides. He was known to have a temper, was exceedingly ambitious, and had flirted with the Clinton-ite forces in the election of 1808. Monroe, ever sensitive to his political prospects, would become convinced that Armstrong was using the job as a stepping-stone to the White House. Gall-atin likewise had his doubts that Armstrong would "bring in the administration that entire unity of feeling, that disinterested zeal, that personal attachment, which are so useful in producing hearty co-operation and unity of action." But desperate times called for desperate measures, and so the choice was made.[12]

On the congressional front, the Republicans realized that af-ter the shellacking taken in the 1812 campaign, the army needed to be reorganized. The administration proposed creating mil-itary districts for the whole country, with regular troops and commanders overseeing militia defenses. Congress agreed to this, as well as to the administration's call for another expansion of the army.

Public finance was also a problem. Gallatin warned Congress that the public debt in 1813 would increase by nearly $11 mil-lion, requiring a substantial loan. But the bond market was not obliging. The government was able to get only about $4 million in subscriptions for a loan of $16 million at an effective inter-est rate of 6 percent, so Gallatin had to up the offer to 7.5 per-cent. This unresponsiveness was due to a lack of confidence in the administration, as well as the deep-seated opposition to the war in New England, where much of the nation's hard cash was located.[13]

The Twelfth Congress expired on March 4, 1813, but the press of business was so great that Madison called the new

Thirteenth Congress into special session in May. Federalists in the House, led by a young Daniel Webster, took the opportunity to offer a fresh attack on the very premise of the war, demanding information about the details of the revocation of the Berlin and Milan Decrees, and by implication whether the administration had any business going to war against Britain in the first place. Nothing came of these rhetorical assaults, but it set the tone for an unhappy session, which dragged on into August, when the heat in Washington, DC, left many officials, including Madison, sick. Always prone to episodes of "bilious fever," Madison fell prey once more to it in June 1813. This would be one of the worst attacks in his life, and there were worries that he might not survive, but he did.[14]

Madison had three major agenda items for the session. First, he asked for a new round of taxes to alleviate the deficit problem, to which Congress agreed, but only after lots of squabbling along regional and party lines. Second, he asked for a new embargo to tamp down trading between New England and Canada, a commerce that effectively meant American farmers were feeding British soldiers. The House agreed, but the Senate—where the Federalists were stronger—voted it down. Third, Madison asked the Senate to approve members for a peace delegation, which would participate in talks with the British mediated by the Russians. The president nominated Gallatin; John Quincy Adams, who was already serving as minister to Russia; and James Bayard, a Federalist senator from Delaware. The Senate approved Adams and Bayard, but the Malcontent forces conspired to reject Gallatin's nomination.

Congress was just as dysfunctional as ever. The reality was that a substantial Federalist minority did not want to fight this war at all, and the Republican commitment to it was tenuous at best. The Malcontents in the Senate were still pursuing their petty political agenda, while many more could not shake off the old Jeffersonian shibboleths that a republican nation can fight a war on the cheap.

———————

WHEN ARMSTRONG TOOK over as secretary of war, he judged that there was no way to make an effective assault on Montreal in the spring of 1813, though doing nothing was politically perilous. Federalist Rufus King had just been selected by the New York legislature to serve in the Senate, and the Republicans feared that, should Governor Tompkins lose reelection to the Federalists in the spring, the entire war effort would be seriously endangered. So, the administration agreed on another assault on the Niagara Peninsula, with its first target being York (present-day Toronto). The city had little strategic value, but a victory there in late April was crucial for public relations. In a fateful move, the Americans burned the public buildings at York, an insult that the British would not forget when they invaded Washington, DC, the following summer. In May, an American force led by Winfield Scott took Fort George on Lake Ontario, a triumph whose strategic value was wasted when his commanding officer ordered him not to pursue fleeing British forces, which might have tipped the scales on the Niagara Peninsula. When the Americans began to prepare for their assault on Montreal, they abandoned Fort George, which the British quickly retook and used to attack Fort Niagara and then raid hamlets on the American side of the Niagara River, including Buffalo. As Tompkins wrote Madison in January, "The panic which these events have spread amongst the inhabitants for a number of miles within that frontier is so great that they are abandoning their possessions and retiring into the interior."[15]

If the Niagara campaign of 1813 was bloody and indecisive, the Americans could at least celebrate an unambiguous triumph on Lake Erie. Lake Ontario had more strategic value for the goal of taking Montreal, but Isaac Chauncey, the American commanding naval officer on the lake, never could acquire superiority over the British. It was a different story on Lake Erie, where the British forces were not as strong. Commodore Oliver Hazard Perry built a small but sturdy naval force at Presque Isle, a fleet crowned by the brigs USS *Lawrence* (named after the commander of the *Chesapeake*) and USS *Niagara*. In September 1813, Perry met the British forces, and despite being heavily outnumbered, scored what William Jones told Madison was "a naval victory . . . complete, glorious, and important in the effects it must inevitably produce." The British fleet was defeated, and Lake Erie would be under American control for the rest of the war. Perry's triumph enabled William Henry Harrison to reassert American power in the northwest, culminating in a decisive victory at the Battle of the Thames in early October. The British would never again threaten the American position west of the Niagara River, and Tecumseh's Native revolution was crushed.[16]

But the subsequent assault on Montreal was a disaster. The administration had grown tired of Dearborn's inability to bring victory in the region and replaced him with James Wilkinson, who was little better. He had a dubious reputation and was addicted to laudanum, an opium tincture. This was hardly a man to inspire confidence, but such was the sorry state of military leadership in 1813. Unsurprisingly, the Americans under his command were brutalized at the Battle of Crysler's Farm in November, despite heavily outnumbering their British adversaries. A corresponding attack by American general Wade Hampton moving north from Lake Plattsburgh also ended in defeat at the Battle of Chateauguay.

The 1813 campaign demonstrated that the Americans could fight and win battles in this war when placed under competent commanders with clear strategic objectives. Still, the only thing the Americans had done was retake territory that had been lost the previous summer. There were no lasting gains on the Niagara, and the prospect of taking Montreal now seemed fanciful at best. Worse for the United States, Napoleon's fortunes were sinking rapidly. Whether they cared to admit it or not, the Americans had always depended on the emperor's ability to tyrannize Europe, thereby drawing the balance of British power onto the Continent. Napoleon's invasion of Russia in 1812 had gone badly, and in October 1813 the anti-French coalition scored a decisive victory at the Battle of Leipzig. Early in 1814, the coalition invaded France, triumphed over the emperor's armies, and sent him into exile on the island of Elba. With Napoleon out of the picture, the British planned to beef up their forces in North America for the 1814 campaign.

WHEN CONGRESS ASSEMBLED for its regular session in the fall of 1813, public finances had sunk to a precarious state. The Treasury Department reported revenue of just $16 million against spending of $45 million—a deficit so large that the government would have to borrow to pay back the interest owed on its debt.

Diplomatic prospects seemed a bit less bleak. The British had rejected the Russian offer to mediate but had proposed direct peace talks with the United States. The two sides agreed to hold them in Gothenburg, Sweden, although they eventually moved to Ghent, Belgium. Madison renominated Adams, Bayard, and Gallatin (who was confirmed this time around), and supplemented them with Jonathan Russell, who had served as chargé d'affaires for the American mission in Great Britain, as well as Clay.

By the spring of 1814, the United States was ready for another campaign along the Niagara River, this time under the command of Major General Jacob Brown, who had distinguished himself in the previous year's campaign. The brave and intrepid Scott, meanwhile, was promoted to brigadier general. The Americans easily recaptured Buffalo and then took Fort Erie on the southern end of the Canadian side of the river. But subsequent battles that fall were equal parts bloody and indecisive. By the end of the fighting season, they had made no progress beyond Fort Erie, and they were no further along in their plan to invade Montreal, let alone Quebec.

While the Americans pressed the issue on the Niagara, the British were preparing a multipronged invasion of the United States. The British had grown extremely resentful that this war had ever taken place. Their view was that they were standing up to Napoleonic tyranny, and rather than taking their side, the United States had selfishly looked to enrich itself through the carrying trade. Moreover, the American land campaign in Canada looked to them like a savage war of territorial conquest. The burning of York especially rankled British feelings. With Napoleon having been pacified (at least temporarily, for he would later break free from his exile on Elba, reassemble his army, and force the coalition of nations arrayed against him to battle him once more), the British planned a vicious counterattack in the summer of 1814, in the hopes of winning significant concessions from the American diplomats at Ghent. The British forces moved simultaneously on two fronts. The main thrust came down from Montreal into upstate New York, engaging the Americans at the town of Plattsburgh along Lake Champlain. Meanwhile, they launched an attack in the Chesapeake Bay. Both assaults would be supported by seasoned British redcoats who had served under the Duke of Wellington in the Napoleonic Wars.

The United States was badly fortified at Lake Champlain, with much of the region's forces involved in that summer's Niagara campaign. Fortunately, the Americans had a brilliant naval commander on the lake, Commandant Thomas Macdonough, whose smaller force outmaneuvered the British squadron to win a smashing victory on September 11, 1814. Macdonough's triumph on the lake spooked the commander of British land forces, George Prévost, into withdrawing. The American victory at Plattsburgh had upended a major element of the British counterattack strategy and likely saved upstate New York and perhaps much of New England from falling into enemy hands.

The Chesapeake region had long been vulnerable to attack, given the lack of American frigates available to patrol the Atlantic. The USS *Constellation* was hemmed in by a British blockade of Norfolk, as were the USS *Erie* and USS *Ontario*, which basically left a hodgepodge of small vessels to guard the regional waterways. By early July, Madison had received intelligence from spies within British ranks that an attack was coming not only against the region but upon the capital itself. Armstrong did not buy it. He reckoned that Washington, DC—a tiny hamlet with no strategic value—would not be worth the efforts of the British. He wagered that Annapolis—a larger commercial town on the Chesapeake Bay just downstream of Baltimore—would be the target.

Armstrong miscalculated. The British were sore over the brutality of the Niagara campaign, especially the burning of York, and from their point of view this whole war was an American temper tantrum that had to be dealt with severely. In August, Vice Admiral Alexander Cochrane floated a naval flotilla up the Chesapeake Bay. The corresponding land forces, under the command of Major General Robert Ross, who had served under the Duke of Wellington, disembarked at Benedict, Maryland, on August 19. At that point, it was still unclear if British forces would march northeast to Annapolis or northwest to Washington. But soon enough they turned toward the capital and met a force of local militia at the Battle of Bladensburg on August 24. Coincidentally, Madison had been there just a few hours before, arriving to inspect the regiments. But, he recollected, when apprized that the fight was about to begin, he decided "it would be proper to withdraw to a position in the rear, where we could act according to circumstances." It was a lucky thing too. The militia, badly trained and poorly disciplined, was routed despite the inferior size of the British force.[17]

That gave Cochrane and Ross a clear shot at Washington, DC, which, thanks to Armstrong's miscalculations, had largely been left unprepared. The British arrived late on August 24 and proceeded to burn down the House and Senate, the Treasury and State Departments, the Library of Congress, and other public buildings. A garrison of British regulars found the White House abandoned, but with a large dinner feast that had been left behind in the haste to flee. The men stuffed themselves, toasted the health of the prince regent, and burned the executive mansion to the ground too. Fortunately, they did not come upon the copy of Gilbert Stuart's famous portrait of George Washington, for Dolley Madison had made sure it was safeguarded before she abandoned the capital.

About twenty-four hours after they had arrived, the British departed. Armstrong was right in one regard: the city had little strategic value. The point of the attack was to send a message to the Americans. The invading force rejoined the main British squadron by September 11. At this point, Cochrane was unsure about his next move. He eventually decided to press on to Baltimore, but his indecision gave the city time to prepare. Managing the city's defenses was Samuel Smith, the former senator and Malcontent rival of Madison who had taken charge of the local militia. By the time the British came upon the city on September 12, the Americans were ready.

The British attack upon Baltimore came from two directions. Ross took his land forces in from the east, while the Royal Navy made a move on Baltimore Harbor. On land, the two sides clashed at the Battle of North Point, during which Ross was killed, and on September 13 at the Battle of Hampstead Hill. The American lines held, while the British troops received no naval support. Though the Royal Navy blasted heavy artillery for hours on end upon Fort McHenry, located on the harbor, they could not break through. By September 15, it was clear that the Americans had triumphed in the series of engagements that came to be known as the Battle of Baltimore, which would be memorialized by Francis Scott Key in "The Star-Spangled Banner." Trapped on a ship while the Royal Navy pounded Fort McHenry, Key was left wondering anxiously whether the American position would hold. By the morning of the fourteenth, he had his answer:

> O say can you see, by the dawn's early light,
> What so proudly we hailed at the twilight's last gleaming,
> Whose broad stripes and bright stars through the perilous fight,
> O'er the ramparts we watched, were so gallantly streaming?
> And the rocket's red glare, the bombs bursting in air,
> Gave proof through the night that our flag was still there;
> O say does that star-spangled banner yet wave
> O'er the land of the free and the home of the brave?

This famous stanza, known by virtually every American to this day, is a perfect encapsulation not only of the Battle of Baltimore but the War of 1812 itself. The United States celebrated not because it had won, but because it had not lost. And to add insult to injury, the Americans set Key's poem to an old British drinking song.

———————

WHEN THE DUST settled after the Chesapeake campaign, Madison took the opportunity once again to reshuffle his cabinet. Armstrong had to go, of that there could be no doubt. He had to answer not only for the burning of Washington but also for another year of stalemate in Niagara. Moreover, his political scheming had become intolerable. Monroe complained bitterly that he was allocating War Department patronage for his own political future. Armstrong had also threatened to launch a formal investigation into William Henry Harrison, one of the few American military leaders who could actually win. Armstrong and Harrison disliked each other, and Armstrong perhaps feared the popular general as a future rival for the presidency. In any case, the proud general resigned in protest, after which Armstrong awarded a major generalship to Andrew Jackson without getting Madison's approval. Enough was enough. Armstrong was out, and Madison gave Monroe the dual task of managing the State and War Departments, thereby ensuring that he had no major rivals for the presidency.

Meanwhile, the peace negotiations in Europe moved slowly. The British, despite proffering the invitation for direct negotiations, did not seem eager to engage. When the two sides finally met in August 1814, the British made a series of outrageous requests. They wanted control of portions of Maine and Minnesota, a demilitarization of the Great Lakes, a renegotiation of American fishing rights off the coast of Newfoundland, and a Native American buffer state in the northwest. The Americans rejected these demands outright. Adams, who headed the

American delegation, complained in his diary that the British were "arrogant, overbearing, and offensive" in their attitude toward the Americans. Clay, an expert card player, sensed they were bluffing. He wrote Monroe on August 18 that the British were "attempting an experiment upon us, under the supposition that a panic has seized us, and that their policy is to consume as much time as possible . . . under the hope that they will strike some signal blow during the present campaign." As Adams recollected, Clay suspected that the British were playing a game of Brag with the Americans. "He said the art of it was to beat your adversary by holding your hand with a solemn and confident phiz; and out-bragging him." Clay reckoned "it was time for us to begin to play Brag with them." He was right. After the British campaign of 1814 failed to produce any breakthroughs, their diplomats in Belgium became much more amenable to making a deal. On Christmas Day, the two sides signed what came to be known as the Treaty of Ghent, which enshrined the status quo antebellum. Nobody gained anything of substance.[18]

In the meantime, Admiral Cochrane—unaware that a deal was about to be struck—had sailed the British fleet down to New Orleans to engage the American forces now under the command of Jackson, fresh off a decisive victory over the Creek Indians, whom the Americans feared might join in alliance with the British. When the British landed in early January, Jackson's motley assortment of regulars, Tennessee volunteers, freedmen, and Natives was ready. On January 8, British forces under the command of Edward Pakenham marched on several well-fortified lines of American artillery and riflemen. The Americans slaughtered them. Pakenham was killed, and all told the British suffered some two thousand casualties to just three hundred on the American side.[19]

President Madison was unaware of the events in Ghent or New Orleans until weeks after they happened, so slow was communication in the early nineteenth century. By the end of January he had been a wartime commander for two and a half years, and it looked like the conflict would continue on. The country had grown weary of the fight, and New England in particular was getting restless. Fervently opposed to the war from the beginning, its governors would frequently withhold the assistance of their state militias, its creditors would refuse to loan money to the government, and its merchants would trade surreptitiously with the enemy. In December 1814, delegates from Connecticut, Massachusetts, and Rhode Island met in Hartford to discuss their situation, with rumors circulating that they might advocate a break from the union. As it turned out, no such call was made. Instead, the Hartford Convention advocated for a series of constitutional amendments to limit the power of the South and West and recommended a second meeting in June should the "exigency of a crisis so momentous may require." Its bark had been louder than its bite, and Madison reportedly laughed when he read the report on January 12.[20]

The president would soon have more reasons for cheer. Word soon came of Jackson's triumph at New Orleans, and of the peace forged at Ghent. In seemingly an instant, the nation's war weariness disappeared, and the Americans could celebrate a kind of victory. Ghent produced no substantive concessions from the British, but the fact that the Americans yielded none of their own, combined with Jackson's triumph at New Orleans, gave the United States a sense of a moral victory. The nation had once again stood up to the most formidable power on the face of the earth and held its own.

———

JUDGED IN HISTORICAL retrospect, the euphoria of early 1815 seems fanciful, if not downright delusional. From 1812 through the middle of 1814, the war could scarcely have gone worse for the United States. Not only had the country not accomplished any of its goals, but it also had to face a Britain freed from having to battle Napoleon. If Prévost had succeeded at Plattsburgh or if Cochrane had won at Baltimore, there is no way the British negotiators would have agreed to the peace terms signed at Ghent. The war would have dragged on, and who knows what would have come of it. As German chancellor Otto Von Bismarck is once reputed to have said, "God has a special providence for fools, drunkards, and the United States of America." The events in the last half of 1814 had proved that adage right.

No doubt, many Americans fought valiantly. In fact, the War of 1812 revealed a stark generational gap in American talent. By the time the war began, Madison was sixty-one, while Monroe and Gallatin were in their late fifties. All three were seasoned leaders. But after them, what senior government or military officials from their age cohort stood out? Hardly any. It was the younger generation that was so impressive in the war. At the time the fighting began, Winfield Scott was twenty-six. Oliver Hazard Perry was twenty-seven. Thomas Macdonough was twenty-eight. William Henry Harrison was thirty-nine. So it went with the political talent as well: John C. Calhoun was thirty, and Henry Clay was thirty-five. While there were certainly exceptions to the rule—including Andrew Jackson, who was forty-five—it was generally true that there was a gap in political talent between the founding generation, which had mostly retired or died by that point, and the Jacksonian era, and that the administration of government suffered as a consequence. One reason Madison struggled so mightily to find good leaders to prosecute the war was because there just were not that many to be found in the senior ranks. If one looks at the people tasked with running the military, managing the executive, or legislating from Congress at the beginning of the war, one sees a rogue's gallery of drunkards, fools, cowards, schemers, and Malcontents.

The conflict further revealed the inadequacy of the Republican Party's agenda. That the war even happened demonstrated that commercial discrimination had been a dismal failure. Beyond that, the army was not up to the task at hand, the navy was basically nonexistent, and the militia was a paper tiger. These problems could have been addressed a decade earlier, but Republican leaders never invested the money or the effort needed to do so. Nor did they push hard enough for federal sponsorship of internal improvements, like roads and canals, which would have been useful for moving troops through the country. Madison's failure to get behind a recharter for the Bank of the United States left the federal government persistently pinched for cash and—with the proliferation of state banks in the absence of a national bank—wreaked havoc on private credit markets too. The Republicans had likewise never made significant provision to develop domestic industries, even those necessary for national defense, leaving the country badly provisioned when it declared war against Great Britain, which had always supplied most of its manufactured goods.

The ultimate responsibility for these problems rested squarely on the shoulders of James Madison. He had been by Jefferson's side advocating for these policies for decades. He had petitioned Congress for a war that the country was not ready to fight. He had the misery of serving as commander in chief to a fighting force that was not up to task. The good fortune of 1814 notwithstanding, the war taught the president and his allies that they had to do more to strengthen America's domestic economy, and in his final two years as president he would propose policies to do exactly that.

14

NATIONAL REPUBLICANISM

THE PEACE AT Ghent brought about a tremendous surge of nationalism, the likes of which had not been felt in a generation. Even the ever-cautious Gallatin, the biggest skeptic of the war in Madison's cabinet, felt the change. Writing to longtime Republican activist Matthew Lyon in the spring of 1816, Gallatin thought that though "the war has been productive of evil and good . . . the good preponderates." The country, he believed, had become "too selfish, too much attached exclusively to the acquisition of wealth, above all, too much confined in our political feelings to local and state objects. The war has renewed and reinstated the national feelings and character which the Revolution had given." Likewise, James Monroe believed that the war had been a "trial of the strength and efficiency of our government for such a crisis," and had demonstrated that the United States could handle the challenge. Afterward, the country "had acquired a character and rank among other nations, which we did not have before." South Carolina's John C. Calhoun, who would become secretary of war during Monroe's presidency, said the nation now found itself "in possession of a physical and moral power of great magnitude."[1]

A consistent theme in these nationalist rhapsodies was that the government now had a duty to meet the moment. The country had defended its republican character, and now it was up to the state to build up the national vigor. Nobody captured this sentiment better than Henry Clay, returned to the House after his stint on the Ghent peace commission. In a lengthy stemwinder given in the winter of 1816, he appealed to those "who nobly, manfully vindicated the national character by a war, waged by a young people, unskilled in arms, single handed, against a veteran power." He asked them to join together "to ameliorate the internal condition of the country" with a "liberal and enlightened policy" that would "entitle ourselves, upon our return home, to that best of all rewards, the grateful exclamation, 'Well done thou good and faithful servant.'" Republican self-praise notwithstanding, the subtext was that America had vindicated itself during the conflict in spite of, not because of, its government. The old Jeffersonian political economy of minimal spending, reliance on militias, and confidence in the agricultural yeomanry was not sufficient to secure the country's position in the long run.[2]

Madison was never one to give a speech like Clay's, but he knew how to read a political moment as well as anybody. When Congress assembled in the fall of 1815, Madison offered his seventh annual State of the Union message. Though often overlooked, this address was one of the most important of its kind in the nineteenth century. For in it, he subtly abandoned much of the old Jeffersonian orthodoxy, and instead proposed a series of policy reforms that effectively merged Alexander Hamilton's ambition to invigorate the national economy with his own insistence that the benefits and burdens of public policy had to be distributed equitably. The new Fourteenth Congress eagerly enacted most of Madison's policies, which would influence the National Republican Party of the 1820s, the Whigs of the 1830s and 1840s, and eventually the Republican Party of Abraham Lincoln in the 1860s and beyond.

He began the message by thanking "the goodness of a superintending Providence" for the present state of the American union. "Whilst other portions of mankind are laboring under the distresses of war or struggling with adversity in other forms, the United States are in the tranquil enjoyment of prosperous and honorable peace." Having been instrumental in framing the country's government, Madison must have been especially pleased to write that Americans could "rejoice in the proofs given that our political institutions, founded in human rights and framed for their preservation, are equal to the severest trials of war, as well adapted to the ordinary periods of repose." Now, "the nation finds itself possessed of a growing respect abroad and of a just confidence in itself, which are among the best pledges for its peaceful career."[3]

Though Madison was a lame duck president by contemporary standards, his seventh State of the Union was hardly a valediction. There was important business for the government to undertake. At the top of his list was establishing "an efficient military peace establishment." William Crawford—Madison's new, energetic secretary of war, who took control of the department in August 1815—proposed an expanded Army Corps of Engineers as well as a substantial investment in West Point. Congress agreed to both, as well as a ten-thousand-soldier peace establishment, a permanent general staff, and reorganization of the militia. The Republicans had learned, as Clay put it to the House, that "the vicissitudes of human affairs" were so uncertain that "some tempest may suddenly arise, and bring us into a state requiring the exertion of military force," and the country would have to be ready. When the United States next went to war, against Mexico in 1846, the regular army would perform with distinction. This would be another great irony of Madison's career. A longtime skeptic of standing armies, he was the president who established important foundations for what would become the world's greatest fighting force.[4]

Madison also proposed a stronger emphasis on internal improvements, like roads and canals. "No objects within the circle of political economy," he wrote, "so richly repay the expense bestowed on them." Moreover, there was no country but the United States "which presents a field where nature invites more the art of man to complete her own work for his accommodation and benefit." Internal improvements had long been of interest to the Republican Party, but they had never been much of a priority. Party leaders, including Jefferson and Madison, felt constrained by the lack of an authorizing clause in the Constitution to allow for such expenditures, and up until the War of 1812, their fiscal priority had been paying down the debt. Still, they found ways to spend money at the margins. In 1803, when it admitted Ohio into the union, Congress had set aside money from land sales in the state for building roads. By 1806, enough funds had been collected that Congress authorized the construction of the Cumberland Road—connecting Cumberland, Maryland, to Wheeling, Virginia. Jefferson had approved all of this, and Madison had likewise approved an expansion of the road. Congress also spent money on improvements in Washington, DC, authorized post roads (or roads for the delivery of mail), and built lighthouses. In 1808, Gallatin had laid out an expansive plan of internal improvements to connect the regions, which included a post road from Maine to Georgia and canals to connect the tributaries of the Mississippi River to the Atlantic coastal plane.[5]

Now that the crisis with Great Britain was over, Republicans were ready to make improvements a priority. As Clay told the House in January 1816, he "desired to see a chain of turnpike roads and canals from Passamaquoddy to New Orleans; and other similar roads intersecting the mountains, to facilitate intercourse between all parts of the country, and to bind and connect us together." Calhoun argued that "the strength and political prosperity of the republic are intimately connected with this subject," for "good roads and canals judiciously laid out" could overcome the weakness caused by the problem of Americans occupying "a surface prodigiously great in proportion to our numbers." If a population so spread out across a continent was going to come together as one people, they would need ways to do it. So, after the war, Congress authorized $100,000 to expand the Cumberland Road once again, spent more on transportation improvements within the District of Columbia, built additional lighthouses, and built roads through the Illinois Territory as well as the Chickasaw Nation.[6]

Madison also called for a protective tariff. He had, since the start of his career, been a free trader, and he still thought it generally wise to leave "to the sagacity and interest of individuals the application of their industry and resources." But there had to be "exceptions to the general rule." The United States could not continue to import "articles necessary for the public defense or connected with the primary wants of individuals." The war had given a spur to American manufacturing. As trade with Great Britain had tapered off, American industry arose to fill the needs of the nation. But with commerce between the two countries once again flowing, British merchants began dumping their excess goods into the American markets, potentially overwhelming the nascent industrial sector. These new endeavors, the president believed, had to be nurtured. Madison also recommended additional protection for "particular manufactures where the materials for them are extensively drawn from our agriculture, and consequently impart and insure to that great fund of national prosperity and independence an encouragement which can not fail to be rewarded."[7]

Industrial protection was potentially a delicate subject for Republicans, who had initially opposed Hamilton's system in the early 1790s because they felt it was too partial to a handful of capitalists over the agricultural majority. But times had changed, and the Republicans wanted to expand the field of protection, as Clay put it, "not so much for the sake of the manufacturers themselves, as for the general interest." In the spring of 1816, Congress enacted the first truly protective tariff in the country's history, imposing levies on all manner of imported goods, including ironware, hemp, glassware, and woolen items. Judged against future tariffs, the rates imposed were mild, temporary, and carefully balanced to benefit different regions and sectors of the economy. Though protection would become a hotly contested issue in the 1820s, the Tariff of 1816 passed overwhelmingly, with strong support from the mid-Atlantic, where the industrial base was beginning to blossom. It even garnered the support of Calhoun, who would in the next decade become the great opponent of protectionism.[8]

In his own roundabout way, Madison even managed to swallow his pride and recommend that Congress charter another bank, though he could not bring himself to state it outright, telling the legislature in December 1815, "The probable operation of a national bank will merit consideration." This had been a long time coming. The failure to recharter the Bank of the United States in 1811 had dealt a severe blow to the country during the War of 1812. The government's most immediate problems then had been the inability to secure loans to finance the war and the very high rates of interest on the money that could be found. The absence of the bank also distorted private credit markets, for in its place sprung up a multitude of state banks that lent money far in excess of their specie reserves. If the bank had still been in operation, it could have curtailed this activity because it usually held large quantities of state-bank notes that could be called in. But without the national bank's moderating influence, the state banks behaved with reckless abandon. Eventually, a dearth of hard cash resulted in the suspension of specie payments outside of New England. And without the anchor of precious metals, banks refused to accept the notes of other banks as payments, meaning that for all intents and purposes the United States did not have a uniform currency by the end of the war. This left the government in a pinch, for federal deposits stored in banks in one region could not be transferred to banks in regions where they were needed to buy provisions.[9]

By 1814, there was a growing consensus that the government had to charter a new bank—a view most strongly advocated by prominent merchants like Stephen Girard, John Jacob Astor, David Parish, and Jacob Barker. The bank initiative also had the backing of prominent Philadelphia lawyer Alexander Dallas, a friend of Gallatin who had helped him scrape together funds during the war. In September 1814, Dallas had told acting treasury secretary William Jones that "the state of public credit admits of no palliative remedy. There must be established an efficient, productive system of taxation. There must be established a national bank to anticipate, collect and distribute the revenue." When Madison brought Dallas into the cabinet as secretary of treasury that October, the president indicated that he, too, thought a bank was necessary.[10]

Dissension among the pro-bank faction kept a new institution from being chartered during the war itself. Dallas's top priority was getting the government access to necessary funds, while Calhoun, the most energetic advocate of the bank in the House, wanted above all to restore a national currency. The two could not come to an agreement on the details of an institution that did both, and Madison vetoed a charter in January 1815 on purely practical grounds, without respect to "the question of the constitutional authority of the Legislature to establish an incorporated bank." When news of peace at Ghent finally arrived a few weeks later, the question of wartime borrowing was rendered moot, and Dallas and Calhoun crafted an alternative that Congress passed with only a few adjustments in April 1816.[11]

The Second Bank of the United States, as it has since been styled, looked much like the first, although there were some notable differences. Its starting capital was larger: $35 million instead of $10 million. The government would receive a bonus from the new bank for chartering it and have the authority to select five of its twenty-five directors. The bank would also have a mandate to place branches in areas of the country that had been under-banked, whereas Hamilton had wanted to keep the number of branches to a minimum. This last difference illustrates the fact that it was the Jeffersonian coalition in the South and West that now needed the bank more than the Federalists of New England and the mid-Atlantic, where a number of responsible state banks undergirded a reasonably stable financial system. The Second Bank, in this respect, was truly a Republican bank, and it received overwhelming support in the House from those regions, forty-five votes in favor to just twenty-six opposed.

Madison disappointed his nationalist allies when, on March 3, 1817—his last full day as president—he vetoed the so-called Bonus Bill, which would have applied the bonus coming to the government for chartering the bank to an expansive fund for internal improvements, not just on federally managed property like Washington, DC, but for the nation at large. Clay begged him not to veto it. He could easily have set the bill aside until Monroe took the presidency the next day and approved it, but Madison felt compelled to admonish Congress that Article I, Section 8 did not offer an unlimited grant of power. His recommendations for internal improvements had usually corresponded to a reminder that some kind of constitutional amendment would be required if Congress were to engage in a broad-based spending campaign. As far as the president was concerned, it was one thing to improve roads and canals in territories or the District of Columbia but quite another to spend willy-nilly. "The legislative powers vested in Congress are specified and enumerated," he cautioned the legislature in his veto message, "and it does not appear that the power proposed to be exercised by the bill is among the enumerated powers, or that it falls by any just interpretation within the power to make laws necessary and proper for carrying into execution those or other powers vested by the Constitution in the Government of the United States."[12]

If the veto of the Bonus Bill disappointed Clay, Madison also had his moments of frustration with the Fourteenth Congress. In his seventh State of the Union, he had called for the creation of a national university in the District of Columbia, something that he had first suggested to Congress twenty years prior, but Congress had once again ignored his entreaty.

Still, the accomplishments of the final two years of Madison's term can hardly be understated. With the president's encouragement, men like Dallas, Clay, and Calhoun charted a new course for the nation, to lasting effect. James Monroe and John Quincy Adams, who followed Madison in the presidency, would advocate the same policies. Over the next generation, Clay would place them at the center of the "American System," his political alternative to the Democratic Party of Andrew Jackson.

Eventually, the Republican Party of Abraham Lincoln and Ulysses S. Grant would call for internal improvements, a strong monetary system, and industrial protection—ideas that can all be traced to the policy initiatives Madison championed following the War of 1812.

To be sure, later generations of nationalists would not be nearly as moderate as Madison, especially with respect to the tariff. Madison was in favor of mild protectionism, but by the end of the century the Republican Party would favor very high tariffs on all manner of industrial goods. Moreover, until the Progressive movement of the early twentieth century, it would be the Democratic Party that gave voice to Madison's anxieties about the limits of congressional authority. Still, the Fourteenth Congress created the basic outline of how the United States would evolve over subsequent decades into a modern, commercial republic. The old ideal of an agrarian republic, once touted by Jefferson and Madison, had shown itself to be insufficient for the national purpose. So, the government would promote policies designed to diversify the economy and bind regions together in a shared quest for prosperity. A strong financial system would create a uniform currency that facilitated economic exchange across regions. Good roads and waterways would likewise enable Americans to better trade with one another. And the protective tariff would encourage risk takers to invest in industries that would diversify the economy and ensure the country had the goods it needed in case of another war.

———————

AT FIRST BLUSH, Madison's late presidential agenda looks like warmed-over Hamiltonianism. Hamilton had called for all of these ideas, in some version or another, in the early 1790s. This in itself is remarkable. Madison was never one to admit that he was wrong, at least not explicitly. That he could embrace a series of policies that originated from his old rival was a tacit admission, late in life, that he understood that his old vision of political economy—which privileged independent farmers as the center of civic life and a thriving international trade based on southern exporters and New England shippers—did not work. But to give all the credit to Hamilton is to overlook Madison's unique stamp on how these policies would be enacted. Madison's most persuasive criticism of Hamiltonian finance was a political one, focused on its unequal distribution of benefits and concentration of government power. A narrow caste—mainly, in Madison's view, a handful of northern financiers—would be the beneficiaries of Hamilton's agenda, and in turn would acquire undue influence in the government. Madison chalked this up in part to Hamilton's elitism, which had been on full display at the Constitutional Convention in 1787. Madison believed that Hamilton was looking to swap American republicanism for a new monarchy. Madison misjudged Hamilton's intentions but not his methods. His program did enrich and empower wealthy men of commerce, purposefully so, as Hamilton sought to bind their interests to the government.

This was always Madison's strongest ground of opposition to the Federalist agenda, and this was precisely what the national Republicanism of the postwar era corrected. It reworked the Hamiltonian economic agenda to make it consistent with Madison's political vision of justice in an extended republic. Consider the bank. In the original Hamiltonian version, its main beneficiaries lived in or around the major commercial cities of Boston, New York, and Philadelphia. But the Second Bank expanded branches across the country, precisely so that it would benefit more people in more places. Additionally, the government had greater leverage over the institution, receiving a bonus for chartering it (a response to an original Madisonian critique of Hamilton's plan) as well as the right to name five of its directors. Hamilton believed that though his bank would benefit the commercial sector in the short term, it would eventually benefit the entire country. No doubt this had been the case, but an animating idea behind the Second Bank was to benefit more of the country immediately, rather than waiting for it to trickle down from a handful of elites.

The same was true of the Republican version of industrial protection. Hamilton's *Report on Manufactures*, released in 1792, promoted diversifying the American economy primarily through bounties, or cash payments to those who made specific goods. The Tariff of 1816, on the other hand, substantially broadened the scope of government munificence. It set aside bounties in favor of a wide range of import duties on manufactured and agricultural goods. More factions in society therefore benefitted from it, and none drew a direct government payment. And though Hamilton's *Report on Manufactures* called for internal improvements, the Federalists—being a party primarily of New England—were never enthusiastic about roads and canals that would drain population from their region. The Republicans, by contrast, made this a policy priority after the war.

It was not just in these adjustments that Madison and the Republicans improved upon Hamilton's ideas. They also saw in them a way to create the kind of balance that Madison had long believed was a hallmark of republican government. Internal improvements and the Second Bank were good for the South and West. Industrial protection was good for the mid-Atlantic and New England. Roads would connect the settlers on the frontier beyond the mountains to the coastal plains. Every geographical faction could gain something from the Republican plan. Each sector would advance with the others, regional economies would become more integrated, and ultimately the bonds of the union would become stronger.

This was the political pathway to the economic integration that Hamilton had touted long before. In *Federalist* 12, he envisioned the "prosperity of commerce" providing resolution to the long-standing rivalry between different economic groups. Yet in the immediate aftermath of his proposals, the farmers and commercial men became political enemies—for Hamilton, in his efforts to harmonize their interests, had rewarded one group at the expense of the other. The late secretary was right on the economics, but he got the politics wrong. That was what Madison got right. He grasped that economic development, if it was to be facilitated by the national government, had to be done in such a way that no groups were privileged over others. This was the essence of Madison's *Federalist* contributions: how to set up a government that would write laws consistent with "justice and the general good." That was a matter not only of constitutional design, but also policy implementation, for as Madison wrote, "What are many of the most important acts of legislation, but so many judicial determinations, not indeed concerning the rights of single persons, but concerning the rights of large bodies of citizens?" Ultimately, subsequent generations would tout the brilliance of Hamiltonian economics, but it was Madison who stamped upon it a truly republican character.[13]

MADISON'S PRESIDENTIAL TERM expired on March 4, 1817, the day his longtime friend (and sometimes rival) Monroe became the fifth president of the United States. James and Dolley headed back to Montpelier in early April 1817. Though Madison's presidency had been tumultuous, the happy conclusion to the war and the productivity of the Fourteenth Congress prompted a nationwide celebration of his administration. He had seen the country through the war, and enacted a bold new program to make sure that, should conflict come again, the United States would be ready for it.

It is fair to wonder if the country's immediate judgment on Madison's tenure is closer to the mark than most historical re-evaluations have been. Madison had sought peace first and foremost, turning to war in 1812 not in pursuit of military glory but as a final vindication of American rights. Though the war had been difficult, it had also been instructional, at least for Madison. He realized that the country had to modernize—militarily, financially, and economically. At the president's encouragement, Congress passed a flurry of legislation that would define public policy for more than a century.

Perhaps the most remarkable quality of this period is the relative absence of partisan strife. This was Madison's vision of republican balance at work. The Tariff of 1816 was moderate. The new Second Bank of the United States had more clear lines of federal authority. Internal improvements would help bring far-flung geographical sectors of the country together. Policymakers in the twentieth century who accomplished as much as Madison did from 1815 to 1817 usually faced some kind of backlash for having moved too far too fast. Some factions would feel alienated by all the changes, and party politics would heat up once again. But that did not happen after Madison left office. Indeed, Monroe faced only token opposition from the Federalists in 1816 and ran unopposed in 1820. Federalism died because Madison co-opted Hamilton's best economic ideas, blended them with his own political insights, and produced a fusion that the overwhelming majority of the country could support. Few presidents leave office with a country as united, secure, and prosperous as Madison did.

The weak link in Madison's chain between Federalism and Republicanism was the matter of constitutionality. Did the Constitution give the federal government authority to facilitate economic development? Madison never had a particularly coherent answer. His positions on the bank and internal improvements at the end of his presidential term were unpersuasive to the point of incomprehensible, and the resulting confusion contributed to later political battles between the National Republicans (later the Whigs) and the Democrats.

The constitutionality of the bank had been a hot-button issue back in 1791, but Madison had little interest in dealing with it a quarter century later. In his veto of Calhoun's bank plan, he waived the matter aside, arguing that the constitutional issue was "precluded . . . by repeated recognitions under varied circumstances of the validity of such an institution in acts of the legislative, executive, and judicial branches of the Government." This posture—that of a judge who, having been overruled, assents to the will of the majority—was a convenient way of accepting a Hamiltonian bank without admitting a Hamiltonian construction of the Necessary and Proper Clause. But it was hardly persuasive. Madison was basically acknowledging that there was a kind of statute of limitations for constitutional violations. Hamilton had broken the rules in 1791, but because he had never been caught, his crime became legal. If nothing else, this posed a moral hazard. Future politicians who wanted to expand the power of the federal government could, if they were brazen enough, get away with it.[14]

In a speech in support of the bank in June 1816, Clay offered a different explanation for his own change of heart. A friend to the state banks, he had opposed Gallatin's recharter plan in

1811, but he had since become one of the bank's greatest champions. How to account for the evolution without conceding that the Constitution gave Congress an unlimited grant of power? Clay answered that the Constitution "vests in Congress all powers necessary . . . to put into motion and activity the machine of government which it constructs." These constructive powers "are from their nature, indefinable," and can be hard to specify in a given policy question. "It is manifest that this necessity may not be perceived, at one time, under one state of things, when it is perceived at another time, under a different state of things." Though the Constitution is immutable, "the force of circumstances and the lights of experience may evolve to the fallible persons, charged with its administration, the fitness and necessity of a particular exercise of constructive power today, which they did not see at a former period." Thus, the constitutionality of the bank had changed with the times. According to Clay, the circumstances of 1816 made it necessary for the government to charter a bank; it was the only way to facilitate a uniform currency, a key delegated power under Article I, Section 8 of the Constitution. Yet it is hard to see how Clay's position is not susceptible to backsliding into Hamilton's original view. Where are the hard limits on congressional power? If the answer is how members of Congress view the matter, then there is no limit at all. After all, Congress judged the bank necessary in 1791, and Gallatin had argued ever since for its utility. Hamilton, were he still around, might have retorted that Clay's failure to appreciate the bank's necessity in 1811 was precisely that—Clay's failure—rather than a meaningful constitutional limitation.[15]

In truth, Madison and Clay had previously established such clear constitutional objections to the bank that the only way for them to accept it without abandoning their principles would have been to propose an authorizing amendment. Neither was willing to do that. Instead, Madison chose to protect the notion of constitutional limits by vetoing the Bonus Bill. But the constitutional distinction between the bank and the Bonus Bill was so fine as to be imperceptible. The bank, according to Madison, had been sanctioned by "repeated recognitions under varied circumstances" that signaled a "concurrence of the general will of the nation." The same could certainly be argued for the internal improvements that the Bonus Bill would have authorized, especially the Cumberland Road. If anything, these were less controversial than the bank, which was still a source of great skepticism among conservative Republicans who feared its oligarchic tendencies.[16]

Though unfortunate, it was strangely fitting that Madison's last major act as president was to throw more confusion into the meaning of the Constitution. In the 1790s, he was a zealous constitutional opponent of Hamilton's innovations but did not hesitate to advocate for federal support of education and scientific research. In 1804, he admitted the potential constitutional problems of integrating the Louisiana Territory into the union, but decided to let the matter lie, so great was the opportunity. And in his presidency, he allowed the bank to be grandfathered into the Constitution, but not internal improvements—despite the fact that he had long ago opposed Hamilton's bank but agreed to expand the Cumberland Road. It is impossible to make rhyme or reason out of these distinctions, at least based on a purely legalistic understanding of the Constitution. His mind was sharpest when considering the nature of republican politics: what it required and what it prohibited. His policy positions were intelligible when considered alongside his theoretical understanding of a just government: that it should act in the public interest, that it should not play favorites, and that it should respect limits to its power. Yet he could offer no clear, constitutional rules for

future policymakers to follow. And the more he tried to articulate such a logic, the more tangled his thinking became.

Madison's failure on this front was a consequential one, re-
verberating through the next generation of American politics.
By the 1820s, two distinct political coalitions would form: the
National Republicans (later the Whigs) under Adams and Clay,
and the Democrats under Andrew Jackson. Two key points of
disagreement between the sides were the legality of internal improvements and the bank, in large measure because Madison left
no clear guidance on how to interpret the Constitution on these
matters.

———————

THE CONSTITUTIONALITY OF internal improvements became
an especially fraught issue during Monroe's tenure. There was
a fairly broad policy consensus within the Republican Party of
the "expediency of vesting in Congress a power as to roads and
canals," as Madison wrote Monroe in the fall of 1817. Both he
and Monroe thought an amendment was necessary to give Congress such a power. But there were other views. In December
1817, Madison received a letter from Henry St. George Tucker,
a congressman from Virginia who believed that the Cumberland Road, along with other federal improvement projects that
had already been signed into law, had sufficiently demonstrated
that no amendment was necessary. This line of argument was
quite similar to the one Madison himself had made in support of
the Second Bank of the United States, but the ex-president was
unconvinced. He wrote a polite but firm response in disagreement, arguing that his "knowledge of those who proposed the
Constitution, and what is of more importance . . . those who
bestowed on it the stamp of authority" induced him to reject

such an inference. In private to Monroe, Madison felt compelled to admit that perhaps Jefferson had only "slightly if at all examined" the constitutionality of the Cumberland Road and that his assent was "doubtingly or hastily given," while Madison had agreed to "additional appropriations . . . with less of critical investigation than was due the case."[17]

Feeling pressure from the nationalist wing of the party, Monroe all but gave up thwarting Congress's repeated efforts to spend on internal improvements by the spring of 1822. Having vetoed a law to collect federal tolls on the Cumberland Road, he submitted to Congress a prolix message that, in effect, granted Congress the power to subsidize internal improvements, but left the implementation and regulation to the states. To Madison, it seemed as though his friend wanted to have his cake and eat it too. It was a loose interpretation of the clause giving Congress the power to "lay and collect Taxes . . . for the common Defence and general Welfare of the United States," but a strict construction of the rest of Congress's powers. "A general power merely to appropriate," he wrote the president in December, "without this auxiliary power, would be a dead letter; and with it an unlimited power."[18]

John Quincy Adams succeeded Monroe to the presidency in 1825 in a hard-fought, four-way battle between Andrew Jackson, William Crawford, and Henry Clay. Madison, as befitting an ex-president in this era, gave no indication of his support, but Adams's supporters believed he was on their man's side. In his first annual address to Congress, Adams proclaimed, "The great object of the institution of civil government is the improvement of the condition of those who are parties to the social compact. . . . Roads and canals, by multiplying and facilitating the communications and intercourse between distant regions and multitudes of men, are among the most important means of improvement." This capacious view of federal power prompted a backlash from Madison's more conservative friends and allies. Thomas Ritchie, the influential editor of the *Richmond Enquirer*, fretted to Madison that "the principles of the Constitution are about to be violated in a most serious manner." Jefferson, whose endorsement of the Cumberland Road got the country started on this project, was also anxious about the "desperate" situation. To Ritchie, Madison countenanced a patient "appeal . . . to the recollections, the reason, and the conciliatory spirit of the majority of the people against their own errors." This was unlike the crisis of 1798, when the Federalists had passed the Alien and Sedition Acts. That was a moment when the power of government expanded at the expense of the people. Here, the government was reacting to public clamor. The proper course, he believed, was once again to call for an amendment.[19]

In 1828, Adams lost the presidency decisively to Jackson, who brought to the office a stricter construction of the Constitution. In 1830, he vetoed a bill to authorize the purchase of stock in the Maysville, Washington, Paris, and Lexington Turnpike Road Company. President Jackson declared in his "Maysville Road Veto," as it came to be called, that the bill was a "measure of purely local character" and thus incompatible with the General Welfare Clause. Jackson's veto cited Madison's "Report of 1800" and his veto of the Bonus Bill approvingly, and afterward Jackson's top lieutenant, Martin Van Buren, wrote the former president asking for guidance on how to differentiate public projects of national versus local character. Madison replied with a long note delineating how the Constitution might be interpreted on that count. Consistent with his lack of clarity on the precise legal boundaries, he made an overfine distinction between national and local purposes that, in practice, could be used to accept or reject any given proposal.[20]

That Madison could remain in correspondence with both the advocates and opponents of national improvement projects spoke to his carefully cultivated reputation as a nonpartisan sage. But it also was a testament to the ambiguity in his thinking on the relationship between the Constitution and internal improvements, for both sides could find something in his views to celebrate. The National Republicans could point to his expansion of the Cumberland Road and claim it granted Congress a wide berth. The Democrats could cite the veto of the Bonus Bill as proof of the legitimacy of strict construction.

The bank was likewise a source of continued constitutional debate into Madison's retirement. In 1791 Hamilton justified the bank by virtue of the Necessary and Proper Clause of the Constitution. It was, the late secretary had argued, essential for the performance of basic governmental tasks; therefore, it was constitutional. Madison had argued vigorously in the opposite direction, and though he later admitted the constitutionality of the bank, he never adopted Hamilton's interpretation of the Necessary and Proper Clause. In 1819, the Supreme Court under Chief Justice John Marshall did precisely that. In the landmark ruling of *McCulloch v. Maryland,* the Court ruled that the Necessary and Proper Clause did in fact justify the bank's existence. Far from being pleased that the cornerstone of his postwar political economy had survived the constitutional challenge, Madison was agitated—not at the ruling, but the logic behind it. He told Virginia judge Spence Roane that Marshall had taken too many liberties. "The occasion did not call for the general and abstract doctrine interwoven with the decision on the particular case," he wrote. If followed to its logical conclusion, Marshall's argument would mean that any "legislative power . . . not expressly prohibited by the Constitution" could, "according to the doctrine of the Court, be exercised as a means of carrying into effect some specified power."[21]

Maybe so, but what was the Madisonian alternative? That Hamilton had seized a power that did not belong to the government some thirty years earlier, but because the theft had gone unpunished, it was in effect constitutional? This was a view that virtually nobody but Madison seemed to accept. Marshall implicitly dismissed it, and in his 1832 veto of a bill to recharter the bank, Jackson explicitly rejected it. "It is maintained," he wrote, that the bank's constitutionality "ought to be considered as settled by precedent and by the decision of the Supreme Court. To this conclusion I can not assent. Mere precedent is a dangerous source of authority, and should not be regarded as deciding questions of constitutional power except where the acquiescence of the people and the States can be considered as well settled." That, in Jackson's mind, had not happened. "One Congress, in 1791, decided in favor of a bank; another, in 1811, decided against it. One Congress, in 1815, decided against a bank; another, in 1816, decided in its favor." Given that there was no precedent that "ought to weigh in favor of the act before me," Jackson felt free to strike it down on the very grounds that Jefferson and Madison had staked out in 1791.[22]

FOR NEARLY FORTY-ONE years, from the spring of 1776 until the winter of 1817, James Madison had committed himself to politics. There was really just one brief interlude, in the mid-1790s, when he was either not serving in an official capacity or preparing to do so. That is a long time for any person to be within government, and in the United States it was an unpredictable and dynamic epoch. When he entered politics, just before the official declaration of independence, the United States did not yet technically exist. When he left, it was a rising economic power with a stable, and at the time revolutionary, vision of republicanism and liberty. And this new nation bore his imprint, not just for the ideas he articulated about how government should be designed but the actions he took after it came into being.

His career was not without its mistakes. No career of such length and substance is. The great mistake in the second half of his career was his belief, held alongside Thomas Jefferson, that as an agrarian republic the United States could dictate terms to the European powers. They believed that because they provided food to Europe, and Europe supplied mostly manufactured goods, they were in the catbird seat. They fervently held to this doctrine, and when troubles with Great Britain arose, they sought to use their country's supposed commercial advantages for foreign policy gains. This was wrong—disastrously wrong. Great Britain was a world-spanning power that could endure the supposed privations imposed by the United States. Republican commercial discrimination hurt America much more than Great Britain. Left with no choice but submission or war, Madison selected war in 1812, only to discover that other shibboleths of Republican political economy were likewise faulty. The military was woefully unprepared after years of inattention. The militia was not up to the task. The credit markets were a wreck and unable to supply needed funds.

It was these mistakes that made his final two years in the presidential office so remarkable. Madison was never one to admit that he was wrong—it just was not in his character. Nevertheless, actions speak louder than words, and it is clear that he had learned from his mistakes. He abandoned the idyllic mythology of a virtuous republic populated with independent farmers—or at least, he finally acknowledged that such yeomen were not a sufficient condition for American security and prosperity. There had to be more. The economy had to be diversified, industry had to be supported, and domestic credit markets had to be strengthened. And the government had to play a role in all of this.

These were all notions that Hamilton had advanced a quarter century earlier, but while Madison accepted his old foe's basic ideas about economics, he freely intermingled them with his own views of politics. If the government was going to involve itself in national economic development, it had to do so in a mild, fair, and reasonable way that respected the constitutional boundaries of federal authority. What emerged from the final two years of Madison's term, therefore, was a hybrid—Hamiltonian economics combined with Madisonian politics. While subsequent political leaders would cast aside his constitutional scruples and abandon his moderate views of industrial protection, they nevertheless followed the same, essential Madisonian playbook—endeavoring to develop the national economy by distributing the benefits of public policy in a more democratic manner than Hamilton proposed.

It was in this way that Madison's vision of republican politics stretched beyond its constitutional structure to inform the substance of public policy, and even the political psychology of the United States. The people of America expect the government to accomplish big things, but to do so in a fair, evenhanded, and moderate manner, with respect for the limited power granted under the Constitution. James Madison, more than any other Founder, was the architect of this design. No doubt, there were weaknesses in this view—obviously, fairness is easier to talk about than to realize, and the constitutionality of many government actions is as hotly contested today as it was in 1815. Nevertheless, the boundaries of American political discourse have been distinctively Madisonian ever since.

15

"THE SERPENT CREEPING"

IN HIS FIRST inaugural address, President James Monroe spoke for many in the country when he said he hoped the now former president Madison would "long enjoy in his retirement the affections of a grateful country, the best reward of exalted talents and the most faithful and meritorious service." Indeed, Madison was blessed with such a retirement. Though his face had aged noticeably, the sixty-six-year-old former president was as lively as he had ever been when he returned to his beloved homestead. For the next decade, he enjoyed reasonably good health, the company of dear friends and close family from both his and Dolley's side, and a lively correspondence with Americans of all political stripes. He helped Thomas Jefferson found the University of Virginia, of which he became the rector in 1826. And in 1829 he traveled to Richmond as a delegate to a convention to redraft the state's constitution—a conclave that brought together the living legends of the Old Dominion, including Monroe and John Marshall.[1]

Madison's Montpelier estate was always busy during his lengthy retirement. Guests of all sorts—family, extended family, political acquaintances, and even perfect strangers—would visit often, as Montpelier was not far from Washington, DC. The Madisons hosted them all, entertaining them lavishly, regardless of the ex-president's financial condition. In retirement, free of the burdens of government, Madison could fully relax. One visitor remembered sitting with the former president on Montpelier's portico: "He spoke without reserve . . . sometimes on literary and philosophical subjects and not infrequently—for he was a capital story teller—he would relate anecdotes highly amusing as well as interesting. He was a man of wit, relished wit in others, and his small, bright blue eyes would twinkle most wickedly when lighted up by some whimsical conception." Perhaps the highlight of his retirement came in November 1824 when Lafayette came to the Virginia Piedmont for a two-week visit. The Frenchman was staying with Jefferson, and Madison went to Monticello to see him, writing to Dolley, "My old friend embraced me with great warmth. He is in fine health and spirits but so much increased in bulk and changed in aspect that I should not have known him." Later, Lafayette would stay with the Madisons at Montpelier for a week before continuing his nationwide tour.[2]

There were hard times for the Madisons as well. An agricultural depression following the Panic of 1819 exacerbated the underlying problems of the plantation economy: overreliance on the international market for southern staples, soil depletion, the hefty fixed costs of maintaining the slave population, the increasing glut of American-made farm products, and more. Madison's efforts to diversify his crops beyond tobacco, as well as his scrupulous attention to scientific principles of agriculture, were insufficient to stem the tide. The estate that his grandfather

Ambrose had established nearly a century ago was slowly failing. Since Madison refused to sell young enslaved people to make ends meet, as many planters did, he was forced eventually to sell off large swaths of land at Montpelier, as well as some he had purchased as investments in Kentucky. Making matters worse was his stepson, Payne, who, despite James and Dolley's best efforts, refused to settle into a responsible adulthood. An inveterate gambler, Payne had to rely on his parents time and again to bail him out, at a total price tag upward of $40,000. Though Madison's presidential stipend was generous for its age—$25,000 per year—it was not enough for all these costs.

By the end of the 1820s, Madison's health began to fail. A bad case of influenza was followed by severe bouts of rheumatism, and for the last three years of his life, he was basically bedridden. Dolley relished the role of caretaker and tended to his every need. But living as long as he did, until the age of eighty-five, he saw many of his dearest friends pass before him. Jefferson died in 1826, and Monroe in 1832. Even Anna Cutts—Dolley's younger sister, who had been like a daughter to the couple—died suddenly in 1832.

Yet even as Madison's health failed, his mind remained as sharp as ever, as evidenced by the voluminous correspondence he kept up during his nearly twenty-year retirement. The ex-president was generally content to stay out of the public side of politics, keenly aware that his age would make him a target. As he wrote to Nicholas Trist, the grandson of Eliza Trist, who had managed the Philadelphia boardinghouse Madison had stayed in all those years ago, "A man whose years have but reached the canonical three score and ten . . . should distrust himself whether distrusted by his friends or not, and should never forget that his arguments whatever they be will be answered by allusions to the date of his birth." However, a new constitutional heresy arose in the late 1820s that drew him back into the fray. South Carolina had come to detest the protective tariff, and under the leadership of Vice President John C. Calhoun argued for the doctrine of nullification, which claimed to allow a state to void federal laws. Calhoun invoked Jefferson and Madison and their Kentucky and Virginia Resolutions as proof of nullification's legitimacy. This, Madison could not abide, and so he entered the public debate one last time to correct the record and stand up for his beloved union.[3]

At the end of the 1810s, nobody could have predicted that the tariff would provoke a constitutional crisis—Madison especially, for the tariff law he signed in 1816 had broad regional support. Granted, like any tax debate, the issue was fraught with parochial concerns, but as Madison in 1820 wrote to Richard Rush, who had served as his attorney general and was by then minister to Great Britain, "The tariff . . . divides the nation in so checkered a manner, that its issue cannot be very serious; especially as it involves no great constitutional question." Madison was spot-on about the constitutional issue, or lack thereof. The original impost of 1789 had some mildly protective elements contained within it, although in general its purpose was merely to raise revenue. While Madison had argued privately in 1792 that Hamilton's protective plan was unconstitutional, the secretary had emphasized industrial subsidies rather than tariffs. The legality of the latter had never seriously been in doubt.[4]

The constitutional controversy over the tariff that developed during the 1820s was downstream of its political character. After the census of 1820, congressional representation shifted toward the mid-Atlantic and the West, where support for more protection was greater than in the South. In 1824, Congress—reflecting the evolving dynamics of regional power—enacted a new tariff law that substantially raised rates. Southerners were outraged by this, and they had fair reasons to be. With little industry, the South had nothing to gain and a lot to lose from higher tariffs. It would have to pay higher prices for imported goods, while its export staples (like cotton and tobacco) received no support from the government, and there was always a risk that foreign nations would enact retaliatory tariffs upon southern crops. Many southerners accepted this in 1816 for the sake of national defense, but the rates put in place back then were moderate and had been designed with an eye to the public interest. The Tariff of 1824, on the other hand, looked like a logroll: congressmen in the North and West stitching together a bill that served no greater public purpose than enriching their own constituents. Virginia senator John Taylor of Caroline denounced the law as a "bill of bargains, to enrich a pecuniary aristocracy . . . courting a number of local interests, with a design to marry them for the sake of their fortunes."[5]

Madison did not think this tariff was prudent. In a letter to Clay, who had become the great champion of industrial protection, Madison warned that "the bill" had "lost sight too much of the general principle which leaves to the judgment of individuals the choice of profitable employments for their labor and capital." He still considered himself a free trader at heart, and that what was needed was "a judicious explanation of the cases constituting exceptions to the principle of free industry," as he wrote in 1824 to Thomas Cooper, a professor at the new University of Virginia. This would provide a great "service . . . to the science of political economy."[6]

The passage of the 1824 bill radicalized southern planters, who had to confront the harsh reality that there was now a majority coalition in the national legislature in favor of tariffs that, in effect, drained wealth from their region and supplied it to others. Increasingly, they came to see the tariff not only as injudicious but unconstitutional. After all, they argued, Congress had the power to tax strictly for "the common Defence and general Welfare," as it said in the Constitution. How could a regional logroll such as the 1824 tariff possibly be justified by those terms? Even an aged Jefferson fell prey to this reasoning, despite the fact that he had long ago advocated discriminatory duties against British imports. Writing to William Branch Giles in 1825, he observed "with the deepest affliction, the rapid strides with which the federal branch of our government is advancing towards the usurpation of all the rights reserved to the states." He feared that the tariff was just another iteration of the "Federal party . . . founded on banking institutions and monied in corporations under the guise and cloak of their favored branches of manufactures, commerce, and navigation, riding and ruling over the plundered ploughman and beggared yeomanry."[7]

There was something else going on with the tariff debate. It was under the surface and not really discussed at the time, but it is clear in historical retrospect: slavery was turning the South into a nation within a nation. Without the numbers to defend its economic institutions in the councils of government, the South would begin to lash out at the republican principle that the majority should rule.

This was the opposite of what delegates from the region anticipated at the Constitutional Convention in 1787. They gazed westward and saw seemingly endless tracts of land for settlement, assuming these new regions would look much like the Carolinas or Georgia. No doubt they looked upon the Louisiana Purchase with similar excitement. But this expansion of the South did not materialize. Between 1800 and 1830, the population of

Massachusetts increased by 44 percent, Pennsylvania by 124 percent, and New York by a whopping 225 percent. Virginia increased by just 29 percent, a growth driven largely by the expansion of the slave population. By 1830, both New York and Pennsylvania had more people than Virginia. Because many of the Old Dominion's residents were slaves, who only counted for three-fifths of a person for the purposes of apportionment, its political influence was correspondingly weaker. Meanwhile, the population of the free states that had been added to the union since 1800 had come to vastly outstrip the population of new slave states. Ohio alone had more residents than Alabama, Mississippi, and Louisiana combined—and had come to rival Virginia in terms of its representation in government.

Immigration was a key force in inverting the population dynamics in the 1780s. Unlike the South, the North and West were a lure for European migrants hoping for a better life. It was hot in the South, excruciatingly so for those not used to such climates, and the highly stratified society and culture were hardly welcoming for new arrivals. Moreover, the North had diversified economically, while the South had lashed itself to the mast of cotton and by extension the institution of slavery. A lot of that had to do with Eli Whitney's cotton gin. Patented in 1794, the cotton gin mechanized the process of separating the cotton seed from the fiber. This made it economically feasible to grow short-staple cotton, which could be planted throughout much of the region. It also reinforced the region's hierarchical economic organization, as a relative handful of southern planters owned the largest plantations and the most slaves.

The reign of "king cotton" likewise exacerbated the long-standing factional differences between the South and the rest of the country. In rebutting the argument of the small states that a large-state axis would dominate the federal government,

Madison noted at the Constitutional Convention, "It seemed now to be pretty well understood that the real difference of interests lay, not between the large and small but between the northern and southern states. The institution of slavery and its consequences formed the line of discrimination." This had become truer in the intervening years. In 1787, all regions of the United States were dominated by farming, with the main difference being whether the type of labor was free or slave. By 1830, the North had diversified its economy and the West was on its way to doing so, while the South had doubled down on its old practices.[8]

This was the underlying cause of what would become the Nullification Crisis. The South was becoming a minority region with a vastly different set of interests than the rest of the country, and its leaders apprehended that the other regions might implement their agenda over uniform southern opposition. In 1824, the issue at hand was industrial protection. But what would it be in 1834 or beyond? Possibly slavery itself. Ultimately, the Nullifiers were looking for a way to stop a national majority from actually governing, at least when it came to their region's priorities. If their demand threatened the republic itself, they seemed prepared to take that risk.

Madison looked upon these political developments with anxiety, especially as the anti-tariff argument appeared to be gaining ground in Virginia. As the Virginia legislature debated a resolution declaring the tariff unconstitutional in 1827, he warned his friend Joseph Cabell that this was "a ground which cannot be maintained, on which the state will probably stand alone, and which by lessening the confidence of other states in the wisdom of its councils, must impede the progress of its sounder doctrines." But the anti-tariff party seemed to have momentum, and when Jefferson's letter to Giles was posthumously released to the public, Madison worried that the comments, written "confidentially, and probably in haste," would not only damage his late friend's reputation but also encourage the Old Dominion to launch this ruinous quest.[9]

In the fall of 1828, Madison wrote a series of letters to Cabell laying out a systematic rebuttal of the anti-tariff argument on both constitutional and prudential grounds. For Madison, it was a simple inference. The power to regulate trade with foreign nations, which the Constitution clearly gave to Congress, "embrace[d] the object of encouraging by duties, restrictions and prohibitions the manufactures and products of the country." This was not only a plain meaning of the text but was also evident from the long history of such regulations in foreign nations as well as within the United States. Madison further explained that though, "as a general rule, individuals ought to be deemed the best judges" of what they should do with their capital and labor, free of protective duties that channeled commerce into certain areas rather than others, there had to be exceptions so long as war remained a prospect and nations refused to "concur in a perfect freedom of commercial intercourse." Cabell, who had been fighting the anti-tariff forces in the state capitol in Richmond, was overjoyed to have the former president's assistance. "It is a paper so important, and so especially calculated to correct the unhappy state of the public mind to the South, that you must consent to its publication. I felt strongly inclined to send it directly to the editors of the *National Intelligencer* and nothing but my respect for you prevented me from doing so." But Madison begged off temporarily. The presidential election was approaching, and "every political subject brought before the public" would inevitably be "judged according to the bearing ascribed to it by the imaginations or suspicions of heated partisans." Better to wait until after the contest.[10]

So, a few weeks after Jackson's victory, the *National Intelligencer* published Madison's letters, bringing him back into the political fray at exactly the right moment. South Carolina was about to begin its most aggressive push against the tariff, but now it would do so alone. The combination of widespread esteem for Madison and the careful precision of his arguments muted criticism of the tariff in Virginia, ensuring that the Old Dominion would not join in the call for nullification.

The leader of the Palmetto State's defiance was Calhoun, whose career had mimicked the growing economic and social ostracization between the South and the rest of the nation. He had begun his stint in Congress as an ardent nationalist, having helped create the Second Bank of the United States and having supported the Tariff of 1816. He had then served for eight years as secretary of war for Monroe and four as vice president under Adams. By 1828, he had once more been elected to the vice presidency, under Jackson. But he had undergone a significant change in his perception of where the South fit in the national schema, coming to believe that the economic agenda of the National Republicans was harmful to his home region and seeking to grind the old nationalist project to a total standstill. Calhoun was a deep thinker, but he was hindered by a too-rigid mind. He was convinced that South Carolina's rights had been violated, and he searched for an argument—any argument—to make the case. The fruit of his labor—the *South Carolina Exposition and Protest*—was released by the South Carolina legislature in December 1828. Though it was published anonymously, Calhoun was widely known to be its author.

The *Exposition and Protest* was written in direct response to the Tariff of 1828, dubbed by its critics the "Tariff of Abominations." Adams, Clay, and the National Republicans had sought a new tariff law in advance of the 1828 presidential election, designed especially to appeal to the mid-Atlantic states of Pennsylvania and New York. Jackson was forced to hedge on the issue; his electoral base was in the South, which opposed increased protection, but he, too, needed to win the mid-Atlantic to guarantee an Electoral College victory. To outflank the National Republicans, Jackson's allies in the House proceeded to draft a tariff they believed could never pass the Senate. It combined extremely high duties on all manner of imported goods with a series of "poison pills" on imports like woolen goods and rope that the Jackson men believed many senators from the North would oppose. But the Jacksonians miscalculated. The bill was amended in the Senate to win over the New Englanders, and Adams signed it.

Southern planters had good reason to be outraged. The tariff raised taxes on dutiable imports to levels that would not be seen again until the Great Depression. It was the political version of Frankenstein's monster, doing violence to the ideal of moderate protection that Madison had promoted after the War of 1812. But rather than arguing a calm, prudential case against it and endeavoring to build a coalition to reform it—something that, back in his prime, Madison would have done—Calhoun and his allies promulgated a novel doctrine of constitutional governance backed by an implicit threat of secession.

Calhoun made two claims, both incorrect. First, he argued that the tariff was unconstitutional—that it could not be justified under the General Welfare Clause because it rewarded some factions in the country over others. He was right that the Tariff of 1828 was deeply unfair to the South, but wrong to suggest that Congress therefore could not enact it. Madison had already laid out the case for the constitutionality of the tariff succinctly, and anyway the Constitution was never supposed to defend against every ill-considered piece of legislation. The power to enact protective duties was bound up inextricably with the responsibility to manage international relations, a clear job for the national government. This had been long understood, given that various protective duties had been implemented as early as 1789. Granted, the Tariff of Abominations was egregiously harsh compared to its predecessors. But just because a law was unwise or even unjust did not necessarily make it unconstitutional.

Second, Calhoun asserted that South Carolina had the right to nullify the law within the state. The premise of his argument was the theory of the "concurrent majority." Calhoun's idea was that a national majority had the authority to govern only when it came to the powers that were explicitly vested in Congress by the Constitution. For all other matters, the proper authority was vested in the majority of a state. Just as the states "cannot, without violating the constitutional compact, interpose their authority to check, or in any manner to counteract [the federal government's] movements . . . so also, the peculiar and local powers reserved to the states are subject to their exclusive control; nor can the general government interfere, in any manner, with them, without violating the Constitution." This gave each state a veto power over federal laws that encroached its jurisdiction, for it was the supreme power in matters delegated to it under the Constitution. The only legal way for the federal government to override the veto of a state was to pass a constitutional amendment.[11]

To buttress the argument for nullification, Calhoun and his allies selectively cited not only the *Federalist Papers* but also the Virginia and Kentucky Resolutions, as well as the "Report of 1800." This may have been a good rhetorical strategy—quote an odd line here, join it to some random consideration there, and make it appear like the framers had actually been Nullifiers all along. But Calhoun's problem was that Madison was still alive, and still sharp. Though he had for most of his post-presidency been satisfied to live a happy retirement and offer advice from behind the scenes, Madison saw the writing on the wall. Calhoun's theory of nullification, by giving the states a veto over the federal government, would destroy the system of republican politics that he had labored for a lifetime to bring into being. Old as he was, he could not let this stand.

In March 1830, Senator Robert Hayne of South Carolina sent Madison a copy of two speeches he gave in January while debating Daniel Webster of Massachusetts over the *Exposition and Protest*. The immediate subject under discussion in the Senate was the disposition of the western territory. There had been stirrings of an alliance between southern and western senators like Hayne and Thomas Hart Benton of Missouri, wherein the South would back easy access to land and the West would favor reduction in tariffs. To preempt such a coalition, Webster changed the subject to the *Exposition and Protest*, which he denounced as an assault on the union itself. This drew Hayne into the debate. In lengthy remarks, Hayne claimed that "the South Carolina doctrine . . . is the good old Republican doctrine of '98, the doctrine of the celebrated 'Virginia Resolutions' of that year, and of 'Madison's Report' of '99." He also approvingly cited Jefferson's letter to Giles, which by that point had been circulated widely in the South to justify the argument that the tariff was unconstitutional. Hayne claimed that South Carolina had "hitherto gone no further than to petition, remonstrate, and solemnly protest against a series of measures which she believes to be wholly unconstitutional, and utterly destructive of her interest." He concluded by arguing that the real issue was not so much the tariff, but whether "the states and the people" would be brought "to the feet of the federal government," left with "nothing they can call their own."[12]

If Hayne thought Madison would applaud this speech, he was wildly off base. The former president took a little over a month to reply, and his response—while written in the respectful manner that had long marked his correspondence—eviscerated the doctrine of the Nullifiers. It was not so much a letter as a 3,500-word treatise on the proper understanding of the Constitution, the relationship between the states and the federal government, and the ways the former could redress grievances caused by the latter. Madison took the further step of supplying a version of the letter to Edward Everett, publisher of the *North American Review*. Everett begged Madison to allow him to publish it, extolling that "nothing more important to the country has been written since the date of the *Federalist*." Madison agreed, but he reworked the arguments as a letter to Everett rather than Hayne, which he sent at the end of August 1830.[13]

Madison began by noting the "characteristic peculiarities of the Constitution," that it was formed neither by the governments of the states nor by the people of the entire country, but rather by "the people in each of the states." It also "divides the supreme powers of government" between the federal and state governments, making it neither a strictly national nor a confederated government. This gave rise to the inevitable question of how to "provide for a peaceable and authoritative termination of occurring controversies" between the states and the federal government. For this, the Constitution provided a number of avenues for recourse. Chief among them was the courts, whose job was to arbitrate disputes arising under the Constitution, even if "the power has not always been rightly exercised"—a not-so-subtle rebuke of the Federalist-dominated judiciary. There were additional safeguards as well: the duty of senators and representatives to represent the people as well as the states, the job of the president to represent the national interest, the power of impeachment to remove executive and judicial officials who fail in their duty, the power to amend the Constitution, and, "in the event of a failure of every constitutional resort," the right to armed resistance.[14]

These were the proper ways to police abuses of power through a robust, national political process that carefully balanced the various forces in society against one another. The South Carolina doctrine of nullification was a repudiation of this whole system of politics. Not only did it have no basis in the Constitution, but it was completely impractical, for "it puts it in the power of the smallest fraction over one fourth of the United States . . . to give the law, and even the Constitution" to the majority. If anything, it would revive all the old problems of the Articles of Confederation, under which a minority of states could obstruct the necessary actions of the majority. It would, in a word, destroy national politics. Moreover, in Madison's judgment, Hayne fundamentally misunderstood the Virginia Resolutions and the "Report of 1800." These had called for "proper measures to be concurrently and cooperatively taken" among a majority of the states, not for a single state to annul a federal law. The "interposition" that Madison had suggested was completely consistent with the regular constitutional means of political action. It was premised on "the ordinary control of the people and legislatures of the states, over the government of the United States," rather than "the doctrine under consideration."[15]

For Madison to come out against the Nullifiers in this way—in a calmly reasoned and tightly argued essay—did enormous damage to Calhoun and Hayne's cause. Nevertheless, the Nullifiers could still hang their hat on Jefferson, much to Madison's chagrin. Not only had his intemperate letter to Giles been publicized, but the Kentucky Resolutions, authored by Jefferson, had inarguably included a clear reference to nullification. Madison

believed that it was "unreasonable . . . disrespectful and unfriendly" to use the Giles letter against Jefferson, for it "set up
against such evidence of Mr. Jefferson's direct and settled opinion, the unstudied and unguarded language incident to a hasty
and confidential correspondence." As for the Kentucky Resolutions, Madison told Nicholas Trist that the draft with the word
"nullification" "belongs to those of [17]99 with which Mr. Jefferson had nothing to do. . . . The Resolutions of [17]98 drawn by
him, contain neither that nor any equivalent term."[16]

The nullification issue turned into a full-fledged crisis in December 1832 when South Carolina passed an ordinance declaring the Tariff of 1828 void in the state. The specter of disunion
now appeared on the horizon, to Madison's horror, and he increased his rate of correspondence to lobby against such a ruinous idea. The letters he wrote during the Nullification Crisis
previewed many of the arguments that Abraham Lincoln would
make in defense of the union during the Civil War: for republican government to work, the union had to be perpetual; otherwise, a minority could thwart the rule of the majority at any
point simply by withdrawing from the compact. Madison, as
one of the key architects of the Constitution, understood this as
well as anybody. To Virginia statesman William Cabell Rives,
Madison argued that "whilst a state remains in the Union, it
cannot withdraw its citizens from the operation of the Constitution and the laws of the Union. In the event of an actual secession without the consent of the co-states, the course to be
pursued by these, involves questions painful in the discussion
of them." To Trist, Madison gave voice to those fears that the
"innovation" of nullification would be "fatal to the federal government, fatal to the Union, and fatal to the hopes of liberty and
humanity." To Clay, Madison hoped that the Nullifiers would
wake up to the fact that this was a path to the destruction of the

union and that "the deluded will recoil from its horrors, and that the deluders, if not themselves sufficiently startled, will be abandoned and overwhelmed by their followers."[17]

These were arguments Madison did not want to take further into the public realm. He was too old to continue this fight, believing "the task of combating such unhappy aberrations belongs to other hands." Still, Madison offered plenty of indirect support to opponents of nullification. The great defender of the national interest against the Nullifiers during the crisis of 1832–1833 was President Jackson, and since 1830 Trist had been a close advisor to the current occupant of the White House. During this time, Madison and Trist exchanged a flurry of letters, as the ex-president was eager to offer Jackson whatever logical or rhetorical aid he could. Ultimately, Jackson stared down the Nullifiers in South Carolina, and in 1833 Clay worked out a compromise tariff with Calhoun that put the issue to rest for the time being.[18]

Madison's efforts against nullification make his one of the most consequential post-presidencies in the history of the United States. In his public rebuttals of the specious case for the unconstitutionality of the tariff, as well as his forceful arguments demonstrating the ahistoricity and illogicality of nullification, Madison employed his reputation as the Father of the Constitution to great effect, helping save the union from the mania of Calhoun and Hayne. Behind the scenes, he was vigorous in supporting any politicians—be they Whigs like Clay and Webster or Democrats like Jackson—who opposed this dangerous strain of thought. In so doing, he would lay down arguments that, thirty years later, Abraham Lincoln would use to justify the Civil War. It was his last, great service to his country.

MADISON'S RHETORICAL BATTLE for the union came amid rapidly declining health. Though his mind never failed him, his
body slowly gave out. A man who in youth believed he was not
long for this world ended up being the last of the Founding Fathers to pass from this world to the next, which he did peacefully in his eighty-fifth year at Montpelier, on June 28, 1836.
It might be said that he lived too long. Not only did he have to
endure the loss of all his closest compatriots from the Founding Era, but he also saw the first glimpses of the sectional conflict that would lead to the Civil War—a horrifying vision for
a man who had dedicated his life to creating and sustaining a
national union.

But though Madison was no doubt aggrieved for his country
in his final years, the United States was fortunate to have him in
the fight against the Nullifiers. Around 1834, he penned one final essay, perhaps the most eloquent and succinct missive he ever
wrote. Entrusted originally to Edward Coles, Madison's private
secretary during his presidency and later governor of Illinois,
Madison's "Advice to My Country" read:

> As this advice, if it ever see the light will not do it till I am
> no more it may be considered as issuing from the tomb where
> truth alone can be respected, and the happiness of man alone
> consulted. It will be entitled therefore to whatever weight can
> be derived from good intentions, and from the experience of
> one, who has served his Country in various stations through a
> period of forty years, who espoused in his youth and adhered
> through his life to the cause of its liberty, and who has borne
> a part in most of the great transactions which will constitute
> epochs of its destiny.
>
> The advice nearest to my heart and deepest in my con-
> victions is that the Union of the States be cherished and

perpetuated. Let the open enemy to it be regarded as a Pandora with her box opened; and the disguised one, as the Serpent creeping with his deadly wills into Paradise.[19]

"Advice to My Country" is a perfect encapsulation of Madison's political thought: the binding together of the thirteen states into a single union that could secure justice and the general welfare through a well-structured political process. This was, from the time he first entered politics in 1776 until he wrote these words around 1834, his guiding principle. His efforts to enact the impost in the 1780s; his alliance with Washington, Robert Morris, and other nationalists; his "Memorial and Remonstrance Against Religious Assessments"; his extended republic of *Federalist* 10; his system of checks and balances of *Federalist* 51; the *National Gazette* essays against Hamilton; his postwar economic agenda; and his fight against nullification—all of these were, at their core, about how to strengthen the union, under the belief that the people of the United States could properly govern themselves. Though his tactics varied over the years and his strategies were often unsuccessful, he never deviated from this basic idea.

Yet Madison's final warning to the country illustrated the tragic error that he and his fellow Founders made. For "the Serpent creeping with his deadly wills into Paradise" had never been the anti-tariff coalition, nor even the doctrine of nullification. It had always been the institution of slavery, which Madison did nothing of substance to destroy.

Slavery has been an endemic feature of human existence since virtually the beginning of time. From a European perspective, it was an outgrowth not only of European racial chauvinism but of the inherently hierarchical society that had developed on the Continent in the millennia since the fall of Rome. Everybody had their place in the order of things, and some were placed higher than others. It was mainly through the Enlightenment, particularly its radical politics that postulated the natural equality and liberty of all human beings, that these long-received notions could be challenged seriously.

The American colonists, in their search to justify the radical step of independence, latched on to these ideas with vigor. "We hold these truths to be self-evident," Jefferson proclaimed in the Declaration of Independence, "that all men are created equal, that they are endowed by their Creator with certain unalienable Rights, that among these are Life, Liberty and the pursuit of Happiness." Jefferson knew that this was an implicit indictment of slavery, which is why in his rough draft he blamed King George III for promoting slavery in the colonies. "He has waged cruel war against human nature itself," Jefferson asserted, "violating its most sacred rights of life and liberty in the persons of a distant people who never offended him, captivating and carrying them into slavery in another hemisphere, or to incur miserable death in their transportation thither." As Madison put the matter bluntly at the Constitutional Convention, "Where slavery exists, the republican theory," or the idea that the people should rule, "becomes still more fallacious," for a part of the community is denied all of its rights by another part.[20]

Confronting this contradiction during the Founding Era was too inconvenient for the nation, especially the South. Thomas Jefferson, James Madison, George Mason, George Washington—their livelihoods depended on the institution. So, they let it remain even though they knew it was wrong. And, for a time, republican government seemed to function well. But just as a cancer can grow for a long time without being noticed, so did the institution of slavery rot the country from the inside out.

Ultimately, the problem was that a republican system of government was not compatible with a profoundly anti-republican society, which is what the South was by the 1830s. Madison's *Federalist* 10 envisioned an extended republic that balanced factions against one another, but how is that balance possible when the primary demand of a faction is the maintenance of an institution that ensured the systematic suppression of another? Ultimately, the only hope was the forbearance of the other factions in society, their willingness to look the other way. But if the Nullification Crisis teaches anything in historical retrospect, it is that those days were coming to an end. The rest of the country was coming into its own as a modern, integrated, and free nation, while the South sank further and further into an economic system dependent upon slavery.

Lincoln framed the Civil War as a consequence of that ancient deal that the Founders had made with the same serpent in the garden that Madison was warning about in 1836. "If we shall suppose," Lincoln said in his second inaugural address, "that American slavery is one of those offenses which in the providence of God must needs come but which having continued through His appointed time He now wills to remove and that He gives to both North and South this terrible war as the woe due to those by whom the offense came shall we discern therein any departure from those divine attributes which the believers in a living God always ascribe to Him." Madison, like all Americans up to the time of that great and terrible war, must take responsibility for this sin. Indeed, he more than most, for he never wielded his enormous powers to check the growth of what he knew to be a scourge upon the land.[21]

———

JAMES MADISON'S LAST words were said to his niece. When asked if anything was the matter, he responded that it was "nothing more than a change of mind, my dear." Soon after, he was gone. One would like to think this a final and fitting Madisonian elocution, a clear-eyed understanding of the thin veil that separates life and death, but it is impossible to say.[22]

His death effectively brought the Montpelier venture to an end. In due course, Dolley sold the estate and moved to Washington, DC, where—in her own Dolley sort of way—she once more became the toast of the town. When she passed away in 1849, President Zachary Taylor, himself a distant relation of James Madison, eulogized her as "the first lady of the land for half a century," a term that has stuck ever since.[23]

Madison died never having children of his own. His stepson, Payne, wasted his life with drinking and gambling and died in 1852 with no heirs. But in a way, we Americans are all the children of James Madison, and not only because of his role in creating our founding document. Madison also did more than any of his contemporaries to inform our understanding of politics. Ask yourself how self-government is supposed to function, and you will inevitably find yourself pondering an idea that was articulated most cogently by James Madison. The people, through the process of bargaining, negotiating, and compromising, can come upon solutions that advance the general welfare while respecting the rights of the individual? Madison. Self-government can span a continent? Madison. The benefits and burdens of policy should be distributed evenly? Madison. Rich citizens should have no greater access to government than the poor? Madison. Government should endeavor to pursue the national interest while respecting constitutional limits? Madison. Many Founders at many points in time advocated all of these ideas, but look through the first forty years of our nation's history, and you will invariably find Madison as these concepts' greatest champion. Nobody was more thoughtful, reasoned, and forceful in his defense of what we today take as common sense but what in his age were contestable notions. Madison won most of his political battles, and we are all the better for it.

James Madison had his faults, as all of us do. And like all statesmen of substantial rank and influence, his errors often had substantial consequences. But if you participate in politics in this country, either as a voter or a politician, you are almost by definition a *Madisonian*—so great and consequential were his contributions to how our politics work. "The great little Madison," as Dolley once called him, still towers over the American body politic.

ACKNOWLEDGMENTS

A PROJECT SUCH as this cannot be completed without a wide circle of supporters to whom I owe an enormous debt of gratitude. First, I would like to thank my wife, Lindsay, for her years of support and encouragement in my intellectual journey, as well as her fantastic suggestions for this manuscript, especially on the subject of Dolley Madison. I would like to thank my parents, John and Lyn Cost, likewise for helping me so much through the years, and recently for their eager babysitting assistance! Thanks as well to my mother-in-law, Kaye McKenzie, who also was always happy to watch "her kiddos" with virtually no notice while I finished up a chapter.

Professionally, I would like to express my gratitude to the American Enterprise Institute, especially to Ryan Streeter and Yuval Levin, for its support of my research. AEI has served as an invaluable venue for me to explore more deeply a lot of the ideas that appear in these pages, and I am so humbled and thankful that the institute thinks enough of my work to let me participate in its community of scholars. Likewise, my thanks go out to Paul Kengor of the Institute for Faith and Freedom at Grove City College for the opportunity to teach college students about our political institutions and the nature of civic virtue. Conversing with such bright young people has helped sharpen my own thinking. I would also like to thank my research assistants, Anna Plank and Ruth Shindledecker, for their careful review of my manuscript.

Thanks as well to the team at Basic Books, for their years of support and encouragement. Thanks to Dan Gerstle, who first brought me to this wonderful publisher, to Lara Heimert, whose confidence in me to complete such a project was emboldening, and to Emma Berry for her truly superb last-minute suggestions to bring into existence the work that is now in front of you. Thanks as well to Kelly Lenkevich, Michael Kaler, Liz Wetzel, Katherine Hill, Jessica Breen, Meghan Brophey, and Kara Ojebuoboh for helping finish the project and getting it into the hands of the readers.

Finally, I would like to thank the scholars and archivists who have labored over the last half century to collect, organize, interpret, and publish the papers of James Madison. I am proud to say that I am an alumnus of the University of Virginia, where the project has been housed for the last forty-five years. And I owe a special debt of professional gratitude to Professor J. C. A. Stagg for his monumental efforts over more than thirty years of work on the Madison papers. I would also like to thank David S. Ferriero and Kathleen Williams of the National Archives for their commitment to making those papers widely available to both scholars and interested citizens alike. The last half century has seen a truly amazing effort to organize the documents of our nation's founding, and this book quite simply would not be possible without that essential work.

NOTES

ABBREVIATIONS

AG   Albert Gallatin
AH   Alexander Hamilton
EP   Edmund Pendleton
ER   Edmund Randolph
GW   George Washington
JM   James Madison
JMe   James Monroe
TJ   Thomas Jefferson

COLLECTIONS

AP. The Adams Papers. Edited by L. H. Butterfield et al. Cambridge, MA: Harvard University Press, 1961. founders.archives.gov.

PAH. The Papers of Alexander Hamilton. Edited by Harold C. Syrett et al. New York: Columbia University Press, 1961–1979. founders .archives.gov.

PGW. The Papers of George Washington. Edited by Donald Jackson et al. Charlottesville: University Press of Virginia of Virginia, 1976. founders.archives.gov.

PJM. The Papers of James Madison. Edited by William T. Hutchinson et al. Chicago: University of Chicago Press; Charlottesville: University Press of Virginia, 1962. founders.archives.gov.

PTJ. The Papers of Thomas Jefferson. Edited by Julian P. Bond et al. Princeton: Princeton University Press, 1950. founders.archives .gov.

PREFACE

1. Max Farrand, *The Records of the Federal Convention of 1787* (New Haven, CT: Yale University Press, 1966), 3:550.

CHAPTER 1: BORN FOR POLITICS

1. Quoted in Robert Beverley, *The History of Virginia* (Richmond, VA: J. W. Randolph, 1855), 5.

2. Quoted in Alan Taylor, *American Colonies: The Settling of North America* (New York: Penguin, 2001), 151.

3. James Harrington, *"The Commonwealth of Oceana" and "A System of Politics"*, ed. J. G. A. Pocock (Cambridge: Cambridge University Press, 1992), 4–5. Byrd quoted in Brent Tarter, *The Grandees of Government: The Origins and Persistence of Undemocratic Politics in Virginia* (Charlottesville: University of Virginia Press, 2013), 86.

4. JM quoted in Irving Brant, *James Madison* (Indianapolis, IN: Ivan R. Dee, 1941–1961), 1:33.

5. JM, "Autobiography," December 1830, and JM to Richard D. Cutts, January 4, 1829, *PJM* Early Access.

6. JM to Thomas Martin, August 10, 1769, *PJM* 1.

7. Quoted in John Maclean, *History of the College of New Jersey*, (Philadelphia: J. B. Lippincott, 1877), 1:362.

8. JM to James Madison Sr., July 23, 1770, *PJM* 1. See also JM to James Madison Sr., September 30, 1769, *PJM* 1.

9. JM to William Bradford, November 9, 1772, *PJM* 1, and Paul Jennings, *A Colored Man's Reminiscences of James Madison* (Brooklyn: George C. Beadle, 1865), 17–18.

10. JM to James Madison Sr., July 23, 1770, *PJM* 1.

11. William Bradford to JM, October 13, 1772, *PJM* 1, JM to Edmund Randolph, June 3, 1783, footnote 6, *PJM* 7, JM to William Bradford, November 9, 1772, *PJM* 1, and William Bradford to JM, March 1, 1773, *PJM* 1.

12. JM to William Bradford, January 24, 1774, JM to William Bradford, July 1, 1774, and JM to William Bradford, August 23, 1774, *PJM* 1.

13. "Virginia Declaration of Rights," June 12, 1776, Avalon Project, https://avalon.law.yale.edu/18th_century/virginia.asp.

14. JM, "Madison's Amendments to the Declaration of Rights, [May 29–June 12, 1776]," *PJM* 1.

15. JM to William Bradford, January 24, 1774, JM to William Bradford, July 1, 1774, and JM to William Bradford, April 1, 1774, *PJM* 1.

16. Mason, "Virginia Declaration of Rights."

17. TJ, "Autobiography," *PTJ* Early Access, and "Article on Religion Adopted by Convention," *PJM* 1.

18. See for instance, "Session of Virginia Council of State," January 14, 1778, *PJM* 1.

19. JM to James Madison Sr., January 23, 1778, *PJM* 1.

20. See "Editorial Note: Revisal of the Laws, 1776–1786," *PTJ* 2.

CHAPTER 2: A POLITICIAN ON THE RISE

1. Luzerne quoted in Brant, *James Madison*, 2:14.

2. Martha Bland quoted in Brant, *James Madison*, 2:33. See JM to James Madison Sr., March 30, 1782, *PJM* 4, JM to ER, August 27, 1782, *PJM* 5, and JM to ER, September 30, 1782, *PJM* 5.

3. TJ to JM, April 14, 1783, *PTJ* 8.

4. JM to TJ, April 22, 1783, *PJM* 6, and JM to TJ, August 11, 1783, *PJM* 7.

5. TJ to JM, August 31, 1783, *PTJ* 6.

6. AH to unidentified recipient, December–March 1779–1780, *PAH* 2.

7. GW to Joseph Jones, May 31, 1780, *PGW* Early Access, and JM to TJ, May 6, 1780, *PJM* 2.

8. GW to Samuel Huntington, April 3, 1780, *PGW* Early Access.

9. JM to EP, September 12, 1780, PJM 2. See "Motion Regarding the Western Lands," *PJM* 2.

10. JM to Joseph Jones, September 19, 1780, *PJM* 2.

11. RM, "Circular to the Governors of the States," in *The Register of Pennsylvania*, vol. 6, ed. Samuel Hazard (Philadelphia: Geddes, 1830), 383. See Nathaniel Greene to AH, *PAH* 10.

12. JM, "Notes on Debates," February 26, 1783, *PJM* 6. See also JM to TJ, April 22, 1783, *PJM* 6.

13. "Report on Address to the States by Congress," *PJM* 6, and GW to the states, June 8, 1783, *PGW* Early Access.

14. JM to TJ, September 20, 1783, *PJM* 7. See "Report on Memorial of Massachusetts General Court," *PJM* 7.

15. TJ to JM, February 20, 1784, *PTJ* 6, JM to TJ, April 17, 1785, *PJM* 8, and JM to ER, July 16, 1785, *PJM* 8. See also TJ to JM, May 8, 1784, *PTJ* 7, TJ to JM, December 8, 1784, *PTJ* 7, and JM to TJ, March 16, 1784, *PJM* 8.

16. See JM to TJ, October 17, 1784, *PJM* 8.

17. Quoted in Ralph Ketcham, *James Madison: A Biography* (Charlottesville: University of Virginia Press, 1970), 158.

18. JM to TJ, March 16, 1784, *PJM* 8.

19. JM to TJ, July 3, 1784, *PJM* 8, and TJ to JM, December 8, 1784, *PTJ* 7.

20. See JM to TJ, January 9, 1785, *PJM* 8.

21. JM, "Memorial and Remonstrance Against Religious Assessments," *PJM* 8.

22. Ibid., and JM, *Federalist* 10, *PJM* 10.

23. Ibid.

24. JM, "Memorial and Remonstrance Against Religious Assessments."

25. JM to GW, December 9, 1785, *PJM* 8. See also JM to TJ, January 22, 1786, *PJM* 8.

CHAPTER 3: THE VIRGINIA PLAN

1. JM to TJ, April 27, 1785, *PJM* 8, JM to TJ, August 12, 1786, *PJM* 9, and JM to GW, April 29, 1783, *PJM* 6.

2. JM to JMe, August 7, 1785, JM to TJ, March 18, 1786, and JM to TJ, January 22, 1786, *PJM* 8.

3. See "The Mount Vernon Compact," March 28, 1785, Con-Source, www.consource.org.

4. JM to GW, December 9, 1785, *PJM* 8.

5. "Address of the Annapolis Convention," September 14, 1786, *PAH* 3.

6. JM to GW, November 8, 1786, *PJM* 9.

7. JM to TJ, February 15, 1787, *PJM* 9.

8. While contemporary interpretations of this period tend to focus on the divide between the North and South, geographical distinctions were often framed at the time in the language of eastern versus southern, reflecting the fact that the rising commercial areas of the North were near the eastern seaboard, while the inland tended to be poor famers. For the convenience of the reader, the contemporary language has been retained throughout.

9. JM to EP, November 30, 1786, *PJM* 9, and JM to TJ, August 12, 1786.

10. JM to James Madison Sr., November 1, 1786, *PJM* 9. See also "Notes for Speech Opposing Paper Money," ca. November 1, 1786, *PJM* 9.

11. Henry Lee to JM, October 18, 1786, *PJM* 9, and Henry Knox to GW, October 23, 1786, *PGW Confederation Series* 4.

12. GW to JM, November 5, 1786, *PGW Confederation Series* 4, JM to GW, December 7, 1786, *PJM* 9, and "Report of Proceedings in Congress; February 21, 1787," Avalon Project, https://avalon.law.yale.edu/18th_century/const04.asp.

13. JM to GW, April 16, 1787, *PJM* 9.

14. JM, *Federalist* 20, *PJM* 10. Madison's *Federalist* 18, 19, and 20 essays were based upon the research he did in preparation for the convention.

15. JM, "Vices of the Political System of the United States," April 1787, *PJM* 9.

16. Ibid.

17. JM to ER, April 8, 1787, *PJM* 9.

18. JM to GW, April 16, 1787, and "The Virginia Plan," *PJM* 9.

19. JM to GW, April 16, 1787, and JM to TJ, March 19, 1787, *PJM* 9.

20. JM to TJ, March 19, 1787, *PJM* 9.

21. Ibid.

22. JM, "Vices of the Political System of the United States."

23. Ibid.

24. Ibid., and JM to Caleb Wallace, August 23, 1785, *PJM* 8. See also JM to ER, April 8, 1787, *PJM* 9.

25. "The Virginia Plan," and JM to Caleb Wallace, August 23, 1785.

26. "Report of Proceedings in Congress," February 21, 1787.

27. Henry quoted in Thomas S. Kidd, *Patrick Henry: First Among Patriots* (New York: Basic Books, 2001), 183.

28. JM to James Madison Sr., April 1, 1787, *PJM* 9.

CHAPTER 4: THE CONSTITUTIONAL CONVENTION

1. Max Farrand, *The Records of the Federal Convention of 1787* (New Haven, CT: Yale University Press, 1966), 3:551.

2. Ibid., 3:77.

3. Ibid., 1:134–135, and 53.

4. Ibid., 2:27–28, and 1:164.

5. Ibid., 2:27.

6. Ibid., 1:288, 512.

7. Ibid., 1:137, and 134.

8. Ibid., 1:575, 533–534, and 2:3.

9. Ibid., 1:584.

10. Ibid., 1:604.

11. Ibid., 1:135.

12. Ibid., 1:580, 592, 596, 593, and 604.

13. Ibid., 1:587, 604, and 3:92.

14. Ibid., 2:373, and 372.

15. Ibid., 2:222, and 220.

16. Ibid., 2:370, 306, 452.

17. Ibid., 1:488.

18. Ibid., 1:8.

19. Ibid., 1:52, 151–152.

20. Ibid., 1:86.

21. Ibid., 1:154.

22. Ibid., 1:177, and 484.

23. Ibid., 1:446–449.

24. Ibid., 2:8–9, 1:486.

25. Ibid., 1:527–528.

26. Ibid., 1:462, 464–465, 492.

27. Ibid., 2:642–643.

28. Ibid., 2:451, 452, 513, 564.

29. Ibid., 3:81.

30. Ibid., 3:78.

CHAPTER 5: THE *FEDERALIST PAPERS*

1. JM to James Madison Sr., September 30, 1787, *PJM* 10, and AH, "Conjectures About the New Constitution," *PAH* 4.

2. Edward Carrington to JM, September 23, 1787, *PJM* 10, and JM to GW, September 30, 1787, *PJM* 10.

3. AH, "Conjectures About the New Constitution."

4. Jonathan Elliott, ed., *The Debates in the Several State Conventions on the Adoption of the Federal Constitution* (Philadelphia: J. B. Lippincott & Co., 1881), 2:164.

5. JM to TJ, October 24, 1787, *PJM* 10, and George Mason to GW, October 7, 1787, *PGW Confederation Series* 5.

6. JM to TJ, December 9, 1787, *PJM* 10.

7. JM to William Short, October 24, 1787, *PJM* 10.

8. JM to ER, October 21, 1787, *PJM* 10.

9. Ibid.

10. JM to Ambrose Madison, October 11, 1787, *PJM* 10.

11. "The Dissent of the Minority of the Convention in Pennsylvania," December 18, 1787, Teaching American History, https://teachingamericanhistory.org/resources/bor/pa-minority-report, and Centinel [pseud.], "Number 1," October 5, 1787, Teaching American History, https://teachingamericanhistory.org/library/document/centinel-i/.

12. Federal Farmer [pseud.], "Letters from the Federal Farmer to the Republican, II," October 9, 1787, Teaching American History, https://teachingamericanhistory.org/library/document/federal-farmer-ii/, and Brutus [pseud.], "IV," November 29, 1787, Teaching American History, https://teachingamericanhistory.org/library/document/brutus-iv/.

13. Brutus [pseud.], "I," October 18, 1787, Teaching American History, https://teachingamericanhistory.org/library/document/brutus-i/, and Brutus [pseud.], "III," November 15, 1787, Teaching American History, https://teachingamericanhistory.org/library/document/brutus-iii/.

14. Centinel, "Number 1," and Federal Farmer, "Letters from the Federal Farmer to the Republican, V," October 13, 1787, Teaching American History, https://teachingamericanhistory.org/library/document/federal-farmer-v/.

15. "The Dissent of the Minority of the Convention in Pennsylvania," and Brutus, "I."

16. Brutus, "I," and Centinel, "Number 1."

17. Brutus [pseud.], "II," November 1, 1787, Teaching American History, https://teachingamericanhistory.org/library/document/brutus-iii/, and Federal Farmer [pseud.], "Letters from the Federal Farmer to the Republican, IV," October 12, 1787, Teaching American History, https://teachingamericanhistory.org/library/document/federal-farmer-iv/.

18. George Mason, "Objections to the Constitution," September 1787, www.archives.gov/files/legislative/resources/education/bill-of-rights/images/mason.pdf, Federal Farmer, "Letters from the Federal Farmer to the Republican, II," and Brutus, "III."

19. George Mason, "Objections to the Constitution," and Centinel, "Number 1."

20. Brutus, "II."

21. JM to GW, November 18, 1787, *PJM* 10.

22. JM, *Federalist 54*, *PJM* 10.

23. JM, *Federalist 62*, *PJM* 10.

24. JM, *Federalist 20*, *PJM* 10.

25. JM, *Federalist 10*, and JM, *Federalist 14*, *PJM* 10.

26. JM, *Federalist 55*, *PJM* 10.

27. JM to TJ, October 24, 1787, *PJM* 10.

28. Ibid.

29. JM, *Federalist 39* and 44, *PJM* 10.

30. JM, *Federalist* 45 and 46, *PJM* 10.

31. JM, *Federalist* 41, JM, *Federalist* 45, and JM, *Federalist* 46, *PJM* 10.

32. JM, *Federalist* 41, and JM, *Federalist* 44, *PJM* 10.

33. JM, *Federalist* 47, *PJM* 10.

34. JM, *Federalist* 48, *PJM* 10.

35. JM, *Federalist* 49.

36. JM, *Federalist* 51, *PJM* 10.

37. Ibid.

38. Polybius, *The Histories: Books 5–8*, trans. W. R. Paton (Cambridge, MA: Harvard University Press, 2011), 345.

CHAPTER 6: RATIFICATION

1. Samuel Adams to Richard Henry Lee, December 3, 1787, in *The Founders' Constitution* (Chicago: University of Chicago Press), http://press-pubs.uchicago.edu/founders/documents/v1ch8s20.html.

2. John Langdon to GW, February 28, 1788, *PGW Confederation Series* 6.

3. JM to Ambrose Madison, November 8, 1787, *PJM* 10.

4. Andrew Shepherd to JM, December 22, 1787, and James Madison Sr. to JM, January 30, 1787, *PJM* 10.

5. Edward Carrington to JM, February 10, 1788, *PJM* 10, and John P. Kaminski et al., eds., *The Documentary History of the Ratification of the Constitution* (Madison: Wisconsin Historical Society Press, 1976–2016), 10:602.

6. JM to ER, April 10, 1788, *PJM* 11.

7. JM to GW, April 10, 1788, *PJM* 11, JM to TJ, April 22, 1788, *PJM* 11, and Kaminski et al., *Documentary History of the Ratification of the Constitution*, 9:611–612.

8. JM to GW, February 20, 1788, *PJM* 10, JM to AH, June 9, 1788, *PJM* 11, Kaminski et al., *Documentary History of the Ratification of the Constitution*, 9:1073, and JM to Rufus King, June 13, 1788, *PJM* 11. See also JM to Rufus King, June 9, 1788, JM to Tench Coxe, June 11, 1788, and JM to GW, June 13, 1788, *PJM* 11.

9. JM to AH, June 16, 1788, and JM to GW, June 13, 1788, *PJM* 11.

10. Kaminski et al., *Documentary History of the Ratification of the Constitution*, 9:963.

11. Ibid., 9:938, 929, 952–953, and JM to GW, June 4, 1788, *PJM* 11.

12. Kaminski et al., *Documentary History of the Ratification of the Constitution*, 10:1375, 1377, 1471, 1560.

13. TJ to Alexander Donald, February 7, 1788, *PTJ* 12, Kaminski et al., *Documentary History of the Ratification of the Constitution*, 10:1210, 1223.

14. Kaminski et al., *Documentary History of the Ratification of the Constitution*, 10:1499, and JM, *Federalist* 37, *PJM* 10.

15. JM, *Federalist* 37, *PJM* 10.

16. Kaminski et al., *Documentary History of the Ratification of the Constitution*, 10:1500.

17. Ibid., 10:1501.

18. JM, *Federalist* 38, *PJM* 10.

19. Kaminski et al., *Documentary History of the Ratification of the Constitution*, 23:2504.

20. ER to JM, August 13, 1788, *PJM* 11, and JM to ER, August 22, 1788, *PJM* 11.

21. Richard Bland Lee to JM, October 29, 1788, *PJM* 11, Gordon R. Denboer, Lucy Trumbull Brown, and Charles D. Hagerman, eds., *Documentary History of the First Federal Elections* (Madison: University of Wisconsin Press, 1976–1990), 2:274, and ER to JM, October 23, 1788, *PJM* 11.

22. JM to ER, October 11, 1788, JM to ER, November 2, 1788, Edward Carrington to JM, November 15, 1788, and Reverend James Madison to JM, November 22, 1788, *PJM* 11.

23. JMe to TJ, February 15, 1789, *PTJ* 14, Edward Carrington to JM, November 26, 1788, *PJM* 11, and JM to TJ, December 8, 1788, *PJM* 11.

24. JM to George Thompson, January 29, 1789, *PJM* 11.

25. JM to Thomas Mann Randolph, January 13, 1789, *PJM* 11, republished in *Virginia Independent Chronicle*, January 28, 1789, JM to TJ, October 17, 1788, and JM to George Eve, January 2, 1789.

26. JM to George Turberville, November 2, 1788, and JM to Thomas Mann Randolph, January 13, 1789, *PJM* 11.

27. Denboer, Brown, and Hagerman, *Documentary History of the First Federal Elections*, 2:348

28. "Observations by Mr. Madison, December 8, 1827," quoted in Henry S. Randall, *Life of Thomas Jefferson* (New York: Derby & Jackson, 1858), 3:255. JMe to TJ, February 15, 1789, *PTJ* 14.

CHAPTER 7: LAUNCHING THE GOVERNMENT

1. JM to GW, March 5, 1789, *PJM* 12.

2. JM to ER, March 1, 1789, *PJM* 12.

3. JM, "Import and Tonnage Duties," April 9, 1789, *PJM* 12.

4. JM, "Tonnage Duties," April 21, 1789, and JM, "Import Duties," April 25, 1789, *PJM* 12.

5. *Annals of Congress*, vol. 1, comp. Joseph Gales (Washington, DC: Gales and Seaton, 1834), 110, 114.

6. JM, "Import Duties," April 28, 1789, and JM, "Import Duties," May 9, 1789, *PJM* 12. See also JM to ER, April 12, 1789, JM to ER, May 10, 1789, and JM, "Import and Tonnage Duties," April 9, 1789, *PJM* 12.

7. JM to TJ, May 23, 1789, *PJM* 12.

8. Fisher Ames to George Richard Minot, May 29, 1789, in *The Works of Ames*, ed. Seth Ames (Boston: Little, Brown and Company, 1854), 1:49.

9. JM, "Amendments to the Constitution," June 8, 1789, *PJM* 12. See also JM to ER, March 27, 1789, *PJM* 12.

10. JM to TJ, October 17, 1788, *PJM* 11, *Annals*, 454–455, and JM, "Amendments to the Constitution," June 8, 1789, *PJM* 12.

11. JM, "Amendments to the Constitution," June 8, 1789, *PJM* 12.

12. Ibid. See "Amendments Proposed by the Massachusetts Convention, February 7, 1788," American History: From Revolution to Reconstruction, University of Groningen, www.let.rug.nl/usa/documents/1786-1800/the-anti-federalist-papers/amendments-proposed-by-the-massachusetts-convention(feb-7-1788).php; "Amendments Proposed by the Virginia Convention, June 27, 1788," American History: From Revolution to Reconstruction, University of Groningen,

www.let.rug.nl/usa/documents/1786-1800/the-anti-federalist-papers
/amendments-proposed-by-the-virginia-convention-(june-27-1788)
-.php; and Richard Labunski, *James Madison and the Struggle for the Bill of Rights* (Oxford: Oxford University Press, 2006), 268.

13. *Annals*, 441–442, 446, 462.

14. JM, "Amendments to the Constitution," June 8, 1789, *PJM* 12, and *Annals*, 731.

15. JM, "Amendments to the Constitution," June 8, 1789, *PJM* 12.

16. JM, "Titles for the President," May 11, 1789, *PJM* 12.

17. *Annals*, 387, 388, 511, and JM, "Removal Power of the President," May 19, 1789, *PJM* 12.

18. JM to EP, June 21, 1789, JM, "Removal Power of the President," June 16, 1789, and JM, "Removal Power of the President," June 17, 1789, *PJM* 12. See also the comments of John Vining of Delaware in *Annals*, 388.

19. JM, "Revisionary Power of the Executive and the Judiciary," July 21, 1787, *PJM* 10, JM to ER, May 31, 1789, *PJM* 12, and JM to EP, June 21, 1789, *PJM* 12.

20. *Annals*, 601.

21. JM, "Location of the Capital," September 3, 1789, *PJM* 12.

22. JM to EP, September 14, 1789, *PJM* 12.

23. AH, *Federalist* 70, PAH 4.

24. *Annals*, 402.

25. Ibid., 468.

26. JM, "Amendments to the Constitution," June 8, 1789, *PJM* 12.

CHAPTER 8: PARTY POLITICS

1. JM, *Federalist* 10, *PJM* 10 AH, *Federalist* 11, *PAH* 6 and AH, *Federalist* 12, *PAH* 6.

2. AH, "Report Relative to a Provision for the Support of Public Credit," January 9, 1790, *PAH* 6.

3. JM, Speech of February 11, 1790, *PJM* 13. See also JM, Speech of February 19, 1790, *PJM* 13. At this point it was Jefferson, not Madison, who was the greater skeptic of debt. In the fall of 1789, Jefferson had told Madison that no generation could contract greater debts than they could pay back, but Madison disagreed, noting that "debts

may be incurred for purposes which interest the unborn, as well as the living"—purposes like the Revolutionary War. JM to TJ, February 4, 1790, *PJM* 13. By 1792, in the heat of the partisan battles between the Federalists and Republicans, Madison would likewise reject the legitimacy of long-term debts. See, for instance, JM, "Universal Peace," January 31, 1792, *PJM* 14.

4. AH, "Report on Public Credit."

5. JM, Speeches of February 24 and April 22, 1790, *PJM* 13. See also JM, Speeches of March 1 and 2, 1790, JM to Henry Lee, April 13, 1790, and JM to Edmund Pendleton, March 4, 1790, *PJM* 13.

6. William Maclay, *The Journal of William Maclay*, American Memory, Library of Congress, http://memory.loc.gov/cgi-bin/query /r?ammem/hlaw:@field(DOCID+@lit(mj0014)). Craigie quoted in Anthony J. Connors, "Andrew Craigie: Brief Life of a Patriot and Scoundrel: 1754–1819." *Harvard Magazine*, November 2011, http:// harvardmagazine.com/2011/11/andrew-craigie.

7. See JM, Speech of March 3, 1790, *PJM* 13.

8. JM to ER, May 19, 1790, and JM to JMe, July 4, 1790, *PJM* 13. Fitzsimons quoted in Jacob E. Cooke, "The Compromise of 1790," *William and Mary Quarterly* 27, no. 4 (October 1970): 540.

9. JM to JMe, July 25, 1790, *PJM* 13. See Jefferson, "Account of the Bargain on the Assumption and Residence Bills," ca. 1792, *PTJ* 17.

10. JM to James Madison Sr., July 31, 1790, *PJM* 13.

11. TJ, "Opinion on the Constitutionality of the Bill for Establishing a National Bank," *PTJ* 19, and Max Farrand, ed., *The Records of the Federal Convention of 1787* (New Haven, CT: Yale University Press, 1911), 3:534.

12. JM, Speech of April 20, 1789, *PJM* 12. See JM, Speech of December 12, 1796, *PJM* 16. During the confederation era, Robert Morris had asked for a congressional charter for the Bank of North America. Madison had supported it, but only because of the exigencies of the situation: Morris was struggling to get subscriptions without government backing, and the Pennsylvania legislature was out of session. See JM to EP, January 8, 1782, *PJM* 4.

13. JM, Speech of February 8, 1791, *PJM* 13.

14. JM to TJ, July 10, 1791, *PJM* 14.

15. Henry Lee to JM, August 24, 1791, *PJM* 14. See AH to Rufus King, August 17, 1791, AH to William Duer, August 17, 1791, and AH to William Seton, August 16, 1791, *PAH* 9.

16. AH to William Seton, January 18, 1792, *PAH* 10.

17. JM to TJ, August 8, 1791, *PJM* 14.

18. JM, *Federalist* 10.

19. TJ to Philip Freneau, February 28, 1791, *PTJ* 19.

20. JM, "Public Opinion," JM, "A Candid State of Parties," JM, "Spirit of Governments," JM, "The Union. Who Are Its Real Friends?" *PJM* 14.

21. TJ, "Thomas Jefferson's Explanations of the Three Volumes Bound in Marbled Paper (the so-called Anas)," February 4, 1818, *PTJ Retirement Series* 12.

22. AH, *Federalist* 11.

CHAPTER 9: BRITAIN AND FRANCE

1. JM, *Federalist* 10, *PJM* 10, and JM, "Memorandum on a Discussion of the President's Retirement," *PJM* 14.

2. JM to Henry Lee, January 21, 1792, *PJM* 14. See also JM to Henry Lee, January 1, 1792, JM to EP, January 21, 1792, and JM, "Bounty Payments for Cod Fisheries," February 6, 1792, *PJM* 14.

3. TJ to GW, May 23, 1792, *PTJ* 23, AH to Edward Carrington, May 26, 1792, *PAH* 11, and AH, "An American No. II," *PAH* 12. For an indication of the common knowledge that Madison was the "friend," see ER to JM, August 12, 1792, and Henry Lee to JM, September 10, 1792, *PJM* 14.

4. JM to Benjamin Rush, October 1, 1792, *PJM* 14. See also John Beckley to JM, August 1, 1792, and JM and JMe to Melancton Smith and Marinus Willett, October 19, 1792, *PJM* 14. A common story is that Jefferson and Madison made the initial efforts at a trans-regional electoral party back in 1792, when they toured upstate New York together. This may be true, but Madison's notes on the trip were dedicated to observations about the soil, the price of land, and the chief agricultural products. See JM, "Notes on the Lake Country Tour," *PJM* 14.

5. See "William Branch Giles's Resolutions on the Secretary of the Treasury, February 27, 1793," and JM, Speech of March 1, 1793," *PJM* 14.

6. JM, Speech of March 10, 1792, *PJM* 14.

7. JM to George Nicholas, March 15, 1793, *PJM* 14, and JM to the Minister of the Interior of the French Republic, April 1793, *PJM* 15.

8. AH to GW, April 14, 1794, *PGW Presidential Series* 15.

9. GW, "Proclamation by George Washington, April 1793," *PAH* 14. See "Treaty of Alliance Between the United States and France; February 6, 1778," Avalon Project, https://avalon.law.yale.edu/18th_century/fr1788-2.asp.

10. JM to TJ, June 13, 1793, and JM to TJ, June 19, 1793, *PJM* 15.

11. See TJ, "Notes on Alexander Hamilton and 'Veritas,'" June 12, 1793, *PTJ* 26, and "Veritas to GW," May 30, 1793, *PGW Presidential Series* 12.

12. AH, "Pacificus I," *PAH* 14, TJ to JM, June 29, 1793, and TJ to JM, July 7, 1793, *PJM* 15.

13. JM to TJ, July 22, 1793, and JM to TJ, July 30, 1793, *PJM* 15.

14. JM, "Helvidius Number I," *PJM* 15.

15. Ibid., and JM, "Helvidius Number IV," *PJM* 15.

16. TJ to JM, May 19, 1793, *PTJ* 26.

17. GW to TJ, July 11, 1793, *PGW Presidential Series* 13, TJ to JM, July 7, 1793, *PJM* 15, and JM to JMe, September 15, 1793, *PJM* 15.

18. JM to Archibald Stuart, September 1, 1793, *PJM* 15.

19. TJ to JM, August 3, 1793, *PJM* 15.

20. See "The Acts, Orders in Council, &c of Great Britain [on Trade], 1793–1812," Napoleon Series, April 2003, www.napoleon-series.org/research/government/british/decrees/c_britdecrees7.html.

21. See TJ, "Final State of the Report on Commerce," *PTJ* 27, and JM, "Commercial Discrimination," *PJM* 15.

22. TJ to JM, August 11, 1793, *PJM* 15.

23. Quoted in "Note 2" of George Clinton to GW, *PGW Presidential Series* 15.

24. JM to Horatio Gates, March 24, 1794. See also JM to TJ, March 26, 1794, and JM to Alexander White, April 14, 1794, *PJM* 15.

25. AH, "Conversations with George Hammond," April 15–16, 1794, *PAH* 16. See also AH to GW, March 8, 1794, *PAH*.

26. GW, "November 19, 1794: Sixth Annual Message to Congress," Miller Center, https://millercenter.org/the-presidency/presidential -speeches/november-19-1794-sixth-annual-message-congress, and JM to JMe, December 4, 1794, *PJM* 15.

27. Mary Cutts, *The Queen of America: Mary Cutts's Life of Dolley Madison* (Charlottesville: University of Virginia Press, 2010), 94–95.

28. Quoted in Ketcham, *James Madison*, 380.

29. Dolley Payne Todd to Eliza Collins Lee, September 16, 1794, *PJM* 15.

30. Quoted in Todd Estes, *The Jay Treaty Debate, Public Opinion, and the Early Evolution of American Political Culture* (Amherst: University of Massachusetts Press, 2008), 108–109. JM to Robert Livingston, August 10, 1795, *PJM* 16. See also JM to an unidentified correspondent, August 23, 1795, *PJM* 16.

31. TJ to JM, September 21, 1795, *PTJ* 28.

32. JM, Speech of March 10, 1796, *PJM* 16, JM to TJ, March 6, 1796, *PJM* 16, and GW to the US House of Representatives, March 30, 1796, *PGW Presidential Series* 19.

33. Fisher Ames quoted in Estes, *Jay Treaty Debate*, 160. See JM, Speech of April 6, 1796, and JM, Speech of April 15, 1796, *PJM* 15.

34. JM to TJ, May 1, 1796, *PJM* 15.

CHAPTER 10: THE VIRGINIA RESOLUTIONS

1. GW to Charles Cotesworth Pinckney, July 8, 1796, *PGW* Early Access, and JM to JMe, September 29, 1796, *PJM* 16.

2. JM to JMe, February 26, 1796, and JM to JMe, September 29, 1796, *PJM* 16.

3. John Beckley to JM, October 15, 1796, *PJM* 16.

4. See JM to TJ, December 5, 1796, *PJM* 16.

5. TJ to JM, December 17, 1796, *PJM* 16, TJ to John Adams, December 28, 1796, *PTJ* 29, and JM to TJ, January 15, 1797, *PJM* 16.

6. JA, *Defense of the Constitutions of the United States*, University of Chicago, http://press-pubs.uchicago.edu/founders/documents/v1ch 15s34.html, and JM to TJ, June 6, 1787.

7. TJ to JM, December 28, 1794, *PTJ* 28, JM to James Madison Sr., March 13, 1796, and JM to James Madison Sr., March 13, 1797, *PJM* 16. See John Taylor to JM, November 16, 1796, *PJM* 16.

8. JM, Speech of June 6, 1787, *PJM* 10, JM, *Federalist* 54, *PJM* 10, JM, "Memorandum on an African Colony for Freed Slaves," *PJM* 12, and JM "Notes on the Lake Country Tour," *PJM* 14.

9. JM to James Madison Sr., September 8, 1783, *PJM* 7.

10. JM to William Bradford, July 1, 1774, *PJM* 1, and JM to Jedidiah Morse, February 26, 1822, *PJM Retirement Series* 2.

11. TJ to Frances Wright, August 7, 1825, *PTJ* Early Access, and JM to Frances Wright, September 1, 1825, *PJM Retirement Series* 3.

12. See Timothy Pickering to AH, June 9, 1798, *PAH* 21.

13. JMe to JM, February 27, 1796, *PJM* 16.

14. JM to TJ, April 15, 1798, *PJM* 17.

15. John Adams to Benjamin Rush, December 4, 1805, *AP* Early Access. See, for instance, AH to Harrison Gray Otis, January 26, 1799, and AH to Theodore Sedgwick, February 2, 1799, *PAH* 22.

16. "An Act in Addition to the Act, Entitled 'An Act for the Punishment of Certain Crimes Against the United States,'" Avalon Project, https://avalon.law.yale.edu/18th_century/sedact.asp.

17. TJ to JM, *PTJ* 30, JM to TJ, May 5, 1798, *PJM* 17, Uriah Tracy quoted in Donald Stewart, *The Opposition Press of the Federalist Period* (Albany: State University of New York Press, 1969), 11.

18. TJ to John Taylor, June 4, 1798, TJ to Nicholas Lewis, January 30, 1799, TJ to JM, January 30, 1799, and TJ to Thomas Mann Randolph, January 30, 1799, *PTJ* 30.

19. "Resolutions Adopted by the Kentucky General Assembly, November 10, 1798," *PTJ* 30, and JM to TJ, December 29, 1798, *PJM* 17.

20. JM, "Virginia Resolutions," *PJM* 17, JM, "The Report of 1800, *PJM* 17, and AH, *Federalist* 26, *PAH* 4.

21. John Quincy Adams quoted in Ralph Ketcham and John Quincy Adams, "Jefferson and Madison and the Doctrines of Interposition and Nullification: A Letter of John Quincy Adams," *Virginia Magazine of History and Biography* 66, no. 2 (April 1968): 182.

22. JM, "Public Opinion," *PJM* 14.

23. JM, *Federalist* 39, *PJM* 10, and JM to Daniel Webster, May 27, 1830, *PJM* Early Access.

24. JM, "The Report of 1800."

25. John Adams to Harrison Gray Otis, April 4, 1823, *AP* Early Access.

26. See JM to TJ, April 4, 1800, *PJM* 17.

27. JM to TJ, January 10, 1801, *PJM* 17.

CHAPTER 11: SECRETARY OF STATE

1. JM to JMe, March 11, 1806, *PJM Secretary of State Series* 11.

2. Quoted in David Johnson, *John Randolph of Roanoke* (Baton Rouge: Louisiana State University Press, 2012), 98.

3. TJ to David R. Williams, January 31, 1806, *PTJ* Early Access.

4. Smith quoted in Catherine Allgor, *A Perfect Union: Dolley Madison and the Creation of the American Nation* (New York: Henry Holt and Company, 2006).

5. Talleyrand quoted in Harlow Giles Unger, *The Last Founding Father: James Monroe and a Nation's Call to Greatness* (Boston: Da Capo, 2010), 151.

6. Robert Livingston to James Madison, September 1, 1802, *PJM Secretary of State Series* 3, and TJ to JMe, January 10, 1803, *PTJ* 39.

7. JM to Robert Livingston and JMe, March 2, 1803, *PJM Secretary of State Series* 4, TJ to Pierre Samuel du Pont de Nemours, April 25, 1802, *PTJ* 37, and JM to Robert Livingston, May 1, 1802, *PJM Secretary of State Series* 3.

8. JM to JMe, June 25, 1803, *PJM Secretary of State Series* 5, TJ to Albert Gallatin, January 13, 1803, *PTJ* 39, John Quincy Adams, *Diaries*, vol. 1 (New York: Library of America, 2011), 100, and TJ to JM, August 18, 1803, *PTJ* 41.

9. See TJ, "Fifth Annual Message to Congress, December 3, 1805," *PTJ* Early Access.

10. James Stapleton, *War in Disguise, or the Frauds of Neutral Flags* (New York and Philadelphia: I. Riley and Co. and Samuel F. Bradford, 1860), 9. See JM to JMe, April 12, 1805, *PJM Secretary of State Series* 9.

11. JM to William Pinkney, March 8, 1808, *PJM* Early Access. See JM, "An Examination of the British Doctrine, Which Subjects to

Capture a Neutral Trade, Not Open in Time of Peace," *PJM Secretary of State Series* 11. For a briefer distillation of Madison's views, see JM to JMe, April 12, 1805, *PJM Secretary of State Series* 9.

12. Thomas Cooper to TJ, March 16, 1806, *PTJ* Early Access, Randolph quoted in the editor's introduction to JM, "Examination of the British Doctrine," and Russell Kirk, *John Randolph of Roanoke: A Study in American Politics* (Indianapolis, IN: Liberty Fund, 1997), 326–327.

13. John Randolph, Speech of March 26, 1806, in *Annals of the Congress of the United States*, Ninth Congress (Washington, DC: Gales and Seaton, 1852), 851.

14. JMe to TJ, June 30, 1806, *PTJ* Early Access. See also TJ to Thomas Paine, March 25, 1806, *PTJ* Early Access.

15. JMe to JM, July 1, 1804, *PJM Secretary of State Series* 7.

16. See JM to JMe, March 6, 1805, *PJM Secretary of State Series* 9, and Tench Coxe to JM, April 1, 1807, *PJM* Early Access.

17. JM to JMe, May 20, 1807, *PJM* Early Access.

18. JM to John Armstrong, February 8, 1808, *PJM* Early Access.

19. JM, "Editorial in the National Intelligencer," December 23, 1807, and JM, "Editorial in the National Intelligencer," December 28, 1807, *PJM* Early Access.

20. See, for instance, JM to George Jackson, December 31, 1807, JM to William Pinkney, May 1, 1808, and JM to William Pinkney, July 3, 1808, *PJM* Early Access.

21. TJ to Levi Lincoln, November 13, 1808, *PTJ* Early Access. See also Thomas Jefferson, "A Proclamation Warning All Persons on Lake Champlain and Adjacent County to Cease Violence and Disperse," April 19, 1808, American Presidency Project, www.presidency.ucsb .edu/documents/proclamation-15-warning-all-persons-lake-champlain -and-adjacent-county-cease-violence-and.

22. JM to William Pinkney, July 15, 1808, *PJM* Early Access, JM to TJ, September 14, 1808, *PJM* Early Access, and JM to Henry Wheaton, July 11, 1824, *PJM Retirement Series* 3.

23. Taylor quoted in John Taylor, Wilson Cary Nicholas, and David N. Mayer, "Of Principles and Men: The Correspondence of John Taylor of Caroline with Wilson Cary," *Virginia Magazine of History and Biography* 96, no. 3 (July 1988): 328, 377.

24. TJ to JMe, March 16, 1806, *PTJ* Early Access, and JMe to Walter Jones, January 24, 1808, in *The Writings of James Monroe*, ed. Stanislaus Murray Hamilton (New York: G. P. Putnam Sons, 1901), 5:22–23.

25. Pinckney quoted in Allgor, *A Perfect Union*, 137.

26. Adams quoted in Burton Spivak, *Jefferson's English Crisis: Commerce, Embargo, and the Republican Revolution* (Charlottesville: University of Virginia Press, 1979), 122, and JM to William Pinkney, February 10, 1809, *PJM* Early Access.

27. TJ to Pierre Samuel du Pont de Nemours, March 2, 1809, *PTJ* Early Access.

CHAPTER 12: THE FAILURE OF DIPLOMACY

1. Barlow quoted in Cutts, *The Queen of America*, 112.

2. JM, "Inaugural Address," March 4, 1809, American Presidency Project, www.presidency.ucsb.edu/documents/inaugural-address-21.

3. Ibid.

4. AG to Joseph Nicholson, December 29, 1808, in *The Writings of Albert Gallatin*, ed. Henry Adams, Online Library of Liberty, https://oll.libertyfund.org/titles/1953#lf1358-01_head_294.

5. William Branch Giles to JM, February 27, 1809, *PJM* Early Access.

6. Ibid. Also, see "Memorandum on Robert Smith, April 11, 1811," *PJM Presidential Series* 3.

7. AG to TJ, November 11, 1809, *PTJ Retirement Series* 1.

8. Robert Smith to David Erskine, April 17, 1809, in *American State Papers: Foreign Relations* (Washington, DC: Gales and Seaton, 1832), 3:291.

9. George Canning to David Erskine, January 23, 1809, in *American State Papers: Foreign Relations*, 3:300.

10. JM to TJ, April 24, 1809, and JM to TJ, July 7, 1809, *PJM Presidential Series* 1.

11. David Erskine to George Canning, April 30, 1809, in *Cobbett's Parliamentary Debates* (London: T. C. Hansard, 1810), 153, and JM to Albert Gallatin, July 30, 1809, *PJM Presidential Series* 1. See also George Joy to JM, May 24, 1809, *PJM* Early Access.

12. JM to Albert Gallatin, July 30, 1809, Robert Smith to JM, September 11, 1809, and JM to Robert Smith, September 15, 1809, *PJM Presidential Series* 1.

13. Francis Jackson to Robert Smith, October 23, 1809, in *American State Papers: Foreign Relations*, 3:315, and Robert Smith to Francis Jackson, November 8, 1809, in *American State Papers: Foreign Relations*, 3:319.

14. JM to George Logan, January 19, 1810, *PJM Presidential Series* 2.

15. JM to TJ, May 25, 1810, *PJM Presidential Series* 2.

16. JM, "First Annual Message, November 29, 1809," American Presidency Project, www.presidency.ucsb.edu/documents/first-annual-message-0, and JM to William Pinkney, January 20, 1810, *PJM Presidential Series* 2.

17. See Albert Gallatin, "The State of the Finances, December 8, 1809," *American State Papers: Finance* (Washington, DC: Gales and Seaton), 2:373–374.

18. JM to TJ, May 7, 1810, *PJM Presidential Series* 2, and JM to William Pinkney, May 23, 1810, *PJM Presidential Series* 2.

19. The Duke of Cadore to John Armstrong, August 5, 1810, *American State Papers: Foreign Relations*, 3:387.

20. JM, "Proclamation—Suspension of Prohibition of Trade with France, November 2, 1810," American Presidency Project, www.presidency.ucsb.edu/documents/proclamation-suspension-prohibition-trade-with-france.

21. JM to John Armstrong, October 29, 1810, *PJM Presidential Series* 2, and JM, "Second Annual Message," December 5, 1810, American Presidency Project, www.presidency.ucsb.edu/documents/second-annual-message-0.

22. Richard Wellesley to William Pinkney, December 29, 1810, *American State Papers: Foreign Relations*, 3:408. See also JM to Henry Dearborn, July 23, 1811, *PJM Presidential Series* 3.

23. JM to Caesar Rodney, September 30, 1810, *PJM Presidential Series* 2.

24. Albert Gallatin to James Madison, March 7, 1811, *PJM Presidential Series* 3. See also JM, "Memorandum on Robert Smith, April 11, 1811," *PJM Presidential Series* 3.

25. TJ to JM, March 30, 1809, *PTJ Retirement Series* 1, and TJ to JM, May 25, 1810, *PJM Presidential Series* 2.

26. Henry Clay, Speech of December 31, 1811, in *The Speeches of Henry Clay* (Philadelphia: H. C. Carney and I. Lea, 1828), 38.

27. JM, "Third Annual Message," November 5, 1811, American Presidency Project, https://www.presidency.ucsb.edu/documents/third-annual-message-0. Albert Gallatin, "Increase of Revenue, January 20, 1812," *American State Papers: Finance*, 2:523.

28. See JM to TJ, February 7, 1812, *PJM Presidential Series* 4.

29. JM, "Special Message," June 1, 1812, American Presidency Project, www.presidency.ucsb.edu/documents/special-message-887.

30. See James Buller, "Order in Council. At the Court at Carlton House, June 23, 1812: Present, His Royal Highness the Prince Regent in Council," Napoleon Series, www.napoleon-series.org/research/government/british/decrees/c_britdecrees45.html.

31. AH, *Federalist* 70, *PAH* 4.

32. JM to Caesar Rodney, September 30, 1810.

CHAPTER 13: THE WAR OF 1812

1. Scott quoted in Steven J. Rauch, *The Campaign of 1812* (Washington, DC: Center of Military History, US Army, 2013), 11, and in Robert Allen Rutland, *The Presidency of James Madison* (Lawrence: University of Kansas Press, 106). Henry Dearborn to James Madison, March 21, 1812, *PJM Presidential Series* 4.

2. Walter Jones to JM, November 8, 1813, *PJM Presidential Series* 7.

3. Elbridge Gerry to JM, July 13, 1812, *PJM Presidential Series* 5, Henry Dearborn to James Madison, June 26, 1812, *PJM Presidential Series* 4, and JM to Richard Cutts, August 8, 1812, *PJM Presidential Series* 5.

4. JM to Henry Wheaton, February 26, 1827, *PJM* Early Access.

5. TJ to William Duane, August 4, 1812, *PTJ Retirement Series* 5. See also AG to JM, July 12, 1812, *PJM Presidential Series* 5.

6. See TJ to JM, August 5, 1812, *PJM Presidential Series* 5.

7. JM to JMe, August 8, 1812, *PJM Presidential Series* 5.

8. Lawrence quoted in "James Lawrence," American Battlefield Trust, www.battlefields.org/learn/biographies/james-lawrence.

9. JM, "Fourth Annual Message," November 4, 1812, American Presidency Project, www.presidency.ucsb.edu/documents/fourth -annual-message-0.

10. Henry Clay to Caesar Rodney, December 29, 1812, in *The Papers of Henry Clay*, eds. James Hopkins and Mary W. M. Hargreaves, vol. 1 (Lexington: University of Kentucky Press, 1959), 750–751, and AG to Joseph Nicholson, in *Writings of Albert Gallatin*, https://oll .libertyfund.org/titles/1953#lf1358-01_head_294.

11. William Eustis to JM, December 3, 1812, *PJM* 5. See also Paul Hamilton to JM, December 30, 1812, *PJM Presidential Series* 5.

12. AG to JM, January 13, 1813, *PJM Presidential Series* 5.

13. See AG to JM, March 5, 1813, *PJM Presidential Series* 6.

14. See JM to William Hill Wells, June 17, 1813, *PJM Presidential Series* 6.

15. Daniel Tompkins to JM, January 3, 1814, *PJM Presidential Series* 7.

16. William Jones to JM, September 21, 1813, *PJM Presidential Series* 6.

17. JM, "Memorandum of Conversations with John Armstrong," August 24, 1814," *PJM Presidential Series* 8.

18. John Quincy Adams, *Diaries 1779–1821*, ed. David Waldstreicher (New York: Library of America, 2017), 326–327, and Henry Clay to JMe, August 14, 1814, *Papers of Henry Clay*, 1:963.

19. See JM to JMe, October 18, 1813, *PJM Presidential Series* 6.

20. "Amendments to the Constitution Proposed by the Hartford Convention: 1814," Avalon Project, https://avalon.law.yale.edu/19th _century/hartconv.asp. For Madison's reaction to the Hartford Convention, see Brant, *James Madison*, 6:361.

CHAPTER 14: NATIONAL REPUBLICANISM

1. AG to Matthew Lyon, May 7, 1816, in *Writings of Albert Gallatin*, https://oll.libertyfund.org/titles/1953#Gallatin_1358-01_2814, JMe to the Chairman of the Military Committee of the Senate,

February 1815, in *Writings of James Monroe*, 5:321, and John C. Calhoun, Speech of January 31, 1816, in *The Essential Calhoun*, ed. Clyde N. Wilson (New York: Routledge, 1999), 116.

2. Henry Clay, Speech of January 29, 1816, in *The Writings of Henry Clay* (Lexington: University of Kentucky Press, 1961), 2:157–158.

3. JM, "Seventh Annual Message," December 5, 1815, American Presidency Project, www.presidency.ucsb.edu/documents/seventh -annual-message-0.

4. Henry Clay, Speech of January 29, 1816, *Writings of Henry Clay*, 2:151.

5. JM, "Seventh Annual Message." See AG, *Report of the Secretary of the Treasury on the Subjects of Public Roads and Canals*, 1808, Online Library of Liberty, https://oll.libertyfund.org/titles/gallatin -report-of-the-secretary-of-the-treasury-on-the-subject-of-public-roads -and-canals.

6. Henry Clay, Speech of January 29, 1816, in *Writings of Henry Clay*, 2:157, and John C. Calhoun, Speech of February 4, 1817, *Annals of Congress*, Fourteenth Congress, Second Session (Washington, DC: Gales and Seaton, 1854), 852.

7. JM, "Seventh Annual Message."

8. Henry Clay, Speech of January 29, 1816, *Writings of Henry Clay*, 2:157.

9. JM, "Seventh Annual Message."

10. Dallas quoted in Raymond Walters, "The Origins of the Second Bank of the United States," *Journal of Political Economy* 53, no. 2 (June 1945): 121.

11. JM, "Message to the Senate Returning Without Approval 'An Act to Incorporate the Subscribers to the Bank of the United States of America,'" January 30, 1815, American Presidency Project, www .presidency.ucsb.edu/documents/message-the-senate-returning -without-approval-act-incorporate-the-subscribers-the-bank-the.

12. JM, "Veto Message," March 3, 1817, American Presidency Project, www.presidency.ucsb.edu/documents/veto-message-246.

13. AH, *Federalist* 12, *PAH* 4, JM, *Federalist* 51, *PJM* 10, and JM, *Federalist* 10, *PJM* 10.

14. JM to the Senate, January 30, 1815, *PJM Presidential Series* 8. See also JM to Charles J. Ingersoll, June 25, 1831, *PJM* Early Access.

15. Henry Clay, Speech of June 3, 1816, in *Writings of Henry Clay*, 2:202–203

16. JM to the Senate, January 30, 1815.

17. JM to JMe, November 29, 1817, JM to Henry St. George Tucker, December 23, 1817, and JM to JMe, December 27, 1817, *PJM Retirement Series* 1.

18. JM to JMe, December 20, 1822, *PJM Retirement Series* 2, https://founders.archives.gov/documents/Madison/04-02-02-0546.

19. John Quincy Adams, "First Annual Message," December 6, 1825, American Presidency Project, www.presidency.ucsb.edu /documents/first-annual-message-2. Thomas Ritchie to JM, December 10, 1825, *PJM Retirement Series* 3, TJ to JM, December 24, 1825, *PTJ* Early Access, and JM to Thomas Ritchie, December 18, 1825, *PJM Retirement Series* 3.

20. Andrew Jackson, "Veto Message," May 7, 1830, American Presidency Project, www.presidency.ucsb.edu/documents/veto-message-471. See JM to Martin Van Buren, July 5, 1830, *PJM* Early Access.

21. JM to Spencer Roane, September 2, 1819, *PJM* Early Access.

22. Andrew Jackson, "Veto Message [of the Re-authorization of Bank of the United States]," July 10, 1832, American Presidency Project, www.presidency.ucsb.edu/documents/veto-message-the -re-authorization-bank-the-united-states.

CHAPTER 15: "THE SERPENT CREEPING"

1. JMe, "Inaugural Address," March 4, 1817, American Presidency Project, www.presidency.ucsb.edu/documents/inaugural-address-23.

2. James K. Paulding quoted in Lynne Cheney, *James Madison: A Life Reconsidered* (New York: Penguin Press, 2014), and JM to Dolley Madison, November 5, 1824, *PJM Retirement Series* 3.

3. JM to Nicholas Trist, February 15, 1830, *PJM* Early Access.

4. JM to Richard Rush, December 4, 1820, *PJM Retirement Series* 2. Madison wrote of Hamilton's proposal "as subverting the fundamental and characteristic principle of the government, as contrary

to the true and fair, as well as the received construction, and as bidding defiance to the sense in which the Constitution is known to have been proposed, advocated and adopted. If Congress can do whatever in their *discretion* can be *done by money*, and will promote the *general welfare*, the Government is no longer a limited one possessing enumerated powers, but an indefinite one subject to particular exceptions." JM to Edmund Pendleton, January 21, 1792, *PJM* 14.

5. John Taylor of Caroline, Speech of May 4, 1824, *Annals of Congress*, Eighteenth Congress, First Session (Washington, DC: Gales and Seaton, 1856), 686.

6. JM to Henry Clay, April 24, 1824, *PJM Retirement Series* 3, and JM to Thomas Cooper, March 23, 1824.

7. TJ to William Branch Giles, December 26, 1825, *PTJ* Early Access.

8. JM, Speech of July 14, 1787, *PJM* 10.

9. JM to Joseph C. Cabell, March 18, 1827, and JM to Joseph C. Cabell, December 5, 1828, *PJM* Early Access.

10. JM to Joseph C. Cabell, September 18, 1828, JM to Joseph C. Cabell, October 30, 1828, Joseph Cabell to JM, September 27, 1828, and JM to Joseph Cabell, October 5, 1828, *PJM* Early Access.

11. John C. Calhoun, "South Carolina Exposition," in *Reports and Public Letters of John C. Calhoun*, ed. Richard K. Cralle (New York: D. Appleton and Company, 1856), 36.

12. Robert Hayne, Speech of January 25, 1830, in *The Webster-Hayne Debate on the Nature of the Constitution: Selected Documents*, ed. Herman Belz, Online Library of Liberty, https://oll.libertyfund. org/titles/webster-the-webster-hayne-debate-on-the-nature-of-the -constitution-selected-documents.

13. Edward Everett to JM, April 22, 1830, *PJM* Early Access.

14. JM to Edward Everett, August 28, 1830, *PJM* Early Access.

15. Ibid.

16. JM to William C. Rives, January 23, 1829, and JM to Nicholas Trist, June 3, 1830, *PJM* Early Access.

17. JM to William C. Rives, March 12, 1833, JM to Henry Clay, April 2, 1833, and JM to Nicholas Trist, February 15, 1830, *PJM* Early Access.

18. JM to Nicholas Trist, February 15, 1830, *PJM* Early Access.

19. JM, "Advice to My Country," *PJM* Early Access.

20. TJ, "The Declaration of Independence as Adopted by Congress, 11 June–4 July 1776," *PTJ* 1, TJ, "Jefferson's 'Original Rough Draught' of the Declaration of Independence, 11 June–4 July 1776," *PTJ* 1, and JM, Speech of July 19, 1787, *PJM* 10.

21. Abraham Lincoln, "Inaugural Address," March 4, 1865, American Presidency Project, www.presidency.ucsb.edu/node/202171.

22. JM quoted in Cheney, *James Madison: A Life Reconsidered*, 453.

23. Zachary Taylor quoted in "The First Ladies: Dolley Madison," July 18, 2013, National Women's History Museum, www.womens history.org/articles/first-ladies-dolley-madison.

INDEX

431

Jay Cost is the Gerald R. Ford visiting scholar at the American Enterprise Institute and a visiting scholar at Grove City College. He has written for the *Wall Street Journal*, *National Review*, and the *Atlantic*. He holds a PhD in political science from the University of Chicago. The author of *The Price of Greatness* and *A Republic No More*, he lives in western Pennsylvania.